POLICING IN AMERICA

Clemens Bartollas
University of Northern Iowa

Larry D. Hahn
Police Sergeant
and National Police Trainer

Allyn and Bacon
Boston • London • Toronto • Sydney • Tokyo • Singapore

Editor-in-Chief, Social Sciences: Karen Hanson
Series Editorial Assistant: Heather Ahlstrom
Marketing Manager: Susan E. Ogar
Composition and Prepress Buyer: Linda Cox
Manufacturing Buyer: Megan Cochran
Production Editor: Christopher H. Rawlings
Cover Administrator: Jenny Hart
Editorial-Production Service: Omegatype Typography, Inc.
Electronic Composition: Omegatype Typography, Inc.

Copyright © 1999 by Allyn & Bacon
A Viacom Company
160 Gould Street
Needham Heights, MA 02494

Internet: www.abacon.com

Library of Congress Cataloging-in-Publication Data

Bartollas, Clemens.
    Policing in America / Clemens Bartollas and Larry D. Hahn.
      p.   cm.
    Includes bibliographical references and index.
    ISBN 0-205-27454-4
    1. Police–United States.   2. Police administration–United
States.   3. Police ethics–United States.   4. Police misconduct-
-United States.   I. Hahn, Larry D.   II. Title.
HV8138.B28   1999
363.2'0973–dc21   98-22355
                                             CIP

Printed in the United States of America
10 9 8 7 6 5 4 3 2 1   03 02 01 00 99 98

CONTENTS

PREFACE

This text examines the scope, possibilities, and problems of policing in the United States. At a time in which the credibility of policing is probably as low as it was during the late stages of the Civil Rights Movement, there are many reasons to justify saying that it is the worst of times. The media have been more than willing to disseminate the horror stories of cops gone bad. Too many police officers justify violating suspects' constitutional rights, giving false testimony in court, complying with the code of silence and protecting wrongdoing in the department, participating in one of the many forms of corruption, using excessive force, and displaying racism toward citizens and sexual harassment toward fellow officers.

We believe it is also the best of times, as exciting changes are in the wind. The emerging emphasis on integrity in law enforcement, which is one of the themes of this text, promises to bring a breath of fresh air to the careers of police administrators, middle managers, and line officers. The continued expansion of community policing has the possibility of healing old wounds between citizens and the police in the inner city and of bringing more effective crime prevention techniques to law enforcement. Another positive development is the realization that police deviancy is a systemic problem and that only a structural approach will have any real impact on reducing it.

The quality of policing among the majority of officers, the quality of management among most top police executives and supervisors, and the quality of services provided the community are higher than they have ever been. It is important to honor the majority of police officers who are trying to make a difference and who are a credit to law enforcement. Their badges have not been tarnished by wrongdoing. Their careers capture a sense of the spirit of law enforcement, a spirit of dedication and of resolve for doing what is right.

The first chapter of this text provides a sense of history which is important—where policing has been in the past tells us much about why it is the way it is now and where it is likely to go in the future. In Chapter 2, the roles and functions of the various types of policing agencies—federal, state, county, local, and private are examined. Chapter 3 looks at the process, both formal and informal, of becoming a police officer. Chapter 4 presents what is involved in the administration and management of a police agency. This chapter develops the theme of integrity and what needs to be done to implement integrity and ethics in police agencies throughout this nation. Chapter 5 examines the operations of line and support functions of police departments. It focuses more on what takes place on a daily basis. The final section of this chapter contains a presentation on community policing, including its strengths and the obstacles to its implementation. Chapter 6 discusses constitutional protections for those who are stopped or arrested for a crime. Chapter 7 examines special or difficult policing problems today. Topics covered in this chapter include the militia movement, violence and migrations of drug-trafficking street gangs, hostage negotiations, hate crime, and organized crime. Chapter 8 focuses on stressors in policing, with information on cumulative and post-traumatic stress disorders. The next three chapters reveal much of the dark side of policing. Chapter 9 takes a careful look at the use of appropriate and excessive force in policing. Chapter 10 examines corruption. It presents the various forms of corruption, stages of corruption, and what can be done about corruption. Chapter 11 discusses female police officers, including a section on sexual harassment—a sad phenomenon in American policing. Chapter 12 examines minorities in policing, focusing on African American, Native American, and homosexual police officers. The final chapter evaluates the present state of policing and makes predictions for the future.

There are several themes reflected throughout this text. Integrity is the first. We believe this is an idea whose time has come. An increased number of top police administrators are attempting to implement integrity as part of the basic mission of their agencies. Contextual analysis is the second theme. We contend that to understand policing we must consider the various contexts in which it takes place. We consider the relationship between the police agency and the wider society and are concerned with how political, economic, legal, sociocultural, and historical factors affect the agency. Class is the third theme. To understand policing, we cannot ignore the fact that there are two Americas and the police's response to each is much different. The final theme is the importance of gender and race in establishing quality policing in the United States. Women did not enter policing until early in the twentieth century. Although female police officers perform in general as well as male police officers, they have not been well received and, in fact, have received considerable sexual harassment. We also discuss how the rights and dignity of minorities are violated by the police. We further examine how minority officers feel about their jobs.

On a hot summer night, a New York City police officer interviewed in Spanish Harlem revealed a flaw in the manner in which criminal justice is often pursued. He said, "I read too many criminal justice books that don't really relate to life on the streets. What I want you to do is tell the students the way it really is on the streets. Students have a right to know this."

The police officer is certainly correct that a student needs to be exposed to what is real in law enforcement. If that officer were to read this text, we hope that he would be pleased. We have given sufficient opportunities for insiders to tell how they feel about policing. We have not tried to hide the blemishes but have also rejoiced in what is right and honorable and just. We have suggested that more good people are being found in law enforcement, that good people make a difference, and that good people are learning that if they join together, their power and influence can be much greater. At a very dark hour of policing in this nation, we see emerging a light, still small but growing, and we believe that this light will bring a better future for policing in the United States.

ACKNOWLEDGMENTS

Many individuals have contributed to the writing of this book. We are profoundly grateful to our wives, Margie Hahn and Linda Dippold Bartollas. Both Margie Hahn and Linda Dippold Bartollas were a constant source of support and encouragement throughout the many phases involved in the publication of this volume. We also appreciate the many hours Linda Dippold Bartollas spent editing and conceptualizing materials throughout the manuscript.

The authors are very grateful to those members of the justice system or university professors who were willing to be interviewed, who contributed materials for this volume, or who critiqued our emerging chapters. Special thanks are due to Charles Remsberg, Dennis Anderson, Gary T. Klugiewicz, Linda Hall, Stephanie Bradley Peterson, Mildred K. O'Linn, Bob Willis, Dave Grossi, William J. Lewinski, Tina LaThrop, Ann Meyer, Celia E. Hahn, Chantal P. Poucek, and Linda D. Burk. We thank Betty Heine for all the tasks that she and her staff did to keep the manuscript moving without interruption. Sonja Ackermann was particularly helpful. Laurie Ann Olson also pitched in when help was needed. Finally, we are grateful to Karen Hanson, our editor at Allyn and Bacon, as well as the reviewers of this volume: Vic Kappeler, Eastern Kentucky University; Jo Ann M. Scott, Ohio Northern University; and Donald Hugh Smith, Old Dominion University.

Clemens Bartollas
Larry D. Hahn

1

THE HISTORY OF POLICING

"To police" means in the most general sense to control by political means the behavior and morality of the members of a politically organized unity. This sense of the word was derived early from the Greek word *polis*, meaning *city*, later roughly translated as *politics*. Policing in this sense means controlling, monitoring (in terms of correcting misguided behavior), tracking, and altering, if required, public conduct.

Policing also refers, in a more specific sense consistent with contemporary usage, to the public's expectations of the police force. That is, it refers to the tasks that people expect the people individually and in the aggregate to perform for them. These expectations are clearly variable within a population and over time. From the perspective of a member of the occupation, police work contains a symbolic conception of what is proper and correct behavior. The term can be applied loosely, such as "That's police work" or can be used in a more specific and laudatory manner, as in, "That's a good piece of police work," or "That's real police work!"...

—Peter K. Manning, *Police Work: The Social Organization of Policing*, 2nd ed. (Prospect Heights: Waveland, 1977) 27–28.

There are four important tasks in understanding the role of the police in the United States. First, policing in this nation must be examined within the context of a free and democratic society. It was decided early in the history of this nation that the prevention of crime was the proper role of government. If that could not be accomplished, then moderate rather than severe punishment was more fitting for a free and democratic society. Another early belief was that government is best that governs the least.[1] A further belief was that the authority of the state should be limited and, until suspects of crime were convicted in a court of law, the freedoms guaranteed them in the Constitution were to be zealously protected. Finally, it was held that police power must be regarded with grave suspicion in democratic societies.[2]

This is particularly true because of the enormous political power given to police officers. They are granted the authority to detain and arrest, to search for and seize evidence, and to use deadly force. Egon Bittner has suggested that the capacity to use force is at the core of the police role.[3] It behooves the police officer, then, to serve and protect in a way fitting the principles on which this society is based.

Second, a study of policing must include an examination of the response of individual police officers. Policing is a "tainted occupation" entailing doing society's dirty work,[4] and officers often spend most of their time with society's rejects, individuals who are caught up in criminal lifestyles, drug use and trafficking, and victimization of others. Policing, then, is not for the faint of heart or those who are tempted by wrongdoing. Police officers vary from those who are extraordinary to those who struggle in one way or another with job-related and personal problems. There are also officers who have retired on duty and others who are involved in some form of police deviancy.[5]

Third, an understanding of policing must consider the various contexts in which policing takes place. A major thread woven throughout this text is that policing in the United States is shaped by five contexts: historical, political, legal, sociocultural, and economic. The conjunction of these contexts on societal, organizational, and personal levels is what produces the police as we know them. The contextual approach is a reminder of how multidimensional policing is and how policing is affected by a variety of forces.

Finally, policing in a democracy requires high levels of integrity if it is to be acceptable to the people. What this means is that the desire to do the right thing must act as an internal compass for police officers. Alarming instances of police deviancy in the 1990s have eroded public confidence in the trustworthiness of police officers. These events have motivated police administrators to make integrity central to the mission of their departments.[6]

To begin this study of policing, we will examine the context of history. It is important to have a sense of five periods of police history to understand the development of policing in the United States: (1) early police; (2) European origins; (3) colonial police; (4) development of municipal police; and (5) twentieth century police. Indeed, too much of the time attempts to account for the origins and emergence of typical patterns of policing rarely locate those origins in a historical context. Such ahistorical approaches to understanding the history of the past can teach us much about the present.[7] The philosopher Santayana reminds us that "those who cannot remember the past are condemned to repeat it.[8]

EARLY POLICE

In the premodern world, policing was a private matter. Citizens were responsible for providing protection for themselves, and for maintaining an orderly society. In fact, the uniformed and organized police departments did not appear until the fourteenth century in France and until the nineteenth century in England.[9]

In about the sixth century B.C.E., unpaid magistrates in Athens adjudicated cases, but it was the responsibility of citizens to arrest and punish offenders. Citizens were actively involved in law enforcement as they frequently grouped together in towns and formed a watch, especially at night. They patrolled the town borders to ensure the safety of the town against invaders.

Rome had the most highly developed police forces in the ancient world. In about the fifth century B.C.E., Rome created *questors,* or "trackers of murder," representing the first specialized investigative unit. By the third century B.C.E., citizens also arrested and punished offenders as they did in Athens, following the unpaid magistrates' adjudication of a case.

The Roman Emperor Augustus, who ruled at the start of the Christian era, selected highly qualified members of the military to form the *praetorian guard,* which could be considered the first police force. Although the job of the praetorian guard was to protect the emperor and the palace, the *praefectus urbi,* or urban cohort, was appointed to protect the city. Moreover, Augustus established the *vigiles,* who patrolled Rome's streets day and night. Known for their brutality, the vigiles were actually the first civil police force designed to protect citizens.

Finally, in Rome later in the first century C.E., public officials called *lictors* were appointed to serve as the magistrates' bodyguards. They also brought prisoners before the magistrates to have their cases heard, and were responsible for carrying out the punishments ruled by the magistrates, including the death penalty.

EUROPEAN ORIGINS

The birth of modern policing can be traced to the reign of Alfred the Great, who ruled England from 871 to 900 C.E. In order to provide a defense against an impending Danish invasion, Alfred instituted a system of **mutual pledge.** Designed to create internal stability, this system organized England from the smallest level to that of counties. The smallest level of this community-based police system was called a *tithing,* made up of ten families who assumed responsibility for each other. Each tithing chose a man whose job was to make certain all members obeyed the law. If a member of the tithing committed a crime, it could affect everybody in that the entire tithing could be fined. The next level was the *hundred,* made up of ten tithings or 100 families. A constable was appointed to be in charge of the hundred. Within a specific geographic area, hundreds were combined to form shires. To maintain order in the shires, the king appointed a *shire-reeve* (later to be called a **sheriff**) to be the chief law enforcement officer. The sheriff traveled on horseback throughout the shire, keeping peace, holding court, and investigating crimes.

During the reign of Edward I (1272–1307), the first official police agency was created in an English town. Groups of men were appointed to patrol the streets at night with the twin function of maintaining a fire watch and arresting those committing crimes. This became known as the **watch and ward** system. In 1326, Edward II created the office of **justice of the peace** to assist the mutual pledge system. Noblemen were first appointed to this position to assist the sheriff in law enforcement functions. The justice of the peace soon took over the role of magistrate and eventually asserted control over the sheriff and constables.

By the eighteenth century, unarmed watchmen were chosen to assist the parish constables by means of lots. The responsibility of the watchmen was to patrol the streets at night. Under Charles II (1660–1685), the number of watchmen was increased. The *Charlies,* as watchmen were called, were also required to perform the duties of lighting lamps, calling the time, and reporting unsanitary conditions. The poorly paid watchmen were frequently aging and sickly persons or those moonlighting in addition to their regular employment.

The ineffectiveness of the magistrate, constable, and watchman arrangements led to the development of a private detective system as a supplement. One such system was that of the **thief taker**, in which private individuals would apprehend criminals for a fee or public reward—40 pounds for a robber down to 1 pound for a simple deserter.

During the period 1715–1725, the leading thief taker in England was Jonathan Wild who, at the same time, was also the directing force of most of the theft activity in London. Wild would receive reports from crime victims, then retrieve the stolen items from one of his warehouses of stolen goods and return it for a fee. Those who violated his rules were delivered to the authorities, and Wild was personally responsible for the hanging of a number of thieves. He himself eventually went to the gallows, because he had committed the unpardonable sin of making a magistrate jealous.[10]

England experienced a major crime wave and widespread civil unrest, including strikes and riots, during the eighteenth century. Crime and disorder were rampant, and the poor and working classes were blamed. The upper classes feared that the lower classes would attack them and seize their property. They also did not want to be contaminated by the supposedly immoral conduct of those they named the "mob" or the "dangerous" and "criminal" elements. Thus began a process, from which we have not yet recovered, of blaming the lower classes for the crime and disorder of society.

Government officials soon discovered that the system of parish constables and local watchmen was unable to deal with this social upheaval. In 1748, Henry Fielding was appointed a magistrate for London. He established the unofficial *Bow Street Runners,* whose primary task was to break up the large number of criminal gangs, to pursue lawbreakers, and to make arrests. Upon his death in 1754, his blind half-brother, Sir John Fielding, took over the operations of the Bow Street Runners. But the use of the Bow Street Runners to settle community disorder quickly came under criticism because they were perceived as making unjustified assaults on citizens. The public demanded a new kind of body to deal with the rising rate of crime and unrest.[11]

In 1763, Sir John Fielding was allotted 600 pounds to set up a civilian horse patrol of eight men to patrol the streets of London. Although it was disbanded nine months later, a foot patrol was established a decade later. In 1804, a new horse patrol of two inspectors and 52 men was set up. With their red vests, blue jackets, and trousers, this became England's first uniformed police.[12]

Patrick Colquhoun, a Glasgow businessman who was appointed to be a London magistrate in 1792, developed and advanced the idea of preventive policing and urged the creation of a centralized and organized force. When his proposal for an organized police force was rejected, he followed the Fieldings' example and created a special force to patrol the Thames.

Sir Robert Peel, who was appointed England's Home Secretary in 1822, responded to the public mandate for greater order by proposing a bill to organize the police system. Although his initial recommendations were rejected by Parliament, a bill entitled "An Act for Improving the Police In and Near the Metropolis" was passed on July 19, 1829. Known as the **Metropolitan Police Act,** the measure set up two justices of the peace, later called commissioners, to establish regulations for the hiring, training, and supervision of police officers.[13]

Many historians of the police have seen a logical progression from the Fieldings and the developments in Bow Street, through the work of Colquehoun, to the appearance of the Metropolitan Police in 1829. Yet the fact is that the force created in 1829 bore little resemblance to what had gone before it in London or little resemblance to the proposals made by Fielding or Colquehoun.[14]

Peel's foresight, along with strong leadership exhibited by commissioners Charles Rowan and Richard Mayen, enabled the police to overcome distrust and hatred from the citizens and to develop the approach to law enforcement that became dominant in England and later the United States. There were 12 principles developed during this period which, for the most part, are still used in the United States:

1. The police must be stable, efficient, and organized along military lines.
2. The police must be under government control.
3. The absence of crime will best prove the efficiency of the police.
4. The distribution of news about crime is essential.
5. The employment of police strength, both by time and area, where and when crime has occurred or may occur is essential.
6. No quality is more indispensable to a policeman than a perfect command of temper. A quiet, determined manner has more effect than violent action.
7. Good appearance commands respect.
8. The selection and training of proper persons are at the root of efficient law enforcement.
9. Public security demands that every police officer be given an identifying number.
10. Police headquarters should be centrally located and easily accessible to the people.
11. Policemen should be hired on a probationary basis before permanent assignment.
12. The keeping of crime records by police is necessary to determine the best distribution of police strength.[15]

The main features of this Peelian police force were that the police force resembled the military in many ways, that there was an attempt to implement a system of community policing, and that police administration was acknowledged as a professional career. First, the resemblance of the Peelian police force to the military began with the fact that its members were uniformed and organized in a hierarchical chain of command with central control and military type discipline. Recruits were also expected to be of an age and physique similar to army men (at least 5'7" and under 35) and, in fact, many were former members of the armed forces.

Yet there were cosmetic and actual differences between Peel's police and the army. Of lessor importance, the police used civil titles (inspector, superintendent, and commissioner) beyond the rank of sergeant, and adopted a blue uniform, copper buttons, and top hat at a time when soldiers wore red coats, brass buttons, and helmets. Of much greater importance, police constables were not issued firearms, were responsible to the civil law rather than the articles of war, and were invested with little authority.[16] In terms of the police's lack of power in the nineteenth century, English jurist Sir James Fitzjames Stephen has this to say:

> The police in their different grades are no doubt officers appointed by law for the purpose of arresting criminals, but they possess for this purpose no powers that are not also possessed by private persons.... A policeman has no other right as to asking questions or compelling the attendance of witnesses than a private person has; in a word, with a few exceptions, he may be described as a person paid to perform as a matter of duty acts, which if he so minded, he might have done voluntarily.[17]

Second, this was the first systematic attempt to implement a system of community policing. The beat was an important feature of this police system in that police constables were assigned relatively permanent posts and were expected to be familiar with them. The virtue of the beat system was that it provided for the continuing presence of a police officer as a part of the community or neighborhood life. It was reasoned that the constable would become known to the public, and that citizens with information about potential criminality would be more likely to convey it to a familiar figure rather than a strange one. By the end of the eighteenth century, the calm, courteous, and restrained "bobby" had become a national symbol and was given credit for making London a relatively safe city.

Third, a major characteristic of policing in London, as well as in Paris, Berlin, and Vienna, was that police administration was acknowledged as a professional career. Appointed by the national government, police administrators were kept in office for many years. They were independent of local politics, and their forces were disciplined as tightly as the military. This was in fundamental contrast to police administration in America where top administrators changed with every political breeze and the rank and file lacked discipline and were corrupt.[18]

In sum, the origins of modern policing in this nation can be linked directly to their English heritage. Ideas concerning crime prevention, community policing, constables, sheriffs, and the posse were developed from English law enforcement.[19] A social context much different from England is one of the reasons that policing in America divorced itself in many ways from its English heritage.[20]

COLONIAL POLICE

In seventeenth century colonial America, the settlers occupied themselves with erecting homes and planting crops. Violations of the law most often involved individuals who ran afoul of community obligations or morals. Accordingly, policing typically concentrated on ordinary people's behaviors. Historian David R. Johnson concluded that "colonists found themselves in court for such conduct as working on the sabbath, failing to pen animals properly, begetting a bastard child, and cursing in public places."[21]

The sheriff, the constable, the watch, and the slave patrol were the principal forms of law enforcement in colonial America. Based on English tradition and appointed by the colonial governor, the sheriff had the authority to protect life and property, enforce laws, and execute the wishes of the court. He also was entrusted with the responsibilities to collect taxes, conduct elections, and maintain bridges and roads. The sheriff was further vested with *posse comitatus,* or the "power of the county," a term that later came to refer to the group the sheriff assembled. The *posse comitatus* allowed the sheriff to deputize able-bodied citizens to perform designed functions, such as pursuing and arresting fugitives from justice.[22]

The constable was initially an elected position but eventually evolved into a semiprofessional appointed office. Although his duties varied from place to place according to the particular needs of the people he was serving, the constable usually sealed weights and measures, announced marriages, surveyed land, and executed all warrants. He also inflicted physical punishment and kept the peace. Joshua Pratt of Plymouth colony was the first constable on record (1634) whose primary responsibility was to oversee the watch and ward—the ward during the day and the watch at night. In Boston and other cities, the office of constable was regarded as a desirable and oftentimes lucrative position. In New York City, a large contingent of constables performed their duties. The legendary Jacob Hays served as high constable for over 40 years and established a reputation for stringent law enforcement.[23]

The watch had much in common with contemporary law enforcement responsibilities. Watchmen were charged to patrol the city guarding against fires, crime, and disorder. Although it was initially a nighttime activity, the larger cities gradually created day watches. These positions were generally unpaid, and serving in them was considered an obligation for young men. It was not long before increasing numbers of young men attempted to avoid duty, either by outright evasion or by paying others to serve in their place. The watch eventually evolved into a paid professional position.[24]

The settlements in New England, more densely populated than those in the South, relied primarily upon the English system of watchmen and constables. In the South, where the population was less dense, counties were formed and each county then elected or appointed a sheriff. Created in the southern states, the **slave patrol** was both a distinctive and egregious form of American law enforcement. Its purpose was to guard against slave revolts and to capture runaway slaves. It can be argued that the slave patrols were the first modern police forces in colonial

America. The Charleston (South Carolina) slave patrol employed about 100 officers in 1837, making it possibly the nation's largest police force at that time.[25]

Colonial law enforcement never had a "golden age" of efficiency and integrity, and was inefficient, corrupt, and subject to political interference. Sheriffs and constables were reactive, responding to complaints brought to them. They did not attempt to prevent crime or apprehend offenders, nor did they place any emphasis on maintenance of order or service.[26] **Corruption** appeared early in colonial law enforcement. The source of corruption can perhaps be traced to the fee system. Tempted by abundant opportunities for personal enrichment through graft, early court records and newspapers are filled with accounts of bribery and other forms of corruption.[27]

DEVELOPMENT OF MUNICIPAL POLICING

During the early nineteenth century, mass immigration from European countries swelled American cities. From 1790 to 1820, 5,000 immigrants per year streamed into the United States. For a while, the rise of industrialization in the shipyards, ironworks, cotton mills, shoe factories, and farm-implement foundries kept up with the number of workers coming into the nation. Skilled workers from England, Scotland, and Germany, especially metal workers and skilled crafts people, initially commanded premium wages and were always able to find jobs. But unskilled laborers, such as the displaced Irish farmers, quickly found that jobs went to those who would work for the cheapest wage. The depressions of 1807, 1819, and 1837 forced many of these unskilled workers out of work. This mass of poor, expendable, unskilled, and unemployed immigrants eventually was seen by the nativeborn and middle classes as an expanding pool of criminality. As a result, early in the history of this nation—as in England—crime was blamed on the poor, especially on the poor who were newcomers to America. Coming from different cultural, ethnic, and religious backgrounds also made these individuals seem suspicious and dangerous. It was reasoned that institutions were needed to protect society against the behavior of the **dangerous poor**.[28]

Significantly, those who were charged to control this behavior themselves came from the working class and often were recent immigrants. Jobs on the police force were a major form of political patronage, and the composition of departments reflected the ethnic and religious makeup of the cities. But compared with the London bobby, the police officer's job in America was definitely desirable. For example, a New York police officer was paid higher wages than skilled mechanics, and though the hours were long (nine hours patrol and seven hours reserve per day), discipline was lax and graft readily available.

As immigration populations grew, so did tensions among various economic, political, cultural, and religious groups. By the middle of the 1830's, riots were occurring in Boston, New York, and Philadelphia. The cities found it difficult to deal with this civil disorder because they had no force of social control available other than the military.

In 1833, the city of Philadelphia separated the watch system into a paid day watch and night watch, but New York City is credited with organizing the first police force patterned to some extent after the British model. In 1844, the New York State Legislature gave cities and towns in that state the power to organize police forces, and the city of New York then consolidated its day and night watches under the leadership of an appointed chief of police. Similar police systems were soon adopted in Baltimore, Boston, Chicago, Cincinnati, Newark, New Orleans, and Philadelphia.[29]

The American police departments borrowed selectively from the organization of the London Metropolitan Police. The most striking difference between the English and American models was in the area of control. In England, the strong central leadership in the Metropolitan Police was able to deal immediately with police problems. The English police also had clear lines of authority leading up to the commissioner, who in turn, answered to the home secretary in Parliament. In contrast, the American system was very disorganized, with unclear lines of authority. A police officer in any given city could be at the command of the chief of police, the mayor, an elected alderman, or all three. Police officers were hired and fired at the will of elected city officials. Favors were rewarded and scores settled through the hiring and firing of police officers. In England policing was a technical task with some political aspects, while in the United States it became a political task with technical aspects.

Nineteenth century police also did not have personnel standards. Nor was there any training, recruits were handed a badge, a baton, a copy of departmental rules, and were sent out to patrol. Police officers lacked job security and could be fired at will. Police patrol was totally inefficient. Officers walked a beat in all types of weather for two to six hours of a 12 hour day. The rest of the time was spent at the station house on reserve. Some entire areas of cities were not patrolled at all, and supervision was nearly nonexistent. Officers easily evaded duty, and some spent much of their time in barber shops and saloons. Citizens could not contact the police because no effective communication system existed. The first communication system involved a network of **call boxes** through which patrol officers could call the station house, but there were numerous ways of sabotaging the system.[30]

Early nineteenth century relations between the police and the community were generally good, because police forces served as social service agencies, providing overnight lodging for persons as well as daily meals to the needy. The police further used horse drawn paddy wagons as ambulances. However, the fact that the police in nineteenth century America were primarily tools of local politicians eventually affected their public relations. This political control led to widespread corruption and brutality and made the police ineffective in preventing crime or providing services. August Vollmer described this scandalous era of policing as one of "incivility, ignorance, brutality, and graft."[31]

The passage of a reform bill called the **Pendleton Act of 1833** finally brought some control to this corrupt system. This act established and set rules for civil service commissions, which governed entrance examinations and promotions and settled grievances within a police organization. Although civil service rules did not completely solve all the problems of hiring and promotion, they did remove much of the serious political interference that had adversely affected police forces in the United States.[32]

Three important issues confronted police officials between 1845–1860: (1) a controversy over the adoption of uniforms; (2) a concern about arming police officers; and (3) the issue of appropriate force in making arrests. Police officers were particularly resistant to wearing a uniform, but officials were eventually able to overcome the opposition in New York, Philadelphia, Boston, and Chicago. Arming the police was an even more sensitive issue, but in view of the abundance of guns in American society (every citizen had the right, and even the duty to own firearms), it was inevitable that there would be an armed police. Indeed, in the 1850s, individual police officers began to carry firearms without official permission, and it was not long before this met public acceptance. The chief reasons for the American police's use of force to make arrests in the years from 1840 to 1870 were the desire of police officers to establish their authority on the streets, and to control the violent turmoil of the era between 1840 and 1870.[33]

In the second half of the nineteenth century, politics affected the performance of the police on several levels. The recruitment of officers was largely determined by politics; an individual with the right connection could be hired despite ignorance, a criminal record, poor health, or old age. Police officials sold promotions to higher ranks within the department and also supported a system of electoral fraud. In return for regular payoffs, they ignored laws related to gambling, drinking, and prostitution.[34]

The New York Police Department had the most systematic arrangement for police corruption. By the late nineteenth century, politicians had established a fee of $300 to walk a beat and $15,000 to become a captain. Captains were in a particularly key position to exploit their offices. Selecting one of his detectives to be his personal bagman, this captain would make the rounds once a month to every saloon, gambling house, and brothel in the precinct to collect a tribute. At the turn of the century, the police assessed poolrooms between $100 and $300 a month; brothels between $50 and $150; and gambling houses from $50 to $300 a month. Bagmen kept around 20% of each month's collection and turned the remainder over to the captains and other supervisors.[35]

Mutual disrespect and brutality also characterized relations between late nineteenth century police and the public in most American cities. Youth gangs took great delight in taunting or throwing stones at the police. The police often used the billy club to gain deference to their authority. Police officers generally tolerated the "curbside justice" of the nightstick, and officers' lack of training and supervision only aggravated the problem.[36] These problems were illustrated in the career of Alexander Williams, a New York police officer who was aptly called "Clubber" (see Box 1.1).

TWENTIETH CENTURY POLICING

In the twentieth century, policing went through a reform and police professional movement, a fighting crime movement, and a public relations and community policing movement. These stages of policing history did not, of course, follow each other in a sequential pattern but often took place at the same time.

BOX 1.1   "Clubber" in Action

Alexander Williams was born in Canada in 1839. Spending a number of years as a ship's carpenter, he became a New York patrol officer in 1866. He was extremely strong and soon earned the title "Clubber." On the first day on the job, he picked a fight with the two toughest thugs in the neighborhood, clubbed them unconscious, pitched them through the plate-glass window of a saloon, and then proceeded to throw six of their buddies who stepped forward through the same window. Brought up on brutality charges before the Board of Commissioners on 358 occasions, he was fined 224 times but never dismissed.

In 1872, he was made captain of the Gashouse District, and in 1876 transferred to the Tenderloin district. From 1886 on, he was an inspector of a group of precincts on the City's East Side. In 1894, he admitted to a legislative committee that he had a personal fortune of $300,000, and an estate complete with a private steam yacht.

But even as an administrator, the "Clubber" continued to prowl the streets of New York. In a demonstration to reporters one day to show that he was still the king of the streets, he hung his watch on a lamppost while a number of local citizens looked on. Although people have been murdered for far less valuable items, the watch was still there when Clubber and party returned from a walk around the block. One of his classic statements was, "There is more law in a policeman's nightstick than the Supreme Court."

Source: Thomas A. Repetto, *The Blue Parade* (New York: The Free Press) 55–57.

Reform and Police Professionalism

A broad reform movement began to develop during the last decades of the nineteenth century. The Progressives—primarily upper-middle class, educated Protestants—sought to rectify societal ills. The Progressives drew their various criticisms of urban life into a program emphasizing honesty and efficiency in government, increased authority for public officials, and the use of experts to handle specific problems.[37]

Progressive-minded persons also attacked social injustice and included the police in the demand for change and accountability. The Progressives believed that the police should enforce the law and not provide the various forms of community service that they had traditionally involved themselves in. These reformers also advocated centralized police operations and held that specialization would be helpful in improving police efficiency. Finally, the Progressives supported upgrading the quality of police personnel and held that the police should be selected, deployed, and promoted on the basis of personal ability, rather than on the basis of partisan politics.[38]

Three of the most noted reform police leaders were **August Vollmer, O. W. Wilson,** and, later, **William H. Parker.** All three worked in California at some stage of their career, and all three believed strongly that a police officer must be carefully selected, well trained, free from political interference, and provided with the most up-to date technology and hardware.

August Vollmer was the first of these reform-minded police administrators. At 29, Vollmer was delivering mail and serving as a volunteer fireman when the publisher of the *Berkeley Gazette* and others persuaded him to run for marshal on an antivice ticket. In 1905, the 20,000 citizens of the sleepy college town of Berkeley elected Vollmer town marshal in charge of a six man force.

At the time he became town marshal, most police agencies were politically controlled extensions of the persons in power. The growth of police professionalism was one of Vollmer's top priorities. As town marshal and then as a chief in Berkeley, he fought hard to change the low image of American policing. His many impressive reforms included the distribution of the force based on better calculations of workload, the use of automobiles, the adoption of scientific detection methods such as the polygraph, and the institution of formal training. He believed that police officers should become college-educated professionals, similar to doctors or lawyers.[39] After his retirement as police chief he wrote:

> One can scarcely believe that such great advances could be made in so short a time. It is a far cry from an old politically controlled police department to the modern, scientifically operated organization. Under the old system, police officials were appointed through political affiliations.... They were frequently unintelligent and untrained; they were distributed through the area to be policed according to a hit-or-miss system and without adequate means of communication; they had little or no record system; their investigation methods were obsolete; and they had no conception of the preventive possibilities of the service.[40]

O. W. Wilson developed a progressive management philosophy while working as a patrol officer under Vollmer. His most noted period as police chief was from 1960 to 1967, when he headed the Chicago Police Department. His management approach mirrored that of Vollmer, as he advocated a professionalized law enforcement, divorced from politics, rigorous police personnel selection and training processes, and the use of the latest technological innovations available for law enforcement (e.g. maximum use of patrol cars, radio systems, and computerization of record keeping).[41]

Under the leadership of **J. Edgar Hoover,** the **Federal Bureau of Investigation (FBI)** also became a proponent of police professionalism. Hoover was instrumental in developing the FBI National Academy, which trains police officers throughout the nation in management and specialized fields. Moreover, he established the FBI Crime Laboratory, which is considered the best in the world.[42]

On a municipal level, the Los Angeles Police Department emerged during the 1950s as one of the most progressive police agencies in the country. William H. Parker, chief from 1950 to 1968, played a key role in its development from a scandal-ridden department to an organization noted for being corruption-free. His innovations included the establishment of internal research and development, strict personnel selection, and training for officers.[43]

This movement toward police professionalism had ten basic goals:

1. eliminate political influence
2. appoint qualified police executives
3. establish a mission of nonpartisan public service
4. raise personnel standards
5. encourage officers to interact with citizens in a neutral and detached manner
6. introduce principles of scientific management
7. emphasize military-style discipline
8. develop specialized units
9. apply innovations in technology to policing
10. develop measures to gauge police effectiveness

Not all of these goals of police reform have been achieved, but combined they have had a profound effect on policing in the United States.[44]

The goals of eliminating politics and hiring qualified leaders went hand in hand. The reformers recommended recruiting chiefs from other professions because they wanted the police to have the leadership of those who had proven abilities to manage a large organization. Both New York City and Philadelphia did this in the second decade of the twentieth century. Reformers also advocated giving police executives job security and/or tenure to better ensure that they would be shielded from political influence. Milwaukee adopted this idea, giving its police chiefs life tenure. What the reformers had in mind with raising personnel standards was to establish minimum recruitment requirements and formal preservice training. New York City created the first police training academy in 1895 (initially restricted to firearms training). The most frequent reason cited for requiring that recruits meet minimum standards of intelligence, moral character, and health was that police officers were public servants. The process of preservice training was painfully slow, and some cities did not offer meaningful training until the 1950s.

The reformers argued for scientific management of police departments because they saw it as a way to centralize command and to make efficient use of personnel. The reformers were sensitive to the fact that too often the decision-making power was held by the captains in the neighborhood precinct stations where politicians had great influence. Reformers closed some of the precinct stations, asserted greater control, and put more emphasis on a chain of command. They also saw technology as a means to expand command and control.

Reformers also advocated military-style discipline. Up to this point, policing had employed many military components, but was distinctly unmilitary in its inefficiency and lack of discipline. In his brief career as New York City Police Commissioner, Theodore Roosevelt placed great importance on injecting a militaristic spirit into policing. He was one of the first to talk about a "war on crime" and emphasized close-order drills, military-style commendations, and parades.

Finally, the reform movement included the development of specialized units. Until then, police departments only had patrol and detective units. The creation of special juvenile units brought the induction of the first female police officers. By 1919, over 60 police agencies employed female officers, usually with limited arrest powers, and by 1925 the number had risen to 144.[45]

On balance, the reformers could claim one success and that was the firm establishment of professionalism as a police force ideal. That agenda has dominated police reform until the present. In the 1970s, minority hiring, more extensive training, utilization of private sector management techniques, and evaluation of police operations, including patrol, were some of the approaches used to advance professionalism in policing. In the 1980s, with the elimination of funding from the **Law Enforcement Assistance Association (LEAA)** and increased economic constraints, police departments across the United States pursued voluntary accreditation as a means to improve police services, and made innovative developments in the areas of data processing and communication.

Yet professionalism yielded some unintended consequences for the police. Agencies tended to divide between old-timers and younger, more progressive police officers, and demands for autonomy, efficiency, and objectivity led to detached and impersonal attitudes toward the community and resistance to any direction from elected political officials.[46] The implementation of ideals into the daily operations of police departments was another problem facing advocates of professionalism. By 1920, only Berkeley and Cincinnati could be labeled professional. Corruption and inefficiency continued to rule the day in most other urban departments. Chicago persisted in resisting all efforts at reform. Philadelphia, New York, and Los Angeles would make some progress under a reform administrator but would then slide back a few years later. For important dates in the history of policing in the United States, see Box 1.2.

Crime Fighters

In the twentieth century, fighting criminals was no new activity for the police. For example, in the undeveloped West bandits and law enforcement officers engaged in continued conflict after the Civil War. American folklore, as well as television and motion pictures, tells of the criminal pursuits of Jesse James and Cole Younger, Butch Cassidy and the Sundance Kid, and other lesser-known outlaws. But what is not commonly known is that as much of the crime of the West was committed by lawmen as by desperadoes. Indeed, many "lawmen" were desperadoes; gunslingers were sometimes marshals, sometimes outlaws, and sometimes both.[47]

In the 1920s and early 1930s, the prohibition of liquor sales in the United States set the backdrop for the rise of the violent gangster. As immortalized in folklore, Federal agent Elliot Ness and his "Untouchables" relentlessly pursued such underworld figures as Al Capone, George "Baby Face" Nelson, and Charles "Pretty Boy" Floyd.[48] The wide open violence of Chicago is represented in the number of police officers shot and killed by gangsters and mob bosses. In the somewhat typical years of 1926 and 1927, 20 police officers were killed, and the police, in turn, killed 89 citizens.[49]

BOX 1.2   Important Dates in Police History in the United States

1600

1631, April   Boston establishes the first system of law enforcement in America—called the "night watch." Officers served part-time, without pay.

1700

1712   First full-time paid law enforcement officers hired in the United States in Boston.

1789, September 24   Congress creates the first Federal law enforcement position, the United States Marshal.

1794, January 11   U.S. Marshal Robert Forsyth becomes the first officer in United States history to be killed in the line of duty.

1800

1835   Texas creates what was later to become the Texas Rangers, the oldest statewide law enforcement agency in the United States.

1858   Boston and Chicago police departments are the first to issue uniforms to their officers.

1863   Boston becomes the first police department to issue pistols to their officers.

1865, April 14   On the day he was shot by an assassin, President Abraham Lincoln approves formation of what is now the U.S. Secret Service.

1870, November 2   Thomas J. Smith of Abilene, Kansas is the first of more than 350 police chiefs to die in the line of duty.

1871, November 11   Portsmouth, Virginia Patrolman John Wilson becomes the first African American police officer to be killed in the line of duty.

1878–1881   Notorious outlaw, "Billy the Kid," kills six law enforcement officers in New Mexico.

1881, October 26   Legendary lawman Wyatt Earp, his brothers, and "Doc" Holiday, win the wild west era's most famous gunfight at the O.K. Corral.

1891   First national police group is formed, the National Chiefs of Police Union, which would later become the International Association of Chiefs of Police. For the first time, police leaders meet regularly to share ideas.

1900

1902   Fingerprinting is first used in the United States.

1910   Alice Stebbins Wells of the Los Angeles Police Department becomes the first female officer with arrest powers.

1924, May 11   Mary T. Davis becomes the first female officer to be killed in the line of duty.

1932–1934   "Bonnie and Clyde" and their gang murder 10 law enforcement officers, more than any other criminal group.

1952, June 25   Dotson "Pop" Sutton, 80, becomes the oldest officer to die in the line of duty.

1959   Last year in United States history that fewer than 100 police officers are killed in the line of duty.

1974   Police start wearing soft body armor for protection against handgun assaults.

1988   The FBI becomes the first law enforcement agency in the country to use DNA test methods to solve crimes.

1991, October 15   The National Law Enforcement Officers Memorial is dedicated in Washington, DC.

Source: National Law Enforcement Officers Memorial Fund, Washington, D.C.

In the 1960s and early 1970s, harmony and order in American society seemed to be in grave jeopardy. The violent reaction to the Civil Rights Movement, urban, college, and prison riots, the expression of antiwar sentiments by American youth in reaction to the Vietnam War, the rise of a drug-using counterculture among young people, and corruption in the Oval Office constituted national emergencies and spurred political leaders and their constituents to seek to quell the unrest.

The turmoil of the 1960s and early 1970s, as well as the supposed resurgence of crime led to a declaration of war on crime. The restoration of "law and order" against street crime emerged as a political issue in the Goldwater and Johnson presidential campaign of 1964. In his acceptance speech before GOP convention delegates, Barry Goldwater stated:

> Tonight there is violence in our streets, corruption in our highest offices, aim-lessness among our youth, anxiety among our elderly, and there's a virtual de-spair among the many who look beyond material success toward the inner meaning of their lives...Security from domestic violence, no less than from for-eign aggression, is the most elementary and fundamental purpose of any gov-ernment that can long command the loyalty of its citizens. History shows us, demonstrates that nothing, nothing prepares the way for tyranny more than the failure of public officials to keep the streets safe from bullets and marauders.[50]

President Johnson launched a **war on crime** two months after his inaugura-tion, part of his larger vision of a "Great Society." Johnson maintained that the best way to halt crime was an all-out war on poverty. To win this war, Johnson's strat-egy included greater federal involvement with increased federal law enforcement efforts and greater assistance to local law enforcement agencies.

On July 25, 1965, Johnson established the President's Commission on Law Enforcement and the Administration of Justice. This commission, better known as the President's Crime Commission, issued a series of task forces covering the po-lice, the courts, corrections, juvenile delinquency, organized crime, science and technology, drunkenness, narcotics and drugs, and the assessment of crime. These individual reports were summarized in a general report, *The Challenge of Crime in the Free Society.*[51]

President Johnson's war on crime also resulted in the passage of the Omnibus Crime Control and Safe Streets Act of 1968. Title I of the Act created the Law En-forcement Assistance Administration (LEAA), which was organized to function in five ways:

1. by supporting statewide planning in the field of criminal justice through the creation of state planning agencies (SPAs)
2. by supplying states and localities with block grants of federal funds to improve their criminal justice systems
3. by making discretionary grants to special programs in the field of criminal justice

4. by developing new devices, techniques, and approaches in Law Enforcement and Criminal Justice, the research arm of the LEAA
5. by supplying money for the training and education of criminal justice personnel[52]

In both the 1968 and 1972 presidential elections, Richard M. Nixon also declared war on crime, lamenting what crime in the streets was doing to the quality of American life. During his terms in office, President Nixon advocated a law-and-order approach to crime. Until his resignation from office as a result of allegations of obstruction of justice, President Nixon continued to maintain that a war on crime could be won by imposing harsher criminal penalties.

Gerald Ford continued the war on crime from the White House, but President Ronald Reagan fought the war with even greater diligence. His emphasis was on violent street crime during his first term in office, but during his second term he focused on violent crime, drug trafficking, and organized crime. His stance was reflected in his words:

> The crime problem has indeed become a matter of widespread concern, even among people of different philosophies. Today's hardliner on law and order is yesterday's liberal who was mugged last night. Some men are prone to evil, and society has a right to be protected from them.[53]

President George Bush also continued the war on crime but his primary concern was with waging the war on drugs. President Bill Clinton, who was sworn in as the 42nd president in 1993, has not abandoned the war on crime and drugs during his two administrations. During his State of the Union address in January 1994, Clinton noted that funds will be available to place more police officers on the streets and to establish boot camps. As did his predecessors during this 30 year war, the president assured the American public that the criminal element will pay for its lawless behaviors.

Fighting this war on crime has led to the growing militarization of policing in the United States. The police have developed various forms of assault teams, have equipped officers with the most high-powered weaponry available, and have even purchased motorized battering rams (tanks) to defeat the enemy.[54] This militarization of policing has also encouraged some police officials and officers to become more aggressive in attacking the bad guys on the streets. This wide-open style, in turn, has been one of the factors contributing to some of the excessive force incidents found in Los Angeles and other urban departments.

Thus, during the twentieth century, cops have been treated as soldiers trying to win the "war on crime" and to control the drug trade. The fact is that the police are fighting for a lost cause. This unwinnable war is a social responsibility that belongs to politicians rather than the police. When asked, "How effective are the police in controlling the drug trade," an experienced New York narcotics officer expressed this predicament well: "We are," he answered, "like a gnat biting on a horse's ass."[55]

Public Relations and Community Policing

Community policing is as old as policing itself. The reform, professionalism, and crime fighting movements had reduced the emphasis on community contacts and relations. In the 1970s, the pendulum swung back to some degree as a number of community-based programs were developed and implemented in police departments across the nation. Team policing was one such program. This was a patrol strategy designed to improve the effectiveness of patrol. Team policing involves the assignment of police officers to a team that becomes responsible for a given geographic area. The team concept generally involves one of four techniques: (1) specialized patrol units; (2) combination of patrol officers and investigators; (3) combination of patrol officers and community services personnel; and (4) combination of patrol, investigation, and community services.[56]

Team policing was designed to bring police personnel and the community closer together, building trust and reducing alienation. Although team policing was hailed as a concept for future policing in the 1970s, two problems in implementation have led to widespread criticism and reduced use during the past two decades. First, team participants were not always fully aware of their roles; second, investigators and uniformed officers (who traditionally have had strained relationships) found it difficult to work together.[57]

"Neighborhood Crime Watchers," another of these programs, are made up of people organized by police in their neighborhoods to help each other in reducing crime—especially property crimes such as burglary and theft. The police provide training on how citizens can secure their homes and protect themselves and on how best to report suspicious activity.

In the 1980s and 1990s, an increased number of police departments have implemented various aspects of community-oriented policing (COP) and problem-oriented policing (POP). There are those who argue that a return to community policing is the most significant change that has taken place in police work. There are also those who look upon community policing as "policing for the twenty-first century," but there is still inconclusive evidence about its effectiveness.[58] Both COP and POP will be extensively discussed and evaluated in future chapters.

LESSONS FROM HISTORY

This brief examination of history offers several insights about the nature and role of policing in the United States.[59] First, modern policing is a product of the complexity and impersonality of an industrial society and is shaped by the political, social, and economic trends of time and place. Urban growth, which has gone hand in hand with industrialization, has involved selective migration to the cities, especially by young people with few ties and fewer resources—a group that in all places is especially susceptible to crime. Migration from other countries has also brought about new mechanisms of social interaction. Some of these new groups have developed deviant, and occasionally predatory subcultures that pose a threat and challenge to public order as conceived by dominant social groups.[60] Thus, industrial society has been unable to assimilate the broad processes of social change, and widespread disruptive behavior has resulted.

Second, the influence of social class has been a dominant theme guiding the role and function of the police. The police were drawn from the lower and working classes. Indeed, early police forces, especially in eastern cities, were largely made up of recent immigrant populations. The lower-class background of the police made them more vulnerable to control by the urban political machines that offered jobs as a form of political patronage. It made them more receptive to graft and other forms of corruption that provided a means to escape their social origins, and made them more open to using force to uphold the law. Accordingly, within United States history, the widespread nature of political control, corruption, and excessive force cannot be separated from the influence of social class.

Third, a review of United States history also leads to the conclusion that police systems are a reflection of the community's social, moral, and economic makeup. What this suggests is that police agencies in communities filled with violence, drug trafficking, and other forms of vice find it difficult to avoid a corruption filled department. Or to express this in another way, policing tends too often to be a microcosm of the larger society.

Fourth, the clash between morality and politics has trapped the police of the United States in an ambivalent posture that ultimately reduces their effectiveness. The control of political machines over the police in some cities may have facilitated the maintenance of order but made it impossible for other sections of the society to view the police as a moral force. The control of the political machine also increases the likelihood of the police's alliance with organized crime, and this, in turn, reduces the credibility of the police even further.

Fifth, the issue of controlling the controllers is always one of great importance in a free and democratic society. History teaches us that the police have abused their power, sometimes in small ways and at other times in major ways. The three traditional mechanisms for control of the police have been law, administration, and politics. Some evidence from the past suggests that the able administrator supporting the rule of law is the most effective way for the police to control its own behavior.

Sixth, professionalism has made major improvements in the nature and function of police operations in the United States. Yet history also reveals that professionalism has resulted in unintended consequences for local police. It has contributed to the widening conflict between administrators and line officers and to the fact that the police have fallen out of touch with the citizens they are supposed to serve.

Seventh, community policing is a widely used term for loosely defined police philosophies, strategies, and tactics known as community-oriented policing, problem-oriented policing, and neighborhood-oriented policing. As one of the major hopes of modern policing, police administrators should study their history to better understand the debates over community policing. Some of the mistakes of the past include lack of planning, mission ambiguity in terms of uncertainty of who to serve and how to serve them, lack of efficiency, and potential for corruption.[61]

Eighth, the presence of women and minorities in police departments has been nearly nonexistent throughout much of police history in this nation. The first female police officer was not appointed until the opening decade of the twentieth century, and it was only in the 1970s because of federal legislation that increasing numbers of women were hired. The police have been involved on too many occasions with discriminatory actions toward racial minorities, and it was not until 1915–1919 in Chicago that African Americans were appointed with any frequency to the police force. Until recent decades, the Chicago Police Department remained one of the few in the United States with any significant representation of African Americans on the force.[62]

SUMMARY

The teleological, the incrementalist, and the conflict views are three general perspectives on the historical roots of policing. The teleological view involves the use of facts to document a set of moral presuppositions. It has been used to present the development of the police as one feature of the steady and inevitable advance of society to a higher, more civilized, and less violent level. The incrementalist view also shares the notion of unilinear development of historical forces. Stripped of the moral tones of the teleological view, the incrementalist view emphasizes the cumulative nature of ideas and events of the past in influencing the present. Conflict-oriented analyses of history present the understanding that interest groups, working through the legislative and legal processes, created the police to serve their own interests over societal needs.[63] For example, Jerome Skolnick argues, "The civil police is a social organization created and sustained by political processes to enforce dominant conceptions of public order."[64]

The development of the history of policing, as presented in this chapter, includes both incrementalist and conflict views. The incrementalist view is revealed in at least two ways. We suggest that the cumulative ideas from the past do influence the structure and functioning of policing from one generation to the next. We also believe that there has been a steady development of the notion of the police since early history and, in the past two centuries, the police as a group have made progress in several significant areas. But this view does not present an inevitable and steady linear improvement of the police. The police vary in quality from one department to another and from one generation and century to another. The conflict view is suggested in this chapter in two ways. We see the political elite's control of the lower classes as one of the underlying forces shaping the police in nineteenth century America. We also are cognizant of the importance of class because the dominant classes used the lower classes to police the poor and immigrant population in this nation.

This chapter further proposes that a contextual analysis is an effective means of understanding policing in the United States. Colonial policing was greatly influenced by what had taken place in England, but the social context in this nation was different than in England. Unlike England, policing in this nation was much more closely linked with local political systems, police officers were typically recruited from the same neighborhoods they were serving, policing provided a variety of social service functions, and police officers enjoyed considerable amounts of discretion.

A contextual analysis also leads us to understand that in every period since the colonies were founded, political and economic forces have combined with socio-cultural and legal forces to shape the development of modern policing. The early development of policing in this nation was scandalous; political control, corruption, and brutality were characteristics of nineteenth century police. The public, not surprisingly, lacked respect for the police, and open conflict with the public has been an enduring characteristic of policing in this nation. This alienation between the public and the police became particularly strident in the 1960s. Both among minorities in the slums and among students on college campuses, open conflict erupted time after time.

Today, the police find they have a severe credibility problem, especially with minority groups. Today, the police are under attack on too many levels and related to too many incidents. Still, the fact remains that great improvement in policing has taken place over the past two centuries. Present day problems are a grim reminder that significant progress must continue to be made. The remainder of this text is devoted to examining the roles and functions of the police at the present time and to suggest promising directions for the future.

KEY WORDS

call boxes	Peel, Sir Robert
corruption	Pendleton Act of 1833
dangerous poor	posse comitatus
Federal Bureau of Investigation (FBI)	sheriff
Hoover, J. Edgar	slave patrol
justice of the peace	thief taker
Law Enforcement Assistance	Vollmer, August
Association (LEAA)	war on crime
Metropolitan Police Act	watch and ward
mutual pledge	Wilson, O. W.
Parker, William H.	

DISCUSSION QUESTIONS

1. What is a contextual approach to understanding policing. Evaluate this approach. What are its advantages and limitations?

2. Are the police better now than they were in the past? In what ways?

3. How did the policing system in London influence the development of policing in the colonies? What was different about the American system?

4. How did class influence the development of policing in the United States?

5 Who were some police officers and officials in the past who made a difference? What common traits did these individuals have?

6. Why was nineteenth century policing so corrupt and brutal?

7. Discuss the lessons that can be learned from the past. How can they be helpful in guiding law enforcement in the present and the future?

FURTHER READING

Emsley, Clive. *The English Police: A Political and Social History.* London: Longman, 1991.

Fogelson, Robert M. *Big City Police.* Cambridge: Harvard University Press, 1977.

Johnson, David R. *American Law Enforcement: A History.* St. Louis: Forum, 1981.

National Constables Association. "Constable." *The Encyclopedia of Police Science,* 2nd ed. Ed. William B. Bailey. New York: Garland, 1995, 114–115.

Reppetto, Thomas A. *The Blue Parade.* New York: The Free Press, 1978.

Richardson, James F. *Urban Police in the United States.* Port Washington: Kennikat, 1974.

Rousey, Dennis C. *Policing the Southern City: New Orleans, 1805–1889.* Baton Rouge: Louisiana State UP, 1996.

Rothman, David J. *The Discovery of the Asylum: Social Order and Disorder in the New Republic.* Boston: Little, Brown, 1971.

Uchida, Craig D. "The Development of the American Police: An Historical Overview." *Critical Issues in Policing.* Eds. R. Dunham and G. Alpert. Prospect Heights: Waveland, 1989.

ENDNOTES

1. Quoted in "The Ethics Roll Call," Law Enforcements Ethics Center, Summer 1997.

2. Paul Chevigny, *Edge of the Knife: Police Violence in the Americas* (New York: The Free Press, 1995) 6.

3. Egnon Bittner, *The Functions of Police in Modern Society* (New York: Jason Aronson, 1975); Egnon Bittner, *Aspects of Police Work* (Boston: Northeastern UP, 1990).

4. See Victor E. Kappeler, Richard D. Sluder, and Geoffrey P. Alpert, *Forces of Deviance: Understanding the Dark Side of Policing* (Prospect Heights: Waveland, 1994).

5. Raymond G. Hunt and John M. Magenau, *Power and the Police Chief: An Institutional and Organizational Analysis* (Newbury Park: Sage, 1993) 6–10.

6. Stephen J. Gaffigan and Phyllis P. McDonald, *Police Integrity: Public Service with Honor* (Washington, DC: USGPO; COPS and NIJ, 1997) iii–iv.

7. Craig D. Uchida, "The Development of the American Police: An Historical Overview,"

Critical Issues in Policing: Contemporary Readings (Prospect Heights: Waveland, 1989) 14.

8. George Santayana, *The Life of Reason* (London: Constable, 1905) 284.

9. For a more extensive examination of early policing, see William G. Bailey, ed., *The Encyclopedia of Police Science,* 2nd ed. (New York: Garland, 1995); and Charles Reith, *The Blind Eye of History: A Study of the Origins of the Present Police Era* (London: Faber, 1912).

10. Thomas A. Reppetto, *The Blue Parade* (New York: The Free Press, 1978) 12.

11. T. A. Critchley, *A History of Police in England and Wales,* 2nd ed. (Montclair: Patterson Smith, 1972) 47. See also Patrick Pringle, *Hue and Cry: The Story of Henry and John Fielding and Their Bow Street Runners* (New York: Morrow, 1965) 29–58.

12. Pringle.

13. Clive Emsley, *The English Police: A Political and Social History* (London: Longman, 1991) 24.

14. Pringle, 50–53.

15. Thomas F. Adams, *Law Enforcement* (Englewood Cliffs: Prentice–Hall, 1973) 60–61.

16. Reppetto, 18.

17. Quoted in Captain W. L. Melville–Lee, *A History of Police in England and Wales* (London: Methuen, 1901) 333.

18. Reppetto, 18.

19. Uchida, "The Development of the American Police," 15.

20. Kappeler, Sluder, and Alpert, 40–41.

21. David R. Johnson, *American Law Enforcement: A History* (St. Louis: Forum, 1981) 4.

22. Johnson, 56.

23. The National Constables Association, "The Constable," in *The Encyclopedia of Police Science*, 115.

24. Reppetto, 18.

25. Robert F. Wintersmith, *Police and the Black Community* (Lexington: Lexington, 1974), 17–21.

26. Samuel Walker, *The Police in America: An Introduction*, 2nd ed. (New York: McGraw–Hill, 1992) 6.

27. Douglas Greenberg, *Crime and Law Enforcement in the Colony of New York, 1691–1776* (Ithaca: Cornell UP, 1976).

28. David J. Rothman, *The Discovery of the Asylum: Social Order and Disorder in the New Republic* (Boston: Little, Brown, 1971).

29. James F. Richardson, *Urban Police in the United States* (Port Washington: Kennikat, 1974) 19–34.

30. Walker, *The Police in America*, 8–12.

31. Quoted in Samuel Walker, *Popular Justice: A History of American Criminal Justice* (New York: Oxford UP, 1980), 61.

32. Johnson, 66.

33. Johnson, 30.

34. Walker, *The Popular Justice*, 64.

35. Johnson, 60.

36. Reppetto, 119.

37. August Vollmer, "Police Progress in the Last Twenty-Five Years," *Journal of Criminal Law and Criminology* 24 (May–June 1933): 161.

38. Robert M. Fogelson, *Big City Police* (Cambridge: Harvard UP, 1977).

39. Craig D. Uchida, "The Development of the American Police: An Historical Overview," in *Critical Issues in Policing*, 3rd ed. edited by Roger G. Dunham and Geoffrey P. Alpert (Prospect Heights: Waveland, 1997) 29.

40. Vollmer, 161.

41. Richardson, 138–139.

42. Adams, 41–50, 88.

43. Richardson, 139–146.

44. This section on the reform agenda is derived from Walker, *The Police in America*, 13–14.

45. Samuel Walker, *A Critical History of Police Reform: The Emergence of Professionalism* (Lexington: Lexington, 1977) 84–94.

46. Jeffrey Patterson, "Community Policing: Learning the Lessons of History," *FBI Law Enforcement Bulletin* 5 (November 1995): 8–9.

47. Patterson, 8–9.

48. Patterson, 328–329.

49. Illinois Association for Criminal Justice, *The Illinois Crime Survey* (Chicago, 1929) 606, 610.

50. "Goldwater Acceptance Speech to GOP Convention," *New York Times*, 17 July 1964.

51. *President's Commission on Crime in a Free Society* (Washington, DC: USGPO, 1973).

52. Twentieth Century Task Force on the Law Enforcement Assistance Administration, *Law Enforcement: The Federal Role* (New York: McGraw–Hill, 1976) 4.

53. Ronald Reagan, Speech before the International Association of Chiefs of Police, New Orleans, Sept. 1981.

54. P. B. Kraska, "The Police and the Military in the Post-Cold War Era: Streaming the State's Use of Force Entities in the Drug War," *Police Forum* 4 (1994): 1–12. See also Peter B. Kraska and Victor E. Kappeler, "Militarizing American Police: The Rise and Normalization of Paramilitary Units," *Social Problems* 44 (Feb. 1997): 1–18; and David B. Kopel and Paul H. Blackman, *No More Wacos: What's Wrong with Federal Law Enforcement and How to Fix It* (Amherst: Prometheus, 1997) 337–342.

55. Quoted in Jerome H. Skolnick and James J. Fyfe, *Above the Law: Police and the Excessive Use of Force* (New York: The Free Press, 1993) 132.

56. Edward A. Thibault, Lawrence M. Lynch, and R. Bruce McBride, *Proactive Police Management* (Englewood Cliffs: Prentice–Hall, 1985) 168–169.

57. Thibault, et al., 168–174.

58. Susan Sadd and Randolph Grinc, "Innovative Neighborhood Oriented Policing: An Evaluation of Community Policing Programs in Eight Cities," *The Challenge of Community Policing*, ed.

Dennis P. Rosenbaum (Thousand Oaks: Sage, 1994) 50.

59. These insights are derived in part from Reppetto.

60. Ted Robert Gurr, "Development and Decay: Their Impact on Public Order in Western History," *History and Crime: Implications for Criminal Justice Policy,* ed. James A. Inciardi and Charles E. Faupel (Beverly Hills: Sage, 1980) 31–52.

61. Patterson, 8–9.

62. Reppetto, 220, 222.

63. Peter K. Manning, *Police Work: The Social Organization of Policing,* 2nd ed. (Prospect Heights: Waveland, 1997) 50.

64. Jerome Skolnick, "Changing Conceptions of the Police," in *Great Ideas Today* (Chicago: Encyclopedia Britannica, 1972) 41.

2

POLICE'S ROLES AND FUNCTIONS IN A DEMOCRATIC SOCIETY

To a police chief, the perfect cop is someone who looks sharp, works hard and doesn't expect overtime pay, makes good arrests without offending anyone, writes detailed reports and keeps a neat, readable activity log. He is also always available when extra help is needed, accepts work assignments willingly and comes up with fast, favorable results. In short, a perfect cop is someone who makes the chief look good.

To a prosecuting attorney, a perfect cop is a meticulous investigator who gathers and documents evidence, obtains confessions to all crimes, and outlines each case in order to make the prosecutor's job easy. He doesn't object when a case is plea bargained so the attorneys can go golfing on Friday afternoon, and doesn't mind if an offender gets probation or a suspended sentence because it is more convenient to make a deal than go to trial.

To a defense attorney, a perfect cop is a bungling idiot who makes mistakes and someone the defense can manipulate and make angry in court. A perfect cop is someone who will agree to any and all plea bargaining proposed, and whom the defense attorney can call when he needs protection from his own client.

To the city council, a perfect cop is someone who does his job well without making waves, who is so grateful for a job that he willingly works nights, weekends, and holidays. He never asks for more than the city is willing to pay, does an exemplary job without adequate equipment and tools. Best of all, he never writes tickets on any council member—or their kids.

To his wife, a perfect cop never lets the job effect his emotions. He can spend his hours dealing with drunks, domestics, drug users, injured or dead people, and then come home and be a loving, well-adjusted husband and father.

I have been a cop for over 20 years, and have never met a perfect cop. Only a few have even come close, being totally honest and truly caring about people and doing the best job they can.

But all the cops I have known are human. They love, laugh, cry, hurt, and sometimes die too young. They try to make it to retirement, although many do not. Divorce is common, some become alcoholics and some suffer from "police stress," seen in a variety of emotional disorders or heart attacks. Our job is often described as 98 percent boredom and 2 percent sheer terror.

Why do we do it? We don't really know. I hope it's because we simply care about right and wrong.

—Keith H. Winger, appeared in *Law and Order, Vol. 41* (March 1993).

Keith H. Winger, chief of the Warroad Police Department in Minnesota, describes the contexts and conflicting demands police officers face as they do their jobs. They must satisfy the police chief and their supervisors within the department, judges and prosecutors within the criminal justice system, politicians in the community, local citizens, and their spouses and families. At the same time, adds Chief Winger, police officers encounter their own problems and personal limitations. Those who persevere on the job and care deeply about doing what is right can make a difference.

Chief Winger is also talking about the role behavior of police officers. He is suggesting that the police sometimes have a dangerous role, a role that may cost officers' lives. It is far more often a boring role, but occasionally within that boredom everything breaks loose. It is a frustrating role, especially in dealing with departmental rules and regulations. Every now and then, it is a rewarding role, in which an officer knows that good has been done, justice has prevailed, and the world is just a little bit better off. The roles of the police are ultimately social roles that are affected both by society's expectations and its norms and values.

The public is, of course, more mindful of the police's functions and responsibilities in deterring crime. Police officer's presence on the streets, their uniforms and marked cars, and their powers of persuasion are some of the means they employ to help deter crime. After a crime has been committed, the police are responsible for questioning the victims, ascertaining what happened, determining whether the victims need help, and providing assistance. As the first official line of decision makers in the criminal justice system, the police are responsible for initiating a process that can either deprive individuals of their freedom or assure that their freedom is not arbitrarily taken away. Police officers are also responsible for safeguarding the rights of citizens and the well-being of communities.

This chapter examines the roles and functions of the police in the United States. Beginning with an examination of policing in a democratic society, citizens' attitudes toward the police, and the functions of the police, there is a description of the various roles of federal, state, city, and county police departments. The scope of private security is also discussed. The chapter further exposes some of the dark sides of policing, vivid and tragic examples of how far the ideal of the perfect cop has fallen.

POLICING IN A DEMOCRATIC SOCIETY

In the United States, policing takes place in a free and democratic society. It is a government made up of those who are elected by the people with the responsibility to comply with the wishes of the people. It is also a government that values human rights and the freedom of the individual. What this means is that democratic systems of government build a delicate balance between individual rights and collective needs. This balance, based on a long history of constitutional government, is weighed on the side of individual rights.

There has always in this nation been a distrust of authority, a sense that too much governmental control will lead to the erosion of individual freedom. David Bayley expressed it this way: "Government in the United States is created by communities to achieve certain limited purposes. Government is a created artifact and is distrusted." Bayley then concludes, "Americans believe that the only way to restrain its power is to ensure that its agents do not exceed the authority of the law. In order to preserve freedom, grants of power must be explicit and unambiguous."[1]

Still, in the midst of the concern about freedom of the individual and the restraint of government, disorder is a serious concern in the United States. Humankind has always sought the ordered society. Prehistoric humans desired order because they feared the catastrophes of nature and the disruption of their already fragmented communal existences. To humans throughout history, the ordered society has meant structured and stable communal lives. In the ordered society, people feel safe; traditional values are preserved; human behavior is predictable; and those who play by the rules are honored as valued members of the community.

An examination of Western society during the nineteenth and twentieth centuries shows that the balance between order and disorder is precarious and temporary, and that the balance can be altered by conditions that cannot always be contained. The competition between the two states is relentless. Too much order triggers disorder and loss of freedom; too much disorder will make the public wonder whether this nation is losing its steering mechanism.

In recent decades, the public has become convinced that an intolerable point has been reached: the rules are no longer clear, the legal constraints are no longer effective, and the moral consensus is no longer present. In this context, rising crime rates have become a source of special concern and fear because they signify, in Richard Quinney's words, "the ultimate crack in the armor of the existing order."[2] Crime has become the symbol of the breakdown of the status quo. The public, whose perceptions have been influence by the media as well as by real increases in the crime rates, have begun to advocate a "get-tough" strategy for dealing with crime.

The police are called on to reestablish order, but police power in democratic societies is regarded with enormous suspicion. Bayley contributes, "police power must be justified by and carried out in accordance with law. Police have no choice but to pay close attention to constitutions, statutes, and judicial opinions." Accordingly, Bayley adds, "For good reason the police become wary of doing anything not covered by written rules and sanctioned by law. It is not surprising, then, if the police conclude that being wrong is much worse than being ineffective."[3]

The fact that the police claim they are apolitical seems to ensure that they will not violate the power entrusted to them. In practice, police organizations are anything but apolitical. They function in a public political arena, and their mandate is politically defined. There are three reasons why the police are of necessity involved in the political system. First, the vast majority of the police in the United States are locally controlled. The sheriff is typically an elected position, and municipal policing is embedded in the context of local political culture. Second, law is a political entity, and the administration of criminal law encompasses political values and political ends. The police are tied to a political system that defines the law, itself a product of interpretations of what is proper and right from the perspective of powerful segments within the community. Third, the police administer the law and, as those who administer the law, the police have the right to take away various freedoms and even life itself from others.[4]

It would seem that in a free and democratic society the performance of the police should be judged in terms of three criteria: effectiveness, efficiency, and rectitude. Effectiveness can be evaluated by whether or not the police achieve the objective of a reduction in crime. Efficiency is involved with the costs of what the police do in relation to what they achieve. Rectitude focuses on whether the police treat individuals properly, legally, and morally.[5] This third criteria becomes particularly important because intensified law enforcement has been perceived as the only remedy for the crime "crises" facing this nation. Giving the police total responsibility for crime control has at times been hazardous to the rectitude of the police.[6] How much the police fulfill these three criteria is an ongoing discussion in this text

CITIZENS' ATTITUDES TOWARD THE POLICE

The vast majority of United States citizens have confidence in the police. Indeed, nine in ten say that increasing the number of police is a very (46 percent) or somewhat (44 percent) effective way to reduce crime.[7] In terms of confidence, 58 percent report that they have a "great deal" or "quite a lot" of confidence in the police; another 30 percent say they have "some" confidence in the police, and only 11 percent express "very little" or "no confidence."[8] Another survey reported that the only major institution that rated higher than the police was the military (64 percent rather than 57 percent). See Table 2.1 for this survey of public confidence in selected institutions. Interestingly, in this survey, only one in five United States citizens expressed strong confidence in the criminal justice system.[9]

African Americans and European Americans differ dramatically in terms of confidence in the police. Although 63 percent of European Americans say that they have a great deal of confidence in the police, only 26 percent of African Americans

TABLE 2.1   Public Confidence in Selected Institutions

"I am going to read you a list of institutions in American society. Would you tell me how much respect and confidence you, yourself, have in each one—a great deal, quite a lot, some, or very little?"

Institution	Percentage of general public having a great deal or quite a lot of confidence in the institution
Military	64
Police	58
Organized religion	57
Presidency	45
Supreme Court	44
Banks	43
Medical system	41
Public schools	40
Television news	33
Newspapers	30
Organized labor	26
Congress	21
Big business	21
Criminal justice system	20

Source: Jean Johnson, "Americans' Views on Crime and Law Enforcement: Survey Findings," *National Institute of Justice Journal* (U.S. Department of Justice, Office of Justice Programs, Sept. 1997): 11.

feel the same way. Perhaps even more importantly, only 8 percent of European Americans say that they have very little or no confidence in the police, while 35 percent of African Americans make this statement.[10]

Surveys of public reaction to the Rodney King beating revealed that the overwhelming majority of people in the United States did not like what they saw. Only 6 percent of those who were surveyed after the officers' initial acquittal said they agreed that the verdict was "right."[11] Only 9 percent said they "sympathize[d]" more with the police than with the beating victim.[12] There was a similar reaction to the tape-recorded comments of Mark Fuhrman that were played during the O. J. Simpson murder trial. At that time, 87 percent of United States citizens, with African Americans and European Americans agreeing in about equal numbers, said they had an "unfavorable impression" of Fuhrman.[13] Only 9 percent of either group said that watching this tape gave them more confidence that "police officers perform their duties in a professional and ethical manner."[14]

Yet, what emerged in subsequent surveys is that for many European Americans, these incidents were simply the regrettable exception to the rule. This was a belief not shared by a majority or near majority of African Americans:

- Only 15 percent of [European] Americans, compared to 53 percent of [African Americans], think that "the kind of improper behavior by police described on the Fuhrman tapes (racism and falsification of evidence)" is common among their local police (Princeton Survey Research Associates, August 1995).
- Twenty-four percent of surveyed European Americans, compared to 43 percent of African Americans, said "police overreaction to crime" is a very serious threat (The Gallup Organization for America's Talking, June 1994).
- Seventy-six percent of surveyed European Americans, compared to 47 percent of African Americans, say police in their community "mostly" treat the races equally (The Gallup Organization for CNN/*USA Today*, September 1995).[15]

There is substantial agreement among African Americans and European Americans concerning what constitutes appropriate police behavior. Nine in 10 United States citizens, with no significant differences between African Americans and European Americans, disapprove of a police officer striking a vulgar and obscene citizen. About an equal number (92 percent), again with no significant differences between African Americans and European Americans, disapprove of an officer striking a murder suspect during questioning.[16] Opinions do differ about what police behavior actually takes place in most communities. Most European Americans who have generally had only positive interactions with the police experience a sense of relief when they see a police officer in their community. In contrast, 43 percent of African Americans, according to one survey, reported that "police brutality and harassment of African Americans [is] a serious problem" in their own community.[17]

Significantly, both African Americans and European Americans are dubious that police departments will act in a forceful way to address problems of dishonesty, racism, and brutality. Only 14 percent of European Americans and 15 percent of African Americans think that it is "very likely" that the controversy surrounding Fuhrman will lead to "significant improvement in the way police in this country treat blacks."[18] What is disconcerting about the information in these police surveys is that "many black Americans are disaffected and suspicious. They are not confident that the police will be fair. They are not confident that the police will be professional. They are not confident that the police will protect and serve."[19]

Vincent J. Webb, Charles M. Katz, and Nanette Graham extended the analysis to Hispanic/Latino Americans as well as to African Americans and European Americans.[20] The previous research had reported that European Americans have the most positive attitudes about policing, African Americans have the least positive attitudes, and Hispanic/Latino Americans have attitudes less positive than European Americans but not as negative as African Americans.[21] Webb, Katz, and Graham found that African Americans and Hispanic/Latino Americans "are similar to whites in their ratings of crime control duties such as investigating street crimes, drug crimes, and gang activity."[22] They add that "Hispanics differed from African Americans in two ways. First, they rated responding to family disputes as being more important than did blacks (or whites). Second, they rated investigating white collar crime as being less important than blacks did."[23]

POLICING THE TWO AMERICAS

It is not surprising that the attitudes of European Americans are much better than those of African Americans and Hispanic/Latino Americans toward the police because they receive a much different type of policing. Early in this nation's history the police were mandated to control the "dangerous classes" (see Chapter 1). Although police officers were frequently from the same class as the immigrant poor they were supposed to be controlling, a clear pattern of attributing violence to the poor was established. Thus, as part of establishing their own legitimacy, and moral and political interests, police departments in nineteenth America applied violence and the norm of state authority against the poor ("dangerous classes").[24] The police, in fulfilling this state action against the poor, are in a variety of ways defending the status quo. Peter K. Manning illuminates how this has been played out in the United States:

- As activities slip either away from popularity, or drift downward to the lower classes, they are defined as criminal and subject to arrest and prosecution.
- Certain "deviant" lifestyles are stigmatized and defined as "criminal." Activities publicly associated with lower class, native peoples, or immigrant pastimes and lifestyles, such as cock fighting, dog fights, and peyote use, are subject to criminal sanctions.
- Space is regulated to maintain control of symbolically valued property and places. Changes in the uses and control of space marginalize certain powerless groups and place them at risk from public and private policing.
- Shared activities are differentially sanctioned. When leisure patterns are shared by middle and lower middle classes, such as sport gambling, the middle class form is legalized while the lower class form(s) are made subject to the criminal sanction and police-initiated control.
- As newly respectable activities gain respectability they are de-criminalized and are diffused widely e.g., marijuana and alcohol use.
- Dissent such as flag burning, public demonstrations and draft evasion, when carried out by members of the dominant coalition, is treated sub rose, and with discretion within the criminal justice system, while marginal groups are given the full benefit and force of the law.[25]

This matter of differential justice for the rich and poor is no new matter. It has always been that way. What generates so many negative feelings toward the police on the part of the poor, especially members of minority groups, is the way in which the police apply to them the heavy heel of the law. The First America is treated with respect, unless they push the police too far, but the Second America, made up of the poor and minorities, are too frequently the recipients of violence and victimization on the part of the police.

FUNCTIONS OF THE POLICE

Police departments are charged to prevent crime and to develop a style of policing acceptable to the community in which they serve.

Prevention of Crime

A long-standing function of the police is to prevent crime. The public may expect this from the police, but one of the best kept secrets of contemporary life is that the police do not prevent crime. The police know it. Experts are aware of it. The public does not know it.[26] Bayley, who examines the police's function in crime prevention, has this to say:

> What is the evidence for this heretical and disturbing assertion? First, repeated analysis has consistently failed to find any connection between the number of police officer and crime rates. Second, the primary strategies adopted by modern police have been shown to have little or no effect on crime.[27]

The police can legitimately argue that crime cannot be prevented exclusively through their efforts. Indeed, the police are aware that they are only a bandage in dealing with the crime problem. The police know that crime prevention must be dealt with through structural means, that crime prevention belongs more to the realm of politics, and that crime prevention will not take place until society's institutions are improved and society's norms and values are changed. However, as long as the police monopolize crime prevention, the pursuit of other means of preventing and reducing crime will be half-hearted. Thus, by pretending to be the solution to crime, the police become part of the problem.[28]

Styles of Policing

A style of policing describes how a particular police agency sees its purpose and the methods and techniques that it undertakes to fulfill that purpose. James Q. Wilson has identified three styles of policing: (1) the watchman style, (2) the legalistic style, and (3) the service style.[29]

The Watchman Style
The watchman style of policing, according to Wilson, is primarily concerned with achieving the goal of "order maintenance." This style makes considerable use of discretion, and its informal approach sometimes takes a different approach in middle-class and lower-class communities. In the lower-class communities, the

persuasion and threats of the watchman style can turn into an ugly form of street justice against those who are deemed to be resisting police authority.[30]

The Legalistic Style
The legalistic style, says Wilson, is committed to the full enforcement of the law. This style makes little use of discretion and, as much as possible, attempts to eliminate discretion. In view of the fact that proponents of this style perceive themselves as doing law enforcement work, these departments tend to avoid becoming involved in either order maintenance or service-oriented policing responsibilities as much as possible. For example, an officer using this style of policing would avoid becoming involved in community disputes arising from violations of social norms that do not break the law.[31]

The Service Style
Those who are involved in this style of policing see themselves as helpers rather than as crime fighters. Officers with this style of policing are more frequently found assisting juveniles than adults and tend to work with social service agencies and other community groups to prevent crime and solve problems. The philosophy of the service style of policing is at the base of community-oriented (COP) and problem-oriented policing (POP).[32]

Wilson's 1968 typology of police departments actually covers the basic areas in which the police have responsibility: (1) law enforcement, (2) order maintenance, and (3) service providing. Box 2.1 provides a partial list of the various tasks or activities involved in each area.

BOX 2.1   Activities Involved with the Functions of the Police

Law Enforcement
Investigate criminal activities
Arrest suspects of crime
Conduct criminal investigations
Interrogate suspects
Serve warrants
Investigate crimes in progress

Order Maintenance
Quell a riot or social protest
Investigate a domestic disturbance
Break up a bar fight
Intervene in neighborhood or party disturbances

Force intoxicated persons or the homeless to leave an area
Direct traffic
Issue parking tickets
Issue traffic citations

Service Provider
Provide assistance during a medical emergency
Look for lost children
Assist stranded motorists
Assist those who locked their keys in their automobiles

The public is in wide disagreement on which of these styles of policing are most important for a community. Business owners, of course, want protection against criminals, but they also desire order maintenance functions to prevent problems from taking place in the vicinity of their stores. All citizens want to feel protected against burglars breaking into their homes, and if there is a problem, they want an immediate police response. They also want to feel safe in their neighborhoods and on their way to and from work. They desire that their children be safe from harm's way as well as from drugs and other debilitating influences. In addition to these law enforcement functions, citizens desire the intervention of the police in case of being stranded on the highway, or locking themselves out of their vehicles, and of needing someone to break up their neighbor's noisy party.

FEDERAL POLICE

Federal police work employs some 25,000 full-time personnel.[33] There are 504,000 state and local police officers providing general purpose law enforcement, with an additional 61,000 officers policing transit systems, state university systems, public housing, and other special areas.[34] There are currently more than one and a half million private police.[35]

Federal police agencies have evolved through the years for the purpose of investigating and enforcing violations of federal laws. The post of United States Marshal, established by Congress in 1879, was one of the first federal police positions. Today, 53 federal agencies have the authority to make arrests and carry firearms. Most of the criminal work done by federal agencies comes under the authority of either the Department of Justice or the Treasury Department.

Department of Justice

The attorney general, appointed by the president, is the chief law enforcement officer of the federal government, and the Department of Justice is under the attorney general's direction. The Department of Justice was formed in 1870, but not until 1908 did President Theodore Roosevelt establish an investigative body under that department, an agency later known as the Federal Bureau of Investigation.

The Criminal Division of the Department of Justice develops, enforces, and supervises federal criminal laws, excluding those specifically assigned to other divisions. The Division and its 93 United States Attorneys are responsible for overseeing criminal matters under more than 900 statutes, as well as civil litigation. The Division also formulates and implements law enforcement policy and provides advice and assistance. For example, the Division approves or monitors such sensitive areas of law enforcement as participation in the Witness Security Program and the use of electronic surveillance; advises the Attorney General, Congress, and the White House on matters of criminal law; provides legal advice and assistance to federal prosecutors and investigative agencies; and furnishes leadership for coordinating law enforcement matters on both the international and national levels.

Federal Bureau of Investigation

The agency now known as the **Federal Bureau of Investigation (FBI)** was founded in 1908 when Attorney General Charles J. Bonaparte appointed an unnamed force of special agents to be the investigative force of the Department of Justice. In 1909, the special agents force was named the Bureau of Investigation. Following a series of name changes, the Federal Bureau of Investigation (FBI) received its present title in 1935.

During its early history, the FBI investigated illegal activities such as bankruptcy fraud, antitrust crime, and neutrality violations, but during World War I, espionage, sabotage, sedition, and draft violations were new federal criminal violations added to the FBI's responsibilities. In 1919, the passage of the National Motor Vehicle Theft Act further broadened the FBI's jurisdiction. In 1934, Congress gave Special Agents the authority to make arrests and to carry firearms. During the 1960s, the Civil Rights Movement and organized crime became major concerns of the FBI, and during the 1970s and 1980s, it was terrorism, drugs, violent crimes, and financial crime that received the most attention.

J. Edgar Hoover, the controversial leader of the FBI (1924–1972), was the director who made the Bureau into what it became. He suffered little criticism during the time he ran the Bureau, perhaps because he terrorized his agents and generally had the media in his pocket. In years subsequent to his resignation, however, a number of stories have circulated about Hoover's flaws, both from special agents and from those outside the Bureau. He has been accused of being very fond of horse racing and, supposedly, was soft on organized crime because of his involvement in gambling. Whatever substantiation there was of the various rumors about Hoover, there was no question about what an able bureaucrat he was. Hoover was instrumental in developing the FBI National Academy, which trains police officers throughout the United States in management and specialized fields. Further, he established the FBI Crime Laboratory, considered the best in the world.

The FBI is a field-oriented organization which has nine divisions and provides program direction and support services to 56 field offices, about 400 satellite offices known as resident agencies, four specialized field operations, and 23 foreign liaison posts. The FBI employs nearly 24,000 personnel, including 10,100 special agents. About 7,300 employees are assigned to the FBI headquarters in Washington, DC, and the rest are assigned to field installations.

Among the duties of the FBI are performing federal criminal investigations, domestic intelligence, and background investigations on various federal appointments. The FBI also operates the National Crime Information Center (NCIC), a nationwide computer network linked to local and state police agencies. The more than 200 specific crimes and broad areas of criminal activity that fall under the jurisdiction of the FBI include kidnapping, aircraft piracy, violations of both Civil Rights Acts, crimes against banks, organized crime, and interstate flight to avoid prosecution. Furthermore, the FBI National Academy annually trains over 1,000 local and state law enforcement officers.

The Drug Enforcement Administration (DEA)

The **Drug Enforcement Administration (DEA)** is another agency under the Department of Justice. The origins of this agency go back to such acts as the Harrison Narcotic Act of 1914, the Volstead Act of 1919, the Narcotic Drugs Import and Export Act of 1922, the Marijuana Tax Act of 1937, the Boggs Act of 1956, and the Comprehensive Drug Abuse Prevention and Control Act of 1970. These acts, in turn, gave birth to the Narcotics Division, the Federal Narcotics Control Board, the Federal Bureau of Narcotics, and the Bureau of Narcotics and Dangerous Drugs in 1968. In 1973, the Drug Enforcement Administration was created and charged with federal drug enforcement efforts.

The Drug Enforcement Administration, as the leading agency responsible for the development of overall Federal drug enforcement strategy, has the following responsibilities:

- Investigation and preparation for prosecution of major violators of controlled substance laws operating at interstate and intrastate levels.
- Management of a national drug intelligence system in cooperation with Federal, state, local, and foreign officials to collect, analyze, and disseminate strategic and operational drug intelligence information.
- Seizure and forfeiture of assets derived from, traceable to, or intended to be used for illicit drug trafficking.
- Enforcement of provisions of the Controlled Substance Act as they pertain to the manufacture, distribution, and dispensing of legally-produced controlled substances.
- Coordination and cooperation with Federal, state, and local officials on mutual drug enforcement efforts and enhancement of such efforts through exploitation of potential interstate and international investigations beyond local or limited Federal jurisdictions and resources.
- Coordination and cooperation with other Federal, state, and local agencies, and with foreign governments, in programs designed to reduce the availability of illicit abuse-type drugs on the United States market through nonenforcement methods such as crop eradication, crop substitution, and training of foreign officials.
- Responsibility, under the policy guidance of the Secretary of State and U.S. Ambassadors, for all programs associated with drug law enforcement counterparts in foreign countries.
- Liaison with the United States, Interpol, and other organizations on matters relating to international drug control programs.[36]

Immigration and Naturalization Service (INS)

Congress was first given the power to establish a naturalization service under Article I, Section 8, of the United States Constitution. In 1798, the Alien Act gave the president the power to expel aliens regarded as a threat to national security. Established in 1864, the Office of Commissioner of Immigration was placed under the Department of State. In 1898, the Commissioner of the Bureau of Immigration was created, and was placed in 1903 under the control of the Department of Commerce and Labor. This agency was divided into a Bureau of Labor and the Bureau of Naturalization in 1913, both of which were placed under the Department of Labor. These two agencies were eventually combined into the Immigration and Naturalization Service (INS) and became part of the Department of Justice in 1940.

The over 10,000 agents of the INS have full powers of arrest, search, and seizure. Their main functions are to check ports of entry as well as persons entering and leaving the country. INS operations are divided between the two major programs of Enforcement and Examination, reflecting the traditional distinction between enforcing the requirements and administering the benefits of immigration law. The primary enforcement mission of the INS is to prevent aliens from entering the United States illegally and to locate and remove those who are living or working here illegally. These functions are performed by the Border Patrol, which has the diverse responsibilities of investigation, intelligence, detention, and deportation.

The Border Patrol performs their duties along 8,000 miles of international boundaries by automobile, boat, aircraft, and afoot. The danger of a Border Patrol agent is illustrated by the fact that over 60 agents have lost their lives in the line of duty. For the story of the death of one of these officers, see Box 2.2. At the end of fiscal year 1994, the Border Patrol had assigned 3,911 of its 4,260 agents to 145 Border Patrol stations. As of September 1995, it had hired and finished training 530 agents and had an additional 369 agents in training.

United States Marshal Service

This federal law enforcement agency was established under the Judiciary Act of 1789. President George Washington appointed a marshal for each of the 13 states. Formally established in 1969, it became a bureau in 1974. It currently has 2,500 full-time employees.

The Marshal Service is responsible to the federal courts for handling prisoners and executing orders issued by federal courts. Its court functions consist of producing prisoners for trial; protecting courts, including judges, attorneys, and witnesses; and tracking and arresting fugitives. The importance of its job is seen in the fact that 2,200 agents produce about 400,000 prisoners for trial, and it makes more than 10,000 felony arrests and 37,000 misdemeanor arrests each year.

In 1971, the Marshal Service created the Special Operations Group (SOG)—an elite group of deputy marshals capable of responding anywhere in the United States within a few hours. Members of the SOG are trained in a variety of skills including helicopter operations, small-unit tactics, bomb recognition, building entry and search procedures, bilingual communication, and the use of night vision devices.

The operation of the Witness Protection Program is also an important function of the United States Marshal Service. Established in 1984, this program is used to protect federal witnesses whose testimony during trial places them at considerable risk. This program has been especially helpful in the past decade in protecting

BOX 2.2   Danger on the Job

EAGLE PASS—Two hours past midnight, the Rio Grande glides serenely between Eagle Pass and Piedras Negras, Mexico, its banks overhung with Carrizo cane and its gray–green surface dappled by reflections of city lights.

But the image of tranquility is an illusion.

In the cold and darkness along the riverbank, U.S. Border Patrol agents in uncomfortable bullet-proof vests and armed with automatic weapons brace themselves against a freezing February rain and a new sense of menace.

"We're not Arizona or Southern California. They get shot at all the time. Here it was almost taken for granted that if you caught dope, they wouldn't have weapons," said agent Adrian Ramirez.

I wish people know what we've been going through down here. When I got here seven years ago, they used to talk about the two dope loads they caught that year. Now, it's the two they caught yesterday. It's gotten out of hand," Ramirez said.

There is a sense here of siege and of manning an outpost that is out-of-sight and out-of-mind.

Because, on January 19 [1996], what for some agents was a boy's game played by men ended forever with the violent death of agent Jefferson Barr.

One of the station's toughest dope busters, Barr was killed in a shootout with drug smugglers in the brush south of town. One man is being held by Mexican authorities, but it is unlikely he will be extradited....

"It used to be a game, and Jeff loved it. All he wanted to do was catch dopers, not aliens. But things have changed. Now the point is to get home safely," said Ramirez.

Source: Todd Martin, *Border Agents Serve as Nation's Gate Keepers,* Associated Press, March 31, 1996.

witnesses who testified in federal court against organized crime figures. What this program provides for those who qualify is a complete change of identity for themselves and their families. This includes residences, employment, and new Social Security numbers.

The United States Marshal Service has further been given the responsibility of managing and disposing of seized and forfeited assets bought with the proceeds of drug trafficking and organized crime. As a result of the President's Organized Crime Drug Enforcement Task Force (OCDETF) program and emphasis by the Department of Justice on organized crime prosecution, asset forfeiture activities have dramatically increased in volume. The Marshal Service is presently managing more than $1.6 billion worth of property seized from criminals.[37]

Office of Community Oriented Policing Services (COPS)

The Violent Crime Control and Law Enforcement Act of 1994 authorized funds to promote community policing and add 100,000 community policing officers over the next six years. The United States Department of Justice established the Office of **Community Oriented Policing Services (COPS)** to carry out this mission.

In 1995 and 1996, COPS has benefited nearly 9,000 agencies and provided funding for nearly 50,000 officers and deputies to supplement the sworn forces on the streets. For qualifying agencies, COPS pays 75 percent of the salaries and benefits for new officers for three years, up to a maximum of $75,000 per officer. Half of the funds are required by the Act to be granted to jurisdictions with populations under 150,000. The director of COPS adds:

> Our work has just begun. As you know, the success of community policing is not attained exclusively through the deployment of more police to neighborhoods. It is also dependent on the commitment of the community and local authorities. It's about personal involvement and empowerment through partnerships. At the COPS Office, we define it as "policing philosophy that promotes and supports organizational strategies to address the causes and reduce the fear of crime and social disorder through problem-solving tactics and community-police partnerships.[38]

COPS has develop a number of initiatives to accomplish the twin goals of putting 100,000 police officers on the streets and promoting community policing strategies:

- *Hiring grants:* COPS created a number of hiring grants that feature streamlined applications and awarded grants to hire more than 23,000 officers in its first year.
- *Equipment, technology, and MORE:* COPS MORE (Making Officer Redeployment Effective) provides funds to acquire new technologies and equipment, hire civilians for administration tasks, and pay for officer overtime. This allows local police agencies to redeploy officers so more of their time is spent on the streets solving problems instead of at the station completing paperwork.
- *Promoting innovations:* The COPS Youth Firearms Violence Initiative supports innovative community policing approaches to fight firearms violence among young people. The Innovative Community Oriented Policing (ICOP) grants encourage organization-wide commitment to community policing, promote problem-solving efforts, and similar initiatives.
- *Training and technical assistance:* Because community policing requires a change in approach for many law enforcement agencies, COPS is dedicated to providing training and technical assistance for agencies receiving COPS grants.[39]

COPS claims to have a number of success stories. In Amsterdam, New York, in the neighborhood of Central Civico (one of the highest crime areas in the city, with a particularly high rate of drug-related crime), COPS runs a substation where it appears to have had marked success in developing an after-school program, tutoring children, and organizing field trips. In Chicago, Chicago's Alternative Policing Strategy (CAPS) reorganized police around small geographical areas, where "beat teams" work with community members to solve problems. Following the initial success of the five prototype areas, Chicago is expanding community policing into 279 police beats that cover the entire city. In El Paso, Texas, police claim that community policing, combined with the targeting of repeat offenders, has led to the lowest crime rate in 10 years.

Police have experimented with a number of innovative programs in community policing. In Hillsborough County, Florida, law enforcement officials work together to attend local community events, identify gang members, and prevent gang crime. One of their programs is to supervise juveniles ordered to perform community service while they clean up vandalized structures. In Lowell, Massachusetts, a city long plagued by heroin use and street gangs, an intensive community policing effort supported by a COPS grant seems to have had a positive effect in reducing crime. Indeed, for the first time in 25 years, 365 days passed without anyone being murdered.[40]

Department of Treasury

The United States Secret Service, Bureau of Alcohol, Tobacco and Firearms, Customs Service, and Internal Revenue Service are the agencies within the Treasury Department having the most pronounced law enforcement roles.

United States Secret Service

The Secret Service Division was created in 1865 on the day of the assassination of President Lincoln. At the time, in spite of the war-time hostility toward President Lincoln, there was only a single officer stationed outside his box at Ford's Theater. John F. Parker, a District of Columbia police officer, wandered away from his post, relieving the assassin of the necessity of killing him.[41]

The early years of the Secret Service Division were not much more effective. In 1881, President Garfield, who was unguarded, was shot in a Washington DC railroad station. President Cleveland received various threats, but the Secret Service Division provided guards only occasionally for the president due to lack of appropriations. In 1901, when President McKinley opened the Pan-American Exposition at Buffalo, he was guarded by three Secret Service men, but this still did not prevent his assassination.

In 1908, the division was transferred to the Department of Justice, and in 1965, the division was renamed the United States Secret Service and placed under the Treasury Department. The Secret Service is authorized to provide protection for high-ranking persons in the federal government and to provide overall security for the White House and the major treasury buildings. Its mission statement is as follows:

> The Secret Service is charged with protecting the life of the President and Vice President of the United States and their immediate families, the President-elect, and Vice-President elect and their immediate families, former Presidents and their wives, the widows of former Presidents until death or remarriage, minor children of a former President until they reach 16 years of age, heads of a foreign state or government, and at the direction of the President official representatives of the United States performing special missions abroad.[42]

The Secret Service also provides security at the White House complex, buildings which house Presidential offices, the Vice President's residence, the Treasury

Building and Treasury Annex, and various foreign diplomatic missions in the Washington, DC metropolitan area. Its mission further encompasses investigations related to certain criminal violations of the Federal Deposit Insurance Act, the Federal Land Bank Act, and the Government Losses in Shipment Act. Moreover, the Secret Service is charged with the direction and arrest of any person committing any offense against the laws of the United States relating to coins, currency, stamps, government bonds, checks, credit or debt card fraud, computer fraud, false identification crime, and other obligations or securities of the United States.[43]

Bureau of Alcohol, Tobacco and Firearms (BATF)
In 1862, this federal agency originated as a unit within the Internal Revenue Service (IRS), when alcohol and tobacco tax statutes were created. First called the Alcohol Tobacco Tax Unit, it eventually became the Alcohol, Tobacco, and Firearm Division within the IRS. In 1972, its jurisdiction was transferred to the Treasury Department.

The Bureau of Alcohol, Tobacco and Firearms has about 2,000 special agents and 850 inspectors and specialists. Its responsibilities, according to the BATF's director, John Magaw, are "dedicated to reducing violent crime, collecting revenue, and protecting the public. BATF enforces the Federal laws and regulations relating to alcohol, tobacco, firearms, explosives, and arson by working directly and in cooperation with [other law enforcement agencies]…"[44]

Some of the most noteworthy efforts of BATF are its programs, especially the Achilles Program, that targets the most violent career criminals. These programs function through task forces comprised of BATF special agents and other federal agents, often with state and local officers. This task force works in neighborhoods in which there are high rates of gang-related violence, drug trafficking, homicides, and other violent crimes. In the 20 cities in which this program has been established since 1988, 17,870 cases have been forwarded for prosecuting involving 26,545 defendants.[45]

BATF has also placed a major emphasis on investigating and arresting arson, high explosives, and automatic weapons violators. In the past 15 years, BATF has conducted investigations of about 8,000 acts of arson resulting in more than 5 billion dollars in property damage. In view of the fact that it is illegal for a private citizen to own or possess an automatic weapon without authorization from the Treasury Department, the opposition of militia and other extremist groups to federal regulation have involved BATF agents in incident after incident.

United States Customs Service
Created by President Washington under the Tariff Act of 1789, the United States Customs Service was authorized by Congress to collect duties on goods, merchandise, and wares. The Bureau of Customs Service, currently employing about 10,000 agents, has the primary responsibility of preventing the smuggling of goods or contraband into or out of the country. During the fiscal year 1994, the United States Customs Service made 10,665 arrests and seized 14,651 aircraft, vessels, and vehicles and

$168 million in various forms of currency. This agency also made 9,372 seizures of illegal narcotics, including 2,000 pounds of heroin, 157,000 pounds of cocaine, and 484,000 pounds of marijuana.[46]

The Customs Service has developed close relationships with other law enforcement agencies, the Coast Guard, and the Navy. It has worked particularly closely with the Coast Guard—which has the power to board any vessel believed to violate the laws of the United States and to examine all the vessel's documents and contents.

A number of weapons have recently been developed by the United States Customs Service and the military for the war on drugs. The Coast Guard put into service Blue Thunder, a high-performance speedboat, and employed an Cessan Citation, a jet aircraft equipped with radar. Later, Customs Service pilots flew the Sikorsky Black Hawk assault helicopter. The United States Navy used their EC–2, an aircraft equipped with such sophisticated radar that it could detect other aircraft from as far as 300 miles away. Furthermore, "Fat Albert" and other aerostat surveillance balloons, equipped with state-of-the-art radar and listening devices, were put into service. These balloons, 175 feet in length, could not only pick up communications from Cuba and from Soviet satellites, but could also detect traffic in Smugglers' Alley, an area of Caribbean sky virtually invisible to land-based radar systems.[47]

Internal Revenue Service (IRS)

The IRS has had a Criminal Investigation division (CI) since 1919, and employs more than 3,000 armed agents who investigate possible criminal violations of income tax laws. If warranted, they recommend appropriate criminal prosecution. CIs have the authority to execute search warrants, make arrests without warrants for internal revenue-related offenses, and make seizures of property related to tax fraud violations. In fiscal year 1994, CI agents working in 34 districts across the United States initiated 5,346 investigations. This included 2,310 money-laundering investigations under Title 18 of the United States Code, resulting in 3,130 convictions and prison terms for 2,420 convicted offenders.

The CIs have a long list of celebrated prosecuted clients. The most famous of all prosecutions was the income tax violations case of Al Capone in 1932. More recently, the long list includes federal judges, politicians (Vice President Spiro T. Agnew and former Secretary of the Treasury Robert B. Anderson), athletes (baseball stars Darryl Strawberry and Pete Rose), organized crime figures (John Gotti), and entrepreneurs (Leona Helmsley).[48]

The Abuse of Power

So far, this description of the roles of the various federal law enforcement agency has sounded like an advertisement or training manual. The fact of the matter is that at times the role behavior of federal law enforcement agencies makes us proud to have this quality of policing in a free and democratic society. At other times, the questionable performance would be an embarrassment for advertisements or training manuals. The performance, in these cases, represents the dark side of federal law enforcement. The most serious dark side of federal policing is presently the abuse of power.

Federal law enforcement agencies are recognized for higher entry requirements than local and state agencies, more extensive training, increased salaries, and less corruption. These agencies supposedly do not have the informal code often found in local departments and, accordingly, such norms as the oath of secrecy do not exist to the degree that they do in local agencies. So far, so good. But then, the bad news comes to the surface. It appears that such federal agencies as the FBI, basking in their former glory, are only more successful in covering up their improprieties than are local agencies.[49] The FBI has victimized the following through surveillance abuses—Dr. Martin Luther King, Jr., the Congress of Racial Equality, Cesar Chavez, the Civil Rights Movement in general and Barry Goldwater. Throughout J. Edgar Hoover's life, critics of the FBI sometimes naively assumed that the bureau would be fine after Hoover left. Kopel and Blackman charge:

> But in fact the scandals, the violations of the Constitution, the obstruction of justice, and the lying to the public have continued in each new regime. When Republican appointee William Sessions was forced out of office and replaced by Democratic appointee Louis Freeh, the FBI continued to obstruct justice and cover up the murders at Ruby Ridge; the FBI's architect of Waco and Ruby Ridge (Larry Potts) was appointed second-in-command; personal files on nearly a thousand people were shipped to political operatives at the White House with no justification; and the FBI continued its incessant demands for greater surveillance powers, more wiretaps, and more money. Perhaps the problem is not that we need a new FBI director. We need a new FBI.[50]

Beyond the FBI, the BATF has become involved in other forms of unacceptable behaviors. The Waco raid was the most spectacular, but there are a number of other instances in which the BATF abused their power (Chapter 7 will document a number of these instances). It is not only that the BATF has a bad record of targeting innocent people somehow associated with guns, it is the fact that they have picked on law-abiding citizens who are not afraid to assert their rights. The Border Patrol has been subjected to more complaints to the Department of Justice than any other justice agency. In an April report of 1995, Americas Watch, the international human rights organization, has provided detailed allegations of unjustified shootings, sex abuse, racism, and torture. The Immigration and Naturalization Service and the Drug Enforcement Administration are also known for their unnecessary violence and contempt for civil liberties.[51]

STATE POLICE

The story of the development of state policing is dependent on a specific state's history and evolution. The Texas Rangers were the first territorial police agency, and the creation of the Pennsylvania State Constabulary in 1905 constituted the beginning of the modern state police force. Today, state police are found in every state except Hawaii.

The 49 state police agencies total less than 10 percent of the total employees and sworn officers of police and sheriffs' departments (see Figure 2.1). The two basic models of state police are the decentralized model and the centralized model. In the decentralized model, the state police are responsible for traffic enforcement on state highways, and another agency in the state is responsible for criminal investigation. Patrol units regulate traffic movement, investigate traffic accidents, and conduct traffic safety programs. The state police may also be assigned other tasks, such as conducting examinations for a driver's license and providing protection for the governor.[52]

In the centralized model, which combines the functions of patrol and investigation, the state police conduct statewide criminal investigations and assist county and local police agencies with investigating criminal incidents occurring within their jurisdictions. State investigative bodies can work separately or with special units. Examples of such special units include the narcotics division, fire marshal division, fraud division, intelligence division, and general criminal investigation division. Some state police agencies in this model provide crime laboratory facilities to local police agencies and state data processing centers, and act as the central collection point for information on missing and wanted persons, stolen property, and uniform crime statistics.

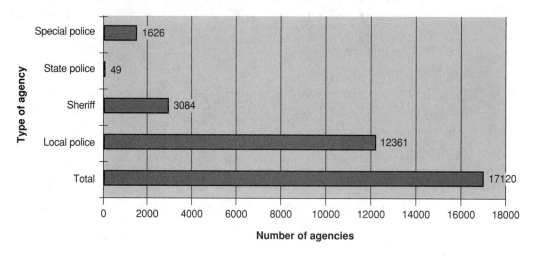

FIGURE 2.1   Employment by State and Local Law Enforcement Agencies in the United States, 1993

Note: The Special police category includes both state-level and local-level agencies. Consolidated police-sheriff agencies are included under the local police category.

Source: Brian A. Reaves and Pheny Z. Smith, "Sheriffs' Departments 1993," U.S. Department of Justice, Office of Justice Programs, Bureau of Justice Statistics (June 1996): 1.

COUNTY POLICE

The **county sheriff** is still an elected official of a county, and sheriffs exist in every state except Alaska. The term *sheriff* to many recalls such largely fictional images as the Sheriff of Nottingham chasing Robin Hood through Sherwood forest; the gun-toting, fast-drawing sheriff of the 19th century Wild West; or the fat, ignorant, and prejudiced Southern sheriff. Past attempts to eliminate the position of sheriff have failed, and the role of sheriff appears to be strong and secure.[53]

Among the 156,000 full-time sworn personnel employed by sheriffs' departments in 1993, about 60,000 were uniformed officers. In addition to such law enforcement duties as crime investigation and patrol, most sheriffs' departments also are responsible for functions related to court and jail operations (see Figure 2.2). The major difference between sheriffs' departments and local police has to do with sheriffs' responsibilities related to jail and court operations.

The size of sheriffs' departments vary greatly. In 1996, the Los Angeles Sheriffs' Department was the largest in the United States, with nearly 8,200 sworn personnel and 4,000 civilians. Their pay range is from $40,349 to $44,909. The LASD also runs the largest jail system in the United States, with a daily inmate population of

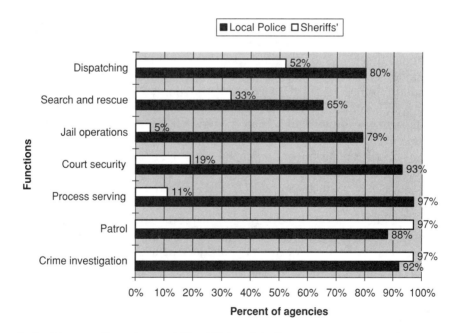

FIGURE 2.2   Functions of Sheriffs' and Police Departments and Their Officers

Source: Brian A. Reaves and Pheny Z. Smith, "Sheriffs' Departments 1993," U.S Department of Justice, Office of Justice Programs, Bureau of Justice Statistics (June 1996) iv.

about 18,000. The department further oversees court services throughout Los Angeles County. In addition, the LASD staffs an Avalon station located on Santa Catalina Island, approximately 25 miles off the coast of Southern California. LASD patrol personnel are commanded by a division chief, and the department is divided into three field operations regions, each of which is staffed by more than 1,100 sworn personnel. More than 2,600 sworn officers are assigned to the various custody facilities operated by the sheriff. In addition, the LASD Reserve Forces Bureau consists of four components: uniformed reserves, search and rescue, mountain posse, and the reserve academy. There are approximately 1,000 female officers. European Americans make up 55 percent of the force; Hispanic/Latino Americans, 37 percent; African Americans, 10.9 percent; Asian Americans, 10 percent; and other, 0.5 percent.[54]

The 1993 survey reported that there were 19 sheriffs' departments throughout the nation that employed 1,000 or more sworn officers and more than 300 that employed at least 100 officers. Yet almost 1,000 sheriffs' departments employed fewer than 10 officers, including 19 with just one sworn officer.

Sheriff's departments across the nation are basically the same in terms of objectives, organizational structure, and assigned functions, but unique differences do exist among sheriffs in the East, the South, and the West. Eastern sheriffs have generally been divested of all law enforcement authority and have been specifically relegated to court security, civil process serving, and allied activities. In contrast, Southern sheriffs continue to be powerful law enforcement figures. In most of the South, sheriffs' offices provide criminal law enforcement and essential public safety services to the unincorporated areas of the county. In the Great Plains region, the Rocky Mountains, and the West coast, the modern political, full-service sheriffs' office prevails. The Los Angeles County Sheriffs' department, a classic example, is known to be one of the finest law enforcement agencies in the nation. This department employs more than 7,500 sworn deputies and non-sworn civilian personnel and is widely respected for its civil service control.[55]

Sheriff's departments, much like municipal police agencies, are making efforts to upgrade the quality of personnel and improve police services. The controversial fee system, by which the sheriff receives a portion of all revenues collected, is now largely a thing of the past. The practice of an incoming sheriff appointing deputies for political reasons is also changing with the advent of protection through civil service. Yet the political nature of this office will likely remain, because sheriffs are aware that one of their primary goals must be to gain and keep public support.

MUNICIPAL AND LOCAL POLICE

Local police agencies make up the largest portion of law enforcement personnel in the United States. As of June 30, 1993, local departments had an estimated 474,072 full-time employees, 3 percent more than in 1990.[56] New York employed over 38,000 full-time officers, while Los Angeles employed over 8,000 officers. But police agencies, for the most part, are still small in size. It is estimated that more than 90 percent of all police agencies in this nation employ fewer than 10 persons.[57]

The 1993 survey also revealed that women comprised 8.8 percent of all full-time officers in 1993; African American officers, 11.3 percent; and Hispanic/Latino American officers, 6.2 percent. Twelve percent of local police departments required new officer recruits to have at least some college education. Eighty-eight percent of local departments authorized their regular field officers to use semiautomatic sidearms; and a third of all departments, including half of those serving a population of 1 million or more, required all regular field officers to wear protective body armor while on duty. Nearly all local departments authorized the use of one or more types of impact devices as a nonlethal weapon, usually in the form of a PR–24 baton or traditional baton. Sixty-eight percent of local departments participated in a 911 emergency telephone system during 1993 and two-thirds were using computers. Departments that were using laptop computers or mobile terminals employed twice as many officers as those that didn't.[58]

A 1996 survey revealed some differences from the 1993 survey. There was a lower average number of sworn officers and civilian employees in the 1996 survey. More officers were being reassigned from traditional patrol to crime prevention (from 64 percent in 1993 to 73.6 percent in 1996). The 1996 survey found less resistance from middle management and confusion over what community policing means, while the concern that community policing is too soft on crime increased from 1993.[59]

The Vancouver, Washington Police Department is a small progressive department. Its 120 sworn officers work five 10.5 hour days, and then have either four or five days off. The pay range for officers is between $3,153 to $3,832 per month. Entry level personnel attend a live-in 11 week academy in Burien, Washington, followed by 14 weeks of field training. The standard sidearm is an issued Sig Sauer P.220 (.45 caliber). Officers are provided body armor on a five year replacement cycle and wear is mandatory for all uniformed officers. Oleoresin (pepper spray) Capsicum spray is authorized and issued. Straight batons and collapsible models are the authorized impact weapons. Mobile computers, consisting of Roadrunner Inc. touch screen Pentium 150 models, are being installed in the squad cars.[60]

Comparisons between large urban departments and small agencies illuminate striking contrasts. The most notable distinction is in the area of assignment. The larger the police organization, the more diversified and technical it becomes. An officer in Detroit, Michigan may be assigned to one specific area, such as narcotics enforcement, whereas an officer in Buena Vista, Colorado may assume all policing functions, including traffic enforcement, patrol, criminal investigations, prisoner maintenance, and budget preparation. Another difference is function. Small agencies tend to be more concerned with crime prevention, medium-sized departments show the greatest concern for providing noncrime services, and large agencies focus on enforcing criminal laws and controlling crime through arrests. People from small communities typically want police to perform a wide variety of functions.[61] For example, in many rural areas, police must provide a wide range of services because other social services are either nonexistent or too remote.[62]

Most small town police officers also receive lower salaries and benefits than their urban counterparts. The states have minimum hour requirements for basic training of officers, and this puts great strain on small communities because they lose the services of the officers while they are training. Larger municipalities, offering larger salaries and more extensive benefit plans, add to the small community problems because they often recruit young, certified police officers away from small municipalities. Small communities must then hire additional persons, pay the cost of certification, and hope they will stay.

Vigilante Justice

The poor and minorities often receive street justice from county and municipal police who take the law into their own hands and, acting like the vigilantes of old, victimize the Second America in ways that are shocking and horrifying in a free and democratic society. How else can what happened in the New York Police Department in the fall of 1997 be explained. Dan Carlson questions:

A toilet plunger?

Honest to goodness, every time you think you have seen it all, something will come along to prove you wrong. Like, for example, the allegation that some NYPD officers used the handle of a toilet plunger to sodomize a man in custody. What is going on here? Is the traditional assortment of devices for "teaching people a lesson" inadequate? Are we no longer able to get the job done with the cattle prod, the Manhattan phone directory, and the "screen test" on the way back to the station? Has law enforcement fallen so far behind the curve of technology?

Bluntly stated, this horrible act, if true, is so completely beyond the realm of rational behavior as to be almost sub-human. The fact is that right-thinking officers, at least in their hearts, wholly deplore such actions, and wish upon its perpetrator(s) the imposition of speedy and stern punishment. But the manner in which this atrocity has unfolded raises a fundamental question from an ethical point of view...where is the outrage? Why has the law enforcement community been largely silent in the face of an act that promises to tarnish, once again, all the good works that police officers do?[63]

Carlson reminds us that some of what takes place in the Second America in the name of "policing" is shocking. Thugs, with a badge on their shirts and a gun on their hips, pretend to be serving and protecting the people. The fact is that officers involved in such sadistic behaviors as the Rodney King beating, the toilet plunger incident in New York, and other well publicized incidents, deserve to be in prison. Then, these aggressors will discover what it is like to be a victim and to be a recipient of various forms of brutality themselves. Unfortunately, such forms of police deviancy are systemic—meaning that the barrel itself is rotten and the problem is not as simple as a few "rotten apples." Such forms of brutality are too frequently protected by the oath of secrecy within the department.

PRIVATE POLICE

Private police agencies have a long history. Indeed, before the nineteenth century, all policing in both England and the United States was private, except for the police duties performed by the military. The Pinkerton Agency, founded in Chicago in the mid-nineteenth century, played a dominant role in the industrial conflicts in the late nineteenth century for management against workers. The Wells Fargo Company was the best known corps of detectives hired by the railroads to protect themselves against train robbery in the "Wild West."

In the twentieth century, the "rent-a-cop" has become a visible feature in corporate America. Indeed, in 1994, revenues in the security guard industry rose from $12.7 billion to $14 billion.[64] There is evidence that private security may be growing at a rate more than 11 times faster than city police.[65]

Private security guards or police can be found guarding shopping centers, apartment buildings, office buildings, factories, sports centers, college campuses, and hospitals. Most have uniforms, some carry weapons, and, for the most part, these private police are organized along the same paramilitary lines as public police.[66] Private police have moved into areas where public police either are not allowed or are not willing to operate.

The main task of security guards is to control risk factors. Instead of roaming far and wide looking for action, as public police officers do, security guards stay within an assigned area, such as an office building or a shopping mall. They are on constant lookout for that which causes elevated risks of harm to the community. When faced with a risk factor, such as a suspicious looking person, the guard either attacks these risk factors directly or summons others with appropriate expertise. When the risk factor has been dealt with, the guards begin looking for other risk factors.[67]

In most states, the biggest difference between private and public police is that public police have arrest powers. The private police, who do not have this authority, are usually paid well below the level of the public police. A study by the Rand corporation found that the average age of private security guards was 52, less than half had high school education, and their training was virtually nonexistent.[68]

SUMMARY

The function of the police is to enforce the law, and the structures described in this chapter are designed to preserve law and order throughout the United States. The roles of police agencies have changed in relation somewhat to the expansion of federal laws, to the changing needs of American society, and to the bureaucratization of police organizations. Police agencies also differ in terms of armament, prevalence of force, efficiency, civility, criteria for recruitment, morale, social status, incidence of misbehavior, and nature of activity.[69] In addition to the rapidly expanding federal role in enforcing crime control in this nation, the role of the private police has also increased significantly in the past couple decades. Private police played a pivotal role in crime control in the nineteenth century. It was frequently a controversial role as private police agencies, including the Pinkerton and Burns Detective Agencies, were employed by industrial owners to stamp out strikes and other forms of working class protest. Currently, private police are performing needed roles in areas in which public police either are not allowed or are not willing to operate. This chapter also explores the dark sides of policing. The dark side may not be representative of every agency, but such miscarriages of justice do take place. These sad performances are a reminder that it is the pursuit of integrity that needs to drive every police agency in all of its roles and functions.

KEY WORDS

Community Oriented Policing Services (COPS)
county sheriff
Drug Enforcement Administration (DEA)

Federal Bureau of Investigation (FBI)
federal police
Hoover, J. Edgar
private police

DISCUSSION QUESTIONS

1. What crimes are the FBI most likely to investigate in your community?

2. Is the DEA effective in winning the war against drugs? Is there any more effective way this war could be won?

3. What are the functions of the United States Marshals Service?

4. The government really needs your testimony. You are a key witness for the government to convict one of the most ruthless leaders of an organized crime family. Yet you know that your life will have absolutely no value if you testify. Would you be willing to testify if you are offered protection by the Witness Protection Program?

5. If you want to work in law enforcement, which job described in this chapter seems most attractive to you?

FURTHER READING

Bayley, David H. *Police for the Future.* New York: Oxford University Press, 1994.

Bayley, David H., ed. *Police and Society.* Beverly Hills: Sage, 1977.

Clark, Constance. *In the Line of Duty: The Service and Sacrifice of America's Finest.* Washington: Potomac, 1989.

Cook, Fred J. *The FBI Nobody Knows.* New York: Macmillan, 1964.

DeToledano, Ralph. *J. Edgar Hoover: The Man in His Time.* New Rochelle: Arlington, 1973.

Jeffreys–Jones, Rhodri. *American Espionage: From Secret Service to CIA.* New York: The Free Press, 1977.

Kopel, David B. and Paul H. Blackman. *No More Wacos, What's Wrong with Federal Law Enforcement and How to Fix It.* New York: Prometheus, 1997.

Manning, Peter. *Police Work: The Social Organization of Policing* 2nd. ed. Prospect Heights: Waveland, 1997.

Mayo, Katherine. *Justice to All: The Story of the Pennsylvania State Police.* 5th ed. Boston: Houghton Mifflin, 1940.

ENDNOTES

1. David H. Bayley, "The Limits of Police Reform," in *Police and Society,* ed. by David H. Bayley (Beverly Hills: Sage, 1977) 224.

2. Richard Quinney, *The Problem of Crime: A Critical Introduction to Criminology,* 2d ed. (New York: Harper & Row, 1977) 13.

3. David H. Bayley, *Police for the Future* (New York: Oxford UP, 1994) 65–66.

4. Peter K. Manning, *Police Work,* 2d ed. (Prospect Heights: Waveland, 1997) 109.

5. Bayley, *Police for the Future,* 179.

6. Bayley, *Police for the Future,* 143.

7. ABC News, Nov. 1994.

8. The Gallup Organization for CNN/*USA Today,* Apr. 1995.

9. Jean Johnson, "Americans' Views on Crime and Law Enforcement," *National Institute of Justice Journal* 233 (Sept. 1997) 12.

10. Johnson, 12.

11. CBS News/*New York Times,* May 1992.

12. Sylvester Monroe, Tom Curry, Soph Fronia, Scott Gregory, "Los Angeles Riots: The Fire This Time," *Time* (11 May 1992): 18.

13. The Gallup Organization, Oct. 1995.

14. The Gallup Organization for CNN/*USA Today,* Oct. 1995.

15. Quoted in Johnson, 13.

16. General Social Survey, 1994.

17. Joint Center for Political and Economic Studies (Apr. 1996).

18. The Gallup Organization for CNN/*USA Today,* Oct. 1995.

19. Johnson, 14.

20. Vincent J. Webb, Charles M. Katz, and Nanette Graham, "Citizen Ratings on the Importance of Selected Police Duties," *Journal of Crime and Justice* 20 (1987): 45.

21. Webb, et al., 45.

22. Webb, et al., 51.

23. Webb, et al., 51.

24. Peter K. Manning, "Violence and Symbolic Violence," *Law Enforcement Operations and Management,* ed. Marilyn McShane and Frank P. Williams, III (New York: Garland, 1997) 156.

25. Manning, 157.

26. Bayley, *Police for the Future,* 143.

27. Bayley, *Police for the Future,* 143.

28. Bayley, *Police for the Future,* 143.

29. James Q. Wilson, *Varieties of Police Behavior: The Management of Law and Order in Eight Communities* (Cambridge: Harvard UP, 1968).

30. Wilson.

31. Wilson.

32. Wilson.

33. David B. Kopel and Paul H. Blackman, "The God Who Answers by Fire: The Waco Disaster and the Necessity of Federal Criminal Justice Reform." Paper presented at the Annual Meeting of the American Society of Criminology in Miami, Nov. 1994: 107.

34. Brian Reaves, *Census of State and Local Law Enforcement Agencies,* 1992 (Washington, DC: Bureau of Justice Statistics, 1993).

35. William C. Cunningham, John J. Struchs, and Clifford W. Van Meter, "Private Security: Patterns and Trends," *National Institute of Justice— Research in Brief* (Washington, DC: U.S. Department of Justice, 1991).

36. DEA Mission Statement found on the DEA Home Page in 1997.

37. *Treasury Home Page,* Internet, (1997).

38. COPS NEWS, COPS Home Page, Internet, (1997) 1.

39. COPS NEWS, 1.

40. COPS NEWS, 1.

41. Interestingly, the police trial board absolved Parker of blame in the Lincoln assassination.

42. *Treasury Home Page.*

43. *Treasury Home Page.*

44. *Treasury Home Page.*

45. *Treasury Home Page.*

46. U.S. Department of Treasury, U.S. Customs Service, *Office of Investigations Accomplishments: FY 1994* (Washington DC: USGPO, n.d.) 17–19.

47. James A. Inciardi, *The War on Drugs II* (Mountain View: Mayfield 1992) 235–236.

48. Internal Revenue Service, *CI Digest* (June 1994): 12.

49. David B. Kopel and Paul H. Blackman, *No More Wacos: What's Wrong with Federal Law Enforcement and How to Fix It* (New York: Prometheus, 1997) 311.

50. Kopel and Blackman, *No More Wacos,* 315.

51. Kopel and Blackman, *No More Wacos,* 318.

52. For an examination of state police agencies, see Mark E. Correia, Michael D. Reisig, and Nicholas P. Lovrich, "Public Perceptions of State Police: An Analysis of Individual-Level and Contextual Variables," *Journal of Criminal Justice 24* (1996): 17–28.

53. See David N. Falcone and L. Edward Wells, "The County Sheriff as a Distinctive Policing Modality," *American Journal of Police 14* (1995): 123–149.

54. Dale Stockton, "A Closer Look: L. A. County Sheriff's Dept.," *Police: The Law Officer's Magazine 20* (1996): 40–42.

55. Clemens Bartollas, Stuart J. Miller, and Paul B. Wice, *Participants in American Criminal Justice: The Promise and The Performance* (Englewood Cliffs: Prentice-Hall, 1983) 53–55.

56. Brian A. Reaves, *Local Police Departments, 1993* (Washington, DC: Bureau of Justice Statistics, 1996) 1.

57. Federal Bureau of Investigation, *Uniform Crime Reports* (Washington, DC: USGPO, 1996) 291.

58. Reaves, 1–2.

59. Nicholas P. Lourich and Brent S. Steel, *Results: National Survey of Municipal Police Departments* (Vancouver: Washington State Univ.–Vancouver, 1997) 1.

60. Dale Stockton, "Vancouver PD: Ambitiously Recruiting Professionals," *Police: The Law Enforcement Magazine 21* (Sept. 1997) 22–24.

61. See John P. Crank, "Police Style and Legally Serious Crime: A Contextual Analysis of Municipal Police Departments," *Journal of Criminal Justice 20* (1992): 401–412.

62. Ralph A. Weisheit, David N. Falcone, and L. Edward Wells, *Rural Crime and Rural Policing* (Washington, DC: U.S. Department of Justice, 1994) 9.

63. Dan Carlson, "Hiding Behind the 'Blue Wall'," *The Ethics Roll Call,* Center for Law Enforcement Ethics, Southwestern Law Enforcement Institute (Winter 1997).

64. *Wall Street Journal,* Mar. 22, 1994, 1.

65. Lawrence W. Sherman, "The Police," *Crime,* ed. James Q. Wilson and Joan Petersilia (San Francisco: Institute for Contemporary Studies, 1995) 338.

66. James S. Kakalik and Sorrel Wildhorn, *The Private Police: Security and Danger* (New York: Crane, Russak, 1977) 150–158.

67. Kakalik and Wildhorn, 150–158.

68. Kakalik and Wildhorn, 155.

3

BECOMING A POLICE OFFICER

How does one explain the raw excitement of being a cop? This is an excitement so powerful that it consumes and changes the officer's personality. For the officer all five senses are involved, especially in dangerous situations. They are stirred in a soup of emotions and adrenaline and provide an adrenaline rush that surpasses anything felt before. You are stronger and more agile; your mind functions on a higher level of quickness and alertness. Afterwards, the grass seems greener; the air fresher; food tastes better; and the spouse and children are even more precious. It is an addictive feeling that makes the runner's high in comparison feel like a hangover. Police work gets into the blood and possesses the spirit. You become the job and the job becomes you, until the day you die.

—Anonymous line police officer, personal interview, 1997.

This veteran police officer is making several important statements about becoming a police officer. He is contending that policing "gets into the blood and possesses the spirit," and that once you become a police officer, "you become the job and the job becomes you." In the words of one sergeant, policing is "not a job but a vocation."[1] It becomes a calling, rather than a set of bureaucratically defined duties.[2] Indeed, it is a calling remaining with officers until the day they die. Like a mental patient and criminal who always take the labels of ex-patient and ex-offender with them, the cop who leaves policing is still the ex-cop.

This veteran police officer also believes that civilians simply do not and cannot understand what it is like to be a police officer. In another part of his interview, he claims that "it is hopeless to attempt to describe what it is like to be a police officer to one who has never experienced it." The reason for this is that "there is a brotherhood and a sisterhood that goes beyond words. It is an emotion, a psychic communication, a shared experience that brings officers from hundreds of miles around to offer emotional support for the family and co-workers of a fallen colleague."[3]

Furthermore, this veteran officer is convinced that "the vast majority of those willing to become police officers, accepting the personal risks and the challenge of maintaining law and order, are special people."[4] They are special because "they are good people who care enough to do the best possible job. They are the people who unanimously respond in the affirmative to the question of whether they would sacrifice their lives to save others. They are the men and women of all nationalities who represent the best America has to offer."[5]

Finally, this veteran officer believes in the importance of the **police spirit** exemplified by honor, courage, and commitment. Policing is perceived as the "'thin blue line' that stands between anarchy and order."[6] Those who hold to the idea of the police spirit generally view the police officer as attempting to stand tall against all those forces interfering with their jobs. He adds that "the breaking of the police spirit is an accruing tragedy in law enforcement. Everyday, peace officers place their careers, financial well-being, family's future, and their lives on the thin blue line." He notes that "one mistake or one wrong decision can destroy all the good they have done and can result in department abandonment, civil suits or criminal charges. This type of situation can destroy an officer's life as surely as a bullet."[7]

Joseph Wambaugh aptly expressed this sentiment when he wrote, "Civilians have seldom understood the real danger inherent in police work. It has never been particularly hazardous to the body, not since Sir Robert Peel first organized his Bobbies. This line of work has always been a threat to the spirit."[8] A national police trainer suggest that the threatened death of the spirit is one of the real trouble spots in policing today:

> We have observed that police officers often suffer a death of the police spirit, brought on by the paradox of their courage and commitment on one hand, but the utter futility of their efforts on the other.
> It is our responsibility as a leader to insure that this does not happen.[9]

A proper response to this opening section is, "Wow, this is quite a speech." It does encapsulate the very best of what policing is supposed to be in the United States. Yet considerable evidence exists that individually and collectively, police sometimes fall short of the high ideals set forth in the opening statement.

EARLY DAYS ON THE JOB

During a police officer's early days on the job, the most influential experiences are the hiring process, academy training, and supervised field training.

Who Is Attracted to Police Work?

There has been considerable debate concerning whether persons attracted to police work have a "police personality."[10]

Those who support this notion of the police personality frequently claim that police recruits are more authoritarian than those who enter other occupations.[11]

The **authoritarian personality** is characterized by aggressive, cynical, conservative, and rigid behaviors.[12] Authoritarian personalities often abuse the authority they have, have difficulty working in situations in which no clear cut answers are readily available, and respond too much of the time in inappropriate ways to those who are different from themselves. However, J. J. Broderick, D. H. Bayley and H. Mendolshohn, and Jerome H. Skolnick and James J. Fyfe are among those who reject the notion that those who go into policing have more of an authoritarian personality than those who go into other occupations.[13]

B. N. Carpenter and S. M. Rasa found that police applicants differ from other occupational groups in several ways. Police applicants, as a group, are usually psychologically healthy. The police tend to be a homogeneous group of people, and the police are much like military personnel in their conformance to authority.[14] Some evidence also exists that police candidates may be lower than average in their desire to do autonomous work and that they favor a more directive leadership style.[15] Jerome H. Skolnick and James F. Fyfe support the notion that those who are attracted to policing have certain personality characteristics. They "do not see themselves as bullies." They "tend to be upright, virtuous, and civic-minded." In addition, "the typical police recruit is white, physically fit and agile, of the lower-middle or working class, male, in his twenties, and with some college education."[16]

There seems to be some clarity on the motivations that attract individuals to policing. Several studies have found that recruits say they were attracted to policing because it is a well-paid and stimulating job and a job in which they felt they could do some good.[17] Another study found that males and females alike generally list six factors that originally attracted them to policing: helping people, job security, fighting crime, job excitement, job prestige, and a lifelong interest.[18]

The Hiring Process

Police officers are granted considerable discretionary power, may work alone, and are placed in stressful, if not potentially dangerous situations in which there is a risk that the officer could act inappropriately. In such situations, the officer's actions are critical for citizen safety and department liability exposure. Misconduct is extremely costly in terms of monetary judgments against an agency, investigative costs, personnel costs, morale, and the public trust. One of the best ways to reduce liability is to hire the best people possible. The importance of proper selection cannot be overemphasized.[19]

Although the steps to becoming a police officer vary with each jurisdiction, the criterion for selection generally includes a written, psychological, and medical examination; drug screening; physical fitness assessment; oral interview; and a polygraph examination. If the testing is successful, most departments conduct a background investigation.

Written Examination

Larger police departments, as well as state police agencies, use some or all of four means of written tests:

1. cognitive tests (measuring verbal and mathematical aptitude and reasoning skills)
2. personality tests (typically the MMPI)
3. interest inventories (the Kuder and the Strong–Campbell)
4. biographic data inventories[20]

Smaller departments will usually administer some form of intelligence test, as well as a psychological screening test. A number of states also require a state mandated competency examination prior to the candidate being hired.

Physical Agility Test
The next stage usually is to determine whether a candidate has the physical agility necessary to be a police officer. There is presently little agreement on a proper physical agility test that would measure an individual's ability to perform the tasks sometimes necessary in police work. Still, at least 80 percent of large police departments and state police agencies require various types of qualifying strength and agility tests.[21] These tests range from a timing running (frequently a mile and a half in 12 minutes) and jumping test, walking on horizontal ladders, crawling through tunnels, dragging weights, leaping over six foot walls, and pushing cars.

Oral Interview
Many departments conduct oral interviews to test the candidate's ability to evaluate and reason through several difficult situations. Some advanced testing may include a interactive training video or role playing, where the applicant is asked at different stages to provide a solution. Ethical questions are always included in the evaluation. A prospective police officer might be asked the following:

- While doing reports, your Field Training Officer retrieves a Coca–Cola for himself and you from the lab refrigerator where a records clerk keeps her case of pop. He takes one, opens it and hands you a can. What would you do?
- Your commanding officer gives you an order that you know violates the law or a departmental policy. What would you do?
- You have only been on the job for a few months when you observe a vehicle driving recklessly. You stop the vehicle and discover that the driver is clearly intoxicated and is a popular fellow police officer. You are aware what a DWI conviction would do to his career. What would you do?

Medical Tests and Drug Screening
Ever since the *Americans with Disabilities Act* (ADA) classified drug and alcohol addiction as a disability, addiction has become a catch-22 in terms of when in the hiring process an applicant can be asked about his or her alcohol or drug use. In applying this Act to law enforcement, Attorney General Janet Reno states that "a law enforcement agency may not ask at the pre-offer stage about the frequency of past illegal drug use or whether the applicant has ever been addicted to drugs or undergone treatment for addiction."[22]

However, there is no indication that the Americans with Disabilities Act has affected departments' drug screening procedures. Departments continue to require that job applicants undergo such testing during the application process. They continue to ask applicants about their previous drug use, a question that is repeated during the polygraph examination. If the use of drugs other than marijuana is found to be more than experimental in the last three to five years, applicants are likely to be eliminated.

Background Investigation
A background investigation involves checking fingerprints for any criminal record; investigating the applicant's driving record, educational background, prior places of employment, and financial stability; and both securing references and interviewing parties who know the applicant. One of the quickest ways for an applicant to be eliminated is to put inaccurate information on the application form for employment.

Polygraph Examination
A survey of the 50 largest police departments found that 57 percent of the respondents conducted polygraph examinations during the hiring process.[23] An updating of this 1980s survey would probably reveal an even larger percentage of large department and state agencies requiring the polygraph examination. Those who defend the use of the polygraph contend that it is an effective means of weeding out questionable candidates. But there are those who strongly question the reliability of the polygraph examination. Its results are not admissible in most state courts, they counter, and neither should they be used to evaluate the suitability of candidates for employment. A student recently informed one of the authors, "I failed the polygraph exam, and I am really upset about it. They asked me about using drugs. I have never used drugs in my life, and the machine said I was lying. I know I was anxious; I really wanted the job."[24]

Academy Training

By 1975 the demographics of the average academy class changed from a class of all white males with little or no education beyond high school to one consisting of females, minorities, and college graduates. The staffing of academies also changed in ways reflecting the demographics of academy classes. College educated instructors, preferably with policing backgrounds, were much more widely used than before. Curriculums have further undergone revisions, reflecting the complicated issues facing modern-day police—such as instruction in cultural diversity, *bloodborne pathogens* (AIDS and Hepatitis B), hazardous materials, domestic abuse, active countermeasures, and verbal judo.

Recruit training varies nationwide, depending on state or agency requirements. Ten percent of police and sheriffs' departments require no academy training.[25] Training requirements are more stringent in larger departments, primarily due to the danger faced by the officers, than in smaller ones. According to a survey of local police agencies across the country conducted by the Bureau of Justice Statistics, departments serving populations of 100,000 or more require over 1,000 total hours of training, compared to under 500 hours in jurisdictions of less than 2,500 residents (see Table 3.1).

Debate over minimum basic training standards continues today as it did when Sir Robert Peel introduced reforms in the 1800s.[26] In 1973, the National Advisory Commission on Criminal Justice Standards and Goals recommended 400 hours of basic training.[27] At first, this amount of training seems adequate until one considers the 2,100 hour requirement to become a licensed beautician in Iowa. This inadequacy in recruit training resulted in one police scholar observing, "Doctors bury their mistakes, while lawyers send theirs to jail. Unfortunately, untrained police officers do a little of both."[28]

Another concern relates to the educational requirement for prospective recruits. The Bureau of Justice Statistics survey found 14 percent of police departments do not require a high school diploma, with only 8 percent requiring some kind of college degree (see Table 3.2).[29] Despite this apparent lack of concern for a higher education entry requirement, Larry Armstrong and Clinton Longenecker report that 65 percent of those employed as police officers have some college and 25 percent have a college degree.[30]

The classical method and the developmental approach are the two basic methods of recruit training. The classical method is adopted from the military model and attempts to develop discipline of recruits through instructor-applied nonspecific stress. Classical training is known for its verbal harassment, criticism, and physical endurance used as punishment. Today, the classical method is being criticized for producing officers who have low levels of self-esteem and motivation, are afraid to make decisions and act independently, and may need constant supervision to perform.[31]

The developmental approach consists of nonstress training relying on adult learning principles. The stress produced is based on the struggle for achievement through pragmatic learning activities rather than the fear and intimidation of the classical method. It has been credited with producing graduates who achieve a higher level of performance and job satisfaction, fewer complaints from citizens and internal discipline difficulties, and better academic and proficiency performance.[32]

Most states require minimum entry-level educational requirements and mandate minimum certification requirements to become a peace officer. States generally approach this centralized control of police professional standards either by creating a Peace Officers Standards and Training Board (POST) or by operating law enforcement academies. Both act as regulatory agencies setting and monitoring standards to become and to remain a police officer. For example, in Minnesota the board requires applicants seeking employment as officers to be licensed before they are hired. This is a unique approach since most departments usually have to pay to train recruits after they have been hired. Before seeking employment, the candidate must pay for and complete Minnesota's clinical program, complete a two-year degree program at a POST-certified college, and pass the Minnesota Peace Officer Licensing Examination.

TABLE 3.1   Training Requirements for New Officer Recruits in Local Police Departments and Sheriffs' Departments by Size of Population Served, 1993

Local Police Departments

| Population served | Percent of agencies requiring training | *Average Number of Hours Required* | |
		Classroom hours	Field training hours
all sizes	90	425	215
1,000,000 or more	100	865	311
500,000 to 999,999	100	757	396
250,000 to 499,999	100	727	551
100,000 to 249,999	99	630	498
50,000 to 99,999	100	494	435
25,000 to 49,999	100	492	393
10,000 to 24,999	98	468	305
2,500 to 9,999	93	455	204
less than 2,500	93	352	105

Sheriffs' Departments

| Population served | Percent of agencies requiring training | *Average Number of Hours Required* | |
		Classroom hours	Field training hours
all sizes	90	366	199
1,000,000 or more	100	615	286
500,000 to 999,999	100	414	331
250,000 to 499,999	96	411	336
100,000 to 249,999	96	388	255
50,000 to 99,999	98	414	242
25,000 to 49,999	92	357	239
10,000 to 24,999	86	343	155
2,500 to 9,999	83	342	109
less than 2,500	93	352	105

Note: Computations of the average number of training hours required excludes departments not requiring training.

Source: Kathleen Maguire and Ann L. Pastore, eds., *Sourcebook of Criminal Justice Statistics 1995.* U.S. Department of Justice, Bureau of Justice Statistics (Washington, DC: USGPO, 1996) 42.

TABLE 3.2   Minimum Educational Requirements for New Officer and New Deputy Recruits by Size of Population Served, United States, 1993[a]

Local Police Departments

Population served	*Percent of Agencies Requiring a Minimum of:*				
	Total with requirements	High school diploma	Some college[b]	2-year college degree	4-year college degree
all sizes	97	86	4	7	1
1,000,000 or more	10	75	25	0	0
500,000 to 999,999	100	85	11	4	0
250,000 to 499,999	98	73	13	9	2
100,000 to 249,999	100	81	9	3	7
50,000 to 99,999	100	72	11	17	1
25,000 to 49,999	100	78	9	9	4
10,000 to 24,999	98	84	5	7	3
2,500 to 9,999	100	90	4	7	1
less than 2,500	94	85	2	5	0

Sheriffs' Departments

Population served	*Percent of Agencies Requiring a Minimum of:*				
	Total with requirements	High school diploma	Some college[b]	2-year college degree	4-year college degree
all sizes	97	89	2	5	(c)
1,000,000 or more	100	96	4	0	0
500,000 to 999,999	93	83	6	2	2
250,000 to 499,999	100	88	7	3	1
100,000 to 249,999	100	88	2	10	(c)
50,000 to 99,999	99	89	5	2	2
25,000 to 49,999	97	88	1	7	0
10,000 to 24,999	95	89	1	5	0
less than 10,000	98	92	1	5	0

Note: [a]Percents may not add to total because of rounding
[b]Non-degree requirements
(c) = less than 0.5%

Source: Kathleen Maguire and Ann L. Pastore, eds., *Sourcebook of Criminal Justice Statistics 1995,* U.S. Department of Justice, Bureau of Justice Statistics (Washington, DC: USGPO, 1996) 42.

Field Training

The emphasis on standards and liability in police work have encouraged departments to spend more money on recruiting and testing police candidates and on upgrading training procedures. Today, most departments have developed a Field Training Officer Program (FTO) to compensate for errors in the hiring process, and to protect themselves from law suits involving negligent hiring, retention, assignment, entrustment, training, and supervision; failure to direct; and failure to follow due process resulting in a termination.

During the **field training,** a rookie is assigned to a field training officer and receives on the job training. Recruits who discover that the values they were taught in the academy are not respected by supervisors under actual working conditions may lose the idealism and initiative fostered during the academy experience. The training officer, then, greatly shapes the climate of the rookie's working environment.[33] As Herman Goldstein put it: "However strongly the head of the agency may elicit a different style of policing, the quality of an officer's daily life is heavily dependent on how well the officer satisfies the expectations and demands of his or her immediate supervisor."[34] The field training officer (FTO) is the probationary officer's teacher and coach whose job it is to tutor the new officer in staying safe, avoiding civil liability, and enhancing the safety and welfare of the community the officer serves.[35]

The earliest formalized Field Training Officer Program began in the San Jose, California Police Department in 1972. This program originated as a result of a 1970 traffic accident that involved an on-duty San Jose police recruit negligently operating a police vehicle. A passenger in another vehicle was killed, while the officer was seriously injured. Subsequent to this accident, the city dismissed the officer and began a process of evaluating the department's recruit training and evaluation procedures."[36]

As a result of this incident, a very formalized and structured post-academy training program was developed. Since that time, San Jose has been used as a basic format to develop other FTO Programs across the nation. In the San Jose model, the recruit has to pass a three phase program lasting 52 weeks to be considered a permanent employee. The first phase consists of academy or in-house training. During the 14 week second phase, a Field Training Officer rides with the probationary officer—completing Daily Observation Reports (DOR) and weekly evaluation reports on the recruit's performance. During the 15 weeks of the final phase, the recruit works a solo beat with first-line supervisors and is evaluated every two to four weeks. The FTO program ends with a meeting of a special board to review the performance and deficiencies of the recruit to determine if the probation period has been successfully completed, remedial training is needed, or termination is necessary.[37]

This is not an easy time for the recruit as the real-life training can have an intensity surpassing anything experienced in the academy's safe training atmosphere. There are few second chances on the streets. What the trainee does next may jeopardize his or her life, a partner's life, an innocent civilian's life, the outcome of a criminal case, or the recruit's career. The recruit will be judged on the legality of his or her actions and whether the trainee's actions followed departmental policy. Unlike the FTO officer who has real-life experiences and training to guide his or her actions, the trainee has only academy training. Under almost constant supervision, the recruit soon feels the stress of every action being evaluated. In Box 3.1 a police officer hired in 1994 describes her FTO training experience in a medium sized department.

FORMAL POLICE DUTIES

The formal duties of a police officer are undergoing a metamorphosis—from the cold exclusive paramilitary model to a more human style of community policing. In the past, law enforcement dictated to the communities just what their duties were. This was often in conflict with what the community valued as important. For example, it was once thought the advantage of the paramilitary model was separation of police and citizens to prevent corruption. This self-imposed "blue wall" blocking communication resulted in suspicion and distrust on both sides. Yet the

---

BOX 3.1   FTO Training

I have been a policewoman for a year now, but the memories of my first few days on the job have not escaped my memory. I remember walking into the police station on my first day feeling afraid and very anxious. My first few days were spent following my field training officer around the police station. It was good training, but somewhat unrealistic because my FTO made everything look easier than it was.

After a few days of watching my FTO, it was finally my turn to show him how I could perform. I remember getting behind the wheel of my squad car with my FTO seated next to me, notebook in hand. The stress was overwhelming. I was very nervous and yet very excited at the same time. I was finally doing what I had always dreamed about doing, but it wasn't as easy as I thought it would be.

As I drove through the city streets attempting to find my way around, my FTO would quietly be writing in his notebook occasionally casting a glance in my direction. I remember all the thoughts racing through my mind.... "Am I doing the right things?" "Does he (my FTO) think I'll make it through the FTO program?" I didn't really know what to think, because my mind was too busy trying to remember proper procedure such as how to talk on the radio and what 10-codes to reply with. That is just one example of the many things that I was thinking about as I drove through the city.

At the end of every day, my FTO would go over my daily performance. I was given a daily score and he would comment on the good and bad things I did. I usually scored pretty well, but I often felt that my FTO was expecting too much out of me too soon. As a recruit, I felt pressure because I knew that my FTO was not only my teacher, he was also my partner. If anything bad would happen, it would be up to me to back him up and keep him from getting hurt or even worse—killed. Because I was very conscious of that fact is why I felt so much pressure to be the best cop that I could be.

Source: Officer Tina Lathrop interviewed July 1995.

residents of a neighborhood served by an officer may value a much closer relationship as that of a friend, a leader, or their personal crime fighter. To them junk cars, abandoned buildings, kids hanging around the street corner, or a simple conversation are more important than a quick response time or a stiff military presence.

The types of calls officers respond to depend largely upon shift assignment: morning to early afternoon (the day shift); afternoon to late evening (the evening shift); and late evening to early morning (the night or graveyard shift). How busy the officer is during his or her shift will depend largely on the demographics of the department or precinct and to some extent on the seriousness of the calls. For example, in small bedroom communities, officers may handle only one or two calls or no calls at all during a shift. They have more time for community policing assignments and traffic enforcement. The complaints are typically minor, with an occasional domestic disturbance to settle.

In larger communities, officers starting their shift often find calls waiting for service. The calls for service are usually more serious in nature, consuming larger amounts of time and placing an increased burden on other officers to answer calls. For example, a drunk driver can take up to three hours to complete the booking, the breath test, statements, and the officer's reports. Usually officers of larger departments spend most of their shifts traveling from call to call, leaving very little time for community policing:

> No challenge is more immediate, no job more demanding, in many police departments than the crushing burden of answering the public's calls for service. Individual officers in busy cities feel the weight on every shift. "If you drive out there and make yourself available for calls, you wouldn't be available one minute that night for anything else," says Los Angeles Police Department patrol officer Joe Ciancanelli. "There wouldn't be a dull moment, no time for anything." Patrol forces have, over the last 10 years, increasingly been restricted to answering the tolling of the 911 bell. Fewer people and less and less time are available for foot patrol, problem solving, crime prevention, or any other important tasks a chief might want the force to perform.[38]

The calls answered by officers from medium to large departments are typically more serious in nature: homicides, stabbings, shootings, robberies, rapes, child neglect and abuse, and gang disturbances and drug sales. More often than not these departments are under-staffed because of forced budget cutbacks. To compound the problem, the public often has an unrealistic perception of the number of officers on patrol in their city at any one time. Regarding this, a community policing officer from a midwestern department noted: "I asked an angry citizen at one of the neighborhood meetings how many police officers he felt were patrolling during a shift. He aggressively responded '150.' He looked at me in disbelief when I told him that there are only eight to ten officers patrolling the streets during an eight hour shift."[39]

Each shift has a different personality. The day shift is the most routine of the shifts and is sometimes called semi-retirement, because there is a lack of criminal activity, at least until noon. In some departments, much of the officer's time is spent "cleaning up" after the other two shifts. They gather preliminary facts and follow-up on complaints from the night before. Officers in small departments fall into the routine of monitoring morning rush hour traffic and school crossings. Officers on the day shift, more than any other shift, occasionally have to respond to bomb threats, school disturbances, or armed robberies. Frequently, they encounter people who are friendlier and more supportive than the evening shifts.

The evening shift is usually the most fast-paced of the three shifts, because citizens are the most active during these hours and the criminal element has awakened after a restful sleep. Generally in smaller departments, officers begin their shifts by making drive-by checks of closed businesses. In medium to large departments, the officers "hit the ground running" as they respond to calls for service. Because problems with teenagers are most common during these hours, officers patrol the areas where teenage groups or gangs meet. Robberies, thefts, vandalism, and domestic abuse calls are common occurrences in urban areas.

During the night shift, the first few hours are usually busy until the bars close. Officers deal with many problems involving persons who have been drinking alcohol or using drugs. After "the bar run" is complete, officers have time for writing reports and taking statements from victims and suspects. Depending on the size of the department, officers will have time to cruise beat areas, check buildings, and note suspicious activity. In urban departments, the "demons" too frequently come out at night, and officers must deal with gang shootings and altercations, knifings, and homicides.

In most departments, the night generally drags after 3:00 A.M. Night shift officers, more than those on the other two shifts, develop close alliances between themselves and coffee shop employees. They are more likely to develop an "us against them" attitude toward administrators. Night shift officers often feel that administrators have insulated themselves from the streets and are "out of touch." They are quick to remind each other that it has been years since administrators have worked the streets and that few administrators, if any, will ride along with them on the shift.

EDUCATIONAL INTERLUDE

In 1967, the President's Crime Commission recommended that the goal of police agencies in the United States should be to have every officer of the peace educated to the baccalaureate degree level.[40] While this goal has not been met, education has played a major role in reshaping policing. Indeed, the assumption that higher education makes for a better police officer is at the center of the *Police Corps Act* and *Law Enforcement Scholarship and Recruitment Act*, both of which are contained in the 1994 Federal Crime Bill.

Education has had the greatest impact at the top level of policing.[41] Human relations training, the findings of social and behavioral sciences, public administration courses, and writing skills learned at the college level have allowed administrators to be more sensitive to the needs of the community and better able to develop and implement new ideas, such as community policing.

The impact of education on line police officers has been widely debated among officers themselves. Leslie B. Buckley et al. found that an officer's attitude toward education seemed to be dependent on the amount of education of the person rendering the opinion. Lesser educated officers tended to have more negative attitudes toward higher education because they believed that university graduates were receiving undeserved advancement.[42] They also endorsed "instincts, common sense and experience over education and claimed that education provided no additional 'perspective' for the police officer's role." In contrast, according to Buckley, et al., "university graduate officers believe that education enhances performance."[43]

There have been four main arguments against mandated college education for police officers: (1) college-educated individuals may not understand the problems and attitudes of lower-class persons with whom police officers must deal; (2) the requirement of a college education might reduce the number of minorities available for recruitment into police work; (3) education beyond high school may produce a higher level of cynicism than would be present among those who have less schooling;[44] and (4) a police career may be unattractive for the college graduate because it is "routine, sometimes dull, frequently unpleasant, and occasionally dangerous."[45]

In contrast, a 1989 Police Executive Research Forum (PERF) study, "The State of Police Education," was supportive of the value of a college education for a police officer. This study, which included both a review of previous research and the results of the PERF survey of police managers, found "that the overall educational level of the police has continued to rise, because 55 percent of the 124,000 offices included in this study had at least two years of college, compared to only 15 percent of police officers in 1970.[46] This study concluded that:

- College-educated officers perform the tasks of policing better than their non-college-educated counterparts.
- College-educated officers are generally better communicators, whether with a citizen, in court, or in written police reports.
- College-educated officers are more flexible in dealing with difficult situations and in dealing with persons of diverse cultures, lifestyles, races, and ethnicities.
- Officers with higher education are more professional and are more responsive to alternative approaches to policing.
- College-educated officers are more likely to see the broader picture of the criminal justice system than to view police more provincially as an exclusive group.[47]

Most other studies have also found that a college education is desirable for a present-day police officer. M. S. Meagher found that the frequency of specific positive acts was statistically different when higher education was controlled. Although Meagher did not claim that higher education was the sole cause, this study revealed a clear relationship between higher education and the performance of desirable police tasks (i.e., improved communication skills, better ability to evaluate characteristics of others, and heightened analytical and conceptual skills).[48]

Micheal G. Breci concurred that a college education improves community policing: "Effective community policing requires skills officers acquire through higher education—critical thinking, problem solving, effective oral and written communication, and an understanding of group and community dynamics."[49] David Murrell, whose dissertation specifically examined whether an educated officer would be a better officer, concluded that "college education makes for superior police work performance."[50]

SOCIALIZATION INTO THE POLICE CULTURE

The process of being introduced into the police culture is called **socialization.** James W. Sterling defines socialization as "a formal or informal learning process by which an individual becomes aware of and committed to behavioral norms which are seen as appropriate and right for specific role performance." He adds that "socialization includes the learning of expected behavioral responses to the performance of specific roles by other people."[51] The process of being socialized into the police culture usually takes place in three steps: the officer's initiation into the culture, the development of a working personality, and the acceptance of the informal system or informal code of behavior.

Initiation into the Culture

One of the most helpful treatments of the initiation into police culture was developed by Ellen Kirschman in her book, *I Love a Cop: What Police Families Need to Know.* Kirschman found that the recruit's initiation into the police organization encompasses the officer's entire career and occurs in several phases: "Falling in love With the Job: The Application Phase, The Academy, and On Probation;" "Phase One: the Honeymoon;" "Phase Two: Settling Down;" "Phase Three: Dealing with Disillusionment;" and "Phase Four: Coming to a Crossroad."[52]

Falling in Love with the Job
According to Kirschman's study, during the initial phase, candidates are proud of their abilities. They have survived the strenuous, time-consuming testing procedure, passing all requirements. They are joining a very elite group, as only two out of 100 applicants were hired. At the academy and on probation, rookies are eager to fit in and become competent. The pressure to succeed is intense because there is no job security until the year long probation is over. Without realizing it, officers are assuming a new identity. Kirschman explains that "for most, the gratification of being part of this accomplished group of professionals far exceeds, for now, the costs of conforming to the group."[53]

Phase One: The Honeymoon
This is the "most delicious" part of an officer's career. Most cannot believe they are being paid to do this job. They would just as soon work than have a day off. The

levels of responsibility and authority far exceed anything felt before. Each call is a challenging and intoxicating experience. The new officers are experiencing worlds never before open to them.

Phase Two: Settling Down
When officers reach phase two, the honeymoon is over. The job is still interesting, but the thrill is gone and the initial signs of cynicism are starting to show. The "rescue" fantasies of the rookie years have been replaced with the realistic acceptance of the boring and frustrating parts of the job. Officers must deal with the mountains of paperwork, the flaws in the judicial system, the influence of politics, and the relentless hammering of the media. The illusions about human beings' basic goodness have been flattened into a persistent skepticism. Some officers conclude that only innocent children and the elderly merit much compassion. During this time, officers may seek promotion or the challenge of a special assignment: drug unit, SWAT team, canine unit, or investigations. The failure to achieve these goals, especially promotion, raises feelings of anger and shame.[54]

Phase Three: Dealing with Disillusionment
By this time, officers have become deeply disillusioned, caught in an "us against them" psychology. A once exciting job is now a trap from which it is impossible to break free. Officers are confronted with their lack of education and financial needs that keep them married to the job and waiting for retirement. Kirschman describes the cynicism:

> Now he or she feels like the best that can be done is to maintain order and hold the line. The judicial system doesn't work, criminals have the advantage over cops, and victim's needs don't count. Neither the community nor the department understands nor appreciates the police. Politics, rather than fairness or justice, dominate the scene. The media are ten times more interested in the occasional police scandal than the thousands of everyday acts of courage and persistence.[55]

Phase Four: Coming to a Crossroad
By the time officers have reached phase four, they have accepted the reality of the situation. Officers at this stage begin to make plans as to what to do next and try to find new challenges to keep them interested in their work. Some will set goals not related to work, which give them the freedom to be themselves and not worry as much about the impact of everything they do or say."[56]

Kirschman is helpful in sketching out a typical career pattern for police officers. She groups the careers of all police officers together, but points out that police careers follow a U-shaped course with satisfaction declining and then increasing in incremental phases. This is only a map, not a timetable, as each officer will chart a different course. She also concludes that there is an inevitable entropy in police officers' careers; that is, a deterministic unraveling of all the positive feelings that they brought into their careers. Facing disillusionment, officers should turn their thoughts to the legacy they want to leave behind.

WORKING PERSONALITY OF THE POLICE

According to Jerome Skolnick's classic typology, the three key elements in the **working personality** of officers are danger, authority, and efficiency.[57] Danger is ever present and only a few seconds away from the criminal element (see Table 3.3 for officers killed in the last century in the United States). S. G. Chapman states that "human error occurs in all occupations, with varying degrees of severity in the results." Yet Chapman adds, "in few callings does it have the potential consequences it has in police work. A glitch in safety, an overlooked precaution, or a departure from proven patrol procedures can cost an officer['s] life."[58] In the FBI study, *Killed in the Line of Duty,* several of the killers admitted watching the demeanor of the officer and looking for mistakes before attacking.[59] Thirty-three percent of the offenders interviewed in the FBI's second study *In the Line of Fire* stated that their attack was intentional and premeditated. Thirty-eight percent wanted to escape or avoid arrest, 14 percent wanted to frighten the officer, 7 percent wanted to wound the officer, 2 percent wanted to immobilize the officer, and 19 percent of the offenders stated that they wanted to kill the officer.[60]

Skolnick adds that "The element of danger isolates policemen socially from the segment of the citizenry which he regards as symbolically dangerous and also from conventional citizenry with whom he identifies."[61] Because police officers operate in dangerous situations, Skolnick suggests, they become suspicious, constantly seeking indications that a crime is about to be committed or that they may become targets of lawbreakers.[62]

The FBI's *Killed in the Line of Duty* study identified behavioral descriptors of victim officers. Surprisingly, some of these characteristics are the same ones screened for during the hiring process and sought out for community policing officers. This study reported: "The most salient behavioral descriptors characterizing these officers appear to be their good-natured demeanor and conservative use of physical force as compared to other law enforcement officers in similar circumstances" (see Box 3.2).[63] Many of the same behavioral descriptors surfaced during the FBI's *In the Line of Fire* study. Victim officers were friendly, hard working, and service-oriented. They felt that they could "read" situations or persons and, as a result, dropped their guard. They also did not follow established rules and procedures in regard to arrest, traffic stops, or waiting for backup.[64]

The rookie soon learns that danger can come from almost anywhere, not just the criminal's bullet. Officers are often called upon to subdue violent people who are bleeding, attempting to bite the officer, or are covered with urine or vomit. Suspects now possess a new element of danger—bloodborne pathogens in the form of AIDS and Hepatitis B and airborne pathogens, such as tuberculosis. The contact with high-risk populations is almost an everyday occurrence. The risk is so great that the Occupational Safety and Health Administration (OSHA) has placed law

TABLE 3.3   State, U.S. Territory, and Federal Death Breakdown

State	Officers killed	State	Officers killed
Alabama	366	Nevada	51
Alaska	28	New Hampshire	24
Arizona	194	New Jersey	318
Arkansas	168	New Mexico	102
California	1205	New York	1031
Colorado	193	North Carolina	298
Connecticut	114	North Dakota	26
Delaware	29	Ohio	621
District of Columbia	105	Oklahoma	234
Florida	512	Oregon	139
Georgia	390	Pennsylvania	601
Hawaii	40	Rhode Island	33
Idaho	40	South Carolina	212
Illinois	834	South Dakota	41
Indiana	259	Tennessee	272
Iowa	128	Texas	788
Kansas	199	Utah	82
Kentucky	280	Vermont	15
Louisiana	284	Virginia	292
Maine	72	Washington	226
Maryland	212	West Virginia	114
Massachusetts	246	Wisconsin	196
Michigan	451	Wyoming	39
Minnesota	186	Territories	270
Mississippi	131	Federal Agencies	822
Missouri	541		
Montana	104		
Nebraska	90	TOTAL	14,248

Source: National Law Enforcement Officers Memorial Fund, Washington, D.C.

enforcement officers in the same high-risk group as emergency room personnel and paramedics. Another area of concern is hazardous materials due to the exposure officers have at industrial spills and traffic accidents.[65]

Authority
The element of authority is essential to the working personality of the police, because the typical response of citizens is to deny recognition of authority. Thus, rookies learn early that the need to take charge of the situation requires using a forceful voice and maintaining a dominant stance.[66] As one of the killers in the FBI

BOX 3.2   Behavioral Descriptor of Victim Officers

Friendly to everyone

Well-liked by community and department

Tends to use less force than other officers felt they would in similar circumstances

Hard working

Tends to perceive self as more oriented to public relations than law enforcement

—service oriented

Uses force only as last resort

—peers claim they would use force at an earlier point in similar circumstances

Doesn't follow all the rules, especially in regard to:

—arrest

—confrontation with prisoners

—traffic stops

—does not wait for backup (when available)

Feels he/she can "read" others/situations and will drop guard as a result

Tends to look for "good" in others

"Laid back" and "easy going"

Source: Federal Bureau of Investigation; Uniform Crime Reports Section, *Killed in the Line of Duty: A Study of Selected Felonious Killings of Law Enforcement Officers* (Washington, DC: U.S. Department of Justice, 1992) 32.

report's *Killed in the Line of Duty* said as he evaluated the officers' actions before taking aggressive action: "The officer was not authoritarian and did not take control of me. He was a willing participant in his death."[67]

This study also found that offenders will often read the body language of the officer, looking for vulnerability before attacking. It notes that "officers should be aware of [their] body language and other signals that they are transmitting to the public."[68] Gary T. Klugiewicz estimates that body language constitutes 55 percent of communication that backs up what is said, 7 percent of the message and how it is said, and 38 percent of the message.[69] In essence, the forceful voice backed by a dominant stance communicates the officer's ability to take control of the situation.

Efficiency

Efficiency is another important aspect of the working personality of the police. Skolnick contends that this demand for efficiency requires that police become craftsmen, thereby meeting the yardsticks for performance placed upon them by the department. In addition, it helps them feel good about maintaining order in the community.

Stephen M. Hennessy's innovative approach categorized officers into four types: (1) Sensing–Thinking Officers; (2) Intuitive–Thinking Officers; (3) Sensing–Feeling Officers; and (4) Intuitive–Feeling Officers. He claims that Sensing–Thinking Officers represent 64 percent of law enforcement officers compared to only 25 percent of the general population. These officers use their five senses to process information making decisions on pure logic or objective reasoning. They are generally extremely good at details and like to organize, control, and run things. Appealing to their feeling side will most likely fall short of the mark as only reasoning based on fact will change their mind. Frequently they are blunt, unfeeling, and lack basic courtesies that are unimportant to them at the time. Intuitive–Thinking Officers, who represent 16 percent of law enforcement personnel and 18 percent of the general population, process information through intuition, their "sixth sense," making decisions based on pure logic and objective reasoning. They dislike detail and routine, often forgetting specifics. Paperwork is not one of their strengths. They use their intuition to process information and do well on complex tasks. They are the ones coming up with new ideas and ways to do things. Like the Sensing–Thinking Officers they are blunt, lacking courtesy, and preferring truth over tact. Sensing–Feeling Officers comprise 16 percent of law enforcement officers compared to 29 percent of the general population. They take in information and process it through the five senses, but make decisions through subjective reasoning and a concern about valuing people. Like the Sensing–Thinking Officers, they focus on detail and concrete reality, but are more interested in people than in things. They excel in community relations, difficult personal matters, and make excellent community oriented police officers. The Intuitive–Feeling Officers, making up 6 percent of law enforcement compared to 28 percent of the general population, prefer to process information using intuition making decisions through a feeling or social value. They excel in long range issues, dislike routine and detail, and are responsive to people's needs most of all. Hennessey concludes that the feeling types make up only 20 percent of the police profession, and he provides insight into why the profession does not appear to be a caring, feeling, and compassionate one.[70]

Charles Remsberg's *Tactics for Criminal Patrol: Vehicle Stops, Drug Discovery & Officer Survival* places the working personalities of officers on a continuum. On one end of the continuum are the "ROD," Retired On Duty, and the other, the "five-percenter mind-set."[71] RODs are not good on aggressive patrol and, because of their lackadaisical attitude, are a danger to themselves as well as other officers, and are a waste of tax payers' money. According to a southern trainer, these officers believe that:

> Their climate-controlled cruiser is a fortress. They roll up the windows and set the temperature at sixty-eight to seventy-four degrees, they adjust the seat just right, they have a soft cushion for their broad ass, they tune in their favorite radio station at a volume that's one decibel below where they can hear their call number. They don't leave this comfortable "home" unless they absolutely have to. Each day to them is just another day toward pulling the pin. They spend their shift going to coffee, coming from coffee, going to bullshit with someone, leaving someone they've just bullshitted with—and occasionally handling a call. When they do stop traffic violators, they're just "mail carriers"—they deliver the ticket. They don't look for anything more, they don't think about anything more. Their philosophy is: "Little cases, little problems…big cases, big problems." They build a career on sliding by.[72]

In contrast, the 5%er is committed to outstanding performance, is aggressive about enforcing the law, and, at the same time, guards civil and human rights.

5%ers seek out proactive rather than skating by on reactive patrol. Remsberg describes the 5%er attitude as enthusiastically embracing the core concept of criminal patrol. They view vehicle stops as "golden opportunities for unique field investigations which, with the right volume of contacts, the right knowledge and creativity, and the right approach, can lead to major felony arrests." Their bodies hum, Remsberg reports, when they are on the streets. They want to see just how sharply they "can hone the fundamental patrol skills of *observation, conversation,* and *tactical thinking.*" To sharpen their "alertness to detail and readiness for trouble, they practice *mental conditioning exercises.*" Remsberg concludes by saying that "the 5%er mind-set is the most essential factor behind successful criminal patrol."[73]

Skolnick's presentation is helpful in portraying some of the aspects of the police personality, but, at the same time, it has several troubling aspects. It is stilted in that it exaggerates the danger of police work, reduces multidimensional concepts (danger, authority, and efficiency) to unidimensional terms, and makes no allowance for variation of response. Hennessy, in examining the variation in feeling among police officers, also makes a contribution to understanding one aspect of the police personality. However, he makes certain assumptions about how individuals make decisions which seem to be both simplistic and incomplete. A number of questions can be raised about his typology: Why only four types? Where is the degree of response? What variability is there with gender, race, stage of the career, and experience in policing? Remsberg's presentation captures the social reality that police officers' commitment, as well as their performance on the job, can be placed on a continuum. Its shortcoming is that it focuses on performance and gives little insight into any other aspect of the police personality.

Informal Code

The **informal code** fills the void that the formal system of rules, regulations, policies, and procedures does not cover. The informal system is taught to young recruits through a variety of socializing experiences—at the academy, riding with a training officer, and interacting with peers on a daily basis. The values of the police culture, such as loyalty and individualism, are reinforced because of the feeling that the formal system does not adequately provide for the needs of the police officer. The informal code provides both status and social satisfaction. Unlike the formal system, the informal system provides a sense of brotherhood and sisterhood that supposedly transverses racial, gender, and jurisdictional boundaries as represented by the slogan "the thin blue line." The solidarity is most evident when officers travel across state lines to share emotions at the funeral of a fallen officer.

The actual content of these informal rules varies among departments, but, according to Skolnick, "one underpinning of the police subculture is the belief among police officers that no one—i.e. management or the public—understands them."[74] Elizabeth Reuss-Ianni found that the police culture of the New York Police Department included such maxims as "watch out for your partner," "don't give up another cop," and "getting the job done" (themes of solidarity); "protect your ass," "don't trust a guy until you have him checked out," "don't trust bosses to look out for your interests," and "don't make waves" (themes of isolationism); and "show balls," "be aggressive when you have to, but don't be too eager," and "civilians never command police"(themes of bravery).[75] Sparrow, Moore, and Kennedy's *Beyond 911* suggests that police culture includes at least six beliefs:

- The police are the only real crimefighters.
- No one understands the work of a police officer.
- Loyalty counts more than anything.
- It is impossible to win the war on crime without bending the rules.
- The public is demanding and nonsupportive.
- Working in patrol is the least desirable job in policing.[76]

The degree to which these informal rules are accepted also varies across departments and even from one police officer to another. Officers who violate these informal rules risk having difficulties with fellow officers. These difficulties range from being the brunt of wise cracks and derogatory comments, to being ignored by fellow officers, to being transferred to another district or area of assignment. These informal norms serve to protect those who become involved in corruption or in the use of unnecessary force. The "blue curtain" or **code of silence** can be a firm barrier against administrative knowledge.[77] It can also be exceptionally effective if it is or is perceived to be largely silent in regard to an act that promises to tarnish all the good works that police officers do.

Ultimately, it can be argued that the informal code represents the line officer's defense against the degrading nature of the paramilitary model. According to former Attorney General Edwin Meese III, "Ironically, one of the principal factors preventing the development of a strong sense of professionalism among police officers—not only in their own eyes, but in the eyes of the public—may be the military form of organization that the police have adopted from their earliest days."[78]

As a system of rigid organizational structure that promotes authoritarian leadership, the paramilitary management style degrades the position of the individual officer, the primary figure in police service.[79] Meese contends that "too often the basic police officer is viewed as comparable to a private in the army, the lowest ranking military person, who has virtually no individual authority...."[80] He adds that it is little wonder, then, that those holding the rank of police officer often are regarded as something less than professionals and that they are denied individual authority, the presumption of expertise, and the discretion that normally would accompany professional status."[81] Herman Goldstein poignantly contributes this:

> The dominant form of policing today continues to view police officers as automatons. Despite awareness that they exercise broad discretion, they are held to strict account in their daily work—for what they do and how they do it...Especially in procedural matters, they are required to adhere to detailed regulations. In large police agencies, rank-in-file police officers are often treated impersonally and kept in the dark regarding policy matters. Officers

quickly learn, under these conditions, that the rewards go to those who conform to expectations—that nonthinking (sic).[82]

SOCIAL ISOLATION

The term "us against them" is often used to describe the cynicism and paranoia of line officers. As the late New Haven, Connecticut Police Chief James Ahern wrote, "The day the new recruit walks through the doors of the police academy, he leaves society behind to enter a profession that does more than give him a job, it defines who he is." Ahern aptly added "for all the years he remains, he will always be a cop."[83]

Inherent in Ahern's statement is a necessary willingness to accept social isolation as the recruit leaves society behind and a self-imposed condemnation to become part of a "brotherhood," suspicious of all others, and fortified by the danger and authority. Most researchers agree that the isolation is self-imposed, but it can also be argued that the very nature of the job forces social isolation on the officer.

In the words of Kirschman, "If it were not such an invasion of privacy, it would be almost comical to think how police officers are treated like public property."[84] Neighbors are quick to point out where an officer lives, and they feel free to knock on his or her door instead of calling 911, almost as though he or she was a private security guard for the neighborhood. Another example of the forced social isolationism of police officers is the 1990s popularity of gangsta rap some of which advocates the killing of police officers. Officers and their families watched as the social leaders of the entertainment industry validated such sentiment. For example, following the debut of his "Cop Killer," Ice–T was awarded with an appearance on Jay Leno and given at least four movie contracts.

POLICE DISCRETION

Discretion, an inescapable element of police work, refers to the unwritten rule that police officers have the right to be selective in how they do their jobs as long as they stay within widely prescribed departmental guidelines. Discretion involves both the power to decide which rules to apply to a given situation and whether to apply them. For example, even if an officer has a quota to fill, it is still up to an officer whether he or she writes this or that ticket.

The decision to arrest has received extensive examination. Nearly all the research has found that the nature and seriousness of the offense is the most important factor affecting an officer's disposition.[85] The other elements that influence an officer's discretion are offender variables, situational variables, and system variables.[86]

The two offender variables that have received the most attention are race and demeanor. Although it is difficult to appraise the importance of race in the disposition of cases involving adult offenders because African Americans and members of other minority groups appear to be involved in more serious crimes more often than

European Americans, it does appear that racial bias makes minority offenders the special targets of the police. Explanations for this include discrimination directed at the individual because of race,[87] and the argument that police officers feel in greater danger in minority neighborhoods.[88] The variable of demeanor has attracted considerable attention recently. One of the most repeated findings about police behavior is that police tend to sanction suspects who display a disrespectful demeanor toward the police.[89] The findings reached over four decades ago that demeanor influences police actions including arrest have recently received new support.[90]

The situation variables that appear to have the greatest influence on police discretion are whether a weapon is present, whether civilians initiated the complaint, and whether the event is concealed or likely to be visible to the public's eye. The presence of a weapon usually results in the officer's taking action.[91] But it seems that the police are less likely to take formal action with action initiated by a citizen's complaint than they are with action initiated by themselves.[92] The decision to arrest is likely to be guided by the officer's belief that the general public or supervisors will become aware of the event.[93]

Three system variables that seem to influence police discretion are the community's standards and expectations, the department's size and structure, and its informal norms. Police officers typically make decisions to support their perceptions of community expectations. For example, officers are more tolerant of minor offenses if they believe that is what the community desires.[94] Officers in large departments tend to have more latitude in decision making than do officers in small departments.[95] Informal norms conveyed by officers' peers can influence subtly or bring direct pressure to behave in a certain way.[96]

The gap between the street officer and the administrator has widened with frequent changes occurring at the top and with demands from the public for a "clean department." The police administrator functions under the formal system by telling the street officer, "You know the rules; you have a policy manual. Follow it!" But the street officer works under an entirely different system—the informal system. This system shows the officer how to survive on the streets and to "cover his or her own ass."

The street officer feels caught in the middle, with the demands from administrators at the top and the demands from the public at the bottom. These officers know they are not expected to enforce the letter of the law all the time, but rather to use a "common sense approach." As one frustrated officer said, "If I enforce the law as it is written, I get hell from the public and pressure from supervisors to cool it. But if I get too easy with my discretion, I get hell from the administrator because I'm not doing my job. The bottom line is production, but within limits."[97]

The chief police administrator also feels the pinch. He or she must somehow balance the needs and demands of line officers on the streets with the needs of the community and the political demands of the city leaders. This administrator learns quickly that his or her job is to support line officers until they step too far out of line.

The fact is that police officers frequently have face-to-face encounters with the public requiring great discretion over important matters (e.g., honor and dishonor, life and death) involving quarrelsome, confused, frightened, injured, intoxicated, or violent people. Discretion is not only an inescapable element of law enforcement, but officers frequently must make decisions in a few seconds (if that much time is even allowed) that may result in civil law suits, departmental suspension or termination, or criminal prosecution of themselves or others.[98]

The misuse of discretion, resulting in police deviancy, has brought wide criticism to the police. The police can be involved in such forms of deviancy as accepting minor sums of money in return for looking the other way or not giving a ticket; ignoring minor laws such as smoking marijuana or drinking; becoming involved in the destruction of evidence or perjury on the stand; engaging in constitutional violations of suspects; accepting large sums of money for overlooking violations of the law; committing such property crimes as burglary and theft; trafficking or protecting drug dealers; participating in sexual harassment or discrimination against fellow officers; using excessive force on suspects or deadly force when it was not necessary; and sexually victimizing women in the community.

Politicians do not want the scandal that arises when such corruption is reported in the police department. Nor do they want an outcry from the community concerning police brutality. Accordingly, they place pressure on police administrators to control two forms of police misconduct: corruption and excessive use of force. Administrators, in turn, expect middle-level supervisors to control this misuse of discretion on the streets.

What makes discretion even more problematic for police officers is that they must decide on how to handle situations or procedures without clear guidelines. The choices (or decisions) of officers are rarely made on the basis of clear-cut legal standards. The law as it unfolds to the average officer is certainly ambiguous. The officer also must decide on procedures that have not been etched in stone by departmental policy or legislative guidelines. Furthermore, administrators lack sufficient resources to deploy specialized units that have received the training to make decisions sometimes required by officers working the streets.[99]

SUMMARY

The working world of police officers, as David Bayley informs us, "is a peculiar combination of impersonal exteriors and intimate interiors."[100] According to Bayley, "Patrol officers spend most of the time driving methodically around, guided by their extensive knowledge of where incidents are likely to occur. Like tour guides of human frailty," they get to know the neighborhoods in which they patrol. At the same time in which officers deal with a largely commercial world, they "may be catapulted instantly into the depths of people's private lives, where they must deal with grief, rage, suspicion, and acute embarrassment."[101]

One of the important functions of police officers is that they become part of a police culture. This chapter examines the various dimensions of this cultural context, an extremely pivotal one in understanding policing in the United States. The culture of line police officers is part of, but yet stands apart from the organizational culture of police departments. The line police culture, then, is a culture within a culture. It is a culture that develops norms and acceptable behaviors, that socializes recruits, that often encourages loyalty at all costs, and that disciplines in one way or another those who violate its precepts.

Proponents of the police culture argue that those seeking to become a police officer are joining a very elite group indeed. One of the real tragedies of policing today, as depicted by this chapter, is that the police spirit is being broken. The breaking of the police spirit can certainly be blamed on "bad apples" who, in both the past and the present, have brought discredit and criticism. It can be blamed on the media who have sensationalized the few who are bad, suggesting, at the same time, that this depicts the average police officer patrolling the streets. It can be blamed on departmental politics, rules, and regulations and how they eat away at a person's spirit. But the police themselves must acknowledge how in turning to a culture within a culture they have created norms encouraging and protecting wrongdoing within the police community. The policy of hiding behind the code of silence and loyalty at all costs is sadly misguided. It promotes engaging in outrageous behavior and defending those who have engaged in such behaviors. This is what ultimately kills the police spirit.

KEY WORDS

authoritarian personality	informal code
code of silence	police spirit
discretion	socialization
field training	working personality

DISCUSSION QUESTIONS

1. Do you believe police officers ought to have higher standards than citizens in the community?

2. If you were designing questions to ask at the time of the oral interview, what questions would you ask candidates?

3. How do police duties vary according to shift assignment?

4. Do you believe that a college education makes for a better police officer? Defend your position.

5. Kirschman suggests that the process of becoming a police officer is one of dealing with disillusionment? Is she always right? Is entropy always found in a police career?

6. Do you believe that Skolnick's classic typology of the working personality of the police is still accurate? What would you add to or detract from his understanding of the working personality of the police officer?

7. Is social isolation a necessary part of policing? Are there any ways that police officers could be better integrated into community life?

FURTHER READING

Alex, Nicholas. *Black in Blue.* New York: Appleton–Century–Crofts, 1969.

Brown, Michael K. *Working the Streets: Police Discretion and the Dilemmas of Reform.* New York: Russell Sage Foundation, 1981.

Carter, David L., Allen D. Sapp, and Darrel W. Stephens. *The State of Police Education: Policy Directions for the 21st Century.* Washington, DC: Police Executive Research Forum, 1989.

Clark, Constance. *In the Line of Duty: The Service and Sacrifice of America's Finest.* Washington, DC: Potomac, 1989.

Fletcher, Connie. *Breaking and Entering: Women Cops Talk About Life in the Ultimate Men's Club.* New York: Harper/Collins, 1995.

Hennessy, Stephen M. *Thinking Cop Feeling Cop: A Study in Police Personalities,* 2nd ed. Scottsdale: Leadership, 1995.

Horne, Peter. *Women in Law Enforcement,* 2nd ed. Springfield: Thomas, 1980.

Kirschman, Ellen. *I Love a Cop: What Police Families Need to Know.* New York: Guilford, 1997.

Leinen, Stephen. *Black Police, White Society.* New York: New York UP, 1984.

Leinen, Stephen. *Gay Cops.* New Brunswick: Rutgers UP, 1993.

Remsberg, Charles. *Tactics for Criminal Patrol: Vehicle Stops, Drug Discovery & Officer Survival.* Northbrook: Calibre Press, 1995.

Reuss–Ianni, Elizabeth. *Two Cultures of Policing: Street Cops and Management Cops.* New Brunswick: Transaction, 1983.

Skolnick, Jerome. *Justice without Trial: Law Enforcement in a Democratic Society,* 3rd ed. New York: Macmillan, 1994.

ENDNOTES

1. Quoted in Steve Herbert, *Policing Space: Territoriality and the Los Angeles Police Department* (Minneapolis: U of Minnesota P, 1977) 151.

2. Herbert, 151.

3. See also Neal Fortin, "The Law Enforcement Attitude," *Total Survival,* ed. Ed Nowicki (Powers Lake: Performance Dimensions Publishing, 1993) 152.

4. Fortin, 152.

5. William Westphall quoted during keynote speech at the Tenth ASLET International Training Seminar, Dallas, Texas Jan. 1997.

6. Victor E. Kappeler, Richard D. Sluder, and Geoffrey P. Alpert, *Forces of Deviance: Understanding the Dark Side of Policing* (Prospect Heights: Waveland, 1994) 105.

7. Anonymous personal interview, 1997.

8. House of Representatives One Hundred Second Congress, first session, Hearing before the Select Committee on Children, Youth, and Families, *On the Front Lines: Police Stress and Family Well-being* (Washington DC: USGPO, 1991) 82.

9. William Westphall quoted during keynote speech at the Tenth ASLET International Training Seminar, Dallas, Texas (January, 1997).

10. G. P. Alpert and R. G. Dunham, *Policing Urban America,* 2nd ed. (Prospect Heights: Waveland, 1992).

11. Kappeler, et al., 92.

12. Kappeler, et al., 92.

13. J. J. Broderick, *Police in a Time of Change,* 2nd ed. (Prospect Heights: Waveland, 1987) 31; D. H. Bayley and H. Mendelsohn, *Minorities and the Police: Confrontation in America* (New York: The

Free Press, 1969); and Jerome H. Skolnick and James J. Fyfe, *Above the Law: Police and the Excessive Use of Force* (New York: The Free Press, 1993) 92.

14. B. N. Carpenter and S. M. Rasa, "Personality Characteristics of Police Applicants: Comparisons Across Subgroups and With Other Populations," *Journal of Police Science and Administration 15* (1987): 16.

15. J. Lefkowitz, "Industrial-Organization Psychology and the Police," *American Psychologist* (May 1977): 346–364.

16. Skolnick and Fyfe, 92.

17. Bayley and Mendelsohn; and Virginia B. Ermer, "Recruitment of Female Police Officers in New York City," *Journal of Criminal Justice 6* (Fall 1978): 233–246.

18. M. Steven Meagher and Nancy A. Yentes, "Choosing a Career in Policing: A Comparison of Male and Female Perceptions," *Journal of Police Science and Administration 14* (1986): 320–327.

19. Gary F. Caulton and Hubert S. Field, "Using Assessment Centers in Selecting Entry-Level Police Officers: Extravagance or Justified Expense?" *Public Personnel Management 24* (1 June 1995): 223–232.

20. Philip Ash, Karen B. Slora, and Cynthia F. Britton, "Police Agency Officer Selection Practices," *Journal of Police Science and Administration 17* (Dec. 1990): 259–264.

21. Ash, et al., 264.

22. Janet Reno, "The ADA and Police Hiring Practices," *The Police Chief: The Professional Voice of Law Enforcement* (June 1997): 24–28.

23. Cited in Charles R. Swanson, Leonard Territo, and Robert W. Taylor, *Police Administration*, 2nd ed. (New York: Macmillan, 1988) 202–203.

24. Student comment, spring, 1997.

25. Kathleen Maguire and Ann L. Pastore, eds., *Sourcebook of Criminal Justice Statistics 1995*, U.S. Department of Justice, Bureau of Justice Statistics (Washington DC: USGPO, 1996) 42.

26. Terry D. Edwards, "State Police Basic Training Programs: An Assessment of Course Content in Instructional Methodology," *American Police Journal 12*, 4, (1993): 24.

27. "Report on Police," *National Advisory Commission on Criminal Justice Standards and Goals* (Washington, DC: USGPO, 1973).

28. Edwards, "State Police Basic Training Programs," 24.

29. Maguire and Pastore, 42.

30. Larry D. Armstrong and Clinton O. Longenecker, "Police Management Training: A National Survey," *FBI Law Enforcement Bulletin* (Jan. 1992): 22.

31. Gary M. Post, "Police Recruits: Training Tomorrow's Workforce," *FBI Law Enforcement Bulletin* (Mar. 1992): 19–24.

32. Post, 19–24.

33. Edwin Meese III, "Community Policing and the Police Officer," *Perspectives on Policing*, U.S. Department of Justice, National Institute of Justice, Program in Criminal Justice, Harvard University (1993): 7.

34. Herman Goldstein, *Problem-Oriented Policing* (New York: McGraw–Hill, 1990): 157.

35. Daniel L. Kalk, "Field Training," *The Law Enforcement Trainer* (Jan.–Feb. 1997): 10–11.

36. Michael S. McCampbell, "Field Training for Police Officers: State of the Art," *Research in Brief*, U.S. Department of Justice, National Institute of Justice (Nov. 1986): 9–10.

37. Glenn F. Kaminsky, *The Field Training and Evaluation Program Concept: A Manual For Development & Implementation* (Longmont: Kaminsky, 1991).

38. David M. Kennedy, "The Strategic Management of Police Resources," *Perspective on Policing*, U.S. Department of Justice, National Institute of Justice, No. 14 (January 1993): 2.

39. Personal interview, July 1995.

40. President's Commission on Law Enforcement and Administration of Justice, *The Challenge of Crime in a Free Society* (Washington, DC: USGPO, 1967) 294–295.

41. J. P. Crank, B. Regoli, J. D. Hewitt, and R. G. Culbertson, "An Assessment of Work Stress Among Police Executives," *Journal of Criminal Justice* (1993): 313–324.

42. Study cited in Leslie B. Buckley, James H. McGinnis, and Michael G. Petrunik, "Police Perceptions of Education as an Entitlement to Promotion: An Equity Theory Perspective," *American Journal of Police 12*, 2 (1992): 79.

43. Buckley, et al., 79, 93.

44. James Q. Wilson, "The Police in the Ghetto," *The Police and the Community*, ed. Robert F. Steadman (Baltimore: John Hopkins UP, 1972) 73–74.

45. Meese, 5.

46. David L. Carter, Allen D. Sapp, and Darrel W. Stephens, *The State of Police Education: Policy Directions for the 21st Century* (Washington, DC: Police Executive Research Forum, 1989).

47. Carter et al.

48. Study cited in William Russell Scott, "College Education Requirements for Police Entry Level and Promotion: A Study," *Journal of Police and Criminal Psychology* (Mar. 1986): 4.

49. Micheal G. Breci, "Higher Education For Law Enforcement: The Minnesota Model," *FBI Law Enforcement Bulletin* (January, 1994) 1.

50. David Murrell, "The Influence of Education in Police Work," diss., Florida State U, 1982.

51. James W. Sterling, "Changes in Role Concepts of Police Officers," *International Association of Chiefs of Police* (1977): 8–9.

52. Ellen Kirschman, *I Love a Cop: What Police Families Need to Know* (New York: Guilford, 1997).

53. Kirschman, 31–33.

54. Kirschman, 39–40.

55. Kirschman, 41–44.

56. Kirschman, 46–48.

57. Jerome Skolnick, *Justice Without Trial: Law Enforcement in a Democratic Society,* 3rd ed. (New York: Macmillan, 1994) 41–68.

58. Chapman, S. G., *Cops, Killers and Staying Alive* (Springfield: Charles C. Thomas, 1986).

59. *Killed in the Line of Duty: A Study of Selected Felonious Killings of Law Enforcement Officers* (Washington, DC: Federal Bureau of Investigation, 1992) 48.

60. Anthony J. Pinizzotto, Edward F. Davis, and Charles E. Miller III, *In the Line of Fire: Violence Against Law Enforcement: A Study of Felonious Assaults on Law Enforcement Officers* (Washington, DC: Federal Bureau of Investigation, 1997) 12.

61. Skolnick, *Justice Without Trial,* 44.

62. Skolnick, *Justice Without Trial,* 44.

63. *Killed in the Line of Duty,* 48.

64. *Killed in the Line of Duty,* 48.

65. Haz-mat training lecture (1996).

66. Skolnick, *Justice Without Trial,* 44.

67. *Killed in the Line of Duty,* 43.

68. *Killed in the Line of Duty,* 42.

69. Gary T. Klugiewicz, *Active Countermeasures Instructional Systems Instructor's Manual* (Greenfield: Active Countermeasures Instructional Systems, 1995) 41.

70. Stephen M. Hennessy, *Thinking Cop Feeling Cop: A Study in Police Personalities,* 2nd ed. (Scottsdale: Leadership, 1995) 15–26.

71. The original concept of RODS and five-percenters was articulated by Trooper Robert V. Stevens of the Ohio State Patrol (not retired).

72. Charles Remsberg, *Tactics for Criminal Patrol: Vehicle Stops, Drug Discovery & Officer Survival* (Northbrook: Calibre Press, 1995) 25.

73. Remsburg, 25–27.

74. Quoted in Stephen J. Gaffigan and Phyllis P. McDonald, *Police Integrity: Public Service With Honor,* U.S. Department of Justice, National Institute of Justice, Office of Community Oriented Policing Services, (Washington, DC: USGPO, 1977) 30.

75. Elizabeth Reuss–Ianni, *Two Cultures of Policing: Street Cops and Management Cops* (New Brunswick: Transaction, 1983) 13.

76. Malcolm K. Sparrow, Mark H. Moore, David M. Kennedy, *Beyond 911: A New Era for Policing* (New York: Basic Books, 1990).

77. William A. Geller and Michael Scott, *Deadly Force: What We Know: A Practitioner's Desk Reference on Police-Involved Shootings* (Washington, DC: Police Executive Research Forum, 1992) 408.

78. Meese, 3.

79. Reuss–Ianni, 116–117.

80. Meese, 3.

81. Meese, 3.

82. Goldstein, 27.

83. Cited in Skolnick and Fyfe, *Above the Law* 91.

84. Kirschman, 13.

85. W. LaFave, *The Decision to Take a Suspect into Custody* (Boston: Little, Brown, 1965); Donald Black, "The Social Organization of Arrest," *Stanford Law Review* 23 (1971): 1087–1111; D. A. Smith and C. Visher, "Street Level Justice: Situational Determinants of Police Arrest Decisions," *Social Problems* 29 (1981): 167–178.

86. The material on arrest and discretion is adapted from Larry K. Gaines, Victor E. Kappeler, and Joseph B. Vaughn, *Policing in America,* 2nd ed. (Cincinnati: Anderson, 1997) 190–193.

87. I. Piliavin and S. Briar, "Police Encounters with Juveniles," *American Journal of Sociology* 70 (1964): 206–214.

88. D. H. Bayley and H. Mendelsohn, *Minorities and the Police* (New York: The Free Press, 1969).

89. Robert E. Worden, Robin L. Shepard, and Stephen D. Mastrofski, "On the Meaning and Measurement of Suspects' Demeanor Toward the Police: A Comment on 'Demeanor and Arrest,'" *Journal of Research in Crime and Delinquency 33* (Aug. 1996): 324.

90. See Richard J. Lundman, "Demeanor and Arrest: Additional Evidence From Previously Unpublished Data," *Journal of Research in Crime and Delinquency 33* (1996): 306–323; Robert E. Worden and Robin L. Shepard, "Demeanor, Crime, and Police Behavior: A Reexamination of the Police Services Study Data," *Criminology 34* (1996): 83–105; Worden, Shepard, and Mastrofski, 324–331. However, for a study that contests this finding, see David A. Klinger, "Bringing Crime Back In: Toward a Better Understanding of Police Arrest Decisions," *Journal of Research in Crime and Delinquency 33* (Aug. 1996): 333–336.

91. Gaines, et al., 192.

92. Black, 1087–1111; A. Reiss, *The Police and the Public* (New Haven: Yale UP, 1971).

93. Gaines, et al., 193.

94. Gaines, et al., 193.

95. S. Mastrofski, R. Ritti, and D. Hoffmaster, "Organizational Determinants of Police Discretion: The Case of Drinking and Driving," *Journal of Criminal Justice 15* (1987): 387–401.

96. Richard Lundman, "Organizational Norms and Police Discretion: An Observational Study of Police Work with Traffic Violators," *Criminology 17* (1979): 159–171; R. Ericson, *Reproducing Order: A Study of Police Patrol Work* (Toronto: U of Toronto P, 1982).

97. Personal interview, 1986. See also Michael K. Brown, *Working the Streets: Police Discretion and the Dilemmas of Reform* (New York: Russell Sage, 1981).

98. For a discussion of the split-second syndrome, see James J. Fyfe, "The Split-Second Syndrome and Other Determinants of Police Violence," *Critical Issues in Policing: Contemporary Readings,* ed. R. Dunham and G. Alpert (Prospect Heights: Waveland, 1989) 465–479.

99. Brown, 4–5.

100. David H. Bayley, *Police for the Future* (New York: Oxford UP, 1994) 24.

101. Bayley, 24.

4

POLICE ADMINISTRATION

What the police chief—behind his big oak desk in his private office, insulated from the outside world by hordes of officious aides and layers of bureaucracy—must do, by all means, is to focus the entire institutional effort around one job; that of the police officer closest to the communities. Everything else should be secondary. It's a bosses' job only if we permit the bosses to make it one, if we permit both the institutions of the police and the officers themselves to become alienated, literally and figuratively, from their primary role in society, which is to keep the peace and maintain order in a sophisticated, humane, and Constitutional way. Policing should not be a bosses' job but rather a cop's job, because it is my view that perhaps the American police officer in this last quarter of the twentieth century has the most important job around.

—Patrick V. Murphy and Thomas Plate, *Commissioner: A View from the Top of American Law Enforcement* (New York: Simon & Schuster, 1977) 270.

This chapter examines how the professional police administrator, whose origins go back to the Progressive Era, has bureaucratized and rationalized the police.* Patrick V. Murphy, former police commissioner in New York and Detroit, chief in Syracuse, and public safety director in Washington, DC, argues in his 1977 autobiography *Commissioner* that able police chiefs should have three attributes.[1] First, given the complex problems and the sheer size of urban departments, they must be good bureaucrats. Murphy recommends putting police chiefs in "gray flannel suits"; that is, training chiefs to be better administrators and equipping them with the techniques and concepts of modern management. Second, police chiefs must control the discretion of officers on the streets by being effective managers and by

---

*We will use the term "police chief" in this chapter, rather than commissioner, public safety director, or superintendent, to refer to the head of a municipal police agency.

emphasizing the importance of good written policies and proper training.[2] Indeed, as Murphy says in the quote beginning this chapter, police chiefs should be evaluated by how well they persuade line officers on the street "to keep the peace and maintain order in a sophisticated, humane, and constitutional way." Third, the police administrator is the custodian of community morals. Murphy's autobiography spoke of there being a "semi-ecclesiastical dimension to the chief's job. He offers an image of the chief as "something akin to a secular pastor." A police chief, according to Murphy, "can be viewed not only as the community's chief law enforcement officer but also as the custodian of the community's morals.... The police chief becomes the focal point not only of a community's sense of physical security but even of its spiritual well-being."[3]

According to Raymond G. Hunt and John M. Magenau, what Murphy is suggesting here is that the internal aspect of this spiritual dimension of a police chief's job description is leadership, which consists of "the will and the ability to articulate a mission, an agenda, and a set of legitimizing values for an enterprise, and to develop operational means for their expression and to which others can commit their energies."[4] The external aspect of this spiritual dimension, Hunt and Magenau add, is to "make clear what is right, what the police stand for in a community, and to act vigorously and consistently, not just in speeches, to support this vision and to cause it to become routinely manifest in police conduct."[5]

The difficulty and high stress level of a chief's job can be readily seen in the high turnover and early burnout rates. A 1992 *New York Times'* article observed that "big-city chiefs are pulling out of intractable wars...tired and beat up from the strain."[6] A 1997 *USA Today* article quotes Charles Mahtesian who claims that "the sacking of the police chief has become part of the routine of the 1990s."[7] The Police Executive Research Forum estimates that the average big city chief lasts between two and a half and four years on the job. Many chiefs are sacked because they cannot satisfy both the politicians and their other constituencies. The politicians tend to measure a chief by reduced crime rates and improvement in the city's image."[8] The former police chief of Milwaukee adds, "To some people, the best chief is always the last one and the next one."[9]

Yet it cannot be denied that some police administrators thrive in their jobs. They are innovative, resourceful, fair, and resilient; indeed, they may remain for 10 or 15 years at the same department or agency. They see police administration as interesting and challenging and speak with pride when they discuss their careers. In addition to Patrick V. Murphy, examples of such administrators are August Vollmer, long time chief in Berkeley, California; O. W. Wilson, commissioner of the Chicago Police Department during the 1960s; Lee P. Brown, chief police executive in Atlanta, Houston, and New York during the 1980s and early 1990s; Reuben M. Greenberg, former chief of the Charleston, South Carolina Police Department during the 1980s and early 1990s; and Anthony ("Tony") Bouza, police commissioner in Minneapolis, Minnesota during the 1980s.

There are three important terms to define when it comes to understanding the administration of a police department. First, **administration** refers to a process whereby individuals are organized and directed toward the achievement of group objectives. Second, **management** is more involved in the day-to-day operations of the organization. Finally, **supervision** involves the direction of the organizational participants in their day-to-day activities. Although we typically look upon the police executive (who usually has the title of chief or sheriff but may also be called superintendent, director, or commissioner) to be the administrator of the department, the police executive is actually responsible for all three tasks.[10]

THE ORGANIZATIONAL CONTEXT OF POLICE ADMINISTRATION

Police organizations are bureaucracies, function as open rather than closed systems, and are complex systems of interacting units. Larger police departments, of course, are more bureaucratic and complex than are smaller ones.

Police Departments Are Bureaucratic Organizations

Bureaucracies were originally developed to make money, not to handle people, but many of the principles used to make profits are now used to manage people-oriented organizations. The purpose behind bureaucracies is to ensure efficient and methodical social organization. Bureaucracies are based on rationalism, the same principle that has been so important in the rise of science and the mastery of the physical and biological worlds. If human social organization could approach the efficiency of a machine, theorists reasoned, profits and the acquisition of capital would be maximized.

Accordingly, bureaucracies were to be so organized that nothing was left to chance. As Max Weber, the German sociologist who provided the theoretical basis for all modern bureaucracies, puts it, "The decisive reason for the advance of bureaucratic organization has always been its purely technical superiority over any other form of organization. The fully developed bureaucratic mechanism compares with other organizations exactly as does the machine with the non-mechanical modes of production."[11]

A modern bureaucracy depends on having a money economy in order to pay salaries. Success and rewards in a money system are supposedly based on merit and hard work rather than on the accident of birth. Furthermore, in a money economy with a democratic political system, it is believed that each person should be provided true equality of opportunity.[12] Weber, in a now classic statement, analyzes the basic components and rules of bureaucracies:

  1. There is the principle of fixed and official jurisdictional areas, which are generally ordered by rules, that is, by laws or administrative regulations.
  2. The principles of office hierarchy and of levels of graded authority mean a firmly ordered system of super- and subordination in which there is a supervision of the lower offices by the higher ones.
  3. The management of the modern office is based upon written documents ("the files"), which are preserved in their original or draft form.

4. Office management, at least all specialized office management—and such management is distinctly modern—usually presupposes thorough and expert training.

5. When the office is fully developed, official activity demands the full working capacity of the official, irrespective of the fact that his obligatory time in the bureau may be firmly delimited.

6. The management of the office follows general rules, which are more or less stable, more or less exhaustive, and which can be learned.[13]

A police organization is clearly a bureaucratic structure. It typically has a budget of hundreds of thousands, or in some cases, millions of dollars. For the complexity of large police organizations, with all their various departments, see Figure 4.1. In police organizations, a hierarchical organization exists, in which chiefs are at the top, generally followed by assistant chiefs, captains, lieutenants, sergeants, and officers. In this paramilitary bureaucracy, officers are centrally commanded, owe allegiance to a commander, and execute orders originating from above. A central communication center directs how and where officers are deployed. The police, according to this bureaucratic model, are supposed to be distant, "professional," cool, and autonomous.[14]

Open Systems

It is possible to view an organization as either an open or closed system. Of the two, the closed system approach is the least satisfactory because of its focus on internal as opposed to external forces. That is, managers who operate from a closed system approach generally want to ignore or minimize external forces that affect their organization; they are aware only of what is happening inside it. The open system approach is more desirable because it focuses upon both external and internal forces and attempts to determine the interplay between the two. What this means is that police chiefs make management decisions by considering both external as well as internal factors. Taking into account the outside environment is necessary if the department intends to respond to community problems.

The open systems approach recognizes that police agencies are influenced by social, political, legal, and economic factors. The police are a reflection of the norms and values of the community. For example, communities with high rates of crime typically have high rates of deviancy within police departments. The public also determines to a large degree what type of police they want. If the public is not pleased with some phase of police operation or is alarmed by an outbreak of crime, pressure will be placed on police administrators to deal with their concerns. Thus, "keeping in tune with the local community" is an early and important lesson that a new chief learns. It does not take long for police executives to become aware that they must constantly monitor the citizenry to determine how each event or community is interpreted. A chief of a small department in a college community explains how he found out quickly that being in tune with the community is important:

> Shortly after becoming chief of police, I read in the local university paper that students were concerned about lighting in the campus area. When asked about

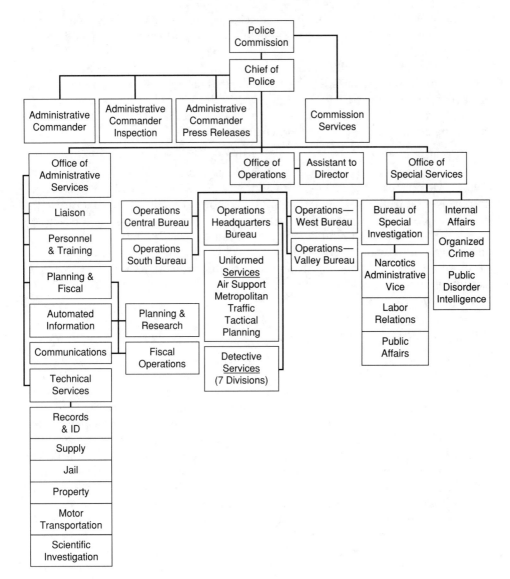

FIGURE 4.1   **Organizational Chart: Los Angeles Police Department**

Source: Sheriff's Departments 1993 (Washington, DC: U.S. Department of Justice, 1996) 2.

it, I responded that no rapes had been reported for some time and students were safe. The response to that remark was immediate and very critical. I was pictured as being insensitive to the needs of women students, as being ignorant to the rape problems in that area, and as not caring for the student population. I learned from that experience that any problem, whether real or perceived, was the same and had to be immediately addressed.[15]

Police chiefs find themselves in a complex political arena in which they are central figures with both power and restraints. Beset on all sides by contending and at times sharply conflicting interests, they are sometimes successful in transforming the nature and forms of policing; at other times, they have no choice but to conserve existing patterns and traditions."[16] Police chiefs are appointed by elected officials and, as much as they might want to be apolitical, they quickly discover that they must win support and respect from these officials. The chief serves at the discretion of the mayor and can be relieved of his or her job simply because the mayor wants the chief out of office. The pragmatic chief knows, then, that the mayor's input must be used to maintain a good working relationship.[17]

Another early lesson that the new police chief learns is to "avoid embarrassing local politicians." The "good old days" of policing, when every police officer, from the top to the bottom, looked out for each other, have given way to the reality of the police manager who must respond to pressure from elected officials to "run a tight ship." Accountability, productivity, affirmative action, and sensitivity to minority groups must all be emphasized. Elected officials bring pressure on police administrators to control the discretionary authority of their departments. These politicians become extremely anxious about complaints concerning police brutality and inappropriate use of deadly force, and they insist that patrol officers maintain good public relations.

The legal context impinges on everything that takes place in policing. Police officers are sworn to enforce the law and yet the law also provides restraints on how they do their jobs. If officers violate the law, they can be arrested, charged, and convicted. The dark sides of policing, including excessive and deadly force, corruption, violations of constitutional rights, and sexual harassment, are increasingly ending up in criminal or civil courts. Police chiefs cannot ignore the recent growth of successful civil lawsuits against officers. For example, in just three years from 1991 to 1993, more than $45 million was paid to people who filed suits against the Los Angeles Police Department officers.[18]

The economic context provides or removes resources from policing agencies. When resources expand, more officers can be hired, equipment can be purchased, and programs can be initiated; when resources shrink, officers must be laid off, old equipment must be kept in service, and programs curtailed. Three of the areas in which the role of the police chief is intertwined with the economic context are the process of negotiating union contracts, of developing annual budgets, and of applying for federal funding.

System Analysis

A major change in administration over the past couple decades has been the advent of system management.[19] This approach recognizes that an organization is affected by other organizations and is therefore made up of interdependent parts. Managers who are not familiar with system management approach organizations as aggregates of components, each of which is separate from and managed independently of the other; the result is a fragmented approach to the management of the total organization. System analysis is ultimately based on awareness of the interrelatedness and interdependence of all components of law enforcement sub-systems. The systems view looks at the world in terms of relationships and integration.[20] It is a dynamic view of the world that emphasizes process and con-nectedness.[21]

System analysis has contributed to the need for a different type of police chief than in the past. Police chiefs have traditionally worked their way up through the ranks.[22] This progression typically provided a limited amount of training and preparation for the chief's position which often resulted in inadequately prepared leaders.[23] Today, although promotions from within the department may be the more traveled route, an increasing number of agencies appear to be hiring from outside the agency.[24] Chiefs are also more likely than in the past to be college grad-uates and a few may even may have graduate degrees. For example, Mark Dantz-ker identified 315 national advertisements for the position of police chief and found that 172, or 54.6 percent, required a bachelors degree; yet only 3, or 1 percent, required a masters degree.[25]

Today, chiefs are more capable of planning for and implementing change in their organization. The effective top administrator of a police department is likely to perceive herself or himself as a generalist rather than as a specialist. The gener-alist is charged with the responsibility of conceptualizing the whole organization and of developing a system-wide plan to manage it. **Conceptualization** involves the ability to see the whole and to rise above organizational parts.

Administrators who have failed to conceptualize the total organization are likely to end up with crisis-centered management. This means that they will spend most of their time "putting out fires." The chances are also good that the adminis-trator who sees only part of the problem or situation will either underreact or over-react to it. Thus, the chief responsibility of the administrator is to think in terms of and to understand the entire organization, while lower-level administrators and managers specialize in the management of their area of responsibility. The general-ist, needless to say, is dependent on specialists to run the various units of the de-partment. This philosophy of administration requires participatory management and input from all levels of staff. The effective generalist does not try to carry the total weight or responsibility of a department on his or her shoulders, knowing that it is necessary to bring others into the decision-making process. The effective gen-eralist carefully selects management staff, encourages them to become involved in staff development programs, reinforces them when they do a good job, and holds them accountable when they do not. This generalist wants to build a team that can be trusted to carry out a stated policy throughout the entire department.

Systems theory is a reminder for police administrators that the best way to im-prove police operations is to examine work flow from beginning to end. For exam-ple, in recent years departments have used systems analysis to examine the effectiveness of one-person versus two-person patrol cars, how calls are answered, and the effectiveness of patrol in reducing crime (see Chapter 5).

Police administrators also use systems analysis to monitor their departments on a daily basis. They do this by reviewing and evaluating information concerning the following departmental activities: the clearance rate for various crime categories, disciplinary actions taken against officers, complaints lodged against personnel, amount of sick time accrued by personnel, number of calls for service by time and geographical area, and conviction rates. The consequence of monitoring such figures is that administrators are able to understand and evaluate the department's performance on a daily basis. It is also possible for administrators through such monitoring to determine whether departmental activities are meeting community expectations and dealing with community problems.[26]

CORPORATE MANAGEMENT PHILOSOPHIES

Many police chiefs, especially those who have had courses in management, know about the periods of history in police management (see Table 4.1). These periods of management can be divided into traditional management, scientific management, human relations and participatory management, behavioral management, systems management, and proactive management.

One of the important concepts typically derived from an examination of the history of police management is that people are as important as the goals of the organization and that organization should "provide employees with satisfying and rewarding work and with conditions which will permit and encourage the fullest development of the individual personalities."[27] Many police executives are aware of the research into humanistic bureaucracy that began to show that as personnel are taken into consideration, their productivity and the quality of their work is increased, their morale is raised, and they are presumably happier in their jobs. Many are also aware that humanistic bureaucracy led to a number of innovations in management practices. Conflict-resolution groups, sensitivity training, human relations courses, group therapy, role-playing, worker participation in decision making, profit-sharing plans, and other techniques were all initiated by organizations to make them more humane. Management by Objectives (MBO), Contingency Management, and Total Quality Management (TQM) are three of the most widely incorporated private sector management techniques.

Management by Objectives (MBO)

Peter Drucker first used the phrase "management by objectives" in 1954, but George S. Odione developed the actual system in 1965.[28] **Management by Objectives (MBO)** differs from other participatory models in that, first, MBO is more concerned with general organizational planning and, second, it de-emphasizes the role of specific personnel in the planning process. MBO is based on the principle that the best way to ensure success is through planning. However, before planning can take place, agreement must be reached upon the goals to be achieved. This is usually not easy because individuals have their own goals, many of which run counter to the goals of the organization. MBO thus attempts to reconcile individual and organizational goals.

TABLE 4.1   Periods of History in Police Management

Years	Period	Major leaders and authors	Major contributions to police management
1750–1900	Industrial revolution, traditional management model	Sir Robert Peel, Charles Rowan, Richard Maynes, John Moore, Henry and John Fielding	Economic man, centralized administration, semimilitary model, ranks, strong leadership, crime prevention objective of policing
1900 to present	Scientific management	Max Weber, O. W. Wilson, Frederick Taylor, Henry Fayol, Raymond Fosdick, Elmer D. Graper, Bruce Smith, August Vollmer, V. A. Leonard, Dwight Waldo, William Parker	Modern bureaucracy, unity of command, civil service, division of labor, specialization, one-way authority, narrow span of control, omnipresent patrol officer, hierarchy
1925 to present	Human relations and participative management	Elton Mayo, Chester I. Barnard, Leonard Fuld, Hawthorne, Frederick Herzberg, R. R. Blake and J. S. Mouton, Rensis Likert	Focus on personnel management, motivation techniques, morale, stress management, participatory and democratic management with team approach, communication models
1945 to present	Behavioral management	Herbert Simon, Douglas Murray McGregor	**PPBS,** organizational development, **PERT, STAR**[a]
1960 to present	Systems management	Patrick Murphy, James McNamara	Zero-based budgeting interfacing of subsystems
1981 to present	Proactive management	J. Q. Wilson, Edward A. Thibault, Lawrence M. Lynch, and R. Bruce McBride	Synthesis of the foregoing theories with emphasis on forward planning and consultative management techniques, high-technology computers, and communication

[a]PPBS, program, planning, budgeting system; PERT, program evaluation and review techniques; STAR, system training and analysis of requirements.

Source: PROACTIVE POLICE MANAGEMENT 4/E by Thibault/Lynch/McBride, © 1998. Reprinted by permission of Prentice-Hall, Inc., Upper Saddle River, NJ.

Several premises are basic in implementing MBO:

1. Top management should, ideally, be committed to the concept.
2. A management philosophy should be developed that brings everyone in the organization into the decision-making process.
3. All personnel should be involved in helping the organization set its goals.
4. Personnel should be evaluated on their ability to achieve the goal that they help to set for both themselves and the department in which they work.
5. Initiators of the process should emphasize that personality differences cannot be permitted to affect deliberations.[29]

William J. Bratton, Commissioner of Police for New York City from 1994–1996, used a combination of Management by Objectives and community policing strategies to attain remarkable reductions of crime. During this period, the city achieved a 36 percent decrease in serious crime, including a 45 percent drop in murder. Bratton contends that traditional policing, with its three R's (rapid response, random patrol, and reactive investigation) has been a failure. Instead, he advocates the three P's of community policing: partnership, problem solving, and prevention. Bratton says, "The police are the most effective when they work in partnership with the community and when they are of the community, not apart from it." He adds, "partnership and problem solving are important, but for what purpose? Prevention—to prevent crime in the first place, and to prevent all those victims."[30] Bratton then gives an unusual twist to his community policing strategy:

> We began to run the NYPD as a private profit-oriented business. What was the profit I wanted? Crime reduction. I wanted to beat the criminals—who were out there working seven days a week, 24 hours a day. I wanted to serve my customers, the public, better; and the profit I wanted to deliver to them was reduced crime. All of my franchises—my 76 precincts in New York City—saw a double-digit decline in crime, so the results were not just happening in the war-torn neighborhoods. Crime reductions were happening throughout the city by our empowering the precincts to act.[31]

Contingency Management

Contingency management theory is based on the notion that organizations will vary the structures they use depending on the decisions that must be made.[32] What this is suggesting is that there is no ideal structural design because structure must be contingent on such variables as tasks, people, environment, and technology. P. Lawrence and J. Lorsch, two of the main proponents of contingency theory, studied a number of different organizations in a variety of fields, with the intent of relating success to type of organizational structure. In finding that there is no best way to structure all organizations, they concluded that the most effective organizations were structured to fit the environments in which they operated. They went on to refine their theory by suggesting that organizations can be located at some point along an environmental continuum, stretching from situations of stability and certainty to situations of instability and uncertainty. Traditional hierarchical structures, they added, are more successful in stable situations, whereas more decentralized and flexible structures do better in situations of instability and uncertainty.[33]

Reuben M. Greenberg, former chief of police of the Charleston, South Carolina, Police Department, used contingency management to develop one of the most innovative police operations in the nation. He suggested in a 1987 interview that his basic broad-based contingency management strategy consisted of the following emphases:

> First,…we have a variety of community service-type projects. We have a domestic violence program, elderly abuse program, police athletic league, boxing club program, crime prevention programs and neighborhood foot patrol. Second, we place a major emphasis on public relations…. Third, we're particularly sensitive to police brutality and corruption. You can't find anyone this town, and I mean no one, who will say that brutality is an issue here…. Fourth, we do not permit our officers to insult or curse citizens…. Fifth, we do not play political favorites…. Finally, we're tough on criminals…. We do it through aggressive enforcement of known criminals. We do it through our quick response time to an incident. We do it through high-quality law enforcement officers. Last year the state of South Carolina had an 8 percent increase in crime, here in Charleston we had a 22 percent decrease.[34]

Total Quality Management (TQM)

Total Quality Management (TQM) is widely acknowledged as the management philosophy that turned the Japanese from a low-tech, substandard industrial nation to one of the foremost economic leaders in the world. This management philosophy, which also provides a set of tools and a process, is designed to move an organization from a focus on production to a culture that encompasses workers, feedback, cooperative teamwork, and customers as critical considerations in organizational enterprise. Efficiency, effectiveness, and responsiveness have resulted from the implementation of TQM in Japan and in organizations in the United States that have adopted it.[35] The key components of TQM are as follows:

- Customer orientation and an idea of production systems as supplier-customer chains.
- Belief in the unacceptability of error and in continuous improvement.
- Proactive problem-seeking, with problems viewed as opportunities for improvement.
- Concentration on work-process control and improvement.
- Emphasis on planning and measurement.
- Long-term perspective on development.
- Stress on human resources excellence, training, development, and empowerment.

- Emphasis on lateral relations instead of hierarchy, cross-functional integration, and teams as problem-solving units.
- Orientation toward management of internal and external relationships via collaboration or partnering.[36]

Total Quality Management is designed to develop a positive, citizen-oriented culture and to create a genuine level of employee commitment pervading the entire work environment. TQM provides employees with opportunities for participation in decision-making, problem solving, and teamwork. Those who have used TCQ have found that employees tend to be motivated and do not need to be pushed or shoved to obtain the department's objectives.[37]

Chief Randall Aragon of the Whiteville, North Carolina, Police Department has implemented TQM in order to develop a positive organizational climate. He states, "One of the most difficult leadership tasks that police administrators face is creating an appropriate culture for their agencies. By developing a healthy culture—which includes values, beliefs, and behaviors," Aragon adds, "effective leaders build a solid foundation that enables them to foster truly committed employees with high morals, and in turn, enhanced departmental performance and genuinely satisfied citizens." He believes that this goal of building a positive organizational climate can be accomplished by developing an understanding of Total Quality Management (TQM), by employing empowerment techniques, by examining the dynamics of performance, and by instituting a system to monitor the department's progress.[38]

David Couper and his wife, Sabine Lobitz, have combined the principles of Community-Oriented Policing (COP) and Problem-Oriented Policing (POP) to the broader managerial ethos of TQM to implement reform in the Madison, Wisconsin, Police Department. In Couper's book, *Quality Policing,* he sees the combination of COP–POP and TQM as producing a leadership style that is nonauthoritarian, problem-oriented, and open to new ideas from both inside and outside the police agency.[39]

SCOPE OF RESPONSIBILITY

The acronym **POSDCORB** is a model of management theory that suggests that the seven functions of an organization are planning, organizing, staffing, direction, coordinating, reporting, and budgeting.[40] Although the chief police executive is responsible for all seven functions, he or she is more directly involved with planning, staffing, directing, controlling, and organizing. In Box 4.1, Dr. Jack Enter suggests a number of principles of effectiveness for police administrators.

Planning

Effective planning is vital for successful police operations. The reason for this is that planning is concerned with formulating and constructing the design of the

BOX 4.1   Can Your Administrators Meet These Key Challenges?

1. Before you can influence others, you must first manage yourself. Never expect things from others until you first see them in your own life. If you want to be a great leader, you have to hold yourself accountable first.

2. Constantly learn and grow. Constantly read. Be better next year than you were last year.

3. Maintain your perspective. In every agency, there are 3 groups of people. 10% of officers are very, very good—employees who will do well regardless of supervision. 10% are very bad. They should have never come to work, we'd be better off…If you want to take away the power of those [bad officers] to influence you, spend time with those who aren't complaining and are doing a good, conscientious job.

4. Rules without relationships do not work. People trust whom they know and distrust whom they don't know. Whenever you spend time with people when there is not a problem, you invest in those people. You make a "deposit" in them, kind of a bank account you can draw on later when you need their help or cooperation because they get to know you.

5. Deal with misunderstandings. If you see 2 [officers] at each other's throats, do not say, "They will work it out." They will not. Get in the middle of it; see what is going on. If you do it "right away," you can normally deal with it. If you let it go for a month or 2 months, the issue will build up so severe you'll never deal with it.

6. Fight rumors. Talk with people…. How you deal with rumor mongers is to talk with people and take away the power [of the rumor mongers] to influence the group.

7. Encourage feedback. Let them talk, especially cops, and get [what's bugging them] off their chests without fear of retribution. You'll de-escalate a lot of the tension in the environment.

8. To find out where your bad supervisors are, look at 3 things: Complaints by the public (if you've got a shift or a precinct that's always generating complaints, that's where your confrontational supervision is); sick leave; requests for transfer.

9. The leader of the future, to be effective, must have the heart of a servant…. Servant-hood, as a leadership style, is the most powerful form of leadership there is. If you ever want to lead people, you must lead them by example. You want them to work harder, you work harder. If you want them to treat people with respect, you treat people [including them] with respect.

10. An agency has 2 parts: a body and a spirit. The body is its facility, its patrol cars, its computer system, its structure…. But then there's the spirit. Do you like to work here? Do you want to come to work every day? We must nourish the spirit with motivation and encouragement. We need to tell people we appreciate them…. When someone tells us that they care, we put it in a permanent fund.

organization and deciding on goals and priorities.[41] Proactive rather than reactive planning is the best means to avoid crisis-centered management. Stephen R. Covey reminds the administrator that proactive means self-awareness, imagination, conscience, and independent will. A proactive response avoids blaming circumstances, conditions, and conditioning for behavior and situations.[42] This process of acting rather than being acted upon consists of distinguishing language.

Reactive Language	*Proactive Language*
There is nothing I can do.	Let's look at our alternatives.
That's just the way I am.	I can choose a different approach.
He makes me so mad.	I control my own feelings.
They won't allow that.	I can create an effective presentation.
I have to do that.	I will choose an appropriate response.
I can't.	I choose.
I must.	I prefer.
If only.	I will.[43]

The planning process is involved in studying every aspect of the department. Specifically, it entails staff supervision of planning activities; development of long-range planning capabilities; analysis of departmental subsystems, policies and procedures; analysis of crime and accident patterns, service needs and personnel deployment; and development of contingency plans for operational activities, crowd control and riots, and natural disasters. Planning is also involved in establishing intracity and intercity roadblock plans to intercept fleeing felons, in studying the feasibility of developing regional police services, in selecting electronic processing systems to streamline record keeping, and in developing a fiscal planning capability for future support of police services. Planning is further involved in evaluating current plans and services.[44]

The Gallagher–Westfall Group has developed what they call "The Six Layers of Success for the Police Leader" (see Figure 4.2). It suggests that planning is involved in everything the police agency does, including policy formulation; training of personnel; supervision of personnel; rewarding and, when necessary, reprimanding personnel; reviewing complaints, lawsuits, discipline, chronic offenders, and incident and activity reports to indicate the areas where change is needed; and providing constant legal updates of new case law and training for officers to understand the new case law.

Organizing

The first step in organizing a department is to develop a supportive staff. The importance of developing a team of supportive staff is absolutely critical if the chief administrator expects to have short- and long-term success. The top police

The First Layer
Policy

Based on the principle of **"foreseeabilty"** policy must flow from the department's mission statements, the vision and values articulated by its chief executive, his/her personal philosophy, the latest in professional research, in an attempt to channel in a positive mode the discretion of the officer while providing the necessary attention to legal and procedural guidelines.

The Second Layer
Training

Training must use **POLICY** as its basis for its curriculum. Through extensive exercises, simulations, applications of relevant principles and essential knowledge provide in context training that represents the real world in which the police officer must function.

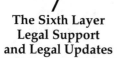

The Sixth Layer
Legal Support
and Legal Updates

This is normally the weakest link. Constant legal update must be provided with aggressive, available, experienced legal support to continuously "scan the legal environment" and alert the agency to new legal decisions, assist it in assimilating these new decisions into its policy and then into its training, and then provide direct support by training the officers in the parameters of the laws and the case law.

THE KEY TO
FIELD LEADERSHIP

"Leadership is not a one-time event. It is an intentional, focused, well planned, well supported, ongoing, step-by-step, never-ending process."

**The Gallagher–
Westfall Group**

The Third Layer
Supervision

Actively essential to that operational structure is the presence of positive, supportive supervision in an envronment that focuses on **"Catching a cop doing something right"** and proactively manages performance with a specific focus on developing people.

The Fifth Layer
Review & Revision

There must be constant review by management and each officer of their "spreadsheet," the overview of complaints, lawsuits, discipline, chronic offenders, incident and activity reports related to High Frequency, Low Frequency/High Severity events to indicate the areas for change and revision.

Revision must take place immediately with attention to the effects primarily on policy and then on training.

It is this **"Kaizen"** approach to managing that keeps an organization from falling victim to dated policies, procedures, legal changes, etc.

The Fourth Layer
Discipline or Reinforcement

Discipline or preferable the three R's of reinforcement consisting of Re-directing, Rewarding and **WHEN APPROPRIATE** Reprimanding.

FIGURE 4.2 The Six Layers of Success for the Police Leader

Source: © Gallagher–Westfall Group, Inc., Indian Valley, VA 24105.

executive wants staff who are loyal, who are responsible to both the real and the imagined concerns of the agency, who are dedicated and are able to convince other personnel that law enforcement is an important profession, and who believe that together they can make a difference.[45] Police executives also want managers on their team who:

1. will challenge them to be their very best
2. are confident and quite capable of making responsible managerial decisions
3. have knowledge, skills, experience, and personal characteristics that they lack
4. have differing perspectives and viewpoints than the chief, and who can articulate these opposing views in a nonadversarial way
5. are supportive of the philosophy and goals of the chief, and who can communicate that they believe in them with sincerity and intensity
6. are not easily provoked and have the capacity to be restrained even under extreme provocation
7. have a track record of demonstrating maturity, good judgment, insight, and wisdom
8. are honest and have integrity so that they will do what is right and will take stands on issues with subordinate staff
9. are tactful and are able to articulate things well so that they can be understood by staff at all levels
10. have perseverance and tenacity
11. are not easily intimidated
12. don't have biases about particular people based on race, gender, or class or other personal biases
13. are not arrogant, pompous, know-it-all, offensive, condescending, caustic, abrasive, and self-righteous
14. have the intellectual depth to know that rarely will we find simplistic solutions to society's and law enforcement's very complex problems[46]

Staffing

Staffing is an important consideration in respect to all work that takes place in a police department. The police executive who usually delegates staffing responsibilities to others is still ultimately responsible for all the decisions that are made. The emphasis on standards and liability in police work encourages departments to spend more money on recruiting and testing police candidates and on upgrading training procedures. Staffing takes place in phases comprised of recruitment, hiring, retention, promotion, and on-going training. Some departments recruit locally, and others, such as the Dallas Police Department, have full-time recruiters who travel nationwide soliciting prospective candidates for employment. If "bad apples" are hired, with sadistic natures, vulnerable to corruption, or racist or sexist attitudes and beliefs, then the department has a long term problem. Promotions continue to be a source of tension and conflict in policing. Politics intrude far too often in promotions in federal, state, and local police agencies. Nearly every police officer, including one of the authors of this book, has a war story or two about unfair promotions in departments they have worked in.

Training is now being perceived as critically important in preparing officers for the challenges of the streets and for upholding constitutional procedures in arrests. The media's chilling announcements of police officers who have fallen by the wayside are vivid reminders of the importance of training. So much of the time, the inappropriately handled incident was a training problem. The fact still remains that training is expensive, and unless the chief executive believes strongly in its importance, training will receive minimal emphasis. The departments that pursue more training for officers, supervisors, and administrators are those that seem to handle the troublesome issues of policing more effectively.

Supervising

There is no question that when it comes to the performance of police officers, no one is as important as the first line supervisor. Yet too many departments give personnel stripes without pre-promotional training. Supervisors may wait months or years before they receive any adequate training directly related to the responsibilities of their new position. It is not surprising, then, that these supervisors often do not have the experience and qualifications they need. As a result, there is a tendency to become hesitant about the role they are supposed to assume as the spectra of liability looms even larger. Lacking any clear indication of what they have to do or having inadequate preparation for what they are supposed to do, many tend to withdraw from active supervision. National trainer G. Patrick Gallagher explains this withdrawal by saying that "they are out of their comfort zones, despite years of experience on the street. They become passive supervisors, or mere observers of the myriad numbers of activities swirling around them."[47]

First-line supervisors stand with one foot in two different worlds: management and operations. It is mandatory that from lieutenant on up there is a realization of the importance of the first-line supervisor's roles. A lieutenant actually should be held responsible for a sergeant's success or failure. Faulty supervision can bring a great deal of grief to a police department. For example, in *Doe v. Calumet City*, a supervisor hypersensitive to liability failed to break down a door to rescue the two children of a woman who had escaped from a rapist who had entered her home. Fearing that the department would be liable for the damages to the door, he was paralyzed by the fear of liability and ended up incurring far greater supervisory liability than that which he feared. The Court of Appeals in *Shaw v. Stroud* (1994) dealt with a case of wrongful death. In this case, the trooper involved in a shooting death had, over his nine year tenure in the department, established a pattern of allegedly using excessive force. Two sergeants had supervised him, one for the first seven years and the other up to the time of the incident. The supervisor for the first seven years had totally ignored his pattern of excessive force.[48] Gallagher suggests the following process to improve the performance of first-line supervisors:

1. The development and implementation of a Field Training Supervisor program patterned on the FTO program.
2. The implementation of the process of Performance Management at all levels within the organization.
3. The establishment of a peak performance-oriented supervisory style.
4. A concentration not only on those whose performance is sub-par, but on protecting and raising the level of performance of every single person without neglecting those who are average or superior.
5. Responsibility and accountability placed on lieutenants measuring their success by the accompanying success of the sergeants reporting to them.
6. Establishment of a basic bias toward the achievement of success by providing support in every form with the provision of a Supervisor's Field Manual Checklist.
7. Careful attention to making sure that all supervisors are trained in all high risk and critical task policies before they are expected to enforce them.[49]

Controlling

The chief police administrator makes policy decisions daily. The decisions concern such important issues as creating a positive departmental culture which requires overcoming the alienation of the line police street culture, preventing and reducing crime, sanctioning those officers who become involved in corrupt or violent behaviors, promoting aggressively the increased employment of women and minority police officers, and reducing civil liability for the police department. In view of the costs to public credibility and trust, one of the top administrator's most important decisions relates to sanctioning those officers who have become involved in unacceptable behaviors. There are also Internal Affairs Units and sometimes Citizens Review Committees that investigate charges of wrongdoing, but the mandate to establish integrity as a basic mission of the department rests squarely on the shoulders of the police executive.

CHALLENGES TO THE POLICE CHIEF

Police chiefs, as well as sheriffs and other top police executives, face six categories of challenges today, and how these challenges are met largely determines the executive's degree of effectiveness. These challenges consist of:

1. Reconciling the conflict between the cop culture and management culture.
2. Implementing successful community-oriented (COP) or problem-oriented policing (POP) policing.
3. Gaining acceptance of a value-driven, or integrity-based approach to police work.
4. Attaining accreditation within that agency.

5. Establishing a good working relationship with the union.
6. Developing the type of policies that reduce the likelihood of widespread police deviancy.

Reconciling the Conflict between Cop and Management Cultures

The professionalization model of police departments developed early in the twentieth century was driven by the desire to create a bureaucratic, technologically sophisticated, standard-based police department. The strategy was for officers to maintain an emotional distance from citizens and act toward them in a professional but impersonal way. One of this model's unintended results was the creation of alienation and lack of communication between management and the line culture. Today, particularly in large urban departments, the police street culture and management culture are in conflict with each other. The tightly knit and unified police departments of the past have increasingly given way to the conflict between these diverging cultures. Elizabeth Reuss-Ianni's study of the New York City Police Department is helpful in terms of understanding this conflict:

> Now there are two cultures which confront each other in the [police] department: a street cop culture of the good old days, working class in origin and temperament, whose members see themselves as career cops; opposed to this is a management cop culture, more middle class, whose members' education and mobility make them eligible for jobs totally outside of policing, which makes them less dependent on, and less loyal to, the street cop culture. In a sense, the management cop culture represent those police who have decided the old way of running a police department is finished.... They do not, like the street cops, regard community relations, for example, as "Mickey Mouse bullshit."... The management culture is sensitive to politics and public opinion [and so cannot be depended upon for support by the street cop]. The street cops who are still into the old ways of doing things are confused and often enraged at the apparent change in the rules of the system. So they fight back in the only way they have at their disposal, footdragging, absenteeism, and a host of similar coping mechanisms and defensive techniques. Nor is all this likely to change soon: the old and the new will continue to coexist for some time because the attitudes and values of doing things have not changed throughout the system.[50]

Three fundamental reasons explain why the unified police culture has diverged into a management and a street culture. First, the increased recruitment of new chiefs outside the department in the 1980s introduced new ideas affecting existing power structures, privileges, and job responsibilities that were previously taken for granted. It was not long before these "outsiders" were accused of being more concerned about satisfying local politicians than they were about gaining the approval of their own officers. Second, federally funded programs in the 1960s and

1970s led to improved training and better educated police officers. The college-educated officer introduced new ideas about leadership, professionalism, and accreditation to police departments. The "old guard" felt increasingly uncomfortable with these college-educated officers, and it was not long before educated officers assumed leadership roles in departments. Third, the affirmative action mandates of the 1970s resulted in the increased hiring of minorities and women. Initially, the changing composition of police departments bred some insecurities, but, in the long run, police officers' need for solidarity only motivated them to entrench themselves even more in the street culture.

The conflict between the street and management cultures is one of the most serious problems facing city and county police departments. However, the fact that these divergent cultures are nearly non-existent in state and federal agencies shows that the feelings of alienation that so often exists in county and city police agencies do not need to exist. New police chiefs or sheriffs in city and county agencies have a difficult task. On one hand, it is necessary for them to demand higher levels of professionalism from their officers, but, on the other hand, these police administrators must take positive and innovative steps to reduce the alienation between the street and management cultures. Possibilities for establishing better rapport and trust with line officers include more organizational decision making, higher status and prestige, increased salaries to match those in state and federal police agencies, and better protection on the street.

Implementing Successful COP or POP Policing

Community-oriented policing is a philosophy of policing. Although it is typically looked upon as a new vision of the role of police in a democratic society, it is actually as old if not older than the crime-fighting role of the police.[51] The implementation of COP or POP does present a strange bed fellow for the bureaucratic reformer, for it was not that many decades ago that police administrators frowned upon unnecessary conversation with the public.[52]

Community-oriented policing is described in much greater detail in the next chapter, but the challenge for the police chief is to overcome the resistance of line officers. An officer in a department that has been undergoing a "conversion" to community-oriented policing made what is probably a statement fairly representative of the opinions of officers in similar situations.

> This is the usual horseshit. The chief tells everybody that we're community-oriented, but we still don't know what that means. The chief goes out and makes speeches about it, but when we ask the sergeant what we should say to people if they ask us about this, he tells us to keep in mind the department's rule that we're not allowed to criticize any department policy or official. I guess it would be critical to tell people we have no idea what the difference between community-oriented policing and what we used to do is, so we just smile and nod.[53]

In addition to widespread confusion among line officers about what COP means, two other problems that police organizations face when implementing COP programs are lack of support of middle management and lack of support of community residents.[54] Indeed, it may very well be that getting middle managers and first-line supervisors to commit to the philosophy of COP will be harder than getting the rank-and-file to commit to it.[55]

Herman Goldstein has observed that not much in the experience or training of sergeants readies them for work in the decentralized POP–COP model. It is, Goldstein adds, threatening to them and, as a result, they tend to resist its implementation. Goldstein believes that training, support, role modeling, and leadership are important in converting supervisors to the new paradigm. Goldstein concludes that in the end, the question of who gets promoted and on what criteria will have the greatest impact because those supervisors who resist POP–COP will be gradually replaced by those who buy into this new paradigm.[56]

Gaining Acceptance of an Integrity-Based Approach

The first wave of reform began in the early 1900s, culminating in what is called the "military–professional model of policing." By the 1950s and 1960s, this became the dominant form of policing and still remains intact today. The 1970s saw the growth of administrative due process. This attempt to increase accountability stemmed largely from the development of policy and procedure manuals, the commitment on the part of police executives to bring officer's discretion more in line with stated policy, and the growth of internal affairs units. The growing concern over police–community relations, especially minority relations, also resulted in many departments' rules being more strictly enforced. The next major move came from the civil process. The concept of police immunity from lawsuits eroded in state courts, and the U.S. Supreme Court opened the floodgates for both personal and departmental liability via civil rights actions. This form of police accountability has been referred to as the "civil due process" revolution.

What does all this have to do with **integrity**? Specifically, all the previous efforts to enhance police accountability relied on rules and punishment. Although each of these reform efforts had an impact, everyone is aware that policing currently has a problem with ethical behavior. In the late 1990s, a movement is beginning to gather momentum across the nation based on the belief that police integrity should represent a basic mission of law enforcement in the future. Increasing numbers of law enforcement administrators believe that integrity is an idea whose time has come.[57] Lee Brown, former chief executive officer of several major police agencies, puts the responsibility for integrity squarely on the shoulders of police executives. "If, in law enforcement, we are to rid ourselves of the specter of wrongdoing, we must fundamentally change the police culture." And then he said, "The leadership of a police organization ultimately will determine the character of the organization."[58]

Police Integrity: Public Service with Honor makes several recommendations for police executives in terms of supporting integrity in their departments. First, police executives are reminded that they must model appropriate behaviors. Second, line officers must know and understand the core values of their organizations. Third, line officers must know that the department will stand by the officers fostering those values. Fourth, police executives have the responsibility to create an environment in which young, morally strong officers can actualize their idealism. Fifth, police executives must know what is going on in their organizations. Sixth, operational strategies should be developed for more positive and creative methods of discipline. Seventh, more time must be allotted to designing and implementing intervention strategies for problem officers. Finally, it is wise to focus on professional integrity rather than political opportunity.[59]

Attaining Accreditation

The process of gaining accreditation has been a promising step in police administration. Standards have been established by the commission for Accreditation since 1979 to improve the delivery of police service. The accreditation process is a joint effort of the commission and four law enforcement membership associations—the International Association of Chiefs of Police (IACP), the National Organization of Black Law Enforcement Executives (NOBLE), the National Sheriff's Association (NSA), and the Police Executive Research Forum (PERF). The commission lists the benefits to police agencies for going through the process of accreditation (which usually takes three years):

1. nationwide recognition of professional excellence
2. community understanding and support
3. employee confidence; esprit de corps
4. state and local government officials' confidence
5. state-of-the-art, impartial guidelines for evaluation, and change, when necessary
6. proactive management systems; policies and procedures documented
7. liability insurance costs contained or decreased
8. liability litigation deterred
9. coordination with neighboring agencies and other parts of the criminal justice system
10. access to the latest law enforcement practices[60]

In 1995, 368 police agencies had received accreditation and hundreds more agencies were in the process of being considered for accreditation. Accreditation is for three years, and reaccreditation must be applied for during the third year. The cost of accreditation depends on the number of sworn and civilian employees. For example, the accreditation costs for an agency of more than 1,000 employees would be $16,000. This is roughly the same cost for the reaccreditation process.[61]

Supporters of accreditation hold that the standardization of police departments across the nation is the most effective means of furthering the professionalization of policing. The underlying objective of accreditation is to encourage more police departments to attain a minimum level of performance, a level that only a few departments across the nation attained until recent years.

Establishing a Good Relationship with the Union

It was not that long ago that police chiefs had nearly unlimited power to run their departments, but today they are severely restrained by police unions. These unions often hammer out collective bargaining agreements and also exert enormous informal influence within the department and the community at large.[62] A. V. Bouza writes from the perspective of being a police chief, "the battle for control of the police agency" is increasingly a struggle between unions and chiefs.[63]

The union movement in policing started slowly. The American Federation of Labor issued initial charters to police unions in Boston, Washington DC, and 30 other cities. When the Boston police commissioner refused to recognize the union, forbidding officers to join it and filing charges against union officials, the Boston police initiated their famous 1919 strike of three days duration. This strike caused major riots in which nine rioters were killed and 23 were seriously injured. The public reaction to the union movement in Boston and elsewhere destroyed at least for a brief period efforts to organize unions in policing. This defunct union movement was revived during the late 1950s and early 1960s by vocal rank-and-file association leaders who came into power. Their support of higher salaries and pensions, free legal aid, low cost insurance, as well as their rejection of civilian review boards, won the support of a large majority of the rank-and-file.[64]

Today, nearly 75 percent of all police officers in the United States hold membership in unions.[65] Some unions continue to hold the threat of work stoppages, and major police strikes took place during the 1970s in Albuquerque, Oklahoma City, Tucson, San Francisco, and New Orleans. Police unions have also flexed their collective muscle in fighting proposals to restrict promotional exams to officers who have completed a year or two of college (Detroit), in blocking plans to introduce lateral entry (Providence, Rhode Island), in preventing several commissioners from changing from two-person to one-person patrol cars, and in stopping the use of polygraph tests to investigate allegations of corruption.[66]

One study that examined police labor contracts in medium- and large-sized cities shed more light on the issues covered by labor contracts.[67] In the 99 police labor contracts examined, the following kinds of provisions were identified:

85%	specified grievance procedures
75%	had management rights clauses
73%	had no-strike clauses
70%	had seniority provisions
58%	referred to employee discipline
57%	had education and training provisions
55%	referred to civil service or related systems
40%	had maintenance of standards provisions
35%	had reductions in force provisions
17%	had transfer provisions
15%	had cost of living adjustments[68]

In sum, the union movement has unquestionably taken some of the power from police chiefs. Some chiefs have much better relationships with the rank-and-file than others, and this usually translates into more harmonious contract negotiations. If a chief fails to convince the rank-and-file union membership that he or she is on their side, then a "no confidence" vote may be taken and the chief will likely be looking for another job.

Reducing Police Deviancy

Police bureaucracies are not easily changed. Unless the chief is an exceptional leader and is able to make systemic changes, this person's influence over this complex organization is likely to be minimal and to a large extent, symbolic and indirect.[69] This minimal influence is most apparent in terms of the chief's influence over police operations in the streets, but yet when it comes to police deviancy, strong leadership has sometimes made a difference in reducing the amount of deviancy within an agency. For example, Jerome H. Skolnick and James J. Fyfe contend that police chiefs have been influential in what they perceive as a decline in brutality in American policing.[70] During the time that he was police commissioner in the NYPD, Patrick V. Murphy instituted systemic changes that reduced corruption in the department.[71]

SUMMARY

This chapter examines the role of chiefs in administering a police department. Chiefs of police function in an organizational context and in this century have bureaucratized and rationalized the police. Daily, police chiefs confront external political, economic, legal, and cultural factors that impinge on their authority and decision making. Nor can they deny the internal political, legal, cultural, and economic factors that they face in administering a police department. The success or failure of chiefs depends in a real sense on how they manage these internal and external factors.

A profile of chiefs of police appears to be emerging across the nation. The chief typically perceives of himself or herself as a professional, is cognizant of public and private sector philosophies of management, pursues various means of participatory management, and has some commitment to community policing. Increased numbers of chiefs are recognizing the importance of integrity as a part of the basic mission of their departments, and they are beginning to reshape the philosophy and structure of their departments around integrity and ethical issues. Nevertheless, especially in large urban departments, many chiefs come to see themselves "in a storm at sea aboard a leaking and rudderless ship with a mutinous crew." It is not surprising that "more than a few of them run into political trouble and lose their jobs simply because they do not understand the nature of those jobs and the forces that bear on them."[72]

One of the underlying themes of this book is that good people make a difference. A long line of chiefs has made a difference. They have been instrumental in developing a healthy police organization.[73] They are persons of integrity who respect and treat others as persons of worth. They have stood tall against corruption and other forms of deviancy within their departments. They have known what they want to accomplish and have had the necessary skills to attain their objectives.

KEY WORDS

administration   management
conceptualization   Management by Objectives (MBO)
contingency management   POSDCORB
integrity   supervision

DISCUSSION QUESTIONS

1. Think for a moment about sharing decision making in a police department. If you were a police chief, which type of participatory management technique would you use?

2. How would a system-wide and nation-wide incorporation of integrity change the face of policing in the United States?

3. What is police culture? If you were the chief of police and the police culture in your department was particularly troubling, what would you do?

4. Would you like to be a chief of police at some point in your career? What aspects of this job would you find fulfilling? What aspects would drive you up a wall?

5. The majority of chiefs support both the professionalism movement in policing and community-oriented policing (COP). The former recommends impersonality of policing while the later focuses on police engagement in a community. Is this a troubling contradiction?

FURTHER READING

Gaffigan, Stephen J., and Phyllis P. McDonald. *Police Integrity: Public Service with Honor.* Washington, DC: National Institute of Justice and Office of Community Oriented Policing Services, 1997.

Hunt, Raymond G., and John M. Magenau. *Power and the Police Chief.* Newbury Park: Sage, 1993.

Lynch, Ronald. G. *The Police Manager,* 4th ed. Cincinnati: Anderson, 1995.

Sheehan, Robert, and Gary W. Cordner. *Police Administration,* 3rd ed. Cincinnati: Anderson, 1995.

ENDNOTES

1. Patrick V. Murphy and Thomas Plate, *Commissioner: A View From the Top of American Law Enforcement* (New York: Simon & Schuster, 1977) 270.

2. Personal interview, November 1986, in Clemens Bartollas and Michael Braswell, *American Criminal Justice* (Cincinnati: Anderson, 1997) 214.

3. Bartollas and Braswell, 56–57.

4. Raymond G. Hunt and John M. Magenau, *Power and the Police Chief: An Institutional and Organizational Analysis* (Newbury Park: Sage, 1993) 145–146.

5. Hunt and Magenau, 121.

6. *The New York Times,* 9 Sept. 1992: B8.

7. "Police Chiefs under Fire: Cities Pay Chiefs Big Bucks So They Expect Big Results," *USA Today* 1997.

8. "Police Chiefs Under Fire."

9. "Police Chiefs Under Fire."

10. Kenneth J. Peak, *Policing America: Methods, Issues, Challenges* (Upper Saddle River: Prentice–Hall, 1997) 118.

11. H. H. Gerth and C. W. Mills (trans. and eds.), *From Max Weber: Essays in Sociology* (New York: Oxford, 1958) 214.

12. Edward A. Thibault, Lawrence M. Lynch, and R. Bruce McBride, *Proactive Police Management,* 2nd ed. (Englewood Cliffs: Prentice–Hall, 1990) 69.

13. Thibault, et al., 196–198.

14. Peter K. Manning, *Police Work,* 2nd ed. (Prospect Heights: Waveland, 1997) 11–12.

15. Personal interview, September 1986.

16. Hunt and Magenau, 5.

17. See Richard Brzeczek, "Chief–Mayor Relations: The View from the Chief's Chair," *Police Leadership in America: Crisis and Opportunity,* ed. William A. Geller (New York: Praeger, 1985) 48–55.

18. Steve Herbert, *Police Space: Territoriality and the Los Angeles Police Department* (Minneapolis: U of Minnesota P, 1997) 53.

19. See Frijof Capra, *The Turning Point: Science, Society, and the Rising Culture* (New York: Bantam, 1988) 265–304; and Michael Beer and Edgar Huse, "A Systems Approach to Organizational Development," *Readings on Behavior in Organizations,* ed. Edgar F. Huse, James L. Bowditch, and Dalmar Fisher (Reading: Addison–Wesley, 1975) 409–426.

20. For the classic work on general systems theory, see Ludwig von Bertalanffy, *General Systems Theory* (New York: Braziller, 1968).

21. Capra, 265–304.

22. Mark Dantzker, "Requirements for the Position of Municipal Police Chief: A Content Analysis," *Police Studies* 17 (1994): 34. See also J. E. Enter, "The Role of Higher Education in the Career of the American Police Chief," *Police Studies* 9 (1986): 110–119; and J. P. Crank, "Professionalism among Police Chiefs," diss., U of Cincinnati, 1987.

23. D. C. Witham, *The American Law Enforcement Chief Executive: A Management Profile* (Washington, DC: Police Executive Research Forum, 1985); D. C. Witham, "Transformational Police Leadership," *FBI Law Enforcement Bulletin* 56 (1987): 2–6.

24. Dantzker, 34.

25. Dantzker, 34.

26. Larry K. Gaines, Victor E. Kappeler, and Joseph B. Vaughn, *Policing in America,* 2nd ed. (Cincinnati: Anderson, 1997) 129.

27. Orlando Belling, "Unification of Management Theory: A Pessimistic View," *Emerging Concepts in Management: Process, Behavioral, Quantitative and Systems,* ed. Max S. Worthman, Jr. and Fred Luthans (Toronto: Macmillan, 1969) 40.

28. Peter Drucker, *The Practice of Management* (New York: Harper, 1954) and George S. Odione, *Management by Objectives* (New York: Pitman, 1965).

29. David Schreiber and Stanley Sloan, "Management by Objectives," *Personnel Administration* 15 (1970): 20–26.

30. William J. Bratton, "Cutting Crime and Restoring Order: What America Can Learn from New York's Finest," speech delivered to the Heritage Foundation, Oct. 15, 1996, 5.

31. Bratton, 9.

32. C. Argris, *Integrating the Individual and the Organization* (New York: Wiley, 1964) 211.

33. P. Lawrence and J. Lorsch, *Organization and Environment: Managing Differentiation and Integration* (Boston: Harvard Univ. Graduate School of Business Administration, 1967).

34. Quoted in Clemens Bartollas and Michael Braswell, *American Criminal Justice: An Introduction,* 2nd ed. (Cincinnati: Anderson, 1997) 185.

35. Gaines, 134.

36. Hunt and Magenau, 127.

37. Randall Aragon, "Positive Organizational Culture: A Practical Approach," mimeograph handout, n.d. See also J. R. Jablonski, *Implementing TQM* (San Diego: Pfeiffer, 1992).

38. Jablonski.

39. D. C. Couper and S. H. Lobitz, *Quality Policing: The Madison Experience* (Washington, DC: Police Executive Research Forum, 1991).

40. Luther Gulick and L. Urwick, eds., *Papers on the Science of Administration* (New York: Institute of Public Administration, Columbia U, 1937) 1–45.

41. Robert Sheehan and Gary W. Cordner, *Police Administration*, 3rd ed. (Cincinnati: Anderson, 1995) 163.

42. Steven R. Covey, *The 7 Habits of Highly Effective People: Powerful Lessons in Personal Change* (New York: Simon & Schuster, 1990) 71.

43. Covey, 78.

44. Sheehan and Cordner, 172.

45. Personal interview, June 1990, in Clemens Bartollas and John P. Conrad, *Introduction to Corrections*, 2nd ed. (New York: Harper/Collins, 1992) 370.

46. Bartollas and Conrad, 370.

47. G. Patrick Gallagher, "Creating a Breed of Super-Sergeants," *Law Enforcement Trainer* (May–June, 1997): 8.

48. Gallagher, 9.

49. Gallagher, 10.

50. Elizabeth Reuss–Ianni, *Two Cultures of Policing: Street Cops and Management Cops* (New Brunswick: Transaction, 1984) 121–122.

51. Jerome H. Skolnick and James J. Fyfe, *Above the Law: Police and the Excessive Use of Force* (New York: The Free Press, 1993) 252.

52. Paul Chevigny, *Edge of the Knife: Police Violence in the Americas* (New York: The Free Press, 1995) 141.

53. Personal communication with James J. Fyfe, 26 July 1991, in Skolnick and Fyfe, 260.

54. Jihong Zhao, Quint C. Thurman, and Nicholas P. Lovrich, "Community-Oriented Policing Across the U.S.: Facilitators and Impediment to Implementation," *American Journal of Police 14* (1995): 21–22.

55. Hunt and Magenau, 134.

56. Hunt and Magenau, 134.

57. Stephen J. Gaffigan and Phyllis P. McDonald, *Police Integrity: Public Service with Honor* (Washington, DC: U.S. Department of Justice, 1997).

58. Gaffigan and McDonald, 26.

59. Gaffigan and McDonald, 26, 27, 33, 49.

60. "Accreditation for Small Police Departments," remarks made by Kenneth H. Medeiros, James V. Cotter, Robert A. Roberts, and Emory A. Plitt, Jr. during the 1984 International Association of Chiefs of Police, Inc. Annual Conference, reprinted in *The Police Chief 52* (Mar. 1985): 40–49.

61. Personal correspondence with a staff member of the Commission on Accreditation for Law Enforcement Agencies, Incorporated, 1995.

62. John M. Magenau and Raymond G. Hunt, "Police Unions and the Police Role," *Human Relations 49* (1996): 1315.

63. A. V. Bouza, *The Police Mystique: An Insider's Look at the Criminal Justice System* (New York: Plenum, 1990) 240.

64. Peak, 134–135.

65. Samuel Walker, *The Police in America*, 2nd ed. (New York: McGraw–Hill, 1992) 372.

66. Peak, 135.

67. S. A. Rynecki, D. A. Cairns, and D. J. Cairns, *Police Collective Bargaining Agreements: A National Management Survey* (Washington, DC: Police Executive Research Forum, 1978).

68. Rynecki, et al.

69. Hunt and Magenau, 44–45.

70. Skolnick and Fyfe, 20.

71. Skolnick and Fyfe, 184–189.

72. Hunt and Magenau, 26.

73. Police Research Institute, "Measuring What Matters" (Washington, DC: National Institute of Justice and Community Oriented Policing Services, 1997) 5.

5

POLICE OPERATIONS

Community policing requires the best efforts of everyone. Whether it is citizens improving the safety of their local communities, officers directing resources to the root problems in their districts, or agency heads and Council members pursing more effective solutions, each individual must feel as if the problem was his or her own, and they must push themselves, and work with others, to solve them.

Community Policing will work to the degree that, we as a community, can assume individual responsibility for making our city work, and to the degree that we, as a community, fulfill our role in helping to make that happen....

No one of us should wait for Community Policing to come to our doorstep, or find its way onto our desk. Rather, we must go out and get started.

The men and women of the Portland Police Bureau. We ask that you be open minded, yet impatient. Success will require your openness to new approaches and your willingness to give those approaches the very best chance to work....

Those who are in a position to influence policy and allocate resources. We ask that you maintain the courage of your commitments to a fully implemented Community Policing, providing resources equal to the job and support for a more active, empowered citizenry....

The citizens of Portland. If you haven't already, get involved! Whether it is through the Police Bureau, the Office for Neighborhood Associations, some other agency, or on your own, learn what you can do to strengthen the safety of your own block, your own community....

—Adapted from Portland Police Bureau,
Community Policing Transition Plan, Portland, 41.

The Portland, Oregon, Police Bureau is one of the police departments in the United States vigorously pursuing community policing. In the above excerpt from its mission and goal statement, the police bureau asks the people of Oregon to commit themselves to community-oriented policing (COP). The mission statement goes on to promise that this partnership between the community and police bureau will work to solve crime-related problems and to improve the quality of life throughout the city. According to Quint C. Thurman and Michael D. Reisig, "Community-oriented policing (COP) represents a new era of police services delivery where the public is asked by local government to take a more active role in identifying and helping to resolve crime-related problems."[1] They add that "coinciding with the Americans' public's growing demand for responsiveness and accountability in local government, citizens who once were assured that experts would solve their problems now are encouraged to participate themselves in community-wide problem solving on a wide range of quality of life issues."[2] They conclude that the police covet the participation of the community "as allies in solving old crimes and preventing the occurrence of new ones."[3]

Within the policing profession itself, there is wide agreement that community-oriented policing (COP) and problem-oriented policing (POP) would change the basic role of the police from crime fighters to service providers.[4] Michael J. Palmiotto and Michael E. Donahue state: "Proponents and detractors alike of community policing agree that it constitutes a revision of the police role, away from that of crime fighter to that of planner, community organizer, problem solver, and broker of government services."[5]

However, although community-oriented policing may have extensive support today and may even be the wave of the future, strong resistance to its implementation does exist throughout the nation.[6] For example, there is consistent resistance from line-police officers, lack of clarity about the practical meaning of community policing, difficulty in involving other public agencies, and problems in organizing and establishing rapport with the community.[7] The degree of COP and POP success depends upon whether these implementation problems can be overcome.[8]

Most police agencies, as suggested in Chapter 2, define their mission as the preservation of public peace and order, the prevention and detection of crime, the protection of persons and property, and the enforcement of the law. To translate these broad functions into police daily operations, they are typically divided into line functions and support functions. One important issue is whether and to what degree COP and POP is flushed out in the daily operations of police departments in the United States. That is, how much has this new approach to policing changed the way the police do their business? The final section of this chapter will attempt to answer this question.

LINE FUNCTIONS

Officers assigned **line functions** provide the primary law enforcement tasks in the community or area served. Line functions include patrol, traffic control, investigation, and work in juvenile and other specialized units (see Figure 5.1).

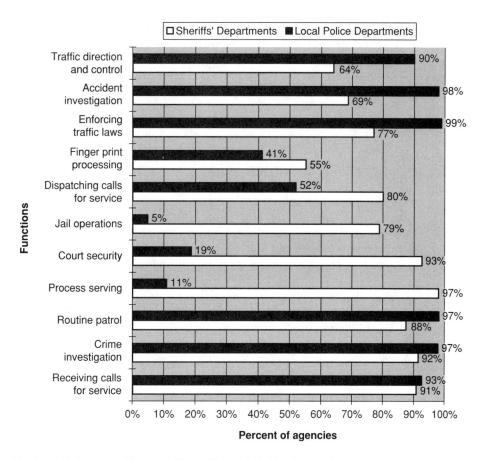

FIGURE 5.1   Functions of Sheriffs' and Police Departments

Source: Brian A. Reaves and Pheny Z. Smith, "Sheriffs' Departments 1993," U.S. Department of Justice, Office of Justice Programs, Bureau of Justice Statistics (June 1996) iv.

Patrol Units

The patrol is the "backbone" of the police department. As the largest and most visible unit, it responds to calls for service 24 hours a day, and requires the most personnel, money, resources, and equipment. According to a Justice Department Study, 67 percent of sworn officers are in uniform patrol. The number of officers assigned to uniform patrol was the highest for jurisdictions serving populations smaller than 25,000. For example, an estimated 75 percent of sworn personnel were assigned to uniform patrol in departments serving a population of 10,000 to 24,999; 85 percent for departments serving a population of 2,500 to 9,999; and about 95 percent for populations under 2,500.[9]

Another significant aspect of patrol is that all other functions of a department are designed to support patrol. Even though citizens and the entertainment industry may perceive that detectives are more important than patrol officers, Gary W. Cordner, Larry K. Gaines, and Victor E. Kappeler correct this viewpoint: "detectives were created to allow patrol officers to remain on patrol rather than leave their beats to investigate crimes. Furthermore, workloads of other units increase when patrol does not function at a maximum level."[10]

Uniformed patrol officers are the first responders of the department. They are the first to arrive at a domestic assault, at a bar fight, murder scene, or bank robbery, and at a hostage situation or a terrorist bombing. As first responders, they arrive when the risk of injury is the greatest. For example, four out of five law enforcement officers assaulted and the largest percent of victim officers slain are on vehicle patrol.[11] The most dangerous time in a barricaded subject or hostage incident is the first few minutes when adrenalin and anxiety levels are in the stratosphere. Usually, by the time the Special Weapons and Tactics Team (SWAT) arrives to take over the incident, uniform officers have set up an inner perimeter containing the armed person and started negotiation.

Uniform officers respond to four types of emergencies:

1. disturbance emergencies such as bar fights and domestic abuse
2. medical emergencies ranging from a baby that has stopped breathing to an accident victim
3. fire emergencies
4. miscellaneous emergencies—the infamous bat in the kitchen call[12]

In a general sense, the responsibilities of patrol personnel include responding to criminal violations, doing preliminary law enforcement, being involved in crime prevention, and answering other calls for assistance.

Officers have frequently found spousal assault calls one of the most problematic for them to handle. Traditionally, they attempted to restore some semblance of order and then leave. However, a study conducted by Lawrence Sherman and Richard Berk in Minneapolis, as well as other supporting studies, found that arresting assailants resulted in the lowest rate of repeated incidents over the following six months.[13] These findings led the departments in Dallas, Denver, Houston, Minneapolis, New York, and Phoenix to use arrest more frequently to handle cases of spousal assault, and states across the nation have enacted laws making spousal assault a separate criminal offense.[14] See Box 5.1 for the findings of these various studies on spousal abuse.

This reporting of the various studies on handling domestic assaults is a reminder that we need to be cautious about simple solutions. The subsequent analysis of the original Sherman and Berk study certainly suggests that arrest is not the panacea that many had hoped in terms of deterring spouse abusers.[15]

The Police Services Study, conducted by Elinor Ostrom, Roger B. Parks, and Gordon P. Whitaker, included 6,000 police–citizen encounters from 60 different neighborhoods and from 24 departments in the Rochester, New York, St. Louis, Missouri, and Tampa—St. Petersburg, Florida metropolitan areas.[16] This study, which examined specific actions police officers took during their patrol encoun-

---

BOX 5.1   Findings on Spousal Abuse and Arresting Assailants

Sherman and Berk concluded from their Minneapolis study that, "The arrest treatment is clearly an improvement over sending the suspect away, which produced two and a half times as many repeat incidents as arrest." This finding held "regardless of the race, employment status, educational level, criminal history of the suspect, or how long the suspect was in jail when arrested."

In replicating this study in a county in California, Richard Berk and Phyllis J. Newton found that arrests substantially reduced the number of new incidents of wife battery; the reductions were greatest for those batterers whom the police would ordinarily be inclined to arrest. The National Institute of Justice decided to test this hypothesis concerning arrest

and reduced domestic violence in other settings. Two studies showed evidence of a deterrent effect of arrest, while three others found evidence of a criminogenic effect. Further analysis revealed that in four of these studies (Colorado Springs, Dade County (Florida), Milwaukee, and Omaha) arrest regularly deterred employed batters but increased repeat violence among unemployed men. Additional analysis of the Milwaukee study added the finding that this pattern may be more related to the neighborhoods where arrests are made than with employment status. The finding that the situation or social context of batterers is an important consideration in the effect of arrests ultimately emphasizes the importance of police discretion.

Source: Lawrence W. Sherman and Richard A. Berk, "The Specific Deterrent Effects of Arrest for Domestic Assault, *American Sociological Review 49* (1984) 261–262; Richard A. Berk and Phyllis J. Newton, "Does Arrest Really Deter Wife Battery? An Effort to Replicate the Findings of the Minneapolis Spouse Abuse Experiment," *American Sociological Review 49* (1984): 253–262; and Lawrence W. Sherman, *Policing Domestic Violence* (New York: Free Press, 1992).

ters, found that crime as a primary problem was involved in only 38 percent of encounters. In John Boydstun and Michael Sherry's study of San Diego's Central Division, 43 percent of calls for service involved crime, 30 percent involved peace keeping, 10 percent were related to traffic, 10 percent to medical emergencies, and the remaining 7 percent to miscellaneous problems.[17] Robert Sheehan and Gary W. Cordner summarize some of the most highly regarded studies concerning the actions taken during patrol (see Figure 5.2):

1. Michael Banton studied policing in England and America and concluded that the patrol officer is more a peace officer than a law officer.

2. Jerome Skolnick studied American police and came to the same conclusion as Banton, "that patrol work is minimally connected with legal processing."

3. James Q. Wilson studied patrol workload in Syracuse, New York, and found that only 10 percent of calls radioed to patrol units involved law enforcement, while 30 percent were for order maintenance and 38 percent were for "service."

4. Albert Reiss studied dispatch records of the Chicago Police Department and found that while citizens defined 58 percent of their calls as criminal matters, the patrol officers who responded classified only 17 percent of these calls as crimes.

5. Thomas Bercal studied calls to police in Detroit and St. Louis and found that only 16 percent of all incoming calls were crime-related.

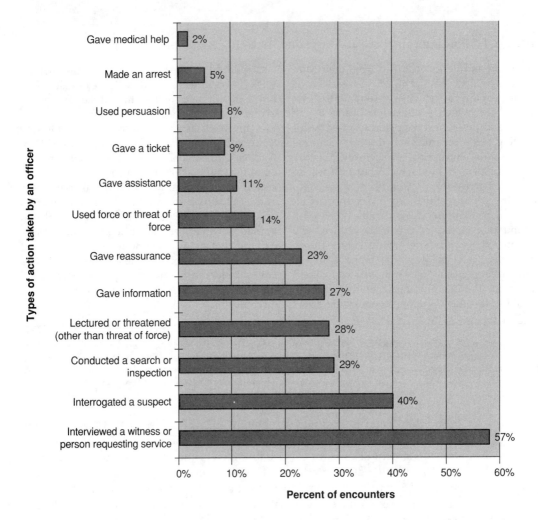

FIGURE 5.2   Officers' Actions Taken in Encounters Involving Each Type of Problem

Source: Gordon P. Whitaker, "What Is Police Work?" *Police Studies* 4(4) (1982). Reproduced with permission, MCB University Press, Ltd.

6. John A. Webster examined activities undertaken by patrol officers in an unidentified city and concluded that less than 16 percent pertained to crimes against persons or property.[18]

Foot patrol or motorized patrol constitute most of the patrol function. For decades, foot patrol was the main form of crime fighting by the police. With the growth of suburban areas and the advancement of police vehicles, foot patrols were believed to be a poor utilization of patrol resources. Such organizations as the International Association of Chiefs of Police came out in support of the motorized patrol:

The more men and more cars that are visible on the streets, the greater the potential for preventing a crime. A heavy blanket of conspicuous patrol at all times and in all parts of the city tends to suppress violations of the law. The most economical manner of providing this heavy blanket of patrol is by using one-man cars when and where they are feasible.[19]

Whether patrol officers should be assigned to one-person or two-person vehicles has been a continuous debate in policing since the 1960s. Police officers argue that two-person vehicles are safer and provide protection from a partner should danger occur. Statistics are misleading concerning the safety of one-officer versus two-officer vehicles.[20] Usually, the two-officer vehicles are assigned to high-risk areas, and backup officers are sent to high-risk calls (see Figure 5.3). Administrators frequently claim that using one-person vehicles, which means that more cars can be out, provides more visibility in a community, and, with more units on the street, respond time to incidents decreases. The most extensive research on this subject has been carried out in San Diego, where one-officer cars were substituted for two-officer cars on a unit-for-unit basis. This study found that one-officer patrol was clearly as effective and more efficient than two-officer patrol.[21]

The police took the importance of patrol for granted, because they believed that saturation policing, or filling a limited area with police, deterred crime by raising the risk of being caught. The public has always viewed the police as the central component in the effort to control crime and urban decay, and, therefore, are consistently calling for more police patrolling the streets.[22] The 1995 Crime Bill which tried to place 100,000 community policing officers on the street operated under the same basic assumptions.

However, a study conducted in Kansas City in 1972–1973 caused many to question the impact of patrol activities. Over the course of the research period, five sections of the city were allocated four times the usual number of cruising squad cars. Five other sections with comparable populations had all cruising cars removed from the streets, and police only responded to calls for assistance. Five additional sections served as a control area in which the normal number of cars was maintained.[23]

The results were somewhat startling. It was found that the crime rates in those areas with intensified policing were nearly identical to those in the normal and "depoliced" sanctions. This was true even of such crimes as auto theft, which generally takes place on the streets. The study concluded that an increase, a decrease, or the discontinuance of patrol activity substantially affected neither the level of criminal activity nor citizens' satisfaction with the police.[24] Although the validity of the Kansas City study has come under heavy criticism, the study still raises questions about the value of preventive and intensified patrol as a deterrent to crime.

In the past two decades, there have been a number of efforts to increase the effect of patrol as a deterrent to crime. The return to popularity of foot patrol accompanied the rise of community policing. It is argued that motorized patrol results in a lack of personal contact with the community and the positive feelings this contact

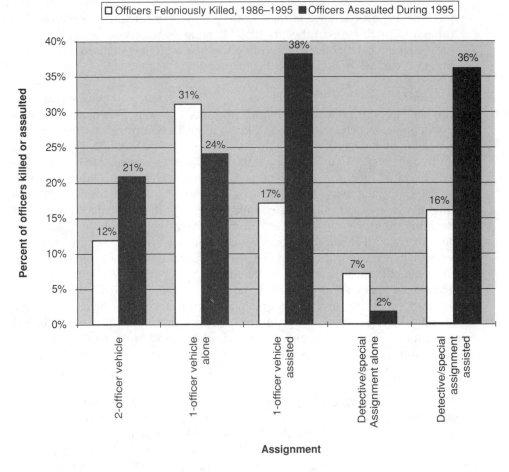

FIGURE 5.3   Officers Killed or Assaulted by Assignment

Source: Uniform Crime Reports, "Law Enforcement Officers Killed and Assaulted 1995," U.S. Department of Justice, Federal Bureau of Investigation (1997).

makes. According to Jerome Skolnick and David H. Bayley, the recent reestablish-ment of the foot patrol in a number of cities has had four meritorious effects:

1. Foot patrol is proactive, so it is more adaptable to street happenings and may stop crime before it occurs.
2. Foot patrol leads to arrests, but also police presence on foot leads to direct and indirect warnings.
3. Foot patrol can generate goodwill in the neighborhood, which raises citizen morale, reduces the fear of crime, and makes it easier for the police to perform other crime prevention functions.
4. Foot patrol seems to raise officer morale.[25]

George L. Kelling's analysis of foot patrol also found that foot patrol reduces levels of fear in a neighborhood, improves citizen satisfaction, and raises morale among officers on the patrol. Kelling adds that foot patrol is much more useful in cities, such as Boston, where population density is high than it is where population density is low and that it is more useful at some times of the day than it is at other times.[26]

Aggressive patrol includes a variety of forms, ranging from programs that encourage citizens to identify their valuables to "sting operations." According to James Q. Wilson and Barbara Bland, patrol tactics increasing the risk of arrest are associated with crime reduction. They contend that the deterrent of the police on crime depends more on what police officers do when employed at a crime scene rather than how many officers are employed there.[27]

Aggressive patrol strategies have been found to be effective in San Diego and New York City. In San Diego, an aggressive patrol strategy of field interrogations and street stops was found to be associated with a significant decrease in burglary, robbery, theft, auto theft, assault, sex crimes, and malicious mischief. This strategy particularly appeared to be an effective deterrent with young and opportunistic offenders. In New York, officers working high crime districts in street clothes constituted only 5 percent of the officers in those districts, but made over 18 percent of the felony arrests. Significantly, these officers made more than half of the robbery arrests and nearly 40 percent of the burglary and auto theft arrests.[28]

Another patrol strategy is directed patrol. This strategy involves redirecting patrol officers to those areas with high crime or the highest calls for service. The Denver Police Department designed a new patrol plan in the 1980s stressing directed patrol. Under Denver's plan, patrol teams are given to lower ranking officers, and their activity is based on the police services needed in that area.[29]

In the 1990s, hitting the "hot spots of crime" and "police crackdowns" are variations of the directed patrol strategy, which have gained popularity.[30] According to Larry Sherman, hitting the hot spots of crime is based on the assumption that "police visibility can make a difference if concentrated at high crime places and times." Sherman adds that "when police have taken that approach, evaluation findings have generally shown police can reduce, or at least displace, the targeted crime problem."[31]

Sherman cites the Minneapolis Hot Spots Patrol Experiment in 1988–1989 to evaluate the effectiveness of increased but unpredictable police presence. In this experiment, there was three hours a day of intermittent and unpredictable police presence applied to 55 of the worst 110 hot spot intersections in the city selected at random. The other 55 received normal patrol coverage, typically in response to citizen calls for assistance or service. This study found that the overall impact on reported crime was modest but statistically significant at 13 percent; some of the more serious crimes like robbery had a 20 percent impact. Further evaluation of this project revealed the value of frequent rotation across different hot spots, rather than long spells of patrol at a hot spot; there were diminishing returns for more than ten minutes of police presence at a hot spot.[32]

In Jersey City, an evaluation was conducted in 1993 of a drug enforcement strategy that focused on "hot spots" of drug activity. Using narcotics sales arrests, drug-related emergency calls for service, and narcotics tip-line information over a six month period, as well as computer mapping techniques, this study identified 56 hot spots of drug activity. Although these hot spots made up only 4.4 percent of the street sections and intersections in the city, they accounted for 45 percent of narcotics sales arrests and 46 percent of emergency services. In the experimental hot spots, it was found that such a drug enforcement strategy can have success in reducing disorder or emergency calls for service without necessarily leading to displacement of crime problems to surrounding areas.[33]

Police crackdowns involve massively increasing police presence or enforcement activity.[34] In refuting the traditional argument that crackdowns merely push crime to other locations, Sherman cites a review of 18 police crackdowns around the United States and in five other countries, which found that 15 were successful and revealed little evidence of displacement. He argues that "the key to making crackdowns work is to keep them short and unpredictable.[35]

The most effective means of patrol remains an on-going debate in policing. What is not debated are the consequences of no patrol at all. In every city which has had a police strike, including Boston and Liverpool in 1919, Montreal in 1969, Helsinki in 1973, and even Copenhagen when it was occupied by the Nazis, the same thing happened: all hell broke loose.[36]

Traffic Units

The primary responsibilities of a traffic unit are the enforcement of traffic laws, the enforcement of parking violations, and the investigation of motor vehicle accidents. Members of the public usually have two questions when they think of traffic enforcement. First, do the police really have a **quota** of tickets they are expected to issue? Second, what will the growing awareness in the 1980s and 1990s about the driver under the influence of alcohol or other substances mean to their chances of being stopped or penalized?

Police administrators will never publicly admit that a quota system exits in the area of traffic enforcement, but they know that violations occur constantly. They also know that the use of enforcement is one of the most effective means to get the bad driver off the road and to keep accidents, injuries, and fatalities to a minimum. To accomplish this objective, many departments set standards that they believe an average officer can achieve, including the number of tickets issued. No problems occur as long as the traffic officer stays close to this standard. However, if the officer should drop substantially in ticket production, the officer is likely to be counselled and later may face some type of discipline. At the same time, the administrator tells the public, "There are no quotas here, only standards."

Some states have laws prohibiting any type of quota requirements. For example on July 1, 1985, a law was enacted in Iowa in response to a requirement from the head of the state patrol that troopers acquire a certain number of points each month. A predetermined number of points had been given for each traffic violation; the more serious the violation, the more points a trooper would collect. The new law stated:

A political subdivision or agency of the state shall not order, mandate, require, or in other manner, directly or indirectly, suggest to a peace officer employed by the political subdivision or agency that the peace officer shall issue a certain number of traffic citations, police citations, memorandums of traffic, or memorandums of faulty equipment on a daily, weekly, monthly, quarterly, or yearly basis.[37]

Organizations such as M.A.D.D. (Mothers Against Drunk Driving) and S.A.D.D. (Students Against Drunk Driving) have spearheaded the public to get tough on the drunk driver. The federal government reacted to this outcry by ordering states to raise the minimum drinking age to 21 by 1986 or lose federal highway construction funds.

Heightened public awareness has also been responsible for tough new laws concerning persons convicted of operating a vehicle while under the influence. Most states are now imposing heavy fines or mandatory jail time on offenders. Police are also conducting planned roadblocks and standardized field sobriety tests. Officers have been trained to watch for involuntary jerking of the eyeballs (Horizontal Gaze Nystagmus), to conduct standard field sobriety tests, and to be alert to subtle movements of a vehicle driven by a drunk driver.

The traffic enforcement unit and its officers are probably the least popular unit of the police department with the public, but yet the most respected because they deal in an area that is still considered in law enforcement circles as pure law enforcement. When a motorist is stopped, the officer has two choices, a citation or warning. The violation carries with it a definite punishment, a scheduled fine imposed by the court. The motorist either pays or goes to court. Plea bargaining is also a choice, but there is usually a fine or jail sentence. As one officer said:

> Imagine how a father feels as he drives down a street with his wife and two children and is stopped. He has a good job and is involved in many volunteer programs throughout the community. On this day, though, he is stopped by a traffic officer for speeding. He is counselled in front of his wife and children, which causes him a great deal of embarrassment. On top of this, he receives a citation and must appear in court, only to find himself in a courtroom with petty thieves and other violators. How would you feel? To maintain his own self-respect, he blames the traffic cop. He reasons, "Why in the hell don't they do real police work and make the streets safe for us to walk at night rather than harass us good citizens who pay their salaries?"[38]

Traffic accident investigation has become as specialized as homicide investigation, and can involve weeks of advanced training. Initially, all officers receive their training while at the academy. The next level of training is Advanced Traffic Accident Investigation School. During this weeklong school, the officer learns how to calculate basic speed skids, detail accident scene measurements, and conduct lamp analysis which determines if the headlights were on or if brake lights were working at the time of the accident. Next, the officer attends a two week Technical Accident

Investigation School. The officer learns how to work with formulas to calculate speed from combination speed skids and critical speed scuffs, speed from uphill or downhill vehicle vaults, and the cause of an accident from almost any conceivable angle. In the next school, the officer learns accident reconstruction. This involves reconstructing an accident from another officer's accident report. The next step for the Accident Reconstructionist is to attend specialized schools in a variety of topics ranging from motorcycle, pedestrian, bus, and construction machinery to bicycle accidents.[39]

Investigation

Patrol officers typically conduct their own investigation, unless the case requires extensive follow-up, search warrants, or specialized training to conduct a thorough investigation or interview. Some specialized areas include arson, homicide, fraud, rape, drugs, kidnapping, and child abuse investigation. The line officer is essentially a preliminary investigator, gathering information, evidence, and witnesses' names and interviews. The officer makes out her or his preliminary case reports and then turns the matter over to the investigator for follow-up. Usually the type of crime determines which investigator takes over the case. Investigations are generally divided into two main groups, property crimes and crimes against persons. Each can be further divided into subdivisions categorized by the crimes investigated. The follow-up investigation process includes four steps:

1. The investigator checks to see that the preliminary information report was thoroughly done.
2. He or she continues investigation of those leads that have surfaced.
3. The investigator works to link the crime with others of a similar type.
4. If an arrest is made, he or she prepares a case for prosecution.[40]

The status of the investigation is determined by how the case is classified. The investigator has three classification options available: (1) closed, which indicates that no further investigation will be devoted to the case; that is, there has been an out-of-court settlement, the victim has refused to pursue charges, or an arrest has been made; (2) suspended, where all solvability factors have been exhausted warranting no further investigation; and (3) open, which indicates a continued investigation.[41] Some major cases may remain open for months or even years.

Despite the glamorous roles portrayed on television and in the movies, the job of an investigator is tedious, with much time spent following-up various leads. A two-year study by the Rand Corporation described a number of shortcomings within the investigative unit. The study involved 23 police departments, and the results showed that investigators gave only slight attention to at least half of all the serious cases reported. Much of the investigator's time was consumed by follow-up duties done after an arrest had been made and a case cleared. Additionally, the study showed that information given to the first officer at the scene was more important to the solving of a crime than the follow-up information obtained by an investigator.[42] Although the validity of this study has been seriously questioned, it does highlight some of the problems of detective work.

The Rand study went on to recommend Managing Criminal Investigations (MCI), a managerial system that grades cases according to their solvability. Solvability factors, such as—Is there a witness? Is a suspect named or known? Can a suspect be identified? Are each given a numerical weight? The total weight of all solvability factors determines the disposition of a case. Cases with little or no evidence to work with receive a low score and are inactivated immediately, conserving investigative resources for cases that are more likely to be solved by investigative efforts. Under this program, the responding patrol officer is responsible for much of the follow-up activity that traditionally has been reserved for detectives.[43]

Skolnick and Bayley contend that "crimes are not solved—in the sense of offenders arrested and prosecuted—through criminal investigations conducted by police departments." It is far more typical to solve crimes "because offenders are immediately apprehended or someone identifies them specifically—a name, an address, a license plate number. If neither of those things happen," they add, "the chances that any crime will be solved fall to less than one in ten."[44]

Even with all the criticisms of investigation, veteran police officers invariably reminisce about the "good old days" when they served in this capacity. One officer said, "The thrill of being assigned a serious crime, with little to go on, and then solving it is hard to match." He told about being assigned a burglary case, in which two safes had been drilled open and a large amount of money taken. Since it was still the middle of the night (about 3 A.M.), he saved some of the metal safe shavings and went to all the motels in the area looking for suspicious persons and checking vehicle plates. Finding that a man suspected of drilling safes had checked into one of the motels, he waited for him to check out, then vacuumed the entire room, and found one metal shaving on the carpet. The shaving was later matched to the shavings from the burglary—the man was arrested and the money was recovered.[45]

The office of investigator is a prestigious position and a mark of success in most departments. He or she who is selected as an investigator, or a detective, has the satisfaction of being elevated above one's colleagues to a job that requires particular skills and that is regarded inside and outside of policing as being police work par excellence. It also usually represents the first step up the promotion ladder. The position provides closure and satisfaction for the investigator who, unlike the line officer, stays involved with a case until prosecution is complete. In addition, being an investigator has a certain anonymity, shedding the stigma and visibility of the uniform. In some departments, punishment for wrongdoing is being placed back into patrol. Finally, being selected as an investigator is like joining an elite club. Hanging around together, detectives develop their own argot and even establish rituals of membership, generally involving drinking.[46]

Investigators do have stressors which line officers do not have. Detectives must produce arrests. For example, an open murder case can bring tremendous public pressure on the chief and therefore the investigator. An ultimate embarrassment is when an investigator is removed from the case because of lack of progress. Child abuse detectives, like homicide investigators, can be traumatized by the constant exposure to violence. Unlike patrol officers, investigators stay in continuous contact with victims, vicariously experiencing their frustrations and pain during the entire case proceedings. What can be more emotionally wrenching than interviewing a four year old about how her stepfather was raping her?

Today, in an attempt to bring about more productive work by investigators, many police agencies are using computer-aided investigative management software to establish solvability factors and to prioritize incoming cases. This software also keeps track of each investigator's caseload and determines the investigator's productivity.

Specialized Units

Large police organizations have a number of specialized units that handle technical or special operational tasks. General terms will be used in our discussion, as departments tend to give various names to these units. Tactical units, or special operations units, are usually assigned special assignments. For example, in a college community a series of rapes occurred near campus. Police formed a special operations unit, the sole duty of which was to patrol the college area and to solve rape cases.

SWAT teams or special weapons and tactics teams are common in most large city police departments. Because of the complex nature of high-risk incidents, SWAT team members are specifically trained to respond to such incidents rapidly. SWAT teams are called to handle hostage situations, cases in which persons have barricaded themselves in a building, terrorist incidents, dignitary protection, serious felony arrest situations, and drug raids. Swat teams in large departments have the luxury of a tactical unit on duty around-the-clock, but in smaller departments, the members may be scattered throughout different divisions, on different shifts, or off-duty. The team may be comprised of six or eight members, as illustrated in Figure 5.4.

Tactical teams are well organized, trained to work as a unit, and equipped with high-powered assault weapons. They have at their disposal chemical agents that can be launched or delivered by hand, and distraction devices that stun the potential assailant with a bright flash and loud bang. The team effort and proper use of equipment provides the safety margin for the team's members. Proper selection of personnel is important for the success of the team. James H. McGee explains the ten commandments for tactical teams:

Commandment #1

Thou shall not select for athletic ability at the expense of experience and maturity.

Commandment #2

Thou shalt select team leaders on the basis of skill and ability, not rank.

Commandment #3

Thou shalt not emphasize equipment over training, nor spend scarce funds on gadgets.

Six-Person Team

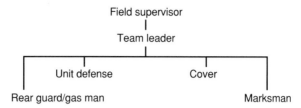

Eight-Person Team

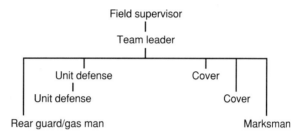

FIGURE 5.4 **Diagrams of Six- and Eight-Person Teams**

Source: Jeffrie Jacobs, *S.W.A.T. Tactics* (Boulder: Paladin, 1983) 1.

Commandment #4

Thou shalt train to produce "situational awareness."

Commandment #5

Thou shalt work with the hostage negotiators, not against them.

Commandment #6

Thou shall not confuse sniper elements with assault or entry elements.

Commandment #7

Thou shalt not "get cute" with assault plans.

Commandment #8

Thou shalt not clear a building in elements of less than two men.

Commandment #9

Thou shalt "go dynamic" at the moment the team is brought under fire.

Commandment #10

Thou shalt not kill, except in accordance with deadly force rules.[47]

Undercover operations can be one of the most exciting and, at the same time, the most stressful of assignments. One example of undercover work is a "sting" operation, in which officers establish a storefront for purchasing stolen goods while secretly videotaping the transactions. In Phoenix, such an operation called Operation Thunderbolt involved 54 police agencies, recovered nearly $2 million of stolen goods, and led to the indictment of 130 suspects.[48]

There has been considerable empirical examination of undercover operations.[49] Gary Marx contends that undercover operations have increased significantly since the 1980s.[50] Jerome H. Skolnick examined the deceptive tactics involved in police covert activities.[51] Several studies have investigated the effects of being assigned to the avidly sought and highly valued undercover police operations. This type of assignment provides many temptations in terms of moral dilemmas,[52] criminal inducements and entrapment,[53] and corruption.[54] Mark R. Pogrebin and Eric D. Poole, in an examination of three federal law enforcement agencies and eight municipal police departments located in the Denver metropolitan area, found that "undercover operatives face both professional and personal risks in the deceptive roles they assume in their assignment."[55] One of the threats of undercover work, especially for those operatives who live under false pretenses for long periods of time, can be such that they take over the role of being a criminal. Two federal agents explain:

> I identified very strongly with the bad guys…Even though these people were breaking the law, they had some fairly good reasons for doing it.… I realized everything wasn't black and white. Everything became kind of gray…
>
> It didn't take me long to get into the way of thinking like the crooks I was running with. I started identifying with these people very quickly.… [P]art of it was identifying with them and part of it was trying to fit in with them.[56]

SUPPORT FUNCTIONS

Persons assigned to **support functions** are those personnel who provide assistance to the line functions or the chief of police. Large departments have a number of support units, including training and staff development, inspection and internal affairs, research and special projects, public relations, budget, and community service.

Community Services

To gain support from the community, police have established community service units. The main emphasis of these units, which is part of the larger emphasis on community-based policing, is to break down the barrier of prejudice and hostility between the police and the public and to assist the members of the public in fighting crime in their own neighborhoods.

Neighborhood Crime Watchers are made up of people organized by police in their neighborhoods to help each other in reducing crime, especially property crimes such as burglary and theft. The police provide training on how citizens can secure their homes and protect themselves and on how best to report suspicious activity to the police.

Operation Identification is a program started in the early 1960s in Monterey Park, California. Versions of this successful program, which involves the engraving of a unique identification number on valuable property, has spread nationwide. The number is recorded by one of three groups: the local police, the national Sheriff's Association, or the International Association of Chiefs of Police. If the property is stolen, the number can help identify the property and aid in its return to its rightful owner. The number can also help police gather physical evidence to prosecute the persons involved.[57]

Community services also takes such forms as fixed substations, as in Santa Ana, California; Directed Response Teams (DART), as in Houston; and ministations, as in Detroit. Santa Ana's substations functions both as community group meeting areas and as centers for the dissemination of crime prevention information; Houston's DART program integrates patrol, criminal investigation, and intelligence collection; and Detroit's mini-stations are the primary response centers for organized community crime prevention programs.[58]

Community service personnel further perform various public-speaking functions throughout the community or assign other police personnel to these duties. In addition, they coordinate open houses, tours, and various police demonstrations. Community policing is more extensively evaluated later in this chapter.

Internal Staff

Internal staff members are those responsible for training and staff development, recruitment, testing of recruits, research and special projects, public relations, budget preparation and purchasing, and internal affairs.

The internal affairs unit causes the most concern among police officers. The unit, usually responsible only to the chief of police, handles complaints against officers and monitors any signs of corruption or misconduct by officers. Some departments have set up integrity tests to check on the officer in an everyday situation. Chapter 10 describes several of these tests. Police unions have reacted to internal affairs units and their activities by establishing guidelines that must be followed during internal investigations. The chief of police in small departments usually assigns the investigation to the detective bureau or to a specific officer. Small departments must also follow guidelines or face appeals or unfair labor practice suits.

Auxiliary Services

Auxiliary services include such areas as records, communications, crime laboratory, jail management, computers, and evidence maintenance. Growth in the application of computers to policing and the advances in communication are making these areas the fastest changing in modern police organizations.

The dominant technical advance in the 1980s and 1990s is the computer. Today computers assist the police in virtually every aspect of the job. The **National Crime Information Center (NCIC)** is a major computer network managed by the FBI, linking police agencies across the country. Information available through this computer network includes wanted persons, missing persons, and stolen property. Box 5.2 presents an example of how police use computers today.

CRIME CONTROL STRATEGIES

This chapter has examined how the police do not prevent crime. The ineffectiveness of the police, according to David H. Bayley, "in preventing crime comes from evaluations of the impact on crime of the three core strategies of contemporary policing: street patrolling by uniformed officers, rapid response to emergency calls, and expert investigation of crime by detectives. These are the activities," Bayley asserts, "that police themselves believe to be essential for protecting public safety. These are the functions they say will prevent crime. Unfortunately, there is no evidence that they do."[59]

It can be argued, of course, that the damning conclusion that the police are not preventing crime is based on flawed research done for the most part during the 1970s. Bayley concludes that researchers at that time or in the past two decades have been unable to show "that the number of police, the amount of money spent on police, or the methods police use had any effect on crime."[60]

There is no question that crime prevention or the reduction of crime in the United States is more difficult now than in the past because of the problems asso-

---

BOX 5.2   Use of a Police Computer

Police are called to the scene of an armed robbery. The computer at the dispatch center is keeping track of the officers' response time to the scene and length of time they will stay. During the initial investigation, police find a fingerprint on an item touched by one of the two robbers and also find that one robber called the other "Steak." Back at the station, officers write their reports on a word processor. By checking the nickname file in the computer, a detective finds that "Steak" is the nickname used by a person known to police to commit violent crimes. The single fingerprint is then placed into an automated fingerprint system, which classifies the print and checks every print in its memory bank. The computer identifies the print as belonging to another person with prior arrests for robbery. Another check of the computer provides addresses on both suspects. At the end of the investigation, both suspects are arrested and a NCIC wanted check is made. It is found that both are wanted in another state for robbery. Even as the suspects are booked into jail, a computer will track them until they are convicted or released.

ciated with the sale and use of drugs, the increased rate of possession of guns among both juveniles and adults, and the ever expanding number of gangs migrating from urban areas throughout the nation. Herman Goldstein explains how these problems are all related to drug traffic and use:

> The police, especially in our large urban areas, are currently struggling with the overwhelming problems associated with the sale and use of drugs. They are under enormous pressure to deal with indiscriminate shootings of innocent citizens, an escalation of violence among drug sellers, frequent involvement of children in both drug use and sale, and the concern of white neighborhoods terrorized by drug-related activities. And all of this has occurred after at least two decades in which violence and street-order problems already ranked high among the nation's major concerns, and police have been under intense pressure to deal with them.[61]

The most hopeful possibility for an effective crime prevention and reduction strategy is expanding community-oriented policing (COP) and problem-oriented policing (POP). The most troubling crime prevention and control strategies are policing repeat offenders (especially those who have been to prison) and controlling violence among juveniles.

Community Policing

The outline of a new direction for policing, broadly termed **community policing,** but also known variously as community-oriented policing (COP) or problem-oriented policing (POP), but also sometimes called strategic policing or neighborhood-oriented policing, emerged in the 1980s in response to a rising tide of crime. This approach affirms the importance of police and citizens working together to control crime and maintain order and is committed to building strong relationships with institutions and individuals in the community. A 1993 survey sponsored by the National Institute of Justice (NIJ) of more than 2,000 law enforcement agencies found strong support throughout the nation for community policing coupled with a need for developing training for practitioners. Almost half the respondents had either implemented community policing (19 percent) or were in the process of doing so (28 percent). The implementation of community policing was most likely to be reported by medium (50 or more personnel) and large (100 or more personnel) agencies. Regionally, community policing was found most frequently in the West, followed by the South, Midwest, and Northeast.[62] Police chiefs and sheriffs overwhelmingly endorsed community policing and were especially positive about such benefits as improved physical environment in neighborhoods, more positive public attitudes toward the police, decreased potential for conflict between citizens and police, increased officer or deputy satisfaction, and reduced crime rates.[63]

There are a number of operational steps in implementing community policing:

1. Police officers must be assigned full-time to beats manageable by foot.
2. Community police officers should establish networks of contacts with citizens throughout their neighborhoods.
3. Police should create precinct and neighborhood committees to consult with about local problems and needs.
4. Community police officers must be given time to carry out their responsibilities for consultation, problem solving, and mobilization.
5. The community must be given the freedom to set their own hours, rather than conform to a mandated shift schedule.
6. Police should make themselves available for meetings with citizens on a daily basis.
7. Police should coordinate police operations so that those officers unfamiliar with a neighborhood would undertake law enforcement action only under the guidance of local community police officers.
8. Local commanders should adapt the use of their resources, especially personnel, to fit the needs of their particular areas and be receptive to suggestions made by community police officers about the use of these resources.
9. Front-line supervisors must understand that they are responsible for facilitating and supervising community police officers' activities.[64]

Problem-oriented policing encourages the police to let the community define the problems receiving their attention, but it is not wedded to a particular strategy. Instead, this problem-oriented approach urges the police to address the underlying causes of problems. Police who practice problem-oriented policing first go through their statistics and group all similar incidents together. They then determine whether the offenses share any common underlying features. For example, knowing that large numbers of robberies or burglaries occur in a specific area shortly after school is dismissed should suggest to the police that students may be responsible for the offenses. Second, the police examine the problem, and collect information from a variety of public and private sources such as school, transportation services, private police, businesses, and citizens. Using these data, police officers analyze the basic character of the problem, try to determine its causes, and develop a range of possible solutions. Third, police officers work with all involved parties to come up with a plan of action. Schools, businesses, services agencies, and citizens are approached to develop a workable plan to solve the problem. Finally, police officers evaluate their results to determine whether the plan actually worked.[65]

Herman Goldstein's *Problem-Oriented Policing* defines the mission of problem-oriented policing:

In a narrow sense, it focuses directly on the substance of policing—on the problems that constitute the business of the police and how they handle them. This focus establishes a better balance between the reactive and proactive aspects of policing. It also creates a vehicle for making more effective use of the community and rank-and-file officers in getting the police job done. In its broadest context, problem-oriented policing is a comprehensive plan for improving policing in which the high priority attached to addressing substantive problems shapes the police agency, influencing all changes in personnel, organization, and procedures. Thus, problem-oriented policing not only pushes policing beyond current improvement efforts, it calls for a major change in the direction of these efforts.[66]

These various approaches in community-based policing are found in efforts by the police to support the development of community-based programs, to pursue activities that improve the social fabric of the community, to undertake projects in conjunction with private industry that improve social control in the community, to have direct contact with citizens in order to reduce the fear of crime, and to provide programs for crime victims and others who need police services. All the efforts are ultimately designed to promote community spirit and empowerment.[67]

One of the major advantages of COP and POP if it was actually implemented throughout police departments in this nation would be that it could have profound implications for reducing the alienation between the police and minority communities. As suggested in Chapter 2, the police bear responsibility for contributing to this alienation by how they have policed the "other America." The service model, purported to be the emerging role of police officers in COP and POP, could do a great deal to heal the hostility felt toward the police in minority communities.[68]

The theory of COP and POP is wonderful but its application to the daily operations of police departments is another matter. As a review of the materials in this chapter reflects, line functions of police departments are related more to law enforcement, and little evidence exists to show that many departments have figured out how to effectively implement COP or POP in many line functions. Support functions, on the other hand, are where COP or POP has been widely implemented throughout the nation.[69]

Even if such implementation problems as the lack of clarity about what COP and POP mean, the difficulty of involving other agencies, and the task of organizing the community could be overcome, the resistance of both line officers and middle managers would likely present an even more formidable obstacle. First, the "tough" image of the cop who is a crime fighter is at the very essence of the police officer's self-image. The role of the tough crime fighter is not one that will be quickly or easily relinquished. Second, the ability of police officers to handle crime in a different way will depend on their being given more conflict and dispute resolution tools than they presently have.[70] Third, there is some question at this time as to how much application a peacemaking approach would have in such crime fighting functions as drug trafficking, vice, homicides and other serious felonies, and sex crimes. Fourth, middle managers tend to have problems with community policing because they believe that it takes away from their authority, and transfers it to line officers.

Policing Repeat Offenders

The fact that a small proportion of criminals commits a disproportionately large number of crimes is a major issue in crime control policies. Several studies found that these chronic offenders commit the majority of violent crimes in their communities.[71] These few are also likely to be deeply involved in gang activity and drug trafficking. Parolees recently released from prisons further present a high-risk factor. The importance of giving close attention to parolees is increasing because of the close relationship in many states between urban gangs and street gangs. Many parolees resume gang involvement and drug trafficking as soon as they return to the community.[72]

Police department programs for repeat offenders use various combinations of reactive and proactive tactics. Reactive tactics include prioritized service of warrants against identified "career" criminals, notification of the prosecutor when an identified career criminal is arrested, and active case supplementation through development of additional witnesses, evidence, or information about other cases against the offender. Proactive tactics include the use of decoys, surveillance, buy–bust schemes (in which police buy drugs and then arrest sellers) and phony fencing operations.[73]

The most comprehensive local strategy for policing repeat offenders is the Repeat Offender Project (ROP), a specialized unit in Washington, DC. In May 1982, the Metropolitan Police Department in Washington adopted a selective approach to apprehending street criminals. Repeat Offender Project (ROP) was dedicated to the arrest and conviction of persons believed to be committing five or more crimes per week. In their evaluation of the program, Susan E. Martin and Lawrence W. Sherman found that ROP substantially increased the likelihood of arrest for persons targeted. ROP arrestees had longer and more serious histories of prior arrests than a comparison sample of persons arrested by officers in other police units. The ROP arrestees were also more likely to be prosecuted and convicted on felony charges and more likely to be incarcerated. Martin and Sherman concluded that the creation of selective apprehension units provides a promising new strategy for urban departments.[74] Although this program was abolished by a new police chief, other police departments across the nation have adopted similar programs.[75]

The expose in Box 5.3 of the Rapid Development Unit in Washington, DC raises enormous constitutional, ethical, and justice questions and reveals policing at its very worse. It represents systemic police deviancy and shows the police to be a thug-like operation oppressing the poor and minorities in order to protect the powerful and wealthy segments of society. Perhaps in a totalitarian state this approach to policing might be acceptable, but it does not appear to have any redeeming features in a free and democratic society.

What then can be said about programs designed to place ex-offenders on strict surveillance; to harass problematic citizens, such as gang members; and to arrest these individuals if there is any cause at all to think that they committed a crime? A functionalist response would be that rigorously policing repeat offenders would seem to bode well for reducing crime in a society. As research has substantiated,

BOX 5.3   Policing the Ghetto Underclass

For several years, William J. Chambliss and students have been riding with the Rapid Deployment Unite (RDU) of the Washington, D.C. metropolitan Police. Members of the RDU are described by other officers on the force as "Dirty Harrys" and "very serious bad-ass individuals."

The RDU is deployed in three patrol cars with two officers in each car. They patrol the urban ghetto, that area of the city where 40 percent of the African American population lives below the poverty level. The RDU uses three activities—the "rip," vehicular stops, and serving warrants—to focus its efforts at crime control. The "rip" involves the use of undercover agents to buy drugs and to identify the person who sold the drugs. The goal of undercover agents, of course, is to maintain their cover. The vehicular stops takes place with the RDU patrolling the ghetto looking for cars with young African American men in them. They initially looked for newer-model cars, but eventually came to the conclusion that drug dealers were leaving their fancy cars at home to avoid vehicular stops. Accordingly, it became commonplace to stop any car with young African American men in it. Any minor infraction is an excuse. The officers reported confidentially to the researchers that if the officers feel strongly that they should stop a car, they will stop it and break a taillight as they approach the car. The third major activity of the RDU is to carry out search warrants. And they are not gentle about it:

Five RDU officers enter an apartment about 10:45 P.M. Before entering the officers draw their guns, break down the door and rush in. The suspect is spotted, guns are pointed at him and he is told to "lie down. NOW." The suspect is handcuffed and taken outside. An elderly woman begins screaming and crying. She tells the officers to put their guns away. An officer goes to her, his gun still drawn, and tells her to "shut up or I'll pop you in the jaw." He physically forces her to lie down on the floor face down. The officers leave the apartment, put the suspect in the car and take him to the precinct for booking.

Chambliss contends that the intensive surveillance of African American neighborhoods and the much different pattern of surveillance of white neighborhoods result in institutionalizing racism by defining the problem of crime generally and drug use in particular as a problem of young African Americans. What this does, he says, is ghettoizes the African American community and destroys any possibility for normal family and community relations. Defining young African American and Latino men as a criminal group, they are arrested for minor offenses over and over again and given criminal records. This accumulation of criminal offenses then justifies long prison sentences. The culture of the African American community and the African American family "is then blamed for high rates of illegitimate children and crime. Crime control polices," argues Chambliss, "are a major contributor to the disruption of the family, the prevalence of single parent families, and children raised without a father in the ghetto" and an inability to get the jobs that are still available.

Source: William J. Chambliss, "Policing the Ghetto Underclass: The Politics of Law and Law Enforcement" © 1994 by The Society for the Study of Social Problems. Reprinted from *Social Problems Vol. 41*, No. 2 (May 1994): 177–194, by permission.

repeat offenders do commit a majority of crimes in a community, but the crime control model seems to replace totally the due process model in these programs. Harassing individuals for what they have done in the past or what they might do in the future is very problematic in a democratic and free society.

The Challenge of Policing Violent Juveniles

In the 1990s, a new troubling problem with juveniles took place when it became evident that violent juvenile crime was increasing. Between 1990 and 1994, the violent crime index for juveniles under 18 increased by 26 percent, which was over four times the increase for individuals 18 years of age or older. Most alarming was that juvenile arrests for murder increased by 14.6 percent, compared with 5.6 percent for adults.[76]

John J. DiIulio, Jr. adds that the United States is "sitting on a demographic crime bomb." By the year 2000, DiIulio predicts that there will be an additional 500,000 youngsters between 14 and 17. He contends that this "large population of seven- to 10-year old boys now growing up fatherless, Godless, and jobless, and surrounded by deviant, delinquent, and criminal adults, will give rise to a new and more vicious group of predatory street criminals than the nation has ever known." He adds that "we must therefore be prepared to contain the explosion's force and limit its damage."[77]

In a 1995 interview, Alfred Blumstein provided good news and bad news about the trends in youth crime. His good news was that "the number of fifteen- to nineteen-years-old males—the group that commits the most crime—is bottoming out this year and has already contributed to recent decreases in homicide rates around the country." The bad news, according to Blumstein, "makes for a grim, chilling picture. Between 1995–2010, this population cohort will grow by some 30 percent, and many of them will have grown up in poverty to single mothers."[78]

Blumstein contends that the crime rate changed dramatically in 1985 with the introduction of crack cocaine, especially in urban areas. This "gave rise to a large demand for crack, and the recruitment of lots of people, particularly young people, into the market to sell the crack."[79] Juveniles soon began carrying guns, adds Blumstein, in order:

> to protect themselves because they were carrying lots of valuable stuff; they were in no position to call the police if somebody set upon them. The more kids started carrying guns, the more the incentive for the other kids to start carrying.
>
> This gave rise to an escalating arms race out in the streets among the kids. Kids are not very good at resolving disputes verbally, as most middle-class folks are. When you look in school yards, we're always seeing pushing and shoving escalate into shooting. That's really contributed to what has been the most dramatic change in the crime story in the past five to ten years: the dramatic growth of homicide by young people of young people.[80]

This highly respected criminal justice researcher is arguing that a long-term decline in homicide rates by young people against young people depends both on getting the guns out of the hands of the young and on addressing the fact that we will have an increasing number of youths who are being socialized into high-risk settings. The police, then, will be handling a two-fold responsibility. First, they will be charged with controlling the juvenile crime wave characterized by increased numbers of offenders and violence. Second, at the same time that there are more children from high-risk settings committing violent acts and trafficking drugs, the police will be asked to get the guns out of the hands of juveniles.

The issue of gun control as it relates to juveniles will be no easier to manage than it has been in adult justice, and it is easy for the police to cross the line of what is constitutionally permitted. Some of the possible strategies to improve gun control with juveniles are more intensive traffic enforcement in gun-crime hot spots; more raiding of crack houses; more targeting of drug trafficking gang members on the streets and an emphasis on building probable cause for a search; more surveillance around gang-controlled and senior high schools; and more community support and emphasis on community policing.[81]

SUMMARY

The methods of policing have changed significantly in the past several decades, especially in terms of the technology the police use for fighting crime. Foot patrols have generally been replaced by police cars, although this trend is now changing. Patrol officers in cars have been linked to headquarters through a radio communications network that permits much closer supervision of police work than was possible before. Computers have been introduced in most cities; some have been placed in patrol cars to allow rapid identification of stolen automobiles. Larger cities have equipped themselves with helicopters to permit rapid movement of police officers. Particularly after the civil disorders of the 1960s, a number of departments also acquired armored vehicles for use in riot situations.

One of the underlying questions of this chapter is whether policing is ready to embark on a new paradigm of community-oriented policing (COP) or problem-oriented policing (POP). This approach has received extensive acceptance across the United States in police departments, yet little evidence exists that it has fundamentally altered daily operations, especially in terms of line functions. Greater operationalization of COP and POP in the daily operations of police departments will require the resolution of several implementation problems. To extend this discussion a step further, there is scattered evidence that COP and POP have reduced crime, but the effectiveness of this community policing paradigm simply has not received sufficient empirical evaluation. Two other crime reduction strategies, policing repeat offenders and reducing juvenile violence, have real constitutional questions about the ethics of their approaches and little evidence of their effectiveness.

KEY TERMS

community policing

community services

line functions

National Crime Information Center (NCIC)

problem-oriented policing

quota

support functions

tactical teams

DISCUSSION QUESTIONS

1. Do you believe community policing will really work? How can it be implemented more fully in police daily operations?

2. If we do not move in the direction of COP or POP, what directions do you suggest?

3. Undercover work has all types of problems. Do we need it? What are its ethical problems? What effect does it have on operatives?

4. Traffic enforcement is one of the more questioned areas of policing. Do you believe that there should be quotas? Are too many tickets being given today?

5. Would you like to be part of a tactical team? Are they too much involved in the militarization of policing?

FURTHER READING

Alpert, Geoffrey P. and Mark H. Moore. "Measuring Police Performance in the New Paradigm of Policing." *Performance Measures for the Criminal Justice System*. Discussion Papers from the Bureau of Justice Statistics—Princeton University Study Group on Criminal Justice, 1993.

Chambliss, William J. "Policing the Ghetto Underclass: The Politics of Law and Law Enforcement." *Social Problems 41* (May 1994): 177–194.

Goldstein, Herman. *Problem-Oriented Policing*. Philadelphia: Temple UP, 1990.

Mastrofski, Stephen D., Robert E. Worden, and Jeffrey B. Snipes. "Law Enforcement in a Time of Community Policing." *Criminology 33* (1995): 539–563.

Trojanowicz, Robert C., and Bonnie Bucqueroux. *Community Policing*. Cincinnati: Anderson, 1990.

Sherman, Lawrence W. "The Police." *Crime*. Eds. James Q. Wilson and Joan Petersilia. San Francisco: Institute for Contemporary Studies, 1995: 327–348.

Skolnick, Jerome H., and David H. Bayley. *The New Blue Line: Police Innovation in Six American Cities*. New York: Free Press, 1986.

ENDNOTES

1. Quint C. Thurman and Michael D. Reisig, "Community-Oriented Research in an Era of Community-Oriented Policing," *American Behavioral Scientist 39* (Mar.–Apr. 1996): 1.

2. Thurman and Reisig, 1.

3. Thurman and Reisig, 1.

4. Stephen B. Perrott and Donald M. Taylor, "Crime Fighting, Law Enforcement and Service

Provider Role Orientations in Community-Based Police Officers," *American Journal of Police 14* (1995): 1,973.

5. Michael J. Palmiotto and Michael E. Donahue, "Evaluating Community Policing: Problems and Prospects," *Policing Studies 18* (1995): 33.

6. Jihong Zhao, Quint C. Thurman, and Nicholas P. Lovrich, "Community-Oriented Policing Across the U.S.: Facilitators and Impediment to Implementation," *American Journal of Police 14* (1995): 11–29.

7. Susan Sadd and Randolph M. Grinc, *Implementation Challenges in Community Policing: Innovative Neighborhood-Oriented Policing in Eight Cities* (Washington, DC: National Institute of Justice, 1996) 1.

8. See Perrott and Taylor, 173–195; and Palmiotto and Donahue, 33–53.

9. Brian A. Reaves, *Local Police Departments 1993*, U.S. Department of Justice, Office of Justice Programs, Bureau of Justice Statistics (April 1996) 3.

10. Gary W. Cordner, Larry K. Gaines, and Victor E. Kappeler, *Police Operations: Analysis and Evaluation* (Cincinnati: Anderson, 1996) 51.

11. "Law Enforcement Officers Killed and Assaulted 1995," *Uniform Crime Reports*, U.S. Department of Justice, Federal Bureau of Investigation (1997): 3, 65.

12. Gary T. Klugiewicz, *Active Countermeasures Instructor Certification Manual* (Greenfield: Active Countermeasures Instructional Systems, 1997) 9.

13. Lawrence W. Sherman and Richard A. Berk, "The Specific Deterrent Effects of Arrests for Domestic Assault," *American Sociological Review 49* (1984): 261–262.

14. Richard A. Berk and Phyllis J. Newton, "Does Arrest Really Deter Wife Battery? An Effort to Replicate the Findings of the Minneapolis Spouse Abuse Experiment," *American Sociological Review 49* (1984): 253–262.

15. Patrick R. Gartin, "Examining Differential Officer Effects in the Minneapolis Domestic Violence Experiment," *American Journal of Police 14* (1995): 107. For the influence of gender and mental state on police discretion, see Mary A. Finn and

Loretta J. Stalans, "The Influence of Gender and Mental State on Police Decisions in Domestic Assault Cases," *Criminal Justice and Behavior 24* (June 1997): 157–176.

16. Gordon P. Whitaker, "What is Patrol Work?" in Cordner, Gaines, and Kappeler, *Police Operations:* 56.

17. Whitaker, 62.

18. Robert Sheehan and Gary W. Cordner, *Police Administration*, 3rd ed. (Cincinatti: Anderson, 1995) 28.

19. International Association of Chiefs of Police, *A Survey of the Police Departments of Youngstown, Ohio* (Washington, DC: International Association of Chiefs of Police, 1964) 89.

20. See Carlene Wilson and Neil Brewer, "One- and Two-Person Patrols: A Review," *Journal of Criminal Justice 20* (1992): 443–454.

21. J. Boydstun, M. Sherry, and M. Moelter, *Patrol Staffing in San Diego: One- or Two-Officer Units* (Washington, DC: Police Foundation, 1977).

22. *Research Preview*, U.S. Department of Justice, Office of Justice Programs, National Institute of Justice (Jan. 1996).

23. George L. Kelling, Tony Pate, Duane Dieckman, and Charles E. Brown, *The Kansas City Preventive Patrol Experiment: A Summary Report* (Washington, DC: Police Foundation, 1974).

24. Kelling, et al.

25. Jerome Skolnick and David H. Bayley, *The New Blue Line: Police Innovation in Six American Cities* (New York: Free Press, 1986) 216.

26. George L. Kelling, *Foot Patrol* (Washington, DC: National Institute of Justice, 1991).

27. James Q. Wilson and Barbara Bland, *The Effect of the Police on Crime* (Washington, DC: U.S. Department of Justice, 1979).

28. James Q. Wilson, *Thinking About Crime*, 2nd ed. (New York: Basic, 1983) 71.

29. Skolnick and Bayley, 128.

30. Lawrence W. Sherman, "The Police," in *Crime*, ed. James Q. Wilson and Joan Petersilia (San Francisco: Institute for Contemporary Studies, 1995) 331–332.

31. Sherman, "The Police," 332.

32. Sherman, "The Police," 333.

33. National Institute of Justice, *Policing Drug Hot Spots* (Washington, DC: USGPO, 1996) 1–2.

34. National Institute of Justice, *Policing Drug Hot Spots,* 1–2.

35. National Institute of Justice, *Policing Drug Hot Spots,* 332.

36. Lawrence W. Sherman, "Attacking Crime: Police and Crime Control," *Modern Policing,* ed. Michael H. Tonry and Norval Morris. Volume 16 of *Crime and Justice: A Review of Research* (Chicago: U of Chicago P, 1992) 192–193.

37. State of Iowa, *Code of Iowa* (Des Moines: Iowa State Printing Division, 1985), chap. 321.492A.

38. Personal interview, Sept. 1986.

39. Chuck Clewell personal interview 1997.

40. Thomas Hastings, "Criminal Investigation," in *Local Government Police Management* (Washington, DC: International City Management Association, 1982) 169.

41. William B. Waegel, "Patterns of Police Investigation of Urban Crimes," in Cordner, Gaines, and Kappeler, *Police Operations,* 190.

42. Edward A. Thibault, Lawrence M. Lynch, and R. Bruce McBride, *Proactive Police Management,* 2nd ed. (Englewood Cliffs: 1990) 138–139.

43. Peter Greenwood, Jan Chaiken, and Joan Petersilia, *Summary and Policy Implications: The Criminal Investigation Process 1* (Santa Monica: Rand, 1975).

44. Skolnick and Bayley, 6.

45. Personal interview, Oct. 1985.

46. David W. Bayley *Police for the Future* (New York: Oxford UP) 57.

47. James H. McGee, "Ten Commandments For Tactical Teams," *The Best of The Police Marksman 1976 to 1994* (Montgomery: The Police Marksman Association, 1994) 41–46.

48. Herbert Jacob, *The Frustration of Policy: Responses to Crime by American Cities* (Boston: Little, Brown, 1984) 115.

49. Mark R. Pogrebin and Eric D. Poole, "Vice Isn't Nice: A Look at the Effects of Working Undercover," *Journal of Criminal Justice 21* (1993): 383–394.

50. Gary T. Marx, "When the Guards Guard Themselves: Undercover Tactics Turned Inward," *Policing and Society 2* (1992): 151–172.

51. Jerome H. Skolnick, "Deception by Police," *Criminal Justice Ethics 1* (1982): 40–54.

52. F. Schoeman, "Undercover Operations: Some Moral Questions About S. 804," *Social Inter-*action, ed. F. A. Elliston and M. Feldberg (Totowa: Rowman and Allanheld, 1985).

53. Gary T. Marx, "Who Really Gets Stung? Some Issues Raised by the New Police Undercover Work," *Moral Issues in Police Work,* ed. F. A. Elliston and M. Feinberg (Totowa: Rowman and Allanheld, 1985); and B. G. Stitt and G. James, "Entrapment: An Ethical Analysis," *Moral Issues in Police Work,* ed. F. A. Elliston and M. Feinberg.

54. M. R. Pogrebin and B. Atkins, "Some Perspectives on Police Corruption," *Legality: Morality and Ethics in Criminal Justice,* ed. N. N. Kittrie and J. Susman (New York: Praeger, 1979).

55. Pogrebin and Poole, "Vice Isn't Nice," 383.

56. Pogrebin and Poole, 388.

57. "I.A.C.P. Operation Identification, An Anniversary Report," *The Police Chief 49* (1982): 30–32.

58. Skolnick and Bayley, 212–220.

59. Bayley, 5.

60. Bayley, 5.

61. Herman Goldstein, *Problem-Oriented Policing* (Philadelphia: Temple UP, 1990) xi.

62. National Institute of Justice, *Community Policing Strategies* (Washington, DC: USGPO, 1995) 1.

63. National Institute of Justice 1.

64. Adapted from David H. Bayley, "The Best Defense," *Fresh Perspectives* (Washington, DC: Police Executive Research Forum, 1992): 7–8.

65. William Spelman and John E. Eck, *Problem-Oriented Policing* (Washington, DC: U.S. Department of Justice, 1987).

66. Goldstein, 32.

67. G. P. Alpert and M. H. Moore, "Measuring Police Performance in the New Paradigm of Policing," Performance Measures for the Criminal Justice System: Discussion Papers from the BJS-Princeton Project (Washington, DC: US Department of Justice, 1993) 123.

68. Perrott and Taylor, 174.

69. Zhao, et al., 16.

70. Christopher Cooper, "Patrol Police Officer Conflict Resolution Processes," *Journal of Criminal Justice 25* (1997): 87–101.

71. The various cohort studies of juvenile crime consistently found this to be true. For an examination of these studies, see Clemens Bartollas, *Juvenile Delinquency,* 4th ed. (Boston: Allyn & Bacon, 1997) 37–45.

72. These observations about parolees and gang involvement are based on Bartollas' work with major Chicago gangs.

73. Susan E. Martin and Lawrence W. Sherman, "Selective Apprehension: A Police Strategy for Repeat Offenders," *Criminology 24* (1986): 155–173.

74. Martin and Sherman, 155–173.

75. Richard J. Lundman, *Police Behavior: A Sociological Perspective* (New York: Oxford UP, 1980) 218.

76. Federal Bureau of Investigation, *Uniform Crime Reports: Crime in the United States, 1994* (Washington, DC: USGPO, 1995) 223.

77. John J. DiIulio, Jr., "Arresting Ideas: Tougher Law Enforcement Is Driving Down Urban Crime," *Policy Review* (Fall 1995): 15.

78. Marie Simonetti Rosen, "A LEN Interview with Professor Alfred Blumstein," *Law Enforcement News,* John Jay College of Criminal Justice, New York, 21 (30 Apr. 1995): 10.

79. Rosen, 10.

80. Rosen, 10.

81. The first two of these are contained in Sherman, "The Police," 339–341.

6

THE RULE OF LAW

On November 22, 1988, a police officer obtained a routine warrant to search Joseph Morris' Philadelphia steak house by claiming he had watched a teenager sell marijuana outside a local high school, had followed him into the restaurant and had seen him hand a roll of cash to Morris. The officer said he saw Morris hand back a brown paper bag. The officer said he then followed the teen to the street and bought some marijuana, which the teen pulled out of the bag. After breaking down the door of the steak house with a sledgehammer, officers said they found marijuana there and arrested Morris. Based on the sworn testimony of officer Steven Brown, Morris was convicted of drug trafficking and sentenced to three years in prison.

But Brown's testimony was a skein of lies. There was no teenager, no exchange of cash or drugs inside the shop, no brown bag, and no drug buy. Last March [1995], Brown a thirteen-year veteran on the force, pleaded guilty to federal charges involving 25 cases, including the illegal search of Morris' steak house. After nearly two and a half years in prison, Morris was released. While he has his freedom, peace of mind is a little harder to come by. "It takes a lot away from you," says the 53 year-old father of five, now a self-employed carpenter. "I can't understand why these people can do anything they want and get away with it."

—Elizabeth Gleick, *Time,* September 11, 1995, 38.

It is said that it is the best of times and the worst of times for police departments in the United States. Certainly, what officer Steven Brown did to Joseph Morris represents the worst of times. It was morally and criminally wrong. Police officers are sworn to protect citizens, not to victimize them. Anytime police officers fabricate or plant evidence, perjure themselves giving court testimony, or are involved in any form of deviancy, it represents another sad day in the history of policing in the United States.

The fact is that the police are faced with certain organizational and personal objectives that encourage them to commit "noble perjury," make "chump" arrests, and "stack" and "jack-up" charges against citizens. First, as one of its basic functions, the police are expected to maintain order. It is no easy task to maintain order and, at the same time, provide suspects all their constitutional rights. Paul Chevigny defines how police sometimes resolve this dilemma: "the police are asked to keep order and control pariah groups that the public fears; at the same time, the public wants to believe that the police act lawfully. One result is that the police harass those who are "out of order," and then try to make the actions look legal."[1]

Second, the feeling exists among police officers that the rules concerning search and seizure favor the criminal and encourage the police to lie and cheat in order to win. Police also argue that the application of the exclusionary rule too frequently leads to suppression of criminal evidence and, as a result, defendants who have committed despicable crimes have their charges dismissed. Furthermore, some officers believe that this nation is losing the war on crime only because the courts have handcuffed them with technicalities and unreasonable limits on their ability to fight the enemy in our midst.[2]

Third, the problem is that the ambiguity in criminal law permits the police to interpret the legal mandates according to the demands of a particular context. Thus, according to Victor E. Kappeler, Sluder, and Alpert, the discretion available to police provides the police an opportunity to use "the law as a tool to facilitate achievement of enforcement objectives rather than as a tool to control the methods by which they reach their goals."[3] For example, they add that "identical legal infractions—can result in different outcomes depending on the motives of the police and their interpretation and application of the law."[4]

The police are charged with protecting citizens against property, violent, and victimless crimes. At the same time, they must maintain a balance between establishing effective law enforcement and ensuring due process rights of individuals. Due process rights are required by the Fourth, Fifth, Sixth, and Fourteenth Amendments to the Constitution. Most due process requirements related to the police pertain to search and seizure, arrest, and interrogation. There have been a number of landmark U.S. Supreme Court decisions in each of these areas. The very integrity of law enforcement depends on upholding constitutional guidelines in its enforcement.

SEARCH AND SEIZURE

The Fourth Amendment defines the "right of the people to be secure in their persons, houses, papers, and effects, against unreasonable searches and seizures." This Amendment sets out the restrictions on the government's ability to search for or seize any item from its citizens and protects their "legitimate expectations of privacy."[5] In addition, the Fourth Amendment states that seizures are reasonable as long as they are based on governmental interest that outweighs the intrusions upon an individual's privacy rights.[6] The government still must have convincing facts and circumstances to support intrusive invasions of an individual's privacy interests.

It is important to remember that the Fourth Amendment "protects people not places."[7] One's person, automobile, or residence are places where one has reasonable or legitimate expectations of privacy, and government intrusions into those areas fall within the meaning of the Fourth Amendment. It remains a basic constitutional rule that "searches conducted outside the judicial process, without prior approval by a judge or magistrate, are per se unreasonable under the Fourth Amendment—subject only to a few specifically established and well-developed exceptions."[8] Notwithstanding an unreasonable search, there is no Fourth Amendment protection in the absence of an expectation of privacy.[9] When officers searched trash bags left on the front curb for collection, *California v. Greenwood* found that there was no reasonable expectation of privacy.[10]

Exclusionary Rule

In a number of cases, the Supreme Court developed the **exclusionary rule,** excluding any illegally seized evidence from use in a criminal trial. The Court reasoned that it was necessary to set the standard for protection of citizens against police misconduct. The exclusionary rule has generated more controversy than nearly any other issue facing the Constitution.

The first landmark case excluding evidence seized by the police was *Weeks v. United States* (1914). Up until this case, no rule existed restricting the use of evidence in a criminal trial. Evidence received illegally was admitted into criminal trials and used to obtain convictions.[11]

Freemont Weeks was arrested for using the mail to sell lottery tickets, a federal crime. Without a warrant, Federal agents went to Weeks' home to conduct a search. They seized various articles and papers that were then turned over to the United States marshal. Federal agents returned later that day with the marshal and again searched Weeks' home without a warrant and seized letters and other articles. The basic issue in this case was whether evidence illegally obtained by federal law enforcement officers was admissible in court. The Supreme Court's decision disallowed the admission of evidence secured by an illegal search and overturned Weeks' earlier conviction. This decision concerning seizure in a federal prosecution applied only to federal cases.[12]

The Court went on to rule in *Silverthorne Lumber Company v. United States* (1920) that evidence illegally seized by federal agents could not be used to uncover other evidence.[13] Frederick Silverthorne and his sons operated a lumber company and were accused of avoiding payment of federal taxes. When federal investigators asked the Silverthornes to turn over the company's books, they refused, citing their Fifth Amendment privilege against self-incrimination. Not long after, federal agents, without a search warrant, went to the lumber company and seized the wanted books.

The Silverthornes's lawyer asked the court that the materials be returned, citing the need for a search warrant. The books were returned to the Silverthornes but not before the prosecutors copied the materials they wanted. Based on these copies, the Silverthornes were convicted. Upon appeal, the U.S. Supreme Court ruled that just as evidence seized illegally cannot be used in a trial, neither can evidence that derives from an illegal seizure. The **poisonous fruit doctrine,** as this ruling is called, states that any evidence found or secured from an illegal search cannot be used because it is like poisonous fruit from a poisonous tree.[14]

In 1949, the Supreme Court applied the Fourth Amendment, Fourteenth Amendment, and the Exclusionary Rule to the *Wolfe v. Colorado* decision.[15] In this decision, based on the seizure of evidence in a state case, a deputy sheriff seized a physician's appointment book without a warrant. He proceeded to interrogate patients whose names appeared in the book, and was thus able to obtain evidence, eventually charging Wolfe with performing illegal abortions. Wolfe was convicted.[16] Upon appeal, the Supreme Court upheld his conviction as it decided that if the evidence were "trustworthy," it would be admissible regardless of how it was obtained.

The Warren Court and the Exclusionary Rule

The Warren Court announced several exclusionary rule decisions that were in accord with what Herbert Packer called the due-process model of the criminal justice system.[17] The **due process model** stresses the possibility of error in the stages leading to trial and thus places an emphasis on the need to protect procedural rights even if the implementation of these rights prevents the legal system from operating with maximum efficiency. This was accomplished as the Supreme Court incorporated one provision after another of the Bill of Rights into the due-process cause of the Fourteenth Amendment, which obligated the states to guarantee criminal defendants many of the constitutional safeguards already routinely accorded those accused of federal crimes.[18] Such landmark decisions as *Mapp v. Ohio* (1961)[19] and *Chimel v. California* (1969)[20] informed state courts that they had to abide by the Constitution in cases involving individual rights or risk the possibility of being overturned on appeal.

The Warren Supreme Court prohibited the use of any illegally seized evidence in *Mapp v. Ohio* (1961): "that all evidence obtained by searches and seizures in violation of the Constitution is, by same authority, inadmissible in a state court."[21] The significance of this decision is that the Court applied the constitutional standards for searches and seizures to both the federal and state systems (see Box 6.1).

In 1965, California police went to Ted Chimel's Santa Ana home with a warrant charging him with burglary of a coin shop. When the police asked permission to "look around," Chimel objected. Nevertheless, the police conducted a search of the entire three bedroom home, including the attic, a small workshop, and the garage, claiming that a search could be conducted based on the lawful arrest. Coins taken from the burglarized coin shop were seized during the hour long search. The property seized was admitted into evidence at Chimel's trial, in spite of his objections of an illegal seizure. Chimel was convicted, but the United States Supreme Court reversed the decision.[22]

According to the Court's decision, valid reasons for conducting a search are to protect the arresting officers, to keep defendants from escaping, and to prevent evidence from being destroyed. But a search becomes illegal when it goes "far

BOX 6.1   *Mapp v. Ohio*

On May 23, 1957, three Cleveland police officers arrived at the home of Darlee Mapp in pursuit of information that "a person [was] hiding out in the home, who was wanted for questioning in connection with a recent bombing," and that there was a large amount of material for operating a numbers game hidden in the home. Upon their arrival, the officers knocked on the door and demanded entrance. Ms. Mapp first telephoned her attorney, and then refused to grant permission for entry without a search warrant. The officers set up surveillance of the house after advising headquarters.

Officers again sought entrance three hours later, seeking permission for admittance. When Mrs. Mapp did not come to the door immediately, they forcibly opened one of the doors to the residence gaining admittance. Meanwhile Mrs. Mapp's attorney arrived, but the officers would not permit him to see her or enter the house. Mapp was halfway down the stairs from the upper floor when officers broke into the hall confronting her. She demanded to see a search warrant. A paper, shown as the warrant, was held up by one of the officers. She grabbed the "warrant" and placed it in her bosom. A struggle ensued in which officers recovered the piece of paper and handcuffed Mapp because she

had been "belligerent" and resisted their official rescue of the search warrant. Mapp was forcibly taken upstairs to her bedroom, where her belongings were searched before the search expanded to the rest of the second floor including the child's bedroom and the basement. During this widespread search, police found alleged lewd and lascivious books and pictures. On the basis of the seized items, Mapp was convicted of knowingly having "in her possession and under her control certain lewd and lascivious books, pictures, and photographs."

"At the trial no search warrant was produced by the prosecution, nor was the failure to produce one explained or accounted for." The prosecution charged that the materials belonged to Mapp; the defense argued that the books were the property of a former boarder who had left his belongings behind. In May 1959 Mapp appealed to the Ohio Supreme Court, claiming that the obscene materials were not in her possession and that the evidence was seized illegally. This appeals court disagreed, finding the evidence admissible. In June 1961 the Warren Court overturned the conviction, holding that the Fourth Amendment prohibition against unreasonable searches and seizure had been violated.

Source: Mapp v. Ohio, 367 U.S. 643 (1961).

beyond the petitioner's person and the area from within which he might have obtained either a weapon or something that could have been used as evidence against him."[23] The significance of the *Chimel v. California* decision is that the **"wingspan search area"** is strictly limited to the area reachable by the suspect and that the search must be made immediately after the arrest.

The Burger (1969–1986) and Rehnquist (1986–Present) Courts

A shift in the court's stance concerning the exclusionary rule gradually took place after Warren Burger became Chief Justice. In a 1971 case, Burger, expressing his dislike of the exclusionary rule, wrote that the exclusion of evidence from criminal trials is a "conceptually sterile and practically ineffective" means of guaranteeing "against unlawful conduct by governmental officials."[24]

The **good faith exception** to the exclusionary rule generated considerable interest and some controversy in the 1980s. What this ruling does is to determine whether the police have acted within the scope of the Constitution and, if not, whether they at least have acted in good faith. The Supreme Court has dealt with the controversial issue of the good faith exception in several cases.

One of the important cases of the good faith exception to the exclusionary rule was ***United States v. Leon*** (1984).[25] This case involved the Burbank, California Police Department and its investigation of a drug trafficking suspect. Following a tip from a confidential informant, Alberto Leon was placed under surveillance. Investigators applied for a search warrant based upon information gathered from their surveillance, and the warrant was issued by a state judge. A search of Leon's resident yielded a sizable amount of drugs and other evidence. The federal district court suppressed the evidence, on the basis that probable cause had not been sufficiently established in the original affidavit. On appeal to the Supreme Court, the Court reinstated the conviction of Leon as it ruled: "When law enforcement officials have acted in objective good faith or their transgressions have been minor, the magnitude of the benefit conferred on such guilty defendants offends basic concepts of the criminal justice system."[26]

The ***Massachusetts v. Sheppard*** (1984) case was decided on the same day as *United States v. Leon* and further reinforced the concept of the "good faith exception." In the *Massachusetts v. Sheppard* case, on the basis of evidence gathered in the investigation of a homicide in the Roxbury section of Boston, a police detective drafted an affidavit to support an application for an arrest warrant and a search warrant authorizing the search of Sheppard's residence. The affidavit was reviewed and approved by the District Attorney. After having difficulty finding a search warrant form because the court was closed on Sunday, the detective adapted a search warrant previously used in another district to search for controlled substances. He then presented it to a judge advising that further changes may be necessary. The judge made some changes, but did not change the substantive portion that authorized the search for controlled substances. He then signed the warrant. Several incriminating pieces of evidence were found, and Sheppard was convicted of first-degree murder. During the suppression hearing, the trial judge "ruled that not withstanding the warrant was defective under the Fourth Amendment in that it did not particularly describe the items to be seized, the incriminating evidence could be admitted because the police had acted in good faith in executing what they reasonably thought was a valid warrant."[27] The Massachusetts Supreme Judicial Court reversed the decision, holding that the evidence should have been suppressed. Upon appeal, the Supreme Court ruled that an error of constitutional dimensions may have been committed issuing the warrant, but it was the judge, not the detective who made the mistake. It would not serve the deterrent function of the exclusionary rule to exclude the evidence seized, because the police had acted on good faith and had used what they believed to be a valid search warrant.[28]

The two cases are perhaps the most important cases decided on the exclusionary rule since *Mapp v. Ohio.* They represent a narrow but significant exception to the doctrine of the exclusionary rule, in that the Court maintained that reasonable grounds existed for the police officers' mistaken belief that the warrants authorized the searches. In both cases the officers took every reasonable step to ensure that the warrants were valid. The difference between the two cases is that in *Sheppard,* the issue focused on the improper use of a search warrant form, whereas in *Leon* the issue involved the use of a questionable informant. What is similar in these cases is that judges made the mistakes, not the police. Accordingly, the Court ruled that the evidence in both cases was admissible because it was the judge, not the police, who erred, and the exclusionary rule is intended to control the conduct of the police rather than the conduct of judges.[29]

In the *Maryland v. Garrison* (1987) decision, the Supreme Court refused to suppress the use of evidence seized by an inaccurate search warrant. The police had requested a warrant to search an apartment believed to be the only one on the third floor. After searching the third floor, officers discovered that it housed more than one apartment. The Court ruled that evidence acquired in the search was admissible based upon the officers' reasonable mistake.[30]

The Supreme Court ruled in *Murray v. United States* (1988) that evidence initially discovered by the police during an illegal entry may still be admissible if discovered from an independent source. The Court reasoned that evidence ought not to have been excluded just because of unrelated illegal conduct by the police. The significance of this case is that it illustrates the **independent source exception** to the exclusionary rule.[31]

The *Illinois v. Rodriguez* (1990) case further defined the scope of the exclusionary rule. In *Rodriguez,* a badly beaten Gail Fischer complained to police that she had been assaulted in a Chicago apartment. She led the police to an apartment that she said she shared with Edward Rodriguez, unlocked the door with her key, and gave the officers permission to enter. Police found the defendant asleep on a bed, with cocaine and drug paraphernalia spread around him. The defendant was arrested, charged, and convicted of assault and possession of a controlled substance. Upon appeal to the Supreme Court, Rodriguez's attorney claimed that Fischer had not lived with Rodriguez for at least a month and no longer had the authority to provide the police with access to the apartment. In dismissing Rodriguez's claim, the Court ruled, "even if Fischer did not possess common authority over the premises, there was no Fourth Amendment violation if the police *reasonably believed* at the time of their entry that Fischer possessed the authority to consent."[32]

In *United States v. Hatchett* (1994), the Supreme Court ruled that an affidavit does not need to state each and every detail regarding a suspected crime.[33] This means that officers do not have to list every detail in a search warrant affidavit to make the warrant valid. It is only necessary to list enough facts to give the probable cause for the court to issue the warrant. Another implication of this ruling is that if a court finds the first nine facts were invalid in the affidavit and the tenth fact was found credible, then the warrant may survive the scrutiny of the court.

In *Arizona v. Evans* (1995), the Supreme Court further addressed the exclusionary rule when it ruled that errors caused by a court's clerical employee resulting in an unconstitutional arrest do not trigger the Fourth Amendment's exclusionary rule. In this case, an officer arrested Evans on a misdemeanor warrant after checking the computer in his squad car. The officer did not know that the arrest warrant had been pulled 17 days earlier, because the computer system that keeps track of such things had not been updated. While being handcuffed, the defendant dropped a marijuana cigarette, and a search of the vehicle turned up a bag of marijuana. The Arizona State Court ruled that the evidence should be suppressed and refused to address the difference between police error and court error. In reversing the verdict of the lower court, the Supreme Court stated that *Arizona v. Evans* did not require suppression of evidence gained as a result of a court clerk's error.[34]

In summary, the Burger Court further defined the Warren Court's landmark decisions on the exclusion of evidence obtained without regard to constitutional rights. The Rehnquist Court appears to be clearly moving even further away from the exclusionary rule.

Search of Persons

Legal searches of persons by the police include those authorized by a search warrant naming a specific person or those where a person gives consent to be searched. The **search warrant,** which is issued by a judicial officer when probable cause exists that a crime has been committed, is the most desirable means of initiating a government search. The advantage of the search warrant is that courts are more likely to admit evidence secured in this way than by other means. The need for obtaining a search warrant depends on the person's reasonable expectation of privacy. For example, a pat down search is less intrusive and therefore has less expectation of privacy than a search for blood. A search warrant is needed if the person does not consent to a search for blood. However, less proof is required for a pat down search because it is less intrusive. The search warrant is frequently not used by the police because of the general inconvenience or delay in obtaining one from a magistrate, especially at night or on weekends.[35]

Person searches are commonly justified using **consent.** A waiver must be voluntary and not obtained under duress,[36] must not exceed the limits set by the consent of the search,[37] and the person giving consent must have the authority to do so. Consent searches are a quick way of obtaining evidence, but many defendants later deny giving consent to the police or they assert that the consent was achieved through duress, threat, or trickery. Furthermore, the burden of proof is placed on the state to prove that the search was in fact voluntary as determined from the totality of the surrounding circumstances.[38]

Search of Vehicles

The preferable means of initiating motor vehicle search is by use of a search warrant. Yet few warrants are issued to search vehicles, because most searches take place when the police have stopped a vehicle for traffic violation or for suspicion of a crime. An important issue in the searches of vehicles is that the person giving the consent must have the authority to do so. When a vehicle is loaned to someone, that person generally can give consent to search the vehicle, unless told by the owner not to grant such a request.

The "automobile exception" to the warrant requirement authorizes warrant-less searches of automobiles where the officers have probable cause to believe that contraband or evidence of criminal activity is located therein and where exigent circumstances exist. The following must be observed for the search to be valid:

1. The vehicle must be mobile and must be lawfully stopped.
2. The officer must have probable cause to justify the search. (The search can be no broader or no narrower than a magistrate could legitimately authorize by search warrant.)
3. The search can include every part of the vehicle and its contents where the object of the search may be concealed.[39]

In the 1981 *New York v. Belton* case, an automobile in which Belton was one of the occupants was stopped by a New York State trooper for traveling at an excessive rate of speed.[40] In the process of discovering that none of the occupants owned the car or was related to the owner, the trooper smelled burnt marijuana and saw on the floor of the car an envelope suspected of containing marijuana. He then directed the occupants to get out of the car arresting them for possession of marijuana. After searching each one of the occupants, he searched the passenger compartment of the car finding a jacket belonging to Belton, unzipped one of his pockets, and discovered cocaine. Subsequently, Belton was indicted for criminal possession of a controlled substance. He pleaded guilty of a lesser-included offense while preserving his claim that the seizure of the cocaine violated the Fourth and Fourteenth Amendments. The New York Court of Appeals reversed the decision, but the United States Supreme Court ruled that a police officer may search the passenger compartment of an automobile and any open or closed containers incident to a lawful custodial arrest. The Court ruled that "the justification for the search is not that the arrestee has no privacy interest in the container but that the lawful custodial arrest justifies the infringement of any privacy interest the arrestee may have."[41] The significance of this case is that it gives the police the right to search an automobile if the following elements are present:

1. The occupant of the vehicle is placed under custodial arrest based on probable cause—which simply means that the person cannot move freely or leave.
2. The search is done at the time of the arrest or as soon as possible after the arrest.
3. The search of the interior of the vehicle may include search of the vehicle's contents and of any closed containers within the arrested person's immediate control—but it *does not* include search of the trunk.[42]

Carroll v. United States (1925) was the first major case that dealt with an exception to automobile search. In *Carroll,* government officers had probable cause to believe contraband was being transported in an automobile, stopped the vehicle, and then seized the illegal liquor they found. George Carroll and another person were arrested following this seizure. On appeal, the Court ruled that a warrantless search of an automobile or other vehicle is valid if it is based upon probable cause that contraband is present.[43]

What has become known as the **Carroll Doctrine** was established by this case. In *Carroll,* the Court held that a vehicle could be searched without a warrant if there was probable cause to believe it contained contraband or evidence. Exigent circumstances must also exist that call for immediate action. For example, in the case of a moving automobile, the urgent circumstances would be that the vehicle was moving. Courts have applied this vehicle exception to uphold warrantless searches of a motor home,[44] a houseboat,[45] and a roomette on a train.[46]

In *California v. Acevedo* (1991), the Santa Ana, California police, acting on information provided by an agent of the Drug Enforcement Administration (DEA), were maintaining surveillance on an apartment known to contain marijuana.[47] One officer left the scene to obtain a search warrant for the residence. While he was gone, the officers who remained on surveillance observed Charles Steven Acevedo leave the apartment after a 10 minute stay. Acevedo was carrying a brown paper bag approximately the size of one of the marijuana packages that the agents believed were in the apartment. He placed the bag in the trunk of a car and started to drive away. The officers stopped him, opened the truck, and found the marijuana in the brown paper bag. They then arrested Acevedo and charged him with possession with the intent to distribute marijuana. The California Court of Appeals upheld the warrantless seizure of the paper bag but concluded that the police required a warrant to open the bag. The Supreme Court reversed and upheld the warrantless search ruling and interpreted "Carroll as providing one rule to govern all automobile searches. The police may search an automobile and the containers within it where they have probable cause to believe contraband or evidence is contained."[48] However, the Court did not allow the search of the entire vehicle absent probable cause.

In 1982, in **United States v. Ross,** a warrantless search of Ross' car occurred after police established probable cause that Albert Ross sold drugs from the trunk of his car. The officers stopped the car, searched it, and discovered drugs in a brown paper bag in the trunk. The Supreme Court ruled that the scope of a warrantless search authorized by the automobile exception is no broader and no narrower than what a magistrate could legitimately authorize by warrant. Probable cause, then, that justifies the search of a lawfully stopped vehicle, justifies the search of every part of the vehicle and its contents that may conceal the object of the search. Thus, the scope of the search is not defined by the nature of the container, but by the object of the search and the place where there is probable cause to believe that it may be found.[49]

The Supreme Court addressed the exterior examination of an automobile in *Cardwell v. Lewis* (1974). In this case, a man's body was found near his car. Tire tracks of another vehicle and foreign paint scrapings from the dead man's vehicle were collected for evidence.[50] A suspect was later found and asked to appear at the police station where he was questioned and arrested. Police seized his automobile for tire comparison purposes. When the tire impressions and paint were found to match those at the crime scene, they were later used as evidence in court to convict the man of murder.[51] On appeal, the Court held that if adequate probable cause exists, a vehicle can be seized. The owner of the vehicle should not expect the same privacy regarding the exterior of the vehicle as that regarding the interior.[52]

The **plain view doctrine** essentially means that objects in plain view of an officer can be subject to seizure and later introduced into court as evidence. The Supreme Court ruled in the *Harris v. United States* (1968) case that anything a police officer sees "in plain view" when the officer has a right to be where he or she is, and that is not the product of a search, is admissible as evidence.[53] The Court reasoned that if contraband is left in open view and is observed by a police officer from a lawful vantagepoint, there has been no invasion of a legitimate expectation of privacy.[54] There are four conditions that must be present for the plain view doctrine to apply:

1. The officer must be lawfully present where the objects are observed.
2. The officer must be in a position to view the objects.
3. The objects must be discovered accidentally and inadvertently.
4. The officer must believe the evidence seen to be illegal.

For example, while on a routine traffic stop, an officer observes a safe in a car's back seat that appears to match one just reported stolen. The officer is lawfully present, the discovery is accidental, and probable cause exists that the safe is stolen. The safe may be seized, and, if positively identified, can be used in court as evidence.

Today, drug deals are made more and more in the public eye. What was once done in the privacy of one's home or out of sight is now often done on public streets. In *Florida v. Jimeno* (1991), police officer Trujillo stopped Enio Jimeno for a traffic violation.[55] He had been following the car after overhearing Jimeno arranging what appeared to be a drug transaction. Jimeno was told the reason for the stop, the traffic violation, and also the suspicion that he was involved in drug trafficking. The officer requested consent to search the vehicle, but stated that Jimeno did not have to consent. Jimeno did give consent. Upon opening the passenger door, the officers found a brown, rolled-up paper bag on the floorboard. The contents were not visible, but when the officers picked up the unsealed paper bag and looked inside, they discovered a kilogram of cocaine.[56]

Jimeno's attorney filed to suppress the cocaine as the search and seizure procedures violated Jimeno's Fourth Amendment rights, because even though he gave consent to search, it was not to include the brown paper bag. The lower courts suppressed the evidence, but on appeal, the Supreme Court reversed the lower courts' decisions. The Supreme Court ruled that Jimeno gave unrestricted search when he consented, and it was reasonable to assume drug carriers carried drugs in a container. Accordingly, visible search extended to include the paper bag.[57]

The hugely disproportionate stopping of African Americans and other minorities has been an issue with people of color. Indeed, the policy of stopping African

American drivers, just to see what officers can find, is so commonly used that "African Americans sometimes say they have been stopped for the offense of 'driving while black.'"[58] The 1996 *Whren* decision of the Supreme Court, which allows police to conduct searches during traffic stops under certain conditions, will probably increase such abuses.[59] David A. Harris interprets this decision by saying "any time we use our cars, we can be stopped by the police virtually at their whim because full compliance with traffic laws is impossible. And we can feel relatively certain that past will be prologue: African Americans and Hispanics will suffer the bulk of this treatment."[60]

Police departments have frequently used the policy of random stopping of automobiles to check drivers' licenses and vehicle registrations. In *Delaware v. Prouse* (1979), the Supreme Court ruled that random spot checks are a violation of constitutional rights.[61] But the Court did allow roadblock inspections, saying:

> Because motorists, apparently like sheep, are much less likely to be "frightened" or "annoyed" when stopped en masse, a highway patrolman needs neither probable cause nor articulable suspicion to stop all motorists on a particular thoroughfare, but he cannot without articulate suspicion stop less than all motorists.[62]

Police have also added roadside sobriety checkpoints in an effort to reduce the number of deaths and injuries resulting from drunk drivers. The Supreme Court has upheld roadblocks as long as vehicles are stopped in a systematic way.[63] The Court did state, however, that officers may not set up roadblock stops for the sole purpose of subjecting all stopped cars to a canine sniff search of the exterior of the car looking for cocaine.[64]

Search of Premises

Legal searches of premises include those authorized by search warrants, consent, and urgent circumstances. The Supreme Court has given considerable latitude to police in the areas of person and vehicle searches, but it has been reluctant to relax the search of premises because of the belief that "a person's home is his or her castle."

One of the rules of the legal search of premises is that only the person in legal control can give consent. If the property is held in common by more than one holder, then any owner can give consent.[65] The courts have also reasoned that if a person can give consent over property jointly owned with others, that person also can tell the police to stop the search. If police deceive a person by telling him or her they have a search warrant when they do not, then the search is illegal because it was done by trickery rather than by consent.[66]

In the *Washington v. Chrisman case* (1982), an officer of the Washington State University police department observed a student (Overdahl) leave a dormitory carrying a bottle of gin. Because the student appeared to be under 21, the officer stopped him and asked for identification. The officer and student went to the student's room to secure his identification. While remaining in the open doorway watching Overdahl and his roommate (Chrisman), the officer noticed what he believed to be marijuana seeds and a pipe lying on a desk in the room. The officer entered the room and seized the evidence. The students waived their *Miranda* rights and consented to a more extensive search of the room. Assisted by another officer, more marijuana was found. The Washington Supreme Court reversed the conviction, holding that the officer had no right to enter the room without a warrant. On appeal to the Supreme Court, the Court held that police officers may stick close to a lawfully arrested person at all times, "literally at his elbow."[67] Although the Court stated that the officer had every right for his safety to stay with Chrisman, this decision still does not give police the right to march someone around his or her house while making a plain view search of each room.

In *Wilson v. Arkansas* (1995), Wilson was convicted on state drug charges after the Arkansas trial court denied her motion to suppress evidence, in which she asserted that the search of her home was invalid because police had violated the common-law principle requiring them to announce their presence and authority before entering. The Supreme Court ruled on the principle of "knock and announce" as part of the Fourth Amendment command that the search and seizure be reasonable.[68] The Court stated that Anglo-American law has a long tradition going back to the thirteenth century of demanding the requirement to knock and announce before entering a person's home. This requires that the police must have just cause to enter a dwelling without prior announcement, including a threat to an officer's safety, an escaped prisoner, or a risk of destruction of evidence.[69] Finally, a police officer may enter premises without a search warrant while in hot pursuit of an armed suspect in a crime. Yet this exception ends when the suspect is located. The search cannot continue until police obtain a search warrant or unless another exception applies, such as that of search incident to arrest.

Use of Informers

The police frequently secure information from confidential informants concerning criminal activity. The informants are generally concerned citizens who for a number of reasons would be reluctant or afraid to supply information without the protection of anonymity. Often the informer is known and involved in the criminal milieu. The information gathered is then used to build probable cause for a search warrant or an arrest based on that hearsay evidence. Without the use of confidential informants, many crimes would remain unsolved. Here a police official describes receiving information from a reliable citizen:

> One night, I was waved over by a concerned citizen who wanted to report a subject carrying a gun without giving his name or becoming more involved. He knew the subject carrying the gun as they both frequented the same restaurant. He gave the subject's name, which I recognized having arrested him before, describing where the subject was sitting in the restaurant, what he was wearing, his age, race and size, and most important where he was concealing the weapon on his person. After supplying this information, he left the area

with his family. Another uniform officer and I entered the restaurant as if on break. When we passed the subject, we grabbed him without warning securing both arms at the same time he was reaching for his gun, which fell on the floor. The subject was arrested for carrying a concealed weapon.[70]

In *Illinois v. Gates* (1983), the Supreme Court abandoned the "two-pronged test" of using the independent channels of the informant's "veracity" or "reliability" and his "basis of knowledge" in determining probable cause for a search warrant developed in *Aguilar v. Texas* (1964)[71] and *Spinelli v. United States* (1969).[72] The Court felt that the two-prong test rigorously applied in every case would seriously impede the task of law enforcement by greatly diminishing the value of anonymous tips. Anonymous tips seldom would survive the rigorous application of either of the *Spinelli* prongs. Simply, ordinary citizens do not provide extensive recitations of their everyday observations and the veracity of persons supplying anonymous tips is largely unknown and unknowable. In addition, the Court concluded that the rigorous scrutiny of the basis of knowledge of an unquestionably honest citizen who comes forth with information is unnecessary. Instead, the Court determined that the *Spinelli* prongs "are better understood as relevant considerations in the totality-of-the-circumstances analysis that traditionally has guided probable-cause determinations: a deficiency in one may be compensated for, in determining the overall reliability of a tip, by a strong showing as to the other, or by some other indications of reliability…. Under the "totality of the circumstances" analysis, corroboration of details of an informant's tip by independent police work is of significant value."[73]

Electronic Eavesdropping

One of the most controversial police activities is the use of wiretapping as part of investigative procedures. Electronic devices have become so sophisticated that they enable the police to listen and record conversations of individuals over the phone, through walls and windows, and from considerable distances. Wireless video surveillance, monitoring pagers, beepers and pen registries that monitor phone numbers being dialed are becoming more and more common.

The Supreme Court has usually held that the use of electronic eavesdropping must be controlled under guidelines established by the Fourth Amendment and that police must acquire a court order based on probable cause before using electronic surveillance. The Court has also ruled that prior to allowing a wire tap or other electronic invasion of a person's privacy, a good faith effort must be made to run the gamut of normal investigative procedures before resorting to wiretapping. Wiretapping, then, is to be distinctly the exception, not the rule.[74] The Court also held that while domestic silent video surveillance is not regulated by statute, it is subject to the Fourth Amendment.[75] The *Katz v. United States* (1967) decision was one of the important Supreme Court cases regarding electronic surveillance. This decision held that any form of electronic surveillance, including wiretapping, that violates a reasonable expectation of privacy constitutes a search under the Fourth

Amendment. No physical trespass is required.[76] The 1984 *United States v. Karo* decision found that the warrantless monitoring of a beeper in a private residence violates the Fourth Amendment.[77]

However, in *United States v. Olderbak* (1992), the Supreme Court ruled that the installation and use of a pen registry is not a search under the Fourth Amendment and does not require authorization by court order.[78] State courts have also found that it is not necessary to obtain a court order for video surveillance of public areas where there is no expectation of privacy.[79] These types of cases have been commonly referred to as "restroom cases," and address the issue of where video surveillance is permissible. In the investigation of sex crimes, state courts have generally held that areas such as restroom stalls cannot be monitored without a warrant.[80]

ARREST

To constitute an arrest or seizure of a person under Fourth Amendment jurisprudence, there must be either some application of physical force or a submission to official authority to restrain a subject's freedom.[81] Regardless of the intent of the officer, a person is arrested in the constitutional sense when a person's freedom is restricted to the extent that he or she is not free to go.[82] Police officers can either make an arrest pursuant to an arrest warrant or without a warrant, but all arrests must be made on probable cause. An arrest warrant is a court order directing any police officer to place the named person in custody and brought before the court. A police officer does not have to have the warrant in hand to affect an arrest, only knowledge that one does exist. Officers can also make warrantless arrests provided they have probable cause that the person committed the act.[83]

In *Payton v. New York* (1980), the Supreme Court applied the Fourth Amendment to states prohibiting the police from making a warrantless and nonconsensual entry into a suspect's home in order to make a routine felony arrest. However, the Court did allow entry into a dwelling in which the suspect lives to make an arrest on a warrant, founded on probable cause, if there is reason to believe the suspect would be present.[84] Furthermore, the Court in *Steagald v. the United States* (1981) held that an arrest warrant was inadequate to protect the Fourth Amendment interests of persons not named in the warrant. To search a third party's home absent exigent circumstances, a search warrant is necessary.[85] **Exigent circumstances** include danger to life or property, hot pursuit, and destruction of evidence.

Once arrested, a person can be searched incident to arrest and following an arrest as the regular booking procedure without the need of a search warrant. The court in *Gustafson v. Florida* (1973) held that "a full search of the person of a suspect made incident to a lawful custodial arrest did not violate the Fourth or Fourteenth Amendments."[86] In *United States v. Robinson* (1973), a police officer made a custodial arrest because Robinson's license was revoked. During a subsequent search of Robinson's coat pocket, the officer found a cigarette package containing heroin.

The heroin evidence was admitted into the District Court trial resulting in a conviction that was later reversed by the Court of Appeals as a search in violation of the Fourth Amendment. The Court held "in the case of a lawful custodial arrest a full search of the person is not only an exception to the warrant requirement of the Fourth Amendment, but is also a "reasonable" search under that Amendment."[87]

Unlike a custodial arrest, investigatory detention is not an arrest because of its less intrusive nature. In *Alabama v. White* (1990), the police received an anonymous phone call that Vanessa White would be leaving number 235-C Lynwood terrace Apartments at a certain time. She would be driving a brown Plymouth station wagon with the right taillight lens broken going to Dobey's Motel, and that she would be in possession of about an ounce of cocaine inside a brown attaché case. Police observed her leaving her apartment without an attaché case and stopped the car before reaching its reported destination. A consensual search of the vehicle found the brown attaché case containing marijuana. After White was arrested, cocaine was found in her purse. The Court of Criminal Appeals of Alabama reversed her conviction on possession charges claiming that the police did not have the necessary reasonable suspicion required in *Terry v. Ohio* (1968). In its ruling that an anonymous tip is reasonable suspicion to justify a stop, the Supreme Court decided that reasonable suspicion is a less demanding standard than probable cause.[88] The Court used the **totality of the circumstances test** developed in *Illinois v. Gates* (1983) in reversing the Alabama court's ruling and upholding White's conviction.

In *California v. Hodari* (1991), narcotics officers of the Oakland, California Police Department in an unmarked vehicle and in plain clothes with jackets marked with "Police" front and back, observed four or five youths gathered around a parked vehicle in an area of high narcotic activity. Officers thought that they had come upon a drug transaction and approached the youth. Seeing the officers, the youths took off on foot and in a vehicle.[89]

Hodari was one of the youths on foot pursued by the Oakland police officer. Nearing a house, with the officer some 11 feet from Hodari, he tossed a rock toward the house, and seconds later was tackled by the officer and handcuffed. A search of Hodari revealed $130 in cash and a pager. The rock Hodari threw was crack cocaine.[90] Hodari's attorneys moved to suppress the crack cocaine as an unlawful search of his person. The trial court denied the motion to suppress, but the California Court of Appeals reversed that decision. They ruled that when the officer chased Hodari, that was seizure of his person, therefore, the crack cocaine was improperly seized. On appeal, the Supreme Court reversed that decision. The Court ruled that suspects who flee from the police and throw away evidence as they retreat may later be arrested based upon the incriminating nature of the abandoned evidence. Justice Scalia wrote:

> That although the police pursuit may have constituted a 'show of authority' enjoining Hodari to stop, Hodari was not 'seized' until physically apprehended, because he did not submit to that injunction.[91]

The police have also been given permission by the courts to **"stop and frisk"** a person, in other words, to stop a person and subject him or her to a "pat down, if they have reasonable suspicion that a crime has just been, is being, or is about to be committed. Less proof is needed because it is less intrusive; you only need reasonable grounds and not probable cause. An officer can also do a pat down search for officer safety. The landmark case regarding this exception to the rules of search and seizure is ***Terry v. Ohio*** (1968).[92] The Supreme Court ruled in this case that police officer McFadden had reasonable grounds to believe that Terry was armed and dangerous and it was necessary to take appropriate action to protect himself and others" (see Box 6.2).[93]

The Court cautioned that before a person can be stopped, detained, and subjected to a pat down, there must be reasonable suspicion that a crime has just been, is being, or is about to be committed. It is important to note that the *Terry* rule allows a pat down for weapons, not a full-scale search of the body. If a weapon is found, the person can be arrested, and a full-scale search can be done incident to the arrest.

There have been several other significant court cases which have added to the *Terry* decision. In *Adams v. Williams* (1972), the defendant was arrested for unlawful possession of a weapon based on information given by a reliable informant. The importance of this case is that it granted the police officer permission to conduct a

---

BOX 6.2   *Terry v. Ohio*

On a downtown beat, a Cleveland detective (Martin McFadden) observed two strangers (John Terry and Richard Chilton) on a street corner, acting suspiciously. He based his judgment on some 39 years as a police officer and 30 years assigned to that area of Cleveland. He saw them proceed alternately back and forth along an identical route, pausing to stare in the same store window. They did so a total of about 24 times. Each completion of the route was followed by a conference between the two on a corner, and a third man (Katz) joined them for a brief period. Suspecting the two men of "casing a job, a stick-up," the officer followed them and saw them rejoin the third man a couple of blocks away in front of a store. The officer approached the three, identified himself as a police officer, and asked their names. The men

"mumbled something," whereupon McFadden spun Terry around, patted down his outside clothing, and found a pistol in his overcoat pocket. He was unable to remove the pistol. The officer ordered the three into the store. He removed Terry's overcoat, took out a revolver, and ordered the three to face the wall with their hands raised. He patted down the outer clothing of Chilton and Katz and seized a revolver from Chilton's outside overcoat pocket. He did not put his hands under the outer garments of Katz (since he discovered nothing in his patdown which might have been a weapon), or under Terry or Chilton's outer garments until he felt the guns. The three were taken to the police station. Terry and Chilton were charged with carrying concealed weapons.

Source: Terry v. Ohio, 392 U.S. 1 (1968).

"stop and frisk" based on information from an informant and not from direct observation.[94]

In *United States v. Hensley* (1985) (a stop and frisk case, not a search case) Hensley was stopped by officers in Covington, Kentucky who recognized him from a "wanted" poster which a police department in St. Bernard, Ohio had distributed to other departments. Although Hensley appealed his conviction with the claim that there had been no probable cause, this case established that the police could stop and detain an individual who is the subject of a "wanted" poster from another jurisdiction.[95]

In *United States v. Sokolow* (1989), Andrew Sokolow was attempting to smuggle drugs through the Honolulu Airport. His behavior was consistent with one of the DEA's "drug courier profiles" such as cash for tickets, a short trip to a major source city for drugs, nervousness, type of attire, and unchecked luggage. The agents who stopped Sokolow knew that: (1) Sokolow purchased round-trip airline tickets for two from Honolulu to Miami with open return dates; (2) paid $2,100 for the tickets from a large roll of $20 bills; (3) was traveling under a false name; (4) only stayed in Miami for 48 hours even though the round trip would take 20 hours; (5) appeared nervous during his trip and was dressed in the same black jumpsuit wearing gold jewelry on the return trip; and (6) neither Sokolow nor his female companion checked in any of their four pieces of luggage. The DEA agents stopped Sokolow and his companion upon their arrival at the Honolulu International Airport. A search warrant was obtained after a narcotics detector dog alerted authorities to Sokolow's carry-on luggage. The agents found 1,063 grams of cocaine. Sokolow was indicted for possession with intent to distribute cocaine.[96]

The District Court denied Sokolow's motion to suppress the evidence finding that the stop was justified. The Court of Appeals disagreed and reversed applying a two-part test for determining reasonable suspicion. First, at east one fact describing "ongoing criminal activity"—such as the use of an alias or evasive movement through an airport—was always necessary to support a reasonable-suspicion finding. Second, "'probabilistic' facts describing 'personal characteristics' of drug couriers...were only relevant if there was evidence of ongoing criminal activity' and the Government offered 'empirical documentation' that the combination of facts at issue did not describe the behavior of significant numbers of innocent persons."[97] The Court of Appeals held that the stop was impermissible because of no evidence of ongoing criminal behavior.

The U.S. Supreme Court reversed and remanded holding that the Fourth Amendment "does not preclude the use of 'probabilistic' facts describing 'personal characteristics' of drug couriers as a basis for finding of 'reasonable suspicion' necessary to justify a brief investigation detention of a drug courier."[98] The fact that the respondent's behavior was consistent with one of the DEA's drug courier profiles did not alter the courts analysis because the factors in question had evidentiary significance regardless of whether they were set forth in a "profile." A stop of this nature must therefore be evaluated considering "the totality of the circumstances—the whole picture."[99] The process as stated in *United States v. Cortez* (1981) "does not deal with hard certainties, but with probabilities."[100]

Yet, the Supreme Court ruled in the *Minnesota v. Dickerson* (1993) decision that a frisk that goes beyond that authorized in *Terry* is not valid. During routine patrol duties, two police officers spotted Dickerson leaving an apartment building known to be a "crack house." Upon seeing the police, Dickerson turned around and walked in the other direction. He was stopped and searched, and the police found a lump of cocaine in cellophane in his pocket.[101] On appeal, the Supreme Court reversed the conviction reasoning that the search went beyond the "pat down search" allowed by *Terry* because the police officer "squeezed, slid, and otherwise manipulated the packet's content" before identifying it was cocaine.[102] There is now the **plain touch exception** that permits further intrusive search, if a pat down search reveals an identifiable object through clothing.

INTERROGATION

There are a number of cases that define what "custody" means in the context of custodial interrogation. These cases generally determine custody as whether the suspect is free to leave or did leave after the interview, whether any physical or verbal restraints are used, whether the person came for questioning voluntarily, whether the suspect is told he or she is under arrest, whether the interview continues for a long period, whether coercive or threatening conditions exist, whether the interrogation is conducted by one or more officers or the prosecutor, whether the person has freedom of movement during the interview, and whether the interview occurred during normal waking hours.[103]

The protections against self-incrimination, the prompt arraignment rule, and the constitutional safeguards related to the use of lineups limit the powers of the police once a person has been taken into custody.

Protection against Self-Incrimination

The Fifth Amendment states that "no person…shall be compelled in any criminal case to be a witness against himself." In 1966, the United States Supreme Court ruled on a case that would be a landmark case in self-incrimination (see Box 6.3).[104] In *Miranda v. Arizona*, the Court ruled that whenever a person who is about to be interrogated by police, "has been taken into custody or otherwise deprived of his freedom of action in any significant way," he or she must be given the following warnings:

1. That he or she has the right to remain silent, and that he/she may choose not to answer any questions.
2. That if the person does answer questions, these answers can be used as evidence against himself or herself.
3. That he or she has a right to consult with a lawyer before or during the questioning of the police.
4. That if he or she cannot afford to hire a lawyer, one will be provided without cost.[105]

BOX 6.3 *Miranda v. Arizona*

Our holding will be spelled out with some specificity in the pages which follow but briefly stated it is this: the prosecution may not use statements, whether exculpatory or inculpatory, stemming from custodial interrogation of the defendant unless it demonstrates the use of procedural safe-guards effective to secure the privilege against self-incrimination. By custodial incrimination, we mean questioning initiated by law enforcement officers after a person has been taken into custody or otherwise deprived of his freedom of action in any significant way. As for the procedural safeguards to be employed, unless other fully effective means are devised to inform accused persons of their right of silence and to assure a continuous opportunity to exercise it, the following measures are required. Prior to any questioning, the person must be warned that he has the right to remain silent, that any statement he does make may be used as evidence against him, and that he has a right to the presence of an attorney, either retained or appointed. The defendant may waive effectuation of these rights, provided the waiver is made voluntarily, knowingly, and intelligently. If, however, he indicates that he wishes to consult with an attorney before speaking there can be no questioning. Likewise, if the individual is alone and indicates in any manner that he does not wish to be interrogated, the police may not question him. The mere fact that he may have answered some questions or volunteered some statements on his own does not deprive him of the right to refrain from answering any further inquiries until he has consulted with an attorney and therefore consents to be questioned.

Source: 384 U.S. 436 (1966).

The background of this case was that Ernesto Miranda, a 23 year old Mexican American, was arrested at his home in Phoenix on March 13, 1963 and taken to a local police station for questioning. He was suspected of having kidnapped and raped an 18 year old woman. Miranda was placed in a lineup and was identified by the victim. The police then interrogated him for two hours, during which time he signed a written confession. The confession was admitted at the trial, over Miranda's objections, and he was convicted of kidnapping and rape and received a 20 to 30 year sentence on each count. On appeal to the Arizona Supreme Court, the conviction was affirmed. But the United States Supreme Court reversed Miranda's conviction, because the interrogation was defined as inherently coercive and because the procedures used violated the constitutional rights of suspects as defined in the Fourth, Fifth, Sixth, and Fourteenth Amendments. In Box 6.3 Chief Justice Earl Warren, in writing the 5–4 majority decision, explained the Court's decision.

In the past 20 years, the Supreme Court made several rulings that modified the *Miranda* decision. In ***Brewer v. Williams*** (1977), a divided Court narrowly held that the defendant's right to counsel under the Sixth Amendment had been violated, and his conviction for murder was overturned.[106]

The case involved Robert Anthony Williams, charged in the State of Iowa with the Christmas Eve murder of a ten year old girl who had disappeared from a YMCA building in Des Moines. Williams was later arrested in Davenport, Iowa.

Before Williams was transported from Davenport to Des Moines, his lawyer told police personnel not to question him on the trip. The police agreed to this, but during the trip a detective played on Williams' emotions and got him to talk.[107]

The detective told Williams that several inches of snow was predicted that night and the snow would cover the body. He went on to say, "And since we will be going right past the area on the way into Des Moines, I feel that we could stop and locate the body, that the parents of this little girl should be entitled to a Christian burial for the little girl who was snatched away from them on Christmas Eve and murdered." This prompted Williams to lead the police to a culvert along a gravel road, where the body was found.[108]

The Court ruled that in obtaining incriminating statements from Williams, the detective had acted in violation of the Fifth Amendment prohibition against self-incrimination and the Sixth Amendment protections concerning interrogating Williams without his attorney present (formal proceedings, including arraignment in court, had begun). The Court reasoned that what really made the evidence inadmissible was the fact that Williams, who was eccentric and a religious zealot, had a history of mental illness and the officers had prior knowledge of this background. Their comments, therefore, were intended to play on the emotions of a weak individual and, as such, resulted in an unlawful inquiry. Williams' statements were suppressed, however, the evidence, the body, and all related evidence, including the body's condition shown by the autopsy, was admitted. Williams was again tried and convicted.[109]

On appeal, Williams asked that the conviction be overturned because the evidence of the body's location and condition introduced at the time of the second trial was obtained as a result of incriminating statements. But, using the **inevitable discovery exception,** the Supreme Court ruled that the evidence found when Williams led police to the body was admissible since some 200 persons were searching the area and the body would have inevitably been found.[110]

In the *Nix v. Williams* (1984) case, the Court upheld the conviction because of the inevitability of discovery exception. Chief Justice Burger's majority opinion stated that *Miranda* was designed to put the police "in the same, not a worse, position than they would have been in if no police error or misconduct had occurred."[111]

The *Rhode Island v. Innis* (1980) case broadened the application of *Miranda* when it required Miranda warnings only in situations of custodial interrogation. The Court ruled that the safeguards against self-incrimination must be observed "whenever a person in custody is subjected to either express questioning or its equivalent."[112]

The context of this case was that a subject was riding with police officers in a squad car after being picked up in a murder investigation. When he overheard an officer comment to the other that because the murder had taken place near a school for handicapped children, he was concerned that some child might find the gun and be injured by it. The subject then informed the officers where the gun could be found.[113] This case gives a rule for deciding whether police officer's "conversation" in the police car is interrogation or just innocuous conversation and whether *Miranda* warnings have to be given.

In *Oregon v. Elstad* (1985), the Court ruled that a confession made after proper *Miranda* warnings and waiver of rights have been given is admissible even if the police obtained an earlier voluntary but unwarned admission from the suspect.[114] In *Colorado v. Spring* (1985), the Court decided that a waiver of *Miranda* rights is valid even if the suspect believes the interrogation will focus on minor crimes and the police later shift their questioning to cover more serious crimes.[115] In *Connecticut v. Barrett* (1987), the Court held that a suspect's oral confession is admissible even if this person informs the police that he or she will not make a written statement without the presence of an attorney.[116] In another important case modifying *Miranda* in the late 1980s, *Duckworth v. Eagan* (1989), the Court ruled that the *Miranda* warnings are not required to be given in the exact wording of *Miranda v. Arizona*; instead, what is required is that they simply convey to the suspect his or her rights.[117]

Illinois v. Perkins (1990)[118] and *Arizona v. Fulminante* (1991)[119] are two more recent cases that further modify the *Miranda* decision. In *Illinois v. Perkins* the police placed an undercover agent John Parisi in the cellblock with Lloyd Perkins who was incarcerated on charges unrelated to the murder Parisi was investigating. The police first learned of Perkins' involvement in the murder from Donald Charlton who was a fellow inmate at Graham Correctional Facility. During their confinement, Perkins admitted to Charlton that he had murdered a man named Richard Stephenson. By the time police heard Charlton's account, Perkins had been released from Graham, but was eventually traced to a jail in Montgomery County, Illinois, where he was being held for an aggravated assault charge. Fearing the use of an eavesdropping device would prove impractical and unsafe, it was decided to place an undercover officer in the cell with Perkins and Charlton. The plan was for Parisi and Charlton to pose as escapees from a work release center arrested for burglary. They were to engage Perkins in casual conversation. While in confinement, the three conspired to escape. During conversations of their planning, Perkins admitted to murdering Stephenson. Based on his admission, he was charged with the murder.[120]

The lower court found that Perkin's admission (confession) was illegally obtained as no *Miranda* warning was given. The Appellate Court of Illinois affirmed ruling that "Miranda prohibits all undercover contacts with incarcerated suspects that are reasonably likely to elicit an incriminating response."[121] The United States Supreme Court reversed the lower court decision, ruling that undercover police officers are not required to give *Miranda* warning to "incarcerated suspects before asking questions that my elicit an incriminating response."[122]

The environmental control of confinement was the basic issue in this case. It was reasoned by the defense that when a suspect is in police custody, he is in a control environment and at a psychological disadvantage, and, therefore, a *Miranda* warning is required. Although Perkins was in confinement, this environment was not controlled by the police. The Court stated further that the police may not use coercion, but can use deception without a violation of *Miranda*.[123]

Under the *Miranda* decision, the rule of thumb is that police must give the Miranda warning when a suspect is in custody (the suspect is not free to leave the area where he or she is being questioned). Simply, without custody there is no need to invoke *Miranda*. Custody is determined to a large extent by the location of the interview and if the suspect feels his or her freedom is being restricted. For example, law enforcement buildings are custodial in nature while hospitals are noncustodial in nature. However, if a suspect drives to the police station and then drives home—there is no custody. The Court will use the "Reasonableness Test" to examine the suspect's feelings of restricted freedom. The trend in recent cases clearly indicates that there will likely be increasing expectations to the *Miranda* warning.

Prompt Arraignment Rule

The rulings of the Supreme Court have long indicated an awareness that the police may subject a suspect to "the third degree" to obtain confessions. Its rulings have also reflected an awareness of the fact that the length of time a suspect is held before the initial court hearing affects whether a confession is voluntary or not. In 1943, in *McNabb v. United States,* the Court held that confessions obtained after unreasonable delay before arraignment (McNabb had been questioned for several days) could not be used as evidence in a federal court.[124] Justice Frankfurter issued the majority opinion and discussed the dangers of unnecessary delay between arrest and arraignment:

> This procedural requirement checks...those reprehensible practices known as the "third degree" which, though universally rejected as indefensible, still find their way into use. It aims to avoid all the evil implications of street interrogation of persons accused of crime. It reflects not a sentimental but a sturdy view of law enforcement. It outlaws self-defeating ways in which brutality is substituted for brains as an instrument of crime detection.[125]

The 48 hour rule was formalized by the Supreme Court in *County of Riverside (California) v. McLaughlin* (1991). In this decision, the Court held that "a jurisdiction that provides judicial determinations of probable cause within 48 hours of arrest will, as a general matter, comply with the promptness requirement."[126] The Court did specify that weekends and holidays could not be excluded from the 48 hour requirement.[127]

In *McNeil v. Wisconsin* (1991), the court ruled that a suspect in custody asking for an attorney at an arraignment or initial appearance is only invoking their Sixth Amendment right to counsel on the charged offense. This person is not invoking the *Miranda's* Fifth Amendment-based right to counsel being present during custodial interrogation about uncharged crimes.[128] In *McNeil,* the suspect was arrested for an armed robbery and had been represented by counsel at his initial appearance. The same day, following his initial appearance, a detective visited the defendant in jail in order to question him about a separate incident involving a murder and another armed robbery. The detective advised McNeil of his rights as per *Miranda* and McNeil waived his rights. McNeil then admitted his involvement in the murder and burglary.[129]

Lineups

The Supreme Court has typically allowed the use of police lineups prior to trial for the purpose of identification. The Court has ruled that simply having someone stand for observation does not have "testimonial significance" (i.e., spoken by live witness), but is considered "nontestimonial" evidence. Other examples of nontestimonial evidence include hair samples, handwriting, blood samples, footprints, fingerprints, and medical records.[130] The Court has additionally ruled that a suspect or defendant has the right to counsel during the lineup, because of the critical nature of the procedure.[131]

The police must use care to insure that the persons in a lineup are of similar size, color, age, and appearance. A police officer told of the time he was picking up a prisoner from another state and found that the local police had used a photo lineup with four white males and one black male, the suspect. When asked why they would do such a thing, a local police officer said, "We don't have blacks living in our city, so white males were all we could come up with."[132] The Court certainly would condemn such a lineup.

SUMMARY

This chapter has examined constitutional protections for citizens against police interference. The police's responsibility for constitutional protections can be grouped into several categories: Fourth Amendment rights, including the exclusionary rule; legal ways to search persons, vehicles, and premises; and Fifth Amendment protections, which include protection against self-incrimination. Understanding these protections is complicated by the fact that earlier rulings are often altered or even reversed by later cases. There was a loud outcry from the police during the 1960s that these protections totally handcuffed them and that the crime rate in this nation would skyrocket accordingly. The fact is, as Skolnick and Ffye aptly expressed it, "No reputable study suggest that any Supreme Court decision has raised crime rates or hampered police effectiveness."[133]

Constitutional protections were expanded significantly in the 1960s but have slowly been decreased by more conservative rulings by the Supreme Court. With the appointment of William Rehnquist as Chief Justice and the other recent appointments to the Court, this conservative trend is likely to continue for some years. The significance of the pendulum swing from extensive to more limited constitutional protections of citizens suspected of crimes relates to the degree to which the due process model is used by the court system. A valid criticism of the due process model is that it permits some guilty persons to go free because "technical violations" of their rights have occurred, which is particularly disturbing when these persons have committed serious crimes. But an even greater problem is that in a free and democratic society, the rights of certain individuals are limited because of society's concern about rising crime rates. The freedom of the individual has long been a fundamental tenet of American society, and it would constitute a great loss to have this freedom compromised.

KEY WORDS

Brewer v. Williams
Carroll Doctrine
Chimel v. California
consent
due process model
exclusionary rule
exigent circumstances
good faith exception
independent source exception
inevitable discovery exception
Mapp v. Ohio
Massachusetts v. Sheppard
Miranda v. Arizona

New York v. Belton
plain touch exception
plain view doctrine
poisonous fruit doctrine
search warrant
"stop and frisk"
Terry v. Ohio
totality of the circumstances test
United States v. Leon
United States v. Ross
Weeks v. United States
wingspan search area

DISCUSSION QUESTIONS

1. What is the exclusionary rule? Cite cases illustrating this rule. What would be the effect on the police if the exclusionary rule would be discontinued?

2. When do the police bend the rules in terms of constitutional protections of suspects? Is there a way for this to be controlled so society does not have the situation found in the opening quote of the chapter?

3. What is the *Miranda* decision? Why are suspects willing to talk with police after being given the *Miranda* rules? In what ways has the *Miranda* decision been "eroded?"

4. Identify the most important Supreme Court decisions discussed in this chapter. Why do you consider them the most important? Are there any Supreme Court decisions that you disagree with? Why?

5. Do you believe that there is currently the proper balance between establishing effective law enforcement and ensuring due process of rights of individuals?

FURTHER READING

Gardner, Thomas J. *Criminal Law: Principles and Cases.* 3rd ed. St. Paul: West, 1985.

Harrison, Maureen, and Steven Gilbert. *Landmark Decisions of the United States Supreme Court.* Beverly Hills: Excellent, 1991.

Lochhead, George S. "Fourth Amendment—Expanding the Scope of Automobile Consent Search." *The Journal of Criminal Law and Criminology* 82 (Winter 1992): 773–796.

Weinreb, Lloyd. *Leading Constitutional Cases on Criminal Justice.* Westbury: Foundation, 1994.

Whitebread, Charles H. "The Burger Court's Counter Revolution in Criminal Procedure: The Recent Criminal Decisions of the United States Supreme Court." *Washburn Law Journal* 24 (1985).

ENDNOTES

1. Paul Chevigny, *The Knife: Police Violence in the Americas* (New York: The New Press, 1995) 141.

2. Jerome H. Skolnick and James J. Fyfe, *Above the Law: Police and the Excessive Use of Force* (New York: The Free Press, 1993) 114.

3. Victor E. Kappeler, Richard D. Sluder, and Geoffrey P. Alpert, *Forces of Deviance: Understanding the Dark Side of Policing* (Prospect Heights: Waveland, 1994) 65.

4. Kappeler, Sluder, and Alpert, 65.

5. *United States v. Chadwick,* 433 US 1, 1977.

6. *Graham v. Conner,* 490 US 386, at 395, 1989.

7. *Katz v. United States,* 389 US 347, 351, 1967.

8. *Coolidge v. New Hampshire,* 403 US 443, 1971.

9. E. A. "Penny" Westfall, "Search and Seizure Issues" (Unpublished paper written for the Prosecuting Attorneys Council, 1997): 1.

10. *California v. Greenwood,* 486 US 35, 1988.

11. *Weeks v. United States,* 232 US 383, 1914.

12. *Weeks v. United States.*

13. *Silverthorne Lumber Company v. United States,* 251 US, 1920.

14. *Silverthorne Lumber Company v. United States.*

15. *Wolfe v. Colorado,* 338 US 25, 1949.

16. *Wolfe v. Colorado.*

17. Herbert Packer, *The Limits of the Criminal Sanction* (Stanford: Stanford UP, 1968) 154–173.

18. James A. Inciardi, *Criminal Justice,* 4th ed. (Forth Worth: Harcourt Brace, 1993) 721.

19. *Mapp v. Ohio,* 367 US 643, 1961.

20. *Chimel v. California,* 395 US 752, 1969.

21. *Chimel v. California.*

22. *Chimel v. California.*

23. *Chimel v. California.*

24. *Bivens v. Six Unknown Agents of the Federal Bureau of Narcotics,* 403 US 388, 1971.

25. *United States v. Leon,* 8 LOB 145, 1984.

26. *United States v. Leon.*

27. *Massachusetts v. Sheppard,* 468 US 981, 1984.

28. *Massachusetts v. Sheppard.*

29. Rolando V. Del Carmen and Jeffery T. Walker, *Briefs of Leading Cases in Law Enforcement* (Cincinnati: Anderson, 1995) 23.

30. *Maryland v. Garrison,* 107 S. Ct. 1013, 1987.

31. *Murray v. United States,* 487 US 533, 1988.

32. *Illinois v. Rodriguez,* 110 S. Ct. 2793, 1990.

33. *United States v. Hatchett,* 31 F. 3d 1411–1417 7th Cir., 1994.

34. *Arizona v. Evans,* 63 LW 4179, 1995.

35. R. Van Duizend, L. P. Sutton, and C. A. Carter, "A Review of the Search Warrant Process," *State Court Journal* (Spring 1984).

36. *Schneckloth v. Bustamonte,* 412 US 218, 1973.

37. *Florida v. Jimeno,* 500 US 248, 1991.

38. *Schneckloth v. Bustamonte.*

39. Westfall, 2.

40. *New York v. Belton,* 453 US 454, 1981.

41. *New York v. Belton.*

42. *New York v. Belton.*

43. *Carroll v. United States,* 267 US 132, 1925.

44. See *California v. Carney,* 471 US 386, 1985; and *United States v. Markham,* 844 F.2d 366, 6th Cir., 1988.

45. See *United States v. Hill,* 855 F.2d 644, 10th Cir., 1988.

46. See *United States v. Tartaglia,* 864 F.2d 837, DC Cir., 1989.

47. *California v. Acevedo,* 500 US 114, L.E. 2d 619, 111 S. CT 1982, 1991.

48. *California v. Acevedo.*

49. *United States v. Ross,* 456 US 798, 1982.

50. *Cardwell v. Lewis,* 417 US 218, 1974.

51. *Cardwell v. Lewis.*

52. *Cardwell v. Lewis.*

53. *Harris v. United States,* 390 US 234, 1968.

54. *Minnesota v. Dickerson,* 508 US, 1993.

55. *Florida v. Jimeno,* 111 S. Ct. 1801, 1991.

56. *Florida v. Jimeno.*

57. Shawn V. Lewis, "Fourth Amendment—Protection Against Unreasonable Seizures of the Person: The Intrusiveness of Dragnet Styled Drug Sweeps," *The Journal of Criminal Law and Criminology 82* (Winter 1992): 797–828.

58. David A. Harris, "'Driving While Black' and All Other Traffic Offenses: The Supreme Court and Pretextual Traffic Stops," *Journal of Criminal Law and Criminology 87* (Winter 1997): 544–545.

59. *Whren v. United States,* 116 S. Ct. 1769, 1996.

60. Harris, 545.

61. *Delaware v. Prouse,* 440 US 648, 1979.

62. *Delaware v. Prouse.*

63. Sandra Guerra, "Domestic Drug Interdiction Operations: Finding the Balance." *The Journal of Criminal Law and Criminology 82* (Winter 1992): 797–828.

64. *United States v. Morales–Zamora,* 974 F.2d 149, 151, 10th Cir., 1992.

65. *United States v. Matlock,* 415 US 234, 1968.

66. *Bumper v. North Carolina,* 391 US 543, 1974.

67. *Washington v. Chisman,* 102 SCt. 812, 1982.

68. *Wilson v. Arkansas,* 63 LW 4456, 1995.

69. *Wilson v. Arkansas.*

70. Personal Interview, Apr., 1998.

71. *Aguilar v. Texas,* 378 US 108, 1964.

72. *Spinelli v. United States,* 393 US 410, 1969.

73. *Illinois v. Gates,* 462 US 213, 1983.

74. *United States v. Hoffman,* 832 F.2d 1299, 1306–07, 1st Cir., 1987.

75. *United States v. Koyomejian,* 970 F.2d 536, 541, 9th., 1992.

76. *Katz v. United States.*

77. *United States v. Karo,* 468 US 705, 1984.

78. *United States v. Olderbak,* 961 F.2d 760, 8th Cir., 1992.

79. *Katz v. United States*; and *People v. Lynch,* 445 N.W. 2d 803, 807, Mich. App, 1989.

80. *People v. Lynch.*

81. *California v. Hodari,* 499 US 621, 1991.

82. Lloyd L. Weinreb and James D. Whaley, "The Field Guide to Law Enforcement" (Westbury: Foundation, 1994) 9.

83. Weinreb and Whaley, 10–11.

84. *Payton v. New York,* 445 US 573, 1980.

85. *Steagald v. United States,* 451 US 204, 1981.

86. *Gustafson v. Florida,* 414 US 260, 1973; see also *United States v. Robinson,* 414 US 218, 1973; and *New York v. Belton.*

87. *United States v. Robinson.*

88. *Alabama v. White,* 496 US 325, 1990.

89. *California v. Hodari D.*

90. *California v. Hodari.*

91. *California v. Hodari.*

92. *Terry v. Ohio,* 392 US 1, 1968.

93. *Terry v. Ohio.*

94. *Adams v. Williams,* 407 US 143, 1972.

95. *United States v. Hensley,* 469 US 2212, 1985.

96. *United States v. Sokolow,* 490 US 1, 1989.

97. *United States v. Sokolow.*

98. Steven K. Bernstein, "Fourth Amendment-Using the Drug Courier Profile to Fight the War on Drugs," *The Journal of Criminal Law and Criminology 80* (Winter): 996.

99. *United States v. Sokolow.*

100. *United States v. Cortez,* 449 US 411, 1981, 418.

101. *Minnesota v. Dickerson,* 113 S.Ct. 2130, 1993.

102. *Minnesota v. Dickerson.*

103. Joseph P. Weeg, John P. Messina, and Associates, *Report on Iowa Criminal Law* (Jan. 1996) 3–5.

104. *Miranda v. Arizona,* 384 US 436, 1966.

105. *Miranda v. Arizona.*

106. *Brewer v. Williams,* 430 US 387, 1977.

107. *Brewer v. Williams.*

108. *Brewer v. Williams.*

109. *Brewer v. Williams.*

110. *Nix v. Williams,* 8 LOB 133, 1984.

111. *Nix v. Williams.*

112. *Rhode Island v. Innis,* 446 US 291, 1980.

113. *Rhode Island v. Innis.*

114. *Oregon v. Elstad,* 470 US 298, 1985.

115. *Colorado v. Spring,* 479 US 564, 1987.

116. *Connecticut v. Barrett,* 479 US 523, 1987.

117. *Duckworth v. Eagan,* 492 US 195, 1989.

118. *Illinois v. Perkins,* 110 S. Ct. 2394, 1990.

119. *Arizona v. Fulminante,* 499 US 279, 1991.

120. *Illinois v. Perkins.*

121. *Illinois v. Perkins.*

122. Michael S. Vaughn, "The Parameters of Trickery as an Acceptable Police Practice," *American Journal of Police xi,* 4 (1990): 71–95.

123. Class notes from Interview and Interrogation class given by John Quinn and Melvin McCleary of the Iowa Division of Criminal Investigation (March 1998).

124. *McNabb v. United States,* 318 US 332, 1943.

125. *McNabb v. United States.*

126. *County of Riverside v. McLaughlin,* 111 S.Ct. 1661, 1991.

127. *County of Riverside v. McLaughlin.*

128. *McNeil v. Wisconsin,* 111 S.Ct. 2204, 1991.

129. *McNeil v. Wisconsin.*

130. *United States v. Wade,* 388 US 218, 1967.

131. *United States v. Wade.* See also *Cardwell v. United States,* 338 F. (2d) 385 8th Cir., 1964; *United States v. Mara,* 410 US 19, 35 LEd (2d) 67, 93 S. Ct 777, 1973; and *Schmerber v. California,* 384 US 757, 1966.

132. Personal interview, July 1986.

133. Skolnick and Fyfe, 194.

7

SPECIAL PROBLEMS FOR THE POLICE

One Christmas eve, several years ago, I was asleep on the floor of my living room after having watched a video with my wife. The TV was still on, the Christmas tree was lit, and the Christmas lights on the house were still fully illuminated. My three boys were all in bed, as were my wife's brother and his family, who were visiting from Detroit.

A knock came at the front door. My wife did not want to wake me, so she decided to see who was at the door.... My wife was able to peek out the door through a small window in the door. Being somewhat cautious, she opened the door just slightly to ask this late night visitor to identify himself. As she did this, the person at the door, "stormed" the door, attempting to force his way in. Others were hiding in the bushes, and soon several persons were attempting to invade.

I awoke to her shouts and screams, including "He's got a gun!" My wife had slipped on the wood floor and fallen to the ground. Her body weight against the base of the door kept it from fully opening, and the invaders had not yet gotten in as I awoke. I was about ten feet from the door, I "stormed" the door myself. I threw my body against the door in an attempt to slam it shut, and after a brief struggle, I was able to do so. I immediately reached for the "dead bolt" and locked the door.

During the brief struggle, all I could hear was my wife's screaming. I did get a glimpse of several individuals with weapons. All were Asian and were dressed in black leather jackets and other dark clothing. Believing that they might begin firing their weapons through the front door, I literally picked my wife up and threw her into the kitchen. I ran to my office located about ten feet from this door to obtain my shotgun. My wife had the presence of mind to call "911."

My wife began to yell as soon as I arrived downstairs that they were at the back door, trying to get in. I exited the front door of my residence, intent on confronting them at the back door if necessary. As I exited my residence with my shotgun, I could see that the get-a-way car was empty and the front yard was "clear." As I got to the rear of my residence, I expected to be met by these invaders and my mindset was a "shoot now and ask questions later frame of mind."

There was nobody at the back door, but I could see numerous footprints in the snow. About that time, I heard a car door slam behind me.
As the get-a-way car began to leave, I fired a round from my shotgun at
it. Return fire came from the car as it sped away.

—Anonymous, interviewed in 1997.

This Wisconsin police officer asked himself the question "Why me?" Why would
this group of individuals conduct a very well organized, "planned" hit on me?
Then, he reflected that he had been involved in several high profile arrests of Asian
gang members earlier that year. Law enforcement in that area had been very successful at making arrests of Asian gang members, and it seemed clear to this officer,
who was particularly well known in the law enforcement community, that this
"hit" was intended to send a message to "stop hassling" the Asian gangs. His very
popularity was viewed as a good "target" to get that message across.

Policing in the United States is a tough job. Previous chapters have reflected how
the job is so much more complicated now than in the past. What adds to this difficulty at the present time, as the opening quote of this chapter aptly illustrates, are
new "crime fighting" challenges facing the police. Some of these challenges are totally new, while others are old challenges shaped in new ways. Some of these challenges provide great temptation for wrongdoing, some are a total nuisance, and
others present increased danger to the police officer. In some of these challenges, the
police are hailed as society's champions; yet others reflect publics who are dissatisfied with police services and regard the police as the enemy. With some of these challenges, the police are having reasonable success, but others must be regarded as
dismal failures. Too many have cost the police dearly in public credibility and trust.

These crime fighting challenges vary from dealing with various forms of domestic terrorism, including anti-government militia movements, hate crimes, and
white supremacists; to the ever-expanding drug trafficking gang problem; to organized crime; and to hostage negotiations. What makes these challenges even more
perplexing is that within each one, there are additional and even more exacting demands placed on the police. The problems within the challenges, on one hand,
show, as Peter Manning has reminded us, that the police have little power to control crime.[1] The problems within the challenges also reveal some of the dark sides
of policing in the United States.

DOMESTIC TERRORISM

The Federal Bureau of Investigation (FBI), the designated leading investigative
police agency on terrorism in the United States, has provided this definition of
terrorism:

> Terrorism is the unlawful use of force or violence against persons or property
> to intimidate or coerce a government, the civilian population, or any segment
> thereof, in furtherance of political or social objectives.[2]

The United States became aware of its vulnerability to international terrorist attack on February 26, 1993, with the bombing of the World Trade Center in New York City. Six individuals were killed and an estimated 1,000 were injured. Yet, as described in Figure 7.1, international terrorist incidents in the United States have decreased rather significantly from the early 1980s. Instead, what has become a major concern are a rapidly increasing number of home grown terrorists groups. According to the FBI, the most troublesome at the present are right-wing extremist groups, basically made up of **militia** groups that adhere to anti-government tactics, and white supremacists who support a racist ideology.[3]

Brent L. Smith's examination of terrorist acts in the United States throughout the 1980s found that significant differences existed between left-wing and right-wing terrorists. At the time of indictment, right-wing terrorists were older (with an average age of 39) than left-wing terrorists (whose average age was 35). Right-wing terrorists were nearly all male, with women being more represented in the ranks of left-wing terrorists. Rightist groups were virtually all white, whereas nearly three-fourths of leftist groups were minorities. In terms of education and occupation, leftists tended to have more formal education and were more likely to have professional work backgrounds.[4]

Joseph R. Carlson's 1993 survey of police chiefs serving a population of over 100,000 (86 out of 140 chiefs responded) asked the chiefs to rank the domestic terrorist groups which they had found to be the most active in the previous two years (see Table 7.1).[5] Interestingly, in addition to the militia groups and white supremacists listed by the FBI, the sample of chiefs of police ranked anti-abortionist

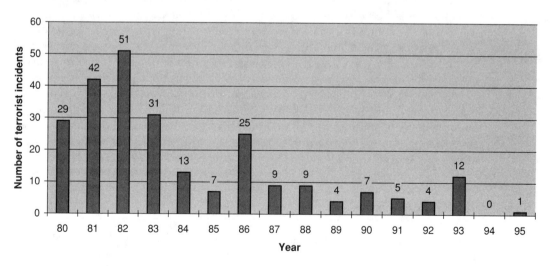

FIGURE 7.1   Terrorist Incidents in the United States: 1980–1995

Source: FBI Homepage, Internet, 1998.

TABLE 7.1 **Rankings of Potential Domestic Terrorist Groups by Chiefs of Police**

Times in top four potential active terrorist groups within two years		Times selected as the #1 most likely group
70 selections	White supremacists	12
67 selections	Anti-abortionists	43
51 selections	Middle East terrorist groups	16
41 selections	Black militants	6
12 selections	Latin American terrorist groups	1
12 selections	European terrorist groups	0
10 selections	Puerto Rican	0
8 selections	Other	1
8 selections	South American terrorist groups	0
6 selections	Anti-Castro Cubans	0
2 selections	Jewish extremists	0

Total number of respondents: 86 or 61%

Source: Joseph R. Carlson, "The Future Terrorists in America," *American Journal of Police 14* (1995): 83. Reproduced with permission, MCB University Press, Ltd.

groups right behind white supremacists as creating the most problems in their communities.

The following section will examine militia groups, hate crimes, and white supremacists, but, as this sample of chiefs of police revealed, violent anti-abortionist groups are becoming a serious form of domestic terrorism. Indeed, on December 8, 1993, television news anchor Ted Koppel presented some documentation of the acts of violence committed by anti-abortionists since 1977 on the nightly news show *Nightline*. He reported that 7,709 incidents of violence were directed at abortion clinics and doctors who performed abortions. Of these incidents, there have been 592 blockages of clinics, 86 bombings, two kidnappings, and one attempted and one completed murder. The attempted murder took place when Dr. George Tiller was shot in both arms on August 19, 1993 outside an abortion clinic in Wichita, Kansas by a protester from Oregon; and the murder occurred in Pensacola, Florida on March 10, 1993, when Dr. David Gunn was shot three times in the back.[6]

Anti-abortionists' acts of violence are currently being handled as individual criminal acts. They are neither being associated with an organized group nor labeled as terrorist acts. But the United States Supreme Court has now ruled that the Racketeer Influenced and Corrupt Organization Act (RICO) statutes can be used against such demonstrating groups. Time will tell how frequently RICO is called upon and how effective it will be in reducing the number of demonstrations and violence at abortion clinics.[7]

Militia Movements

In the spring of 1984, 43 white men from the mountains of Metaline Falls, Washington, most of whom were involved with the Identity Church, began a secret army known as the Order or the Silent Brotherhood. Although only existing for 18 months, the Order committed an unprecedented spree of terrorist acts against what they perceived to be a Jewish-controlled American government.[8]

Randy Weaver, a self-acknowledged white supremacist, played a vital role in the development of the militia movement. On October 24, 1989, while living in Idaho, Weaver sold two sawed-off illegal weapons to federal agents and was arrested for gun charges on January 17, 1991. On February 7, 1991, Weaver was informed by mail that his trial had been changed to March 20, 1991. Yet it had actually been rescheduled for February 20, 1991. When he failed to appear for trial on February 20, a warrant was issued for his arrest.[9]

On August 21, 1992, while checking land around Weaver's cabin in preparation for arresting him, federal marshals encountered Weaver's friend, Kevin Harris and Weaver's son, Samuel, age 14. A shoot-out took place and Samuel and a marshal were killed. Weaver's wife, Vicki, was killed the next day by a federal sniper, who also wounded Weaver and Harris. On August 31, 1992, Weaver surrendered, and his trial began in Boise, Idaho on April 13, 1993. Prosecutors acknowledged during the trial that marshals told an Idaho State Police captain that they fired the first shot on August 21, and on July 8, 1993, the jury found Weaver and Harris not guilty of the death of the agent. Weaver was found guilty of minor gun charges and returned to jail for five months. On August 15, 1995, the federal government agreed to pay the Weaver family $3.1 million to settle the family's claims in the deaths of Vicki Weaver and Samuel Weaver.[10]

What represents a major challenge to both federal and local police agencies is that in the 1990s a subculture perceiving itself as patriot, militia, or citizen guerrilla groups has emerged in American society. Members of this subculture are heavily armed and have a common distrust and even hatred of the federal government and its local enforcement agencies. This militia movement staunchly opposes any form of gun control. To these groups, the Brady Bill and the 1994 federal ban on assault weapons represented the first days of absolute totalitarianism in this nation.

The **Militia of Montana,** or **MOM,** appears to be the "mother" of all militias and has served as an organizational model nationwide. A good many of the most radical militias in this nation owe their existence to MOM's aggressive proselytizing and organizing campaigns since the spring of 1994.[11] The Freemen, one of the Militia of Montana (MOM), occupied "Justus Township" in Jordon, Montana, and engaged the FBI in a long standoff that began in March 1996.

It is estimated that there are 100,000 militia members in 30 states. The Patriot Movement is the largest and fastest growing of the militia groups and is estimated to have over 850 organizations, of which 440 are armed militias. Other militia and extreme anti-government groups include common law courts, "sovereign" citizens, tax protesters, Christian identity religionists, white supremacists, survival-

---

BOX 7.1   Fifteen Years of Violence

Here are some of the more high-profile incidents and developments in the United States involving right-wing extremism since 1982:

1983—Gordon Kahl of the Posse Comitatus shoots it out with federal officers.

1983—Silent Brotherhood/The Order, crime spree fashioned after "The Turner Diaries."

1992, August—Randy Weaver siege at Ruby Ridge; Vicki Weaver, Samuel Weaver, and a federal marshal killed.

1993, April 19—Branch Davidian assault at Waco, Texas.

1995, August 19—Oklahoma City bombing.

1995, May—Larry Harris, alleged National Alliance member, arrested in possession of the Bubonic Plague virus.

1995, June—Frazeyburg, Ohio, Militia Chaplain Michael Hill killed.

1995, October—Amtrak's Sunset Limited train derailed in Arizona desert by Sons of Gestapo.

1996, March—Montana Freemen holed up on Jordan, Montana ranch.

1996, July—Arizona Viper Militia members arrested in weapons and bombing conspiracy.

1996, October—West Virginia's Mountaineer Militia members arrested in conspiracy to sell blueprints of the new FBI fingerprint facility to undercover agents posing as foreign terrorists.

Source: Kathy Marks, "Right-Wing Terrorism's Renewed Threat in the U.S.," *Police: The Law Enforcement Magazine 21* (December 1997): 20. Reproduced by permission of *POLICE: The Law Enforcement Magazine*/Bobit Publishing/Torrance, CA.

ists, Posse Comitatus members, de jure alliances, and jural societies. Most militia leaders are now faithful visitors to Richard Bryan's Aryan Nation compound in Idaho which offers both weapons and spiritual training.[12] For violence incidents involving right-wing extremism in recent years, see Box 7.1.

The common law court movement is exploding in growth at this time and now exists in every state of the nation. Common law courts attempt to impose their own judicial system to handle those who offend against their interpretation of laws. Deriving much of their philosophy from the old Posse Comitatus organization, which arose on the West Coast as a tax protest movement in the 1970s, proponents of common law courts advocate breaking all contracts and going back to the "common law." Then, it is argued, the illegal de facto governments (federal and state) will have no jurisdiction. At this point, a convert can become a sovereign citizen again, subject only to the common law meaning, in effect, no law.[13]

The Bible and a novel called **The Turner Diaries** are the two books most revered in the militia movement. The latter provides a "blueprint for the overthrow of the US—how to blow up buildings, how to set up underground cells, how to establish 'blind pigeon drop' communications and how to wipe out everyone but the white Aryan race."[14] Some of the chilling beliefs common to militia movement members include the following:

- The militia movement's favorite saying is "Freedom is based on respect and respect must be earned by the spilling of blood."
- Many extremists believe that in the year 2000 the United Nations "will wipe out all national governments in the world today."
- Some think that there are "30,000 Russian troops stationed in Mexico, just waiting to invade" the United States.
- It is even thought that the interstate highway system was designed to facilitate foreign occupation.
- Some think that UPC bar codes on the back of traffic signs are there "so that non-English speaking invaders can scan them and read instructions in their own language."
- Many justify violence by saying that they have direction from God to kill people who are not "right."
- A group in Texas, called The Republic, believes that Texas has illegally been held "captive" by the federal government since the 1800s, and it is necessary for their members to work for recognition of the state as an independent nation.
- Many extremists believe that police officers have no right to subject people to searches of their bodies and vehicles.[15]

On April 19, 1995, a car bomb destroyed the Alfred P. Murrah Federal Building in Oklahoma City. Charged and later convicted of various charges related to the crime were two men supposedly angry with the United States government's treatment of the Waco raid: Timothy McVeigh and Terry Nichols. This tragic expression of domestic terrorism caused 169 deaths and 600 more injuries. On April 17, two days before the bombing, McVeigh rented a truck from a Ryder rental agency, which is believed to have carried the bomb.[16]

An interesting sidelight to the matter of the militia movement is the significance of a particular date: April 19. It was on April 19, 1992 that the aborted ATF raid on Randy Weaver's cabin took place. It was on April 19, 1993 that the federal assault of the Branch Davidians in Waco, Texas took place. True believers in the militia are reminded that it was on April 19, 1775 that the Battle of Lexington, the first military engagement of the American Revolution, took place between the colonial Minutemen and the British soldiers. Accordingly, it was on April 19, 1995 that the federal building was bombed in Oklahoma City. Timothy McVeigh appeared to have an obsession with April 19, and even his forged South Dakota driver's license shows the date of issue as April 19, 1993.

Most states have laws against private groups organizing and arming themselves without state sanction, but these groups actively resist any government intervention of any type.[17] In Utah, police officers have been warned by members of a militia group to "start wearing your bulletproof vest off duty as well as on duty" because the militia is "taking a new direction." In neighboring Idaho, a sheriff has been told face to face by a militia leader that "if there is another Waco or Ruby Ridge, we'll seek out the [federal] agents involved and kill their wives and kids."[18]

The challenge posed by militia groups cannot be ignored because they represent a threat to our free and democratic society. Indeed, in 1997 an extremist in

Ohio ordered, and nearly got delivered, three vials of germs capable of causing bubonic plague.[19] Fueled by paranoia and actively promoting fear, militia members "exploit the idea that a limited number of people armed with explosives and a few guns can create problems and affect an entire nation in an hour." They target communication complexes, visible government buildings, and transportation systems, and they propose that "a few well-organized terrorists can disrupt an entire state or nation."[20]

However, no simple solution exists to the ever expanding, national militia problem. The forms of domestic terrorism found in militia movements are tied too closely to cultural and institutional forms in this society. For example, the right to own guns, even if they are assault weapons, is not one which militia groups will easily relinquish. The Weaver and Waco incidents provide examples of how far these groups will go to protect what they consider to be their constitutional rights. In all likelihood, attempts to seize weapons by federal agents will encounter even greater problems in the future.

What adds to the difficulty of controlling these groups is that the militia movement has developed considerable solidarity among its supporters. In several western states, particularly Idaho, militia subcultures are well organized, have financial resources, and benefit from strong leadership. Though not in their conceptions of violence and racial superiority, these subcultures resemble the religious, political, and social communes of the eighteenth and nineteenth centuries in the United States in that they share common belief systems and are openly evangelistic about spreading their beliefs to others.

The growing opposition to and distrust of government that seems to pervade all sectors of American life has also contributed to the popularity of militia groups. Distrust of the government, of course, is not new and has led to various forms of vigilantism in the past. In 1875, the *Chicago Tribune* editorialized: "There is no people so prone as the American to take the law into their own hands when the sanctity of human life is threatened and the rights of property invaded in a manner that cannot be adequately reached and punished by the tortuous course of the law. Judge Lynch is an American by birth and character…"[21]

Controlling the Controllers: A Pressing Challenge

In the first century, the Roman poet Juvenal asked "*Quis custodiet ipsos custodes*"— who guards the guards?[22] In examining federal law enforcement agencies' handling of militia groups, this becomes a very relevant and important question, because it is obvious that these agencies have been involved in the dark side of policing. Combining incompetence, as well as thug-like tactics, federal agents have continually botched the handling of these groups.

The federal law enforcement officers' questionable handling of the Weaver incident is evidenced by the $3.1 million the government had to pay the Weaver family. The Waco disaster involving the Branch Davidians, led by David Koresh, raised even more questions about the competence of federal law enforcement agents and their leaders (see Box 7.2).[23]

BOX 7.2   The Branch Davidian Cult Waco Disaster

The 51 day siege that took place from February 28, 1993, to April 19, 1993, at the compound of the Branch Davidians started with death and ended that way. Beginning with the deaths of four ATDF agents and six cult members, this ordeal ended with the deaths of 86 members of the Branch Davidian cult, including 17 children.

Prior to February 28, evidence was being gathered by the BATF that homemade explosives were being developed that were to be guided by radio-controlled aircraft, that illegal weapons were being stockpiled, and that physical and sexual abuse was taking place with children. One report indicated that David Koresh had spent $199,715 on weapons and ammunition, including parts to convert semi-automatic weapons into automatic weapons.

With the date set to raid the compound, a local ambulance service was retained by the BATF. Someone from the ambulance service leaked information of the impending raid to a local news station, who then proceeded to the area. Being unfamiliar with the area, they asked directions from a postal carrier, who happened to be Koresh's brother-in-law. He informed compound leaders of the impending raid.

An undercover BATF agent who had infiltrated the cult was present when Koresh received word about the raid and ordered preparations to be made to defend the compound. This BATF agent was able to excuse himself from the compound, notifying fellow agents that Koresh was aware of the planned raid and was preparing to defend the compound against the raid.

Yet BATF officials still decided to go ahead with it. Nearly 100 federal agents initiated the raid. They entered the compound in the disguise of ranchers driving two cattle trailers. Driver, agent Dan Curtis of the BATF, realized that cult members were not fooled; gunfire erupted, ending in the deaths of four ATF agents and six cult members.

In the early days of the siege, a full-scale assault was considered, but wanting a peaceful resolution, negotiations with Koresh contin-

ued. Entering the month of April, Koresh agreed to give up after the group's Passover celebration was over, but this turned out to be a false promise. Later in the month, he promised to come out upon completion of a manuscript he was writing, but he provided no time frame for it.

The standoff included negotiations, the surrender of some of the adult and child Branch Davidians, and psychological warfare efforts by the FBI (consisting of bombarding the compound with loud music and with the sounds of rabbits being slaughtered). Then, on April 12, 1993, U.S. Attorney general Janet Reno conferred with FBI officials and experts of the Army's Delta Force in the use of tear gas. Meeting with President Bill Clinton and discussing all alternatives with law enforcement officials, she made the decision in the next several days to use tear gas to end the siege.

The early morning hours of April 19, 1993, found the compound being approached with reconfigured M-60 tanks, with long boom-like arms that extended from them. A phone call was made to the compound, explaining what FBI officials wanted cult members to do. The plan was to punch holes in various parts of the compound, flooding them with gas. It was expected that cult members would flee with the first bursts of gas into the compound; instead, gunfire was directed at the tanks and law enforcement officials. Proceeding to the next level of the plan, the entire compound was gassed. When cult members still refused to flee, another gas strike commenced.

Less than 15 minutes later, 20 to 30 seconds of gunfire was heard within the compound. As seen from an FBI aircraft overhead, three fires began almost simultaneously. In less than one hour, the compound was reduced to a smoldering pile of rubble. What happened to the 86 victims will never be absolutely known. All survivors except one claimed that tanks accidentally started the blaze by knocking over kerosene lamps and a propane tank.

(continued)

BOX 7.2   *Continued*

Questions still remain. Did the BATF have a justifiable reason to enter the compound? If they did, was a proper method of entry used? Once the FBI took over the situation, did they act in proper fashion, or did they provoke mass murder/suicide within the compound? Did Janet Reno, acting out of concern for the children, hastily order the tear gas attack? Or is it true, as David K. Kopel and Paul H. Blackman contend that what happened at Waco shows that the United States has "an increasingly lawless, militaristic, and thuggish set of national police agencies?"

Source: Melinda Beck, et al., "The Questions Live On," *Newsweek,* 3 May, 1993, 28; Howard Chuca-Eoan and Elakine Shannon, "Waco: Tripped Up by Lies," *Time,* 11 October 1993, 39; and David B. Kopel and Paul H. Blackman, "The God Who Answers by Fire: The Waco Disaster and the Necessity of Federal Criminal Justice Reform." Paper presented at the Annual Meeting of the American Society of Criminology in Miami, Florida (November 1994). Copyright © 1997 by Anderson Publishing Co./Cincinnati, OH. Reprinted with permission.

Unfortunately, although the Waco raid was the most spectacular, it is hardly the only instance of the BATF's abuse of power. On September 5, 1991, 60 agents from the BATF, DEA, U.S. Forest Service, and National Guard, wearing painted faces and camouflage, raided the homes of Sina Brush and two neighbors in Mountainair, New Mexico. After kicking the door in, Mrs. Brush and her daughter were handcuffed in their underwear and forced to kneel in the middle of a room while agents ransacked their home. No drugs were found; no apologies were given. On December 16, 1991, 60 BATF agents knocked down the door of John Lawmaster's home with a battering ram. They were acting on a tip that Lawmaster had converted a semi-automatic to a fully automatic weapon. They found nothing illegal but left the house in total disarray. They did leave a note for Lawmaster, who was not at home, saying, "Nothing found." On February 5, 1993, BATF ransacked the home of an African American woman in Portland, Oregon. They terrorized her for hours, refused to allow her to call an attorney, and then left when they discovered that it was a case of mistaken identity. Another in a long list of BATF abuses took place when the lives of Harry and Theresa Lamplaugh were turned upside down on the morning of May 25, 1994. Fifteen to 20 armed men and women burst into their rural Pennsylvania home and treated them with total contempt. Acting like thugs, the federal agents literally trashed their home. Furniture was overturned or smashed and papers were scattered everywhere. Three pet cats were killed and one was literally stomped to death. The agents were looking for a machine gun; unable to find that, they took marriage and birth certificates, school records, insurance information, vehicle registrations, and titles.[24]

A significant issue is that militia groups, in distorted form, represent such basic principles as the freedom to dissent, to speak, and to assemble. The recent history of the militias also reveals the dangers of an overly intrusive state that fails to trust its citizens. The question is whether the danger of the government acting too strongly (and at times like criminals) is greater than the danger of the government failing to act. This argument is much like the debate between proponents of the due-process versus crime control models. The price of liberty would suggest that the greater danger is the government acting too strongly.[25]

Hate Crimes

A perpetual issue in the United States has been the refusal of those in the majority to accept those who are different. This issue is certainly manifested in those who commit hate crimes. **Hate crimes** are legally prohibited activities that are motivated by a person's being different from the person committing the crime. The basis for an attack may be a victim's race, ethnicity, gender, sexual orientation, or religion; that is, any physical or cultural characteristic that, in the minds of the perpetrators, separates the victims from themselves.[26] Hate crimes have been particularly widespread against particular groups, taking the form of racism toward African Americans, anti-semitism directed at Jews, and gay and lesbian victimization.[27]

Jack Levin and Jack McDevitt suggest:

> It has become nearly impossible to keep track of the shocking rise in brutal attacks directed against individuals because they are black, Latino, Asian, white, disabled, women, or gay. Almost daily, the newspapers report new and even more grotesque abominations. These "hate crimes" have become a growing threat to the well-being of our society—on the college campus, in the workplace, and around our neighborhood. As ugly as this situation is now, it is likely to get worse throughout the remainder of this decade and into the next century as the forces of bigotry continue to gain momentum.[28]

Within the context of hate crime, the white supremacist movement is one of the most prolific offenders. Composed of dozens of organizations, some of which have a few members and others tens of thousands, the Center for Democratic Renewal (CDR) estimated in 1993 that there were approximately 25,000 hard core members and another 150,000 people supporting the movement either by attending meetings or making donations.[29] The major groups that make up this movement are the Ku Klux Klan, Neo-Nazis, Aryan Nations, White Aryan Resistance (W. A. R.), the Order, the Christian Patriots, the Christian Identify, and the Skinheads.[30]

According to a study entitled "When Hate Comes to Town: Preventing and Intervening in Community Hate Crime," hate violence is often a response to:

- a growing pattern of economic prejudice built on the stereotype that minorities are making economic gains that threaten the economic and social well-being of whites
- the unprecedented numbers of Latin American and Asian immigrants that have drastically changed many neighborhoods are unprepared for the social, economic, political, and criminal justice system consequences of multicultural living

- the higher visibility of gay men, often identified as "easy targets" who are unable to fight back, combined with the increasing national fear about AIDS
- the increasing lack of social preparedness of most young people when plunged into a multicultural school environment[31]

In the 1980s an increasing number of white youths in the United States were influenced by the British skinhead movement and life-style. The **skinheads** in this nation often wear uniforms consisting of industrial boots, heavy jeans rolled up over the boots, suspenders, green flight jackets, and short or no hair. By the end of the 1980s, the skinheads had achieved the reputation of being the most violent extremist group in the United States.[32]

During the 1980s, the tally of skinhead violence included 121 murders of African Americans, other minorities, and homosexuals in urban areas, 302 racial assaults, and 301 cross burnings.[33] On November 10, 1988 (the 50th anniversary of the Nazi *Kristallnacht*), skinheads in the United States were reportedly involved in more than 60 incidents of anti-Semitic harassment, vandalism, and assault.[34]

Identifying with skinhead groups helps marginal white youths to feel important and accepted, much like gang affiliations for urban youths.[35] In comparison to the media attention they have received, the number of skinheads in the United States is relatively small. In October 1988 it was estimated that there were 1,000 to 1,500 skinheads. This estimate was raised to 2,000 in October 1988, and in June 1989, it was increased to perhaps as many as 3,000 skinheads.[36] In 1992, it was estimated that the number of skinheads had grown to about 3,500 in 40 states.[37]

The challenge to law enforcement is that white supremacist groups and their hate crimes are particularly egregious and cannot be tolerated. They attack and viciously beat, and sometimes kill, the innocent. The victims are usually minorities who are young or female, suspected homosexuals or Jewish, or the homeless. Indeed, five members of the Confederate Hammer Skins were found guilty of putting poison gas into a Dallas synagogue's air-conditioning system. The problem for the police is that, like serial murderers, they choose their victims with some care. The attacks typically take place on the streets at night, in bars, parks, and other isolated locations. Several skinhead youths typically swoop down on the victim, and the sometimes fatal beatings take place very quickly. Then, these skinhead youths go calmly off into the night.

There has been more than sufficient state and federal legislation against hate crimes. Indeed, by 1994, all but Alaska, Nebraska, Utah, and Wyoming had some form of hate crime legislation. The most common elements of these laws include enhanced penalties for common law crimes against persons or property motivated by bias based on race, ethnicity, and religion (31 states); gender (13 states) or sexual orientation (14 states); criminal penalties for vandalism against religious institutions (37 states); and collection of hate crime data (18 states). In addition, Congress enacted the federal Hate Crime Reporting Act in 1990, designed to collect statistics on hate or bias-motivated crimes from local law enforcement departments.[38]

What makes the solution of the hate crime challenge so problematic is that some questions exist about how much commitment there is in police departments to deal with hate or bias-crimes. Samuel Walker and Charles M. Katz identified 16 police departments in the central region of the United States that reported having special bias crime units in the Law Enforcement Management Administrative Statistics (LEMAS) survey in 1990. In surveying these departments, they found that four, or only 25 percent, had a special bias crimes unit. Another six departments, or 37.5 percent, designated officers in other units to handle bias crimes; and six, or 37.5 percent, had neither a special unit nor special procedures for handling these crimes. Walker and Katz conclude: "Even among the departments that have either a special unit or special procedures related to bias crimes, the level of department commitment appears weak."[39]

Administration of Street Justice: A Return to Vigilantism

The police currently face the problem that there is an increasing lack of acceptance toward minority groups in this society. It is quickly apparent that this is true with those who commit hate crimes. Perhaps, the underlying nature of their violent actions relates to their frustration with their own lack of social mobility, but deeper than status inconsistency is a tendency to scapegoat others merely because they are different.

The dark side of policing found within the challenge is that this tendency to reject those who are different and to victimize them in violent ways is very similar to what the police do in administering "street justice" or "curbside justice" against the poor and minorities in urban areas. What the police are actually doing is returning to that sorry legacy of dishonorable vigilante justice found throughout the history of this nation.[40] In order to justify "street justice" or "curbside justice," it is necessary for the police to define those "others" as evil, vile, dirty, and verminesque. The very fact that these individuals are viewed as inferior beings enables the police to define themselves as moral agents.[41]

Thus, when a police officer says that a situation calls for "a little street justice," what this officer usually means is that someone should be hurt a little for what he or she did or was about to do. Officers often find "street justice" appropriate and necessary—morally justifiable and socially desirable—in situations where the courts would be likely to refuse punishment with the severity that the officer believes the offense warrants.[42]

Those who practice street justice tend to reserve it for those acts that openly defy police authority, for those individuals who insult a police officer or cause an officer to lose face, and for those who need to be taught a lesson. For example, if you run away from an officer and make him or her give chase through backyards, over fences, and down back alleys, this offense warrants a "little street justice" of at least one or two good punches when you are finally caught. Now, if you should assault an officer, then more severe street justice is warranted. Assaulting an officer might justify a beating severe enough to require a trip to the hospital. If you should kill or shoot at an officer, this more serious offense might merit a trip to the morgue.[43] This "street justice" rationale largely explains many of the incidents of excessive force cited in Chapter 9. But the nagging question about street justice is this: How are the good guys (the police) any better than the bad guys (criminals).

THE DRUG TRAFFICKING GANG PROBLEM

Gangs have been around since the Revolutionary War. In the War of 1812, for example, Jean Laffite led his band of pioneers and smugglers against the British in support of Andrew Jackson. The Younger and James' gangs of the Wild West have long been folk heroes. The development of youth gangs occurred in the early decades of the twentieth century. According to Frederick Thrasher's study on youth gangs in Chicago during the 1920s, gang participation was a normal part of growing up in ethnic neighborhoods. They were largely transitory social groupings who bonded together without any particular purposes or goals. The protection of turf was universally expected from gang membership.[44]

The 1960s was the decade in which the major "super-gangs" developed. These gangs were made up of both juveniles and adults and, of course, the leadership roles were assumed by the adult members. Over time, some neighborhood gangs became larger and more powerful than other gangs in surrounding neighborhoods, and they forced these groups to become part of their gang organization. A few gangs eventually controlled the entire city. In the 1960s, the Crips, an African American super-gang, began as a small clique in a section of south Los Angeles.[45] It was not long before the Bloods, another African American gang, developed in a nearby neighborhood. In Chicago, the Vice Lords, Blackstone Rangers, and the Gangster Disciples, all major super-gangs today, also had their beginnings during that decade.

The 1980s were a turning point for ghetto-based street gangs as crack cocaine hit the streets. Urban street gangs soon competed with each other for the drug trade. Several Los Angeles gangs established direct connections to major Columbian smugglers, which ensured a continuous supply of top quality cocaine. In some Chicago neighborhoods, heavily armed teams sold drugs openly on street corners, using gang "peewees" as police lookouts.

At the end of the twentieth century, there is every indication that the gang problem is getting worse. With the most lethal weapons available, gangs are terrifying citizens and spreading from metropolitan areas outward to other communities. If the analogy to Prohibition is accurate, as some analysts believe, the gangs have only begun to consolidate their hold on drug trafficking. These drug trafficking street gangs raise several questions for police departments.

Law enforcement officials are mindful that street gangs with origins in large urban centers, especially Chicago, Detroit, Los Angeles, New York, and Miami, have become criminal entrepreneurs in supplying illicit drugs. They have developed intrastate and interstate networks for the purpose of expanding their illegal drug market sales.[46] For example, a study by the U.S. Congress concluded that during the latter part of the 1980s, the Crips and Bloods controlled 30 percent of the crack cocaine market in the United States.[47] A 1988 report by the Drug Enforcement Administration claimed that Los Angeles street gangs were identified with drug sales in 46 states.[48]

The Miami Boys of South Florida, the Jamaican Posses, and the Vice Lords and Gangster Disciples of Chicago are also among those street gangs that have entered the field on the largest scale. Crack cocaine may be the dominant drug most commonly trafficked, but methamphetamine, PCP, LSD, marijuana, and brown heroin are further represented in this illicit drug market. The nationwide reach of this drug trafficking, as well as the rapidity of its spread, is simply astounding.[49]

The social control of this interstate and intrastate drug trafficking has proven to be no easy matter for law enforcement agencies. The drug suppliers sometimes transport drugs by plane, but, more frequently, they deliver the drugs to those in communities who will sell them. It is impossible to stop every new automobile coming into a community, even small towns, and it is also unlawful to stop a vehicle without cause. Nor can every stranger be accosted or accused of being a drug trafficker. This person may be visiting friends or family or looking for employment in that community.

The drug trafficking gangs have also contributed to the dramatic rise of emerging juvenile gangs in communities across the nation. This nationwide expansion appears to be fueled in several different ways. In some communities, it took place when ghetto-based drug trafficking gangs sent ranking gang members in the community to persuade local youths to sell crack cocaine. Gang-related individuals also operate on their own, establishing trafficking networks among community youths. Furthermore, urban gang members whose families had moved to these communities were instrumental in developing local chapters of urban gangs. Finally, juveniles in communities with little or no intervention from outsiders developed their own versions of gangs. The first two types were more likely to become involved in drug trafficking than were the latter two types.

Police have had considerable success in arresting and convicting street gang leaders. For example, nearly every major Chicago gang leader has been arrested, convicted, and is serving a long prison sentence. Although this is less true in other states, there has been a major emphasis on targeting, arresting, and convicting major leaders of street gangs. However, what has taken place is that either new gang leaders have emerged on the streets to replace those imprisoned or those sent to prison have continued to run the gangs in the community from within the prison's walls. If their phone calls are not monitored, then they have used the phone to give direction on drug trafficking endeavors, policy-making decisions, and gang-related activities. If phone calls are monitored, then they have used visitors to pass the necessary directives to gang leaders in the community.

In the 1990s, federal law enforcement agents, especially the FBI, have joined with state law enforcement officials to convict gangs leaders in the community as well as those in prison. As with organized crime leaders, the Racketeer Influenced and Corrupt Organization Act (RICO) has been increasingly used to convict gang leaders and to sentence them in federal court to the Bureau of Prison facilities. These federal facilities have typically placed gang leaders, some of whom have become gang legends, on 24 hour lockup (23 hours in their cells and one hour of recreation) and restricted their visitation rights to family only.

Fighting the Drug War: A Charade for the Public
Many police officers enjoy working in neighborhoods where gang members gather, because gang members present a real challenge. They are anti-police, and

embrace, like many police, the destructive power of the gun and the thrill of danger. Also, similar to the police, gang members seek the respect of others through acts of courage, daring, and physical prowess, and both the police and gang members are interested in securing control over public space. Furthermore, confrontations with gang members provide the police with a direct challenge and opportunity to prove themselves.[50] As one officer put it, "You can't let them see you slip."[51]

With the size of their membership, as well as the large amounts of drug monies they have, drug trafficking gangs can pose a dangerous threat to both the police as well as the larger society. For example, in 1993, law enforcement officials in one city informed Edwin J. Delattre "that a gang operation there had a multimillion dollar agreement with a foreign power to shoot down a commercial airliner inside the United States. The plot was stopped when gang members were arrested after purchasing weapons from undercover law enforcement personnel."[52]

In addition, gangs are a problem because police chiefs regularly receive pressure from citizens to get the drug dealers and crack houses out of local neighborhoods. The elimination of drive-by shootings is also a priority for many communities. A dark side of the challenge of drug trafficking gangs is the question as to whether or not the United States is actually attempting to win the war on drugs. Rickey D. Lashley who worked as a police officer in Wisconsin for 14 years, six of them in drug enforcement, has written an extremely critical and insightful book about the lack of commitment in this nation to win the battle against drugs. In contrast to the trendy rhetoric of the drug war, Lashley makes the argument that problems exist on several levels.[53]

First, Lashley talks throughout his book about the invasion of drug cartels from Bolivia, Columbia, and Peru. The largest Columbian cartels are the Medellin cartel, the Cali cartel, the Bogota cartel, and the North Atlantic Coast cartel. He contends that drugs will continue to flow freely unless the international connections are removed, but he could have pushed the argument a step further and examined the government's commitment to stopping the invasion of these cartels from South America as well as drug suppliers from Asia, Cuba, Jamaica and elsewhere.[54] One of the widely quoted sayings in the inner cities concerning the government's culpability in this drug invasion, beginning in the 1960s, is, "If the government can keep Cuban cigars out of this country, they could have kept drugs also."[55]

Second, Lashley states that federal agencies are much too busy with the art of survival to make a great deal of progress in the drug war. Like other bureaucracies, the DATF, DEA, FBI, and IRS are in competition with each other for a slice of that ever shrinking federal budget pie. As a result, they are overlapping, decentralized, uncoordinated, and at cross-purposes. Federal task forces, according to Lashley, are constantly increasing in number but not effectiveness; there are now federal drug task forces, federal anti-gang task forces, and federal fugitive task forces.[56]

Third, Lashley argues that drug agents are basically inept. Those who work on drug busts are usually low on the enforcement status, and they frequently make sloppy or illegal arrests. He quotes Patricia Adler, whose study of drug users found the police to be but a minor irritation: "Dealers and smugglers held some agencies in high esteem and feared them (the FBI and IRS), but, according to subcultural lore, members of these agencies were not often assigned to drug work. They thus believed that the main task of catching them was left to the lower-echelon drug task forces and the unspecialized local patrols."[57]

Fourth, pondering his own career of frustration in drug enforcement, Lashley inquires why the "police can never seem to get to the kingpins." He answers that the reason why the police do not focus many resources on the large-scale traffickers or "seek to engage the wealthy businessmen who broker and finance the biggest deals of all" is that all too often "the kingpins are too difficult to outwit."[58] Instead, the police choose to focus their raids in the "homes of lower-level dealers and petty distributors of illegal drugs rather than in the mansions and towers of the entrepreneurs who finance and direct them. It is this reason," adds Lashley, "why hundreds of thousands of the poor are locked up every year in the war on crime while white-collar criminals and millionaire money launderers are rarely incarcerated." He concludes that ultimately what is involved is "a failure to devote resources where they will do the most good and a willingness, instead, to hunt down scapegoats marked for imprisonment."[59]

In sum, Lashley's main points would find agreement among many others who have studied the drug problem in the United States. A dark side of policing is that to this point neither the federal government, its law enforcement agencies, or local police departments have really tried to win the war on drugs.

Dealing with Organized Crime

Organized crime, according to Francis A. J. Ianni, is an "integral part of the American social system that brings together a public that demands certain goods and services that are defined as illegal, an organization of individuals who produce or supply these goods and services, and corrupt public officials who protect such individuals for their own profit or gain."[60] Peter A. Lupsha adds that organized crime brings together individuals who develop "task roles and specializations, patterns of interactions, statutes and relationships, spheres of accountability, and responsibility." With continuity over time, they "engage in acts legal and illegal usually involving

1. large amounts of capital
2. nonmember associates
3. the use of violence or the threat of violence (actual or perceived)
4. the corruption of public officials, their agents, or those in position of responsibility and trust"[61]

Organized crime has existed in one form or another since the early history of this nation. Its roots go back to the ethnic street gangs that appeared in New York City, New Orleans, and elsewhere in the late eighteenth century. Several histories of crime have traced modern syndicates (those that have arisen since 1900) to two traditions. The first Jewish gangster tradition traces its roots to Arnold Rothstein, Lewis "Lepske" Buchalter, Jacob "Gurrah" Shapiro, Meyer Lansky, and a Cleveland bootleg ring called the Mayfield Road Gang. The Jewish mobsters diversified quickly into labor racketeering and invested their money in legal and illegitimate gambling resorts.

In the second tradition, Italian gangsters first became involved in bootlegging and remained closely connected to their own neighborhood. With the demise of bootlegging, Italian gangsters used their control of vice—the numbers racket, backroom gambling, prostitution, pornography, and narcotics—and the payoffs that accompanied them to lay the foundation for the control of city political machines, especially those in old Northern cities.[62]

The challenge is that in addition to such old "standbys" as narcotics, gambling, prostitution, and pornography, organized crime has now diversified into fields involving financial institutions, automobile sales, food industries, travel agencies, scavenger services, cigarette vending machines, pinball machines, beer and liquor sales, union racketeering, service industries (such as those providing linen to hotels and restaurants), boxing, and waste disposal.[63]

Organized crime has flourished for several reasons. First, the advantage of organization is that it provides increased profits and reduced risks for those involved in crime. Second, the public has not generally viewed as a serious crime the provision of illegal but desirable goods and services. Third, the presence of organized crime groups frequently reduces the amounts and severity of other crimes in the neighborhood, because organized crime groups usually police their own territory to eliminate competition. Fourth, organized crime often provides assistance for community residents who are seeking legitimate jobs, as well as those having problems with landlords and other such problems. These groups are also generally receptive to contributing to local political campaigns. Finally, organized crime has flourished because it provides a channel of social mobility to groups excluded from legitimate routes to economic success.[64]

Although history teaches that organized crime is difficult or even impossible to control, federal prosecutors have recently had some success in convicting organized crime figures. In 1988, Anthony (Fat Tony) Salerno, alleged boss of the Genovese crime family, was convicted of racketeering. He died in prison in 1992. In 1989 Gene Gotti and John Carneglia were convicted of drug trafficking charges and each was sentenced to 50 years in prison. They were reported to be officers in the Gambino crime family. In 1991, John Gotti, allegedly the leader of this, the most powerful Mafia family, was finally convicted by the federal government for conspiring to murder and racketeering. He was given a life sentence without parole. In 1992, "Little Vic" Amuso, head of the Alucchese crime family, was convicted of 54 counts of murder and racketeering. In 1993, despite several alleged attempts at jury tampering, Robert Bhisaccia, a captain in the Gambino family, was convicted of racketeering, receiving stolen property, and conspiracy.[65]

Organized Crime and the Police: An Unholy Alliance

According to Lashley, there has been for some time an "unholy alliance between organized crime and those in law enforcement who have sold their souls for money and pleasure."[66] This unholy alliance, in which police officers are in on the "take," has permitted organized crime to survive and even thrive.

Adler discusses the "monopolistic markets" in the drug trade controlled by organized crime families. She explains how these organizations operate: "First, large syndicates such as the Mafia, which seek to dominate a market monopolistically, generally develop connections with law enforcement agents. Syndicates use police to protect their members and operations, while driving their competitors out of business."[67] Lashley adds that the corruption goes beyond law enforcement to public officials:

> What needs to be stressed, however, is that such entities as the Cali cartel and the Mafia could not succeed to the extent that they do without the complicity of supposedly legitimate businesses and the corruption of public officials. They need banks in which to launder money and banking officials who will allow them to do so. They need real estate transactions to hide illicit profits and police departments and enforcement bureaus that find no need to search the records of such commerce. Such criminals rely upon an ideological, and morally flawed, stance in law enforcement that wages war against its own population while honoring an armistice with the most despicable of America's enemies. In this there is a need for change.[68]

It can be argued, as suggested in Chapter 1, that police officers "on the take" have been an enduring characteristic of policing in the United States extending back to the colonial era. In the nineteenth and early twentieth centuries, police corruption in cities, especially in the East, became more systematic and structured. Saloons, poolrooms, brothels, and gambling houses all had to pay their tribute to the police. With the rise of organized crime, it is not surprising that the payoffs with the police frequently became an inevitable operational requirement. What makes this dark side of policing even more daunting is the complicity of legitimate businesses and the corruption of public officials.

HOSTAGE NEGOTIATIONS

Skyjacking, political kidnappings, the tragedy of the Munich Olympics, and incidents of foiled bank robberies ending in hostage taking have presented police agencies with a crisis that demands the training and use of specialized teams to preserve the lives of both the hostages and hostage-takers. Before 1972, departments had little guidelines for handling such incidents. During that year, the New York Police Department spearheaded the development of a plan to handle hostage-related situations coining the term "hostage negotiation." The New York City Police Department first attempted to implement these new guidelines in January 1973 when the N. Y. P. D. Hostage Negotiation Team successfully "rescued thirteen hostages. They had been held by four members of a militant Moslem sect for forty-seven hours inside a weapons-filled sporting goods store in Brooklyn, N.Y."[69] Since that time, the NYPD has assisted agencies throughout the United States in developing hostage-negotiations procedures.[70]

Hostage taking threatens every community and is one of the most emotionally charged situations police face. The first few moments of any hostage incident are the most dangerous for all involved. The first officer on the scene must remember the core formula for these situations: "TIME DECREASES STRESS AND ANXIETY."[71] The actions of the first responding officer are extremely important for a successful hostage-negotiation operation. This officer should:

1. Maintain strict firearms discipline once the hostage situation is confirmed.
2. Seek to contain the suspect(s) to the smallest area possible, without unduly endangering officers' or hostages' lives.
3. Identify and detain all possible witnesses.
4. Relay all essential information to the dispatch officer.
5. Establish an inner perimeter as additional backup units become available. They will continue to man the containment area until relieved by the hostage tactical squad [Special Weapons and Tactical Team (SWAT)].
6. Evacuate endangered persons.
7. Report for debriefing and further assignment from command post.[72]

Richard Gallagher and Charles Remsberg warn responding officers, "Unless you, the hostages, or innocent bystanders are at the point of being killed or seriously injured, avoid aggressive assaults on the hostage taker until the situation and all police options can be more fully assessed."[73] They continue, "Do not allow any civilian volunteers to attempt negotiating with the suspect. These persons may push the suspect into more extreme behavior."[74] According to Remsberg, the overall tactical priority in a barricaded incident revolves around three options: (1) talk him out; (2) force him out; and (3) take him out.[75]

In hostage negotiation, the first option is the preferred. An assault is extremely dangerous and, for the most part, impractical for the line officer, and it places the hostages in extreme danger. The suspect has the tactical advantage of a wide field of view, good protection, limited assault access that can be protected from entry,[76] and usually the hostage taker is armed with a weapon that exceeds the lethal threat imposed by the officer's weapon. Remsberg warns responding officers to:

Always Assume

1. The subject is dangerous.
2. Anyone exposed to his line of fire will be injured.
3. There is always one more suspect than you know about.

Never Assume

1. He won't hurt anyone.
2. He is alone.
3. He is gone.
4. He has committed suicide.
5. Things can't turn sour in a millisecond.[77]

Hostage negotiation is the art of communication, psychological acumen, and luck. Negotiators rely on communication to establish rapport with the suspect(s). Voice inflection, tone, and speed of delivery all play a vital part in the communication and negotiation process.[78] When the negotiator arrives, one of the responding officers may have already committed to the communication process. In such cases, the officer may remain the primary negotiator with the support of the hostage negotiation team. See Box 7.3 for another important process of hostage negotiation.

Gallagher and Remsberg divide hostage takers into four categories: (1) cornered criminals; (2) the mentally disturbed; (3) terrorists; and (4) inmates of jails or prisons. Police officers are most likely to encounter the cornered criminal and mentally disturbed individual in a hostage taking episode.[79] Criminal hostage takers have usually been "caught in the act." They are the easiest to negotiate with because the hostage is a shield for safe passage to freedom. Criminal hostage takers are generally rational thinkers who can carefully weigh the odds and recognize the untenability of their situation. For the most part, these hostage takers realize that nothing can be gained by physical violence.

Mentally disturbed individuals, on the other hand, are extremely difficult to deal with and are totally unpredictable. Their actions may be simply a plea for help,[80] or

---

BOX 7.3   The Stockholm Effect or Syndrome

The phrase "Stockholm Syndrome" was developed from an incident which occurred in Stockholm, Sweden, when four bank robbers held four hostages in the bank's vault for several days. Both during and after the incident, strong emotional ties developed between a hostage (female) and one of the captors. Another example of this effect was the conversion of Patricia Hearst from hostage to active participant in the Symbionese Liberation Army. This emotional transfer, or survival identification as it is technically referred to, is a normal and often frequent reaction to continued intense pressure in a life-threatening situation. Those who succumb to this phenomenon eventually demonstrate defenseless and helpless behaviors and see identification with the aggressor(s) as their only option for survival.

In most instances, this phenomenon works both ways. Not only does the hostage identify with his or her captor, but the hostage taker can also identify and develop a relationship with

the prisoner(s). In some extreme cases, the hostage taker and the captives become allies, and the police and the establishment become their enemies. In a negotiable situation, this phenomenon has positive survival value for the hostage(s) because the captors begin to see them as human beings rather than implements of barter, making it difficult to carry through the threats of bodily harm.

A hostage negotiator should not, in any way, try to deter the establishment of such a positive relationship. However, if the tactical alternative is being considered, the negotiator should be aware of the development of such an alliance. It seems wise, in most situations, that captives not be given tactical information, nor should the negotiator seek their cooperation in any tactical operation. In extreme cases of transference, it is highly possible that the hostage would immediately communicate this to his or her captor.

Source: Eugene N. Smith, *Handbook for Hostage Negotiations* (New York: Harper & Row Publishers, Inc., 1979) 9.

they may be acts of desperation in which they are striking out against those who, in their minds, have violated them. Either way, they are capable of changing their minds at a moment's notice. It may be to release the hostages or to kill them. See Table 7.2 for a comparison between mentally disturbed and criminal hostage takers.

Terrorist hostage takers, on the other hand, are the most motivated and typically the most dangerous of the four types. Their operations are generally well-planned and carried out. They are frequently prepared to die for their cause and will kill hostages. They usually have ample weapons and outside support and are well trained. In addition, terrorists are well aware of the Stockholm Syndrome. Terrorist hostage situations are particularly dangerous when the terrorists place hoods over the heads of the hostages and frequently rotate guards. These actions are an attempt to prevent familiarity and the humanization of the hostages.

TABLE 7.2   Mentally Disturbed and Criminal Hostage Takers

Mentally disturbed	Criminal
Common Demands • Revenge for or right of some personal "injustice" • Irrational ultimatums • Press attention	*Common Demands* • Escape • Money • Transportation from scene
Personality Traits • Mental state often confused • May be completely out of touch with reality • Often "inadequate personality"— failure at many things • Wants to prove "manhood" • Often suicidal • May not want to escape	*Personality Traits* • Usually doesn't plan well • May become desperate unless illusion of escape is maintained • Often self-indulgent and impulsive • Lacks conscience or concern for others
Relations with Hostages • Often sees them as symbolic focal points for his rage • Usually presents much more danger to hostages than criminal type does	*Relations with Hostages* • At first uncomfortable with them, worried about what they might do, uncertain how to manage them • Given time, they may begin to relate to them as human beings
Response of Police • May want police to kill him as a form of suicide • Best police approach usually involves being empathic, positive, and interested in listening to his problems	*Response to Police* • Easiest to deal with • Fears police assault and punishment • Knows police tactics and powers • Needs to be persuaded that surrender is in his best interest and reassured that he won't be hurt

Source: Coronet/MTI Film and Video, a division of the Phoenix Learning Group, Inc. 2349 Chaffee Drive, St. Louis, MO 63146.

The fourth type of hostage taker is made up of inmates who take correctional personnel hostage for perceived inhumane conditions in prison and other grievances. They are motivated by temporary mental breakdown connected with the trauma of being incarcerated, of feeling homosexual panic, of reacting to a sense of inadequacy or a craving for power, of suffering chronic and severe mental illness, and of experiencing real or imagined abuse by the system.[81] One problem of this form of hostage negotiation is that the inmates who assume leadership roles are generally unreceptive to peaceful forms of hostage negotiations. Another equally serious problem is that correctional administrators generally refuse by principle to negotiate with inmates.

Negotiations with Extremist Groups: The Gains and the Dark Side

Hostage negotiations have come a long way in the past couple decades. It was not that long ago that there was no training and little ground rules, and, as a result, everyone (hostages, offenders, and officers) were all placed in great danger.

Today, the primary goal of the hostage negotiator is to save lives. To accomplish this task, negotiators rely on proven interviewing "techniques of putting the suspect at ease, eliciting useful information, and keeping communication alive.... The ideal negotiator combines the qualities of a good salesperson, a good actor, and a good psychologist."[82] Box 7.4 lists the ten commandments of hostage negotiation.

Negotiations with Extremist Groups: An Emerging Challenge

The dark side of hostage negotiations, with its sometimes disastrous assault tactics, is primarily in the past. Today, the police usually attempt to make the best of extremely problematic situations in an informed manner. For example, the ten commandments structure and give order to negotiations with hostages. They advise what to do and what not to do in order to get the hostages out alive. They particularly emphasize both the importance of people skills and an awareness of the structural demands and limitations of the hostage negotiation.

BOX 7.4   Ten Commandments of Hostage Negotiation

1. Be conscious of both verbal and nonverbal language.
2. Listen actively.
3. Avoid deadlines.
4. Give hostages only minimal attention.
5. Don't give away what you can use for bargaining.
6. Refuse to negotiate demands for additional weapons or additional hostages.
7. Strive for honesty.
8. Be wary of civilian negotiators.
9. Approach a face to face negotiation situation with caution.
10. Be prepared to be authoritative.

Source: Eugene N. Smith, *Handbook for Hostage Negotiations* (New York: Harper & Row Publishers, Inc., 1979) 14–16.

Waco is a vivid reminder that hostage negotiations still occasionally break down and result in a reversion to the assault tactics of old. The negotiations during this siege was marked by noted conflicts between FBI negotiators and tactical units and communication problems between FBI and BATF agents. There was the FBI's inability to assess so-called "experts" who volunteers their services.[83] Harvard psychology and law professor Alan Stone also took the position that the "active, aggressive law-enforcement mentality of the FBI—the so-called action imperative"— contributed to the outcome.[84]

With the rise of anti-government militia groups across the nation, equipped with high-powered assault weapons, it is likely that increased Wacos will take place in the future. What is disconcerting is the high degree of denial concerning wrongdoing among the federal agencies involved in the siege. The ability of federal agencies to handle more effectively the negotiations involved in such standoffs will depend largely on lessons learned from the Waco disaster.

SUMMARY

With most of these crime fighting challenges, the police find themselves dealing with unmanageable problems. At times in the past, they have handled some of these problems poorly, but are handling them more effectively today. Other problems discussed in this chapter stir debate among various groups, with the result that there is always controversy on how they should be handled. Still others of these problems remain in their emergent state, and the police are attempting to establish policy on how to handle these situations. The overlying theme remains that it will require special and innovative efforts by the police to handle these problems with integrity, efficiency, and effectiveness. Integrity seems to become even more important when there is less clarity about what is to be done and how it needs to be accomplished.

In addition to integrity, this chapter also reflects the importance of class, ethnic, and racial factors. Offenders in hate crimes, drug trafficking, and hostage taking typically feel caught in their social origins. Drug traffickers, especially those who are minorities, often sell drugs because they believe that they cannot make an acceptable living in legitimate ways. Skinheads are typically youths who feel that because of minorities they will have limited upward mobility. The roots of organized crime go back to the ethnic street gangs of the nineteenth century. More recently, modern syndicates, or those which have arisen since 1900, can be traced to a Jewish and an Italian gangster tradition.

This chapter has further examined new problems posed by these crime fighting challenges of the police. One disturbing trend is the thug-like tactics too frequently used by federal agents in arresting suspected violators of guns laws. Local, or municipal, police officers are no better with their administration of street justice. They somehow rationalize that street justice is morally justifiable and socially desirable. Another aspect of this dark side of policing is that street justice is typically dished out to the poor, especially the minority, poor male. The problem beyond the challenge of drug trafficking is that this nation, from the top pinnacles of government to local police administrators, has lacked the type of commitment needed to win this war against drugs. Instead, government and police officials perpetuate the myth that they are doing something about drug trafficking gangs when they continue to arrest street-level dealers. Organized crime and its monopolistic markets in the drug trade only exists to the extent that they maintain an unholy alliance with the police. Public officials are not exempt from corruption with organized crime concerning drugs and the pursuits of other illegal activities. These problems remind us that political, structural, cultural, and organizational changes are needed in order to fight crime more successfully in the United States.

KEY WORDS

hate crimes
militia
Militia of Montana (MOM)

skinheads
The Turner Diaries

DISCUSSION QUESTIONS

1. What would you have done if you were in the shoes of the officer in the opening quote of this chapter?

2. Do you see the militia movement as a serious problem in the United States? If so, how can it be more effectively controlled?

3. The police, as this chapter suggests, sometimes abuse their authority. For example, have some of the lawless actions of federal agents in the militia movement served as a reminder that, once again, the control of the controllers has become an issue in a free and democratic society?

4. Do you see any deeper meaning to the rise of hate crimes? Is there a greater intolerance taking place in this society against those who are different from white males? Are racial tensions in this society increasing?

5. Would you like to be a hostage negotiator? What would make this job satisfying? What would make this job impossible?

6. Why does integrity become more important when there is less clarity about what is to be done and how it needs to be accomplished?

FURTHER READING

Bodansky, Y. *Target America: Terrorism in the US Today.* New York: S.P.I., 1993.

Hamm, Mark S. *American Skinheads: The Criminology and Control of Hate Crimes.* Westport: Praeger, 1994.

Lashley, Rickey D. *Policework: The Need for a Noble Character.* Westport: Praeger, 1995.

Levin, Jack, and Jason McDevitt. *Hate Crimes: The Rising Tide of Bigotry and Bloodshed.* New York: Plenum, 1993.

McMains, Michael J., and Wayman C. Mullins. *Crisis Negotiations: Managing Critical Incidents and Hostage Situations in Law Enforcement and Corrections.* Cincinnati: Anderson , 1995.

Remsberg, Charles. *The Tactical Edge: Surviving High-Risk Patrol.* Northbrook: Calibre Press, 1986.

Shakur, Sanyika. *Monster Cody: The Autobiography of a L.A. Gang Member.* New York: Atlanta Monthly, 1993.

Smith, Eugene N. *Handbook for Hostage Negotiations.* New York: Harper & Row, 1979.

ENDNOTES

1. Peter K. Manning, *Police Work: The Social Organization of the Police,* 2nd ed. (Prospect Heights: Waveland, 1997) 29.

2. Federal Bureau of Investigation, *Terrorism in the United States, 1982–1992* (Washington, DC: U.S. Department of Justice, 1993) 20.

3. "Terrorism: Current Threat," *FBI Home Page,* Internet, 30 Sept. 1997, 1.

4. Brent L. Smith, *Terrorism in America: Pipe Bombs and Pipe Dreams* (Albany: State U of New York, 1994) 37.

5. Joseph R. Carlson, "The Future Terrorists in America," *American Journal of Police 14* (1995): 83.

6. Carlson, 83.

7. Carlson, 76.

8. Mark S. Hamm, *American Skinheads: The Criminology and Control of Hate Crime* (Westport: Praeger, 1994) 50–51.

9. See "Key Incidents in Weaver Case," *The Des Moines Register,* 20 Aug. 1995: 2.

10. "Key Incidents in Weaver Case."

11. Marc Cooper, "Montana's Mother of All Militias," *The Nation,* 22 May 1995: 714, 716.

12. Calibre Press Street Survival Newsline, No. 159, Calibre Press, Inc., Northbrook, IL (15 April 1997).

13. Calibre Press Street Survival Newsline, No. 230, Calibre Press, Inc., Northbrook, IL (23 December 1997).

14. Calibre Press Street Survival Newsline, No. 163, Calibre Press, Inc., Northbrook, IL (28 April 1997).

15. Calibre Press Street Survival Newsline, No. 159, 163.

16. "Ex-GI Charged in Blast," *Chicago Tribune,* 22 Apr. 1995.

17. Kenneth J. Peak, *Policing America: Methods, Issues, Challenges* (Upper Saddle River: Prentice–Hall, 1997) 232.

18. Calibre Press Street Survival Newsline, No. 156, Calibre Press, Inc., Northbrook, IL (4 April 1997).

19. Calibre Press Street Survival Newsline, No. 230, Calibre Press, Inc., Northbrook, IL (23 December 1997).

20. Calibre Press Street Survival Newsline, No. 159, Calibre Press, Inc., Northbrook, IL (15 April 1997).

21. Quoted in Paul Chevigny, *Edge of the Knife: Police Violence in the Americas* (New York: The New Press, 1995) 125–126.

22. Gary T. Marx, "When the Guards Guard Themselves: Undercover Tactics Turned Inward," *Law Enforcement Operations and Management,* ed. Marilyn McShane and Frank P. Williams III (New York: Garland, 1997) 197.

23. For an excellent book on Waco and the Branch Davidian Cult, see David B. Kopel and Paul H. Blackman, *No More Wacos: What's Wrong with Federal Law Enforcement and How to Fix It* (Amherst: Prometheus, 1997). For a follow-up article on Waco, see Richard Abshire, "Waco: Revisited," *Law Enforcement Technology 24* (Apr. 1997): 28–32.

24. Kopel and Blackman, 295–296.

25. Peak, 232.

26. Jack Levin and Jack McDevitt, *Hate Crimes: The Rising Tide of Bigotry and Bloodshed* (New York: Plenum, 1993) 4–5.

27. Robert M. Shusta, Deena R. Levine, Philip R. Harris, Herbert Z. Wong, *Multicultural Law Enforcement* (Englewood Cliffs: Prentice–Hall, 1995) 277–282.

28. Levin and McDevitt, 9.

29. Center for Democratic Renewal, *When Hate Groups Come to Town: A Handbook of Effective Community Response* (Atlanta: Center for Democratic Renewal, 1992) 41.

30. Center for Democratic Renewal, 41.

31. California Office of Criminal Justice Planning, *Emerging Criminal Justice Issues: When Hate Came to Town: Preventing and Intervening in Community Hate Crime 1* (Sacramento: California Office of Criminal Justice Planning, 1989): 1.

32. Jack B. Moore, *Skinheads Shaved for Battle: A Cultural History of American Skinheads* (Bowling Green: Bowling Green U Popular P, 1993) 4.

33. Wayne S. Wooden, "Profiles of Teenage Skinheads and Satanists in South California," paper presented at the Annual Meeting of the American Society of Criminology, San Francisco, Nov. 1991.

34. William A. Marowitz, "Hate or Bias Crime Legislation," *Bias Crime: The Law Enforcement Response* (Chicago: Office of International Criminal Justice, 1991).

35. Levin and McDevitt, 105.

36. Moore, 71.

37. Michael Connely and David Freed, "Breeding Hate," *Gannett Suburban Newspapers*, 1 Aug. 1993, 1E.

38. Samuel Walker and Clarles M. Katz, "Less than Meets the Eye: Police Department Bias–Crime Units," *American Journal of Policing 14* (1995): 29.

39. Walker and Katz, 42.

40. Jerome H. Skolnick and James J. Fyfe, *Above the Law: Police and the Excessive Use of Force* (New York: The Free Press, 1993) 24.

41. Steve Herbert, *Policing Space: Territoriality and the Los Angeles Police Department* (Minneapolis: U of Minnesota P, 1997) 144.

42. Carl B. Klockards, "Street Justice: Some Micro–Moral Reservations Comments on Sykes," *The Police & Society: Touchstone Readings* (Prospect Heights: Waveland, 1995) 156.

43. Klockards, 157.

44. Frederick Thrasher, *The Gang* (Chicago: U of Chicago P, 1927).

45. John C. Quicker and Akil S. Batani–Khalfani, "Clique Succession among South Los Angeles Street Gangs, the Case of the Crips," paper presented at the Annual Meeting of the American Society of Criminology, Reno, Nov. 1989.

46. "Youth Gangs—A Special Problem," *The Christian Science Monitor,* July 1988, 45.

47. General Accounting Office, *Nontraditional Organized Crime* (Washington, DC: USGPO, 1989).

48. Drug Enforcement Administration, *Crack Cocaine Availability and Trafficking in the United States* (Washington, DC: U.S. Department of Justice, 1988).

49. Drug Enforcement Administration.

50. Herbert, 88.

51. Herbert, 88.

52. Edwin J. Delattre, *Character and Cops: Ethics in Policing,* 2nd ed. (Washington, DC: AEI, 1994) xx.

53. Rickey D. Lashley, *Policework: The Need for a Noble Character* (Westport: Praeger, 1995).

54. Lashley, 50, 52.

55. One of the authors has had this statement made to him on several occasions when he has done gang research in urban areas.

56. Lashley, 50, 52.

57. Patricia A. Adler, *Wheeling and Dealing* (New York: Columbia UP, 1985) 109.

58. Lashley, 86.

59. Lashley, 100.

60. Francis A. J. Ianni, *Black Mafia: Ethnic Succession in Organized Crime* (New York: Simon & Schuster, 1974) 15.

61. Peter A. Lupsha, "Networks Versus Networking: Analysis of an Organized Crime Group," *Career Criminals,* ed. Gordon P. Waldo (Beverly Hills: Sage, 1983) 59–86.

62. Frank Browning and John Gerassi, *The American Way of Crime* (New York: G. P. Putnam's Sons, 1980) 438–439.

63. See Howard Abadinsky, *Organized Crime,* 4th ed. (Chicago: Nelson–Hall, 1987).

64. Charles W. Thomas and John R. Hepburn, *Crime, Criminal Law, and Criminology* (Dubuque: Brown, 1983) 314.

65. Sue Titus Reed, *Crime and Criminology,* 7th ed. (Fort Worth: Harcount Brace, 1994) 419, 421.

66. Lashley, 83.

67. Adler, 119.

68. Lashley, 94.

69. Eugene N. Smith, *Handbook for Hostage Negotiations* (New York: Harper & Row, 1979) 1.

70. Smith, 1.

71. Richard Gallagher and Charles Remsberg, *Hostage Negotiations for Police* (Schiller Park: MTI Teleprograms, 1977) 5.

72. Smith, 18.

73. Gallagher and Remsberg, 5.

74. Gallagher and Remsberg, 5.

75. Charles Remsberg, *The Tactical Edge: Surviving High-Risk Patrol* (Northbrook: Calibre Press, 1986) 159.

76. Remsberg, 159

77. Remsberg, 160.

78. Peter V. DiVasto, "Negotiation with Foreign Language–Speaking Subjects," *FBI Law Enforcement Bulletin* (June 1996).

79. Gallagher and Remsberg, 9.

80. Smith, 7–8.

81. Gallagher and Remsberg, 9.

82. Gallagher and Remsberg, 11.

83. Abshire, 30.

84. Abshire, 30.

8

POLICE AND STRESS

It would be impossible to adequately prepare an individual in the police academy for the stress encountered on the street. There is almost continual psychological pressure in police work because the officer must be prepared even if nothing is happening. The constant reminder of the badge and the weight of the pistol on the hip serves notice that at any moment a police officer may be called upon to use deadly force to cope with a sudden life-threatening situation. There is constant exposure to hostility, anger, aggression, depression, and tragedy in the various events and confrontations that occur daily in the police officer's life. The constant exposure to these sorts of stress requires the officer to use all of his adaptive mechanisms to cope....

F. L. McCafferty, E. McCafferty, and M. A. McCafferty (1992), quoted in
Police Suicide: Epidemic in Blue (Springfield: Charles C. Thomas, 1996) 32.

The police officer on the street, as the above quote depicts, is subject to high stress levels.[1] The daily hassles and occasional critical incidents are the main sources of stress. Yet, as intimidating as life-threatening situations on the street may be, organizational stressors usually have greater impact on officers.[2] In some departments, officers feel that they wear their armored vests for what they deal with inside the station rather than what happens on the streets.[3]

Stress has been defined as a response to a perceived threat, challenge, or change; a physical and psychological response to any demand; and a state of psychological and physical arousal.[4] Stressors represent anything in the environment that can cause or set the stage for a stress response. It is when one or more of these events are interpreted as meaningful and potentially challenging, threatening, or otherwise aversive that distress will result.[5] The emotional reaction to the

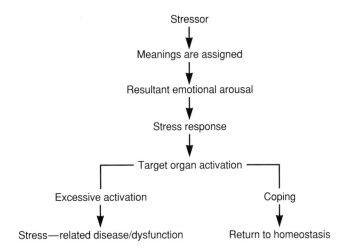

Stressor

↓

Meanings are assigned

↓

Resultant emotional arousal

↓

Stress response

↓

——— Target organ activation ———

Excessive activation   Coping

↓   ↓

Stress—related disease/dysfunction   Return to homeostasis

FIGURE 8.1   The Human Stress Response

Source: Mitchell, J. T. & Everly, G. S. (1995) Critical Incident Stress Debriefing (CISD): An Operations Manual. Ellicott City, MD, Chevron Publishing Corp. Used with permission.

stressor(s) creates a physiological response, and the short and long-term effects depend on the coping mechanism of the individual (see Figure 8.1).

It has long been assumed that police work is more stressful than practically any other occupation and that this stress is due primarily to encounters with violent people and to interactions with those who have been crime victims.[6] Policing may not be the most dangerous occupation, as previously indicated, but the risks that are involved stem from the deliberate acts of other human beings.[7] In recent years, several studies have brought some clarity to how the stress of policing compares to other occupations.[8] Two studies which compared the stress of police officers and teachers found that police officers experience more stress than teachers.[9] Another study found that police officers reported more stress than probation and parole officers but less stress than corrections officers.[10] A further study revealed that police officers reported more stress than firefighters, but less than nonemergency municipal employees.[11]

The severity of a stress reaction depends on the officer's personality, personal support structure, life experiences, law enforcement experience, years on the job, educational background, use of coping resources, the intensity of the stressful event, and the occupational stressors within the officer's agency.[12] This variability of stress among police personnel has received some examination in recent years. John M. Violanti's examination of coping skills in a police academy revealed that recruits who received high scores for personal distress tended to employ "escape-avoidance" and "distancing" coping techniques. This study also found that "the magnitude of personal distress may be an important factor in determining which array of coping techniques is used by an individual."[13] Jerome E. Storch and Robert Panzarella's sample from three departments revealed that those officers focusing on the job's compensations experienced less stress than those pursuing the excitement of the job. They also found that more stress was experienced by officers who thought more frequently about the possibility of being injured and by those who were attempting to adapt to changes in their job or family.[14]

John M. Violanti and Fred Aron found that police "officers with six to ten years of experience reported the highest overall combined stressor mean score."[15] In contrast, Barry J. Evans, Greg J. Coman, and Robb O. Stanley found that officers with more than 12 years of service saw themselves "as more competitive, conscientious, and responsible" and displayed "the traits of cynicism, aloofness, tough-mindedness, independence, aggression, hostility, and authoritarianism."[16] Such traits, according to these researchers, are more likely "to increase the perceived frequency and severity of stressors, rather than helping the officer deal with such pressures."[17]

An assessment of work stress among police executives from two national samples of police executives (one for municipal police chiefs and the other for county sheriffs) reported that police executives with high levels of stress had lower levels of education, less autonomy, and little or no control over the hiring process. This study also found that county sheriffs consistently reported higher levels of stress than did police chiefs. Those executives with lower levels of stress, according to this study, reported greater autonomy and the perception that they had control over the hiring process.[18]

Studies have shown that supervisors also suffer from the adverse effects of distress. Unlike line officers, they receive pressure from all sides—bosses, subordinates, the public, and municipal officials. The most common stressors cited by supervisors are their poorly defined role, lack of support from administrators, little or no input into departmental policy, need to take disciplinary action against a subordinate, and other supervisory functions.[19] It is no wonder that this strain too frequently results in passive–aggressive management styles and alcoholics in supervisory positions.

Both female and minority officers experience unique stressors, which will be examined more extensively in Chapters 11 and 12. The female officer has the stress of gaining acceptance from male officers on the force and, at times, must deal with various forms of sexual harassment from fellow officers. Female officers also report social and marriage problems caused by being a cop. For example, according to Ellen Kirschman, many men are too intimidated to date or marry a female cop.[20]

Minority police officers must deal with the prejudices and hostilities faced by minorities breaking into a profession dominated by white males. In addition, because of the dislike and distrust of the police in minority communities, minority officers face possible negative reactions from their families as well as peers. A minority policewoman expressed how her brother felt about her new occupation: "My brother is a street person and he said, 'O my God, why would you want to do that. It's such a sell out occupation. You'll be doing whitey's work for him.'"[21]

MAIN STRESSORS OF POLICING

There are three basic ways to examine the stressors of policing. First, some studies divide these stressors into organizational practices and the inherent nature of police work.[22] Second, as we have done in this section, it also makes sense to include family stress with that experienced on the streets and in the department. Third, it is possible to develop a more complex scheme for classifying police stress. For example, David Carter devised a typology of police stress consisting of seven categories:

1. "Life threatening stressors" (characterized by the ever-present potential of injury or death).
2. "Social isolation stressors" (includes such factors as cynicism, isolation and alienation from the community, prejudice, and discrimination).
3. "Organizational stressors" (comprising all levels of organizational life).
4. "Functional stressors" (consists of such variables as role conflict, the use of discretion, and legal mandates).
5. "Personal stressors" (originate in the officer's off-duty life).
6. "Physiological stressors" (affected by fatigue, illness or medical conditions, and the physiological impact of shift work).
7. "Psychological stressors" (activated by all of the above as well as exposure to situations that are of a repulsive nature).[23]

Street-Related Stressors

The top **street-related stressors** for police officers include killing someone in the line of duty, experiencing the killing of a fellow officer, being physically attacked or involved in a violent confrontation, and dealing with battered children.[24] These stressors take place in the context of danger, the increased threat of civil and criminal liability, and the negative nature of so many citizen–police contacts. For a study of stress on the street, based on a survey of 103 officers by John M. Violanti and Fred Aron, see Figure 8.2.

The untimely duty-related death is clearly the most tragic for the direct survivors of the fallen officer, and it can also be a profoundly disturbing and unsettling event for surviving officers not present at the tragic event and the officer's family.[25] At least 59 percent of these secondary victims will develop symptoms of post-traumatic stress disorder.[26] Vivian Eney's first flashback happened several years after her husband's death. "I was driving on the Beltway on a beautiful day in August when I felt the blood leave my face. My heart started pounding, and I was crying uncontrollably."[27]

Being involved in a violent confrontation represents another police stressor. Violent confrontations do not take place very frequently, but when they do, a subcultural collection of rules and practices valuing power, courage, and aggressiveness encourages a police officer to be transformed into a heat seeking missile rushing towards the excitement and the danger while others flee.[28]

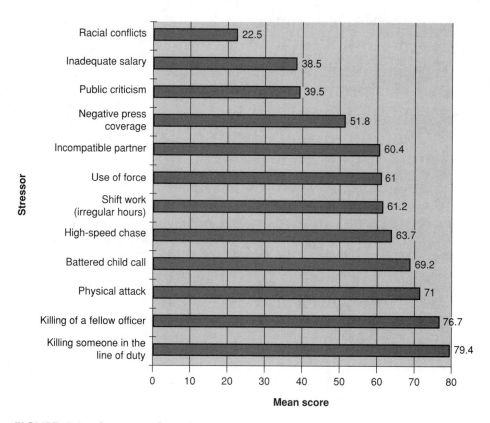

FIGURE 8.2   Stress on the Job

Source: Adapted and reproduced with permission of authors and publisher from: Violanti, J. M., & Aron, F. Ranking police stressors. *Psychological Reports,* 1994, 75, 824–826. © Psychological Reports 1994.

In one dramatic case, a televised shoot-out at the Los Angeles Bank of America allowed Americans to witness men and women police officers responding to life and death stressors. Viewers watched as officers armed with only their sidearms ran into harm's way to aid citizens and fallen officers facing weapons that made their personal body armor useless:

Five months after she gave birth to her son, Ryan, Tracey Angeles was struggling to pull her fellow officer to safety while taking heavy fire.… "Just as Krulac [Detective John Krulac] said, 'You know this is lousy cover,' all you could hear was gunfire.… Officer Zboravan threw me on the ground. We were taking heavy, heavy fire.… I fell face first and my gun went skidding across the cement. I could hear bullets hitting the hard ground and slicing the metal of the cars. I remember thinking we weren't coming out of this alive." When Tracey fell, she was behind the other officers. Unaware that she had fallen, they moved to take cover behind a white van.

But every car they tried to use for cover was fired on with a hail storm of bullets. As they tried to make their way towards a dentist's office, bullets riddled the door frame. The gunman followed every move the officers made firing his automatic weapon.

In the meantime, Guy had fought through the pain and made a tourniquet out of his belt to stop the bleeding in his leg and managed to radio for help. The other three officers were also wounded, with Angeles grazed by either a bullet or shrapnel in the buttocks.

After the longest 20 minutes of both of their lives, Angeles and Guy saw what seemed like a vision. "I saw a Van Nuys police car sneaking up real slowly behind us. I've never been so happy to see a police car in my life." But they were under fire again. Angeles and Guy were joined by Van Nuys officers Todd Schmitz and Tony Cabunoc. They immediately set about getting Officer Guy who was injured, into the back of the cruiser.[29]

In addition, and on a much more regular basis, police officers witness the dark recesses of human behavior. They have to deal with the violence and horror which most citizens only witness on the evening news. Therefore, to function on the job, officers have to suppress the normal emotions of fear, anger, revulsion, and even compassion,[30] but it would be a mistake to assume that an officer would not be affected by this graphic exposure to violence. As described by one officer, "Finding a little baby in the trash, or a little six year old girl asking you 'Is her daddy going to be OK.' You don't leave this at work. You can't!" She adds, "They stay with you no matter how much you try to forget.... You see those faces in your dreams in the middle of the night."[31]

Police Stress and Family Well-Being

Officers' families are secondary victims of the cumulative stress. They vicariously experience the anxiety and frustration of their loved one. According to Richard M. Gist and Vickie Harris Taylor, "public safety work is more than an occupation, more than a career or a profession. The role of police officer...becomes for many the central element in the identity of both the worker and his or her family."[32]

It is not easy being married to a police officer. For one, there is the family disruption due to rotating shift work. While working rotating shifts, female police officers struggle to provide adequate childcare and a family life. For all police families, shift work often means that the officer is unavailable on holidays and for family special events. Shift work over time also begins to exact a physical toll on the officer that is usually accompanied by such emotional changes as irritability and increased tension at home.[33]

The work environment of a police officer poses its difficulties for a spouse. The very nature of the job, filled with unpredictability, crises, and emergency responses, generally communicates to the police family that the job must take priority over their needs. The spouse and children live with the fear of death all the time (see Box 8.1), but are aware that the potential for physical injury is even greater.

BOX 8.1   Of Weeping Adults, Who Wear Badges

On September 22, 1986, Jay Brunkella, a tactical officer in Rogers Park District (Chicago), was killed during a drug arrest. Shortly after Officer Brunkella's death, one of the fellow members of the Rogers Park District tactical unit—Officer Ken Knapcik—returned home after his shift to find a note addressed to him on the dining room table.

"Dad—
    "This poem came directly from my heart.
    "I love you so much it scares and amazes me that you go out every day and risk everything to provide us with all that we have.
    "I didn't write this poem to scare you or Mom, I just wrote to express how lost I'd be without you!
    "I love you Dad!"
    It was signed by his 15 year old daughter, Laura. Laura added a P.S.: "Hey be careful out there."
    With the note was a poem Laura Knapcik had written. Titled "The Ultimate Cop." It was dedicated "To all cops in the world who have daughters who love them with all their hearts. And especially my Dad."
    It reads as follows:

He picked me up from school,
his excitement he didn't hold back
He shared with me his enthusiasm
of our cities' power attack.

Tonight there will be a drug bust
somewhere in an empty lot.
My dad would bust the dealer
and become the ultimate cop.

He dropped me off at home,
he kissed me and held me tight.
As he drove off, he said,
"Say a prayer for me tonight."

At home I went on as usual,
waiting to hear from Dad,
hoping he made the bust,
hoping he nailed them bad.

At 10 I watched the news,
anxious to hear the outcome.
When the newsman read his news
I felt my heart turn numb.

The stern-looking newsman
announced in a voice like thunder.
As my eyes filled with tears,
I said to myself, "Oh why
couldn't Dad be a plumber!"

I screamed at the top of my lungs,
filled with sadness and rage.
I realized then that being a cop
was more than an act on a stage.

Mom awoke with the sound of
    my screams,
running in fear to me.
Before she could ask, she saw
Dad's body lying dead on the ground.

She fell down on the couch
and gasped for a breath
She just couldn't cry—
she was scared to death.

I was running like crazy
throwing things all around
until my mother got up
and tackled me down.

I couldn't stop shaking,
I was nervous and so scared,
I yearned for my Daddy,
and on that thought I blared:
"Oh Daddy, dear Daddy,
where are you now?
I feel so scared and lonely.
Please show me how...

to have faith in God
and in your will to live.
Show me a sign that your life
you'll not give.

Daddy, my Daddy,
can you hear me cry?
Oh God, I need my daddy,
Please don't let him die!!!"

(continued)

BOX 8.1   *Continued*

That night Ken Knapcik stood alone in his house as he read his daughter's note and her poem. He is 40 years old, a 20 year veteran of the Chicago Police Department.

"I started to read it," he said the other day. "I took several minutes. I would get through a part of it, and then I would have to stop and wait awhile before I could go on. I was weeping. She had never told me that she was scared for me. She had told me she was proud of me—but she never told me she was scared. I have three daughters, and I don't recall any of them ever telling me that they were scared.

"I took the poem to work with me the next day and showed it to my fellow officers. I've never seen so many grown men cry. Some couldn't even finish it."…

The poem, by the way, is not framed in the Knapcik's house, and it is not taped onto a page in a scrapbook.

It is in the pocket of Officer Knapcik's police jacket. He carries it with him every time he leaves the house for a new shift.

"I don't want to be out there without it," he said. "I'll probably carry it with me forever."

Source: © Tribune Media Services. All Rights Reserved. Reprinted with permission.

What is unexpected is the ensuing psychological and physiological aftermath of a life-threatening event. Nineteen percent of the 52 officers interviewed in the FBI's 1997 study of feloniously assaulted officers reported strained marital relationships, 12 percent reported strained relationships with other family members and friends, and 4 percent reported problems with children. Eight officers, 15 percent, reported experiencing major changes after the assault in their family structure with one marriage resulting in a divorce.[34]

Spouses are aware that other than the Workman's Compensation Program, there are usually very few financial services or resources available to assist injured officers and their families. Another destabilizing influence is the fear of an officer becoming the target of an internal investigation. Whether due to a serious infraction or to a frivolous complaint, families bear the burden of something for which they had no responsibility and face the possibility of financial ruin or social ostracism.

Another stressor on the family is the personality changes an officer goes through and how these changes affect family relationships. It is not uncommon for officers to hear from their spouses, "You're different," "You've changed," "You've become cold, callous, and unfeeling." "What happened to the person I married?" The officer is usually at a loss of words to explain why he or she has changed and, indeed, probably is not in touch with the fact that he or she is more distant toward the spouse and children. Part of the explanation is found in the disturbing question: "How does an officer who has witnessed violence, brutality, and even death, come home and be warm, sensitive, and loving?"[35]

Finally, the community tends to hold officers to a different standard of behavior in comparison to individuals in other occupations. Officers are often expected to be readily available in off-hours to respond to the slightest neighborhood infraction, and, at the same time, community members expect the officers and their families to be free from family conflicts. Children of officers are frequently expected to behave differently than other children.[36] In addition, law enforcement is the only occupation where an officer is introduced at a party as a cop; this often causes uneasiness and a dampening effect among those attending. Another example of social isolation is that the officer's spouse is often placed on the defensive, having to dodge negative opinions about that bad traffic ticket or the latest police scandal.

As the above material suggests, there are many reasons why communication breaks down between officer and spouse and they end up in a divorce court. A female officer, in explaining her divorce, noted, "I had a husband who would not let me discuss anything with him. This had the effect of pulling the rug out from under me."[37] It is also not surprising that police officers have distant and sometimes alienating relationships with their children. Children, especially adolescents, often rebel against being held to a higher standard than other kids in school. To gain acceptance from peers, they may be pressured to break the law or become more overt in their rebelliousness.

Nevertheless, in spite of these challenges to marriage and family, the police officer needs this support system to remain balanced. It is this balance that is key in functioning effectively as a police officer, in feeling a sense of well being, and in maintaining integrity in policing and in other aspects of life.

Organizational Stress—The Demilitarized Zone

There is wide agreement in the literature that occupational stressors have more negative effects on police officers than dealing with the challenges of the streets.[38] For Violanti and Aron's ranking of some of these occupational stressors, based on their survey of police officers, see Figure 8.3.

One day, a university intern student commented to one of the authors, "I have never seen a place where everyone treats each other so bad." She pointed towards the lieutenant saying, "Doesn't he like anyone?" Julie Klco, founder of My Officer Needs Assistance (MONA), recalls a statement made to her by an officer while noting the accolades, the honor guard, the parade of officers at the funeral of an Illinois officer who died from cancer, "What do we have to do around here—die—before they stop treating us like shit?"[39] Ellen Kirschman's book, *I Love a Cop*, acknowledges that when she walks into a police agency, "I often feel as if I have brought my brief case to a battlefield. I think to myself what I really need now is a flak jacket instead of a flip chart. It is like war inside some agencies."[40] Kirschman writes:

> The law enforcement culture is so rigid and unforgiving that bad situations are made worse for want of an apology. Minor disagreements can push the entire system into legalistic overdrive—people are prepared to do battle at the drop of a hat. Is this the natural consequence of hypervigilance? Or is it a reflection of how embattled and beleaguered many cops feel. They are at war with crim-

inals, at war with drugs, at war with the community, at war with the media, at war with the courts, and, when trouble comes they are at war with each other.[41]

The most detrimental **occupational stressors,** according to Ellen Kirschman, are those violating the officer's value system that demands respect and support. Note how lack of fairness, honesty, and integrity underscores the organizational stressors listed by Ellen Kirschman (see Figure 8.3).

- inadequate training
- poor supervision
- poor equipment
- unfair workload distribution
- inadequate rewards, compensation, or acknowledgment
- poor communication
- lack of administrative support

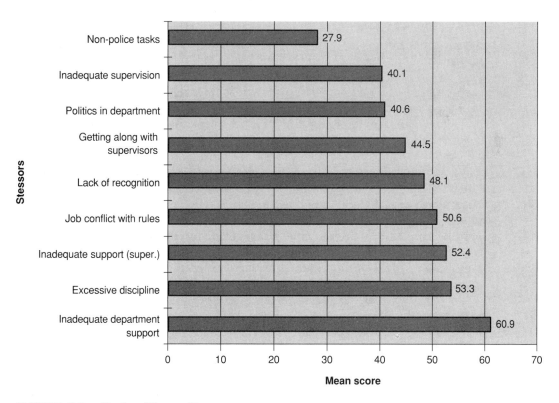

FIGURE 8.3   Station House Stressors

Source: Adapted and reproduced with permission of authors and publisher from: Violanti, J. M., & Aron, F. Ranking Police Stressors. *Psychological Reports,* 1994, 75, 824–826. © Psychological Reports 1994.

- politics
- unfair shift assignments
- few family-friendly policies
- unfair disciplinary practices (performance evaluation and promotional practices)[42]
- poorly managed change
- favoritism
- poor leadership
- lack of clarity and feedback about roles, expectations, and responsibilities[43]

Stress experienced within the department is certainly related to the fact that police bureaucracies are still struggling with the old paramilitary model. In this model, supervisors treat the line officer like a private denying respect and offering little or no support, thereby creating distrust and confrontation.[44] There is considerable role ambiguity found in the fact that supervisors sometimes yell at officers in the station, and then these same officers are expected to go out in the community and administer discretion wisely and treat citizens with respect.

Organizational stressors are also derived from a legion of other factors. Officers typically have performance measures for evaluation. The department may not have a quota, but it has its performance expectations. Then, there is the desire for upward mobility; most entering officers hope to attain rank and job advancement. Peer pressure and need for peer acceptance is a major departmental stressor. When corruption or acts of excessive force are widespread in a department, an ethical officer experiences considerable moral conflict and uncertainty of what to do about it. Every officer faces the stress at times of balancing the constitutional rights of citizens and the protection of society.

Another major stressor takes place when the department is in the process of organizational change, which means that areas of responsibility and role expectation will be altered. For example, community policing is being implemented in the vast majority of police departments in this nation, and this approach requires a different philosophical and organizational approach from more traditional approaches to policing. In a study of the implementation of community policing in the Charlotte–Mecklenburg Police Department, Vivian B. Lord found that community coordinators, radio response officers, and sergeants reported such stress reactions as physiological responses, lack of job involvement, and desire to leave law enforcement.[45]

A final departmental stressor is the fear of being dumped by the department in the event the officer becomes a defendant in a criminal or civil trial. Any incident using force, particularly lethal force, can launch an entire sequence of legal events. Police officials will begin an inquiry with the district attorney, ultimately deciding if the officer was justified, and the media will give the investigation full coverage. Public scrutiny and vigilance over police practices are clearly needed in order to keep borderline officers from stepping over the line and to help remove those who do. Although support from fellow officers assists those who are adjusting to the role of police defendant, officers who lack departmental support often fail to cope with the defendant role and end up compounding their problems.

Recognizing Cumulative Stress

Cumulative stress, more commonly known as "burnout," is a slow erosion of the normal psychological defenses that may go unnoticed until the symptoms manifest. By that time, the officer is already physically sick or has experienced marital problems, alcoholism, or personality changes.[46] Cumulative stress is a collection of work and nonwork-related events, including critical incidents combined with stressors originating in the home and family and stressors left over from one's childhood. Sergeant Steve Albrecht explains the stealthy nature of cumulative stress:

> The uncomfortable truth about this job is that a highly traumatic event can appear before you ... And while you may have been able to successfully cope with the first one, the tenth one, or the 100th bad scene, as the numbers get higher, your internal defense mechanisms can begin to shred. To put this in *Star Trek* terms, your laser shields have failed and the burning hot beams are now penetrating. Things that used to bounce off may now get through and eat at your inner self.[47]

Early warning signs of cumulative stress include vague anxiety, boredom, apathy, emotional fatigue, and depression. They are easy to reverse providing they are recognized and immediate action is taken, perhaps as simple as taking a vacation, a change of job assignment, or open discussions with supervisors, family members or friends. [48] If the early warning signs are neglected or ignored, physical symptoms emerge as cumulative stress becomes fixed and emotions intensify.

Typically, an officer will experience more frequent loss of emotional control; sleep disturbances; headaches, colds, or stomach problems; muscle aches; intensified physical and emotional fatigue; withdrawal from contact with others; irritability; and depression.[49] At this stage, treatment requires a more aggressive life-style change to reduce stress in every area. Short-term counseling would also be beneficial.

An officer who ignores the previous emotional and physical signs of cumulative stress is actually engaging in self-destructive behavior that requires immediate professional help. If cumulative stress is allowed to progress, it becomes ultimately consuming. During this stage, an officer will suffer through the most painful conditions he or she has ever encountered. If the officer does survive, he or she will be emotionally and physically sick, requiring significant professional intervention.

Usually the officer's career is at an end at this point, and any quality of life thereafter may be limited. During this final stage, an officer may suffer from a number of ailments, including muscle tremors; extreme chronic fatigue; over reactions to minor events; chronic feelings of tension; poor concentration and attention span; frequent accidents; carelessness; forgetfulness; feelings of paranoia; uncontrolled emotions of anger, grief, and rage; inability to perform one's job; inability to manage one's personal life; severe withdrawal; suicidal or homicidal thinking;

severe emotional depression; coronary artery disease and heart attacks; diabetes; and cancer.[50]

Cumulative stress reaction takes one to ten years to fully develop. Yet, it is almost totally preventable if officers take "sufficient care of themselves, know the danger signs, and are ready to keep their work and home lives in a state of balance."[51] Possible strategies to mitigate cumulative stress on a personal level are as follows:

1. Maintain a healthy diet avoiding stress producing foods such as caffeine, alcohol, sugars, salt, processed flour, and animal fat.
2. Exercise regularly to burn off the stress producing chemicals. Aerobic exercise is one of the most effective ways to reduce stress.
3. Stop smoking or chewing tobacco; nicotine stimulates the adrenal glands to release stress producing hormones. It also depletes vitamins C and E that help the body cope with stress.
4. Learn to reframe negative stimuli to change the negative impact of an event into a positive experience or perspective.
5. Tap into the inner self through relaxation exercises such as deep breathing, progressive muscle relaxation, biofeedback, hypnosis and meditation.
6. Discuss your reactions to a stressful event with a family member, co-worker, trusted friend, or a mental health professional.[52]
7. Attend the Win® Seminar, the third day of the Calibre Press' Street Survival® Seminar.

THE CRITICAL INCIDENT

In addition to cumulative stress, the police officer can experience a critical incident that can cause an immediate stress reaction. Jeffery Mitchell, who developed a training curriculum for critical incident debriefing teams, defines **critical incident** as any "event which has a stressful impact sufficient enough to overwhelm the usually effective coping skills of either an individual or a group."[53] Roger Solomon, a police psychologist for the Washington State Patrol, defines a critical incident as "any situation beyond the realm of a person's usual experience that overwhelms his or her sense of vulnerability and/or lack of control over the situation."[54]

Critical incidents are particularly damaging to the line officer who has to face the unknown dangers of the street. To face such risks, officers assume a shield of immortality, believing that it cannot happen to them or that they can handle any crisis event. The breaking point of a critical incident entails forcing officers to confront their vulnerability and mortality.

Joseph Wambaugh's *The Onion Field* depicts a gripping account of an actual critical incident.[55] In the mid-1960s, two Los Angeles police officers, Ian Campbell and Karl Hettinger, stopped a vehicle driven by an ex-con, Gregory Powell, who was with another ex-con, Jimmy Smith, on Gower Street in Hollywood, California (see Box 8.2 for how the two police officers gave up their guns).

BOX 8.2 "Give Him Your Gun"

"Would you mind stepping out of the car?" asked Ian, handing back the license.

Greg placed the driver's license in the left front pocket of his leather jacket and lifted and loosened his gun.

"What's this all about?"

"It's just routine."

"Okay. Okay." Greg smiled, shaking his head and sighing, seeing Ian open the door and step back, seeing that Ian held only a flashlight in his hand. Greg turned to his right to back out, then wheeled to his feet.

Ian was looking at the Colt in Greg's hand and stepping backward slowly, unbelieving. Then Greg was behind him, holding him at the back by a handful of jacket, dizzily remembering the things he had learned in the prison yards about police disarming movements. So he clutched the big policeman by the jacket, and if he felt him turn he could push away and step back, and…

Karl had been watching Jimmy, who was licking his lips, cotton mouthed, stone still in the flashlight's glare, asking, "What's the trouble, officer?" And then Karl saw Ian coming around the car, with the suspect walking behind *not* in front, and that was wrong, all wrong. And then Greg peeked behind Ian's back and said, "Take his piece," to Jimmy Smith and fluids jetted through Karl's body and he jerked the six-inch service revolver from the cross-draw holster and pointed it toward the man who was almost completely hidden behind Karl's much larger partner.

"He's got a gun on me," said Ian. "Give him your gun."

And then no one spoke and Karl pointed the gun toward the voice, but the voice had no body. It was like a dream. He was pointing his gun toward Ian, toward a glimpse of black cap and a patch of forehead showing around Ian's arm, and there was no sound but the car sounds, tires, cars humming past on Gower, and headlights bathing them in the beams every few seconds. But no cars stopped or even noticed and Karl found himself now pointing the gun on Jimmy Smith, who was like a statue, and then Karl aimed toward the voice again. It was so incredible! It couldn't happen like this. Back and forth went Karl's gun and he was crouched slightly as on the seven yard line at the police combat range. But this wasn't the combat range. There was no sound except from passing cars.

Ian spoke again. "He's got a gun in my back. Give him your gun."

Then Karl looked at Ian, hesitated, and let the gun butt slide until he was holding it only with the thumb and index finger, the custom wooden grips smooth and slippery between his cold wet fingers. Then he held it up and Jimmy, dark eyes shining, walked toward him and took Karl's Colt revolver.

Source: Joseph Wambaugh, *The Onion Field* (New York: Delacorte Press, 1973) 142–143.

This began two hours of terror for the two officers, followed by 25 minutes of overwhelming horror and shock. Ian was given the task of driving the Ford while Gregory kept careful watch on him from the front passenger seat. Jimmy sat in the back seat while Karl was placed on the floor of the back seat. After nearly two hours of driving, in which the officers had no idea what would happen to them, Ian was told to stop by an onion field in an agricultural area.

"Gregory Powell said to Ian Campbell, 'We told you we were going to let you guys go, but have you ever heard of the little Lindbergh Law?'"

"Ian said, 'Yes.'

Then, as Wambaugh relates it, one of the most horrible and terrifying events in Karl's life took place:

> And Gregory Powell raised his arm and shot him in the mouth.
>
> For a few white-hot seconds the three watched him being lifted up by the blinding fireball and slammed down on his back, eyes open, watching the stars, moaning quietly, a long plaintive moan, and he was not dead nor even beginning to die during these seconds—only shocked, and half conscious. Perhaps his heart thundered in his ears almost drowning out the skirl of bagpipes. Perhaps he was confused because instead of tar he smelled onions at the last. He probably never saw the shadow in the leather jacket looming over him, and never really felt the four bullets flaming down into his chest.[56]

Karl Hettinger took off running down the road at this point. He was shot at, then Greg chased him. He hid in the onion fields, but as he saw car lights, he would get up and run until falling down exhausted. He eventually met a farm hand who helped him escape and be rescued. But Karl met a cool response from fellow officers because to them giving your gun away was simply an unforgivable act. They always contended that he could have done something. Unfortunately, as this book vividly documents, Karl Hettinger never really escaped from the critical incident of that evening, an act that nearly ruined the rest of his life. He began to steal on a regular basis and after getting caught stealing a cigar, he agreed to resign from the police department. He totally lost his confidence, became emotionally withdrawn, had trouble sleeping, and abused alcohol.[57]

Critical incidents have four basic characteristics: (1) they are usually sudden and unexpected; (2) they jeopardize an officer's sense of control; (3) they disrupt an officer's beliefs, values, and basic assumptions about how the world works; and (4) they may include an element of physical or emotional loss.[58]

Traumatic events include the death or serious injury to another officer in the line of duty, suicide of a fellow officer, multi-casualty incident/disaster, death to an innocent civilian caused by the officer's actions, contact with dead or severely injured children, knowing the victim, officer involved shootings, and any event involving intensive media interest.[59] Besides the critical incident itself, as was true with Karl, officers are often traumatized by the department's handling of the event. In some incidences, officers have been driven to the brink of suicide after department abandonment[60] and the news media's adversarial coverage of the event.[61]

Critical Incident Stress

Before the 1980s, it was believed that only ordinary citizens suffered from nightmares, flashbacks, sleep disturbances, and anxiety after facing a crisis event. It was assumed that police officers who were trained to handle emergency situations would not develop stress reactions. The few that were affected would soon heal in a short time because cops were tough, rugged individuals. Nothing could be further from the truth.[62] According to Jeff Mitchell and Grady Bray, several recent studies indicate that better than 85 percent of police officers experience acute stress reactions after working with one or more critical incidents.[63] In fact, numerous studies in the last decade indicate 20 to 46 percent of officers involved in shooting situations, meet the full Diagnostic and Statistical Manual of the American Psychiatric Association criteria for post-traumatic stress disorder (PTSD).[64] Nationally, it has been estimated that 70 percent of the officers who have been involved in shooting situations leave law enforcement within five years, and a Boston area study revealed that 80 percent left within two years.[65]

Charles Remsberg et. al's *Street Survival: Tactics for Armed Encounters* introduced the topic of **after-burn,** more commonly known today as post-shooting trauma or critical incident stress, to the law enforcement community. They write:

> There's a psychological violence connected with gunfights that can be a dangerous enemy, as well as the physical violence. Sometimes the effect makes itself felt almost immediately. The instant the shooting is over, you may burst into tears…throw up…wet your pants…lose control of your bowels…shake so badly you have to put your gun down.…
>
> Most often, though, the impact is not so swift for the officer. It's likelier to set in days, weeks, even months after the shooting, through a phenomenon some therapists call "after-burn." This refers to the tendency of the human mind to dwell on unpleasant, emotion-charged events in the wake of their actual occurrence. In after-burn, you relive and react to an experience, churning over and over what you and others did and what you might or should have done differently. This continual reminding and reassessing can be as vivid as the original event—and even more psychologically upsetting.… *If you continue to deny and repress honest emotions, the effects can escalate into full-blown psychiatric problems* (emphasis in original).[66]

Originally, it was thought that only police shootings were severe enough to produce after-burn, but a recently substantiated conclusion is that police officers suffer the same symptoms as civilians from a wide range of traumatic situations. Consequently, the original idea of post-shooting trauma was broadened to "critical incident stress." Today, a variety of support groups, such as **Critical Incident Debriefing Teams (CISD),** have formed to help officers and their families cope with the stress inherent in the police profession.

How Officers React to a Crisis Event

Officers' reactions to a critical incident usually follow a predictable pattern. The pattern can be broken down into several subsections that Calibre Press in its "The Win® Seminar" calls: "Welcome to Hell"; "What the Hell"; "War is Hell"; "Growing Wings"; and "This Ain't Heaven, But I Sure Feel Strong" (see Figure 8.4).

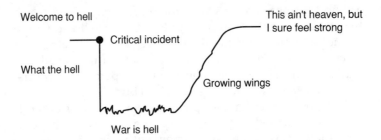

FIGURE 8.4   Reactions to a Critical Incident

Source: From the Street Survival® Seminar, produced by Calibre Press, Inc., Northbrook, IL.

Welcome to Hell

When an officer is confronted with a life-threatening event, the awareness of danger and vulnerability is represented by the universal expression "Oh shit."[67] This triggers the fight or flight response, causing secretion of the adrenal medullary catecholamines, norepinephrine (noradrenalin) and epinephrine (adrenalin).[68] As a result, the officer will start experiencing time, memory, auditory, and visual distortions. Everything will start moving in slow motion or speed up as the officer implements survival tactics. An officer may not remember using his or her firearm or may not hear the sound of a firearm or a partner yelling, but the suspect's gun will sound like a cannon and look like a howitzer. Some officers remember seeing the bullets in the cylinder of the revolver the assailant was pointing at them. Yet, another officer returned to the scene to find a sapling that he thought was a large oak tree he ducked behind as burglars shot at him. Another officer remembers shattering a plate glass window with his gunfire only to return the next day to find the window intact.[69] Impervious to pain, officers report not feeling the blows from a tire iron or the searing pain of a knife cutting. For the perception distortions that may take place at this time, see Box 8.3.

What the Hell

After the euphoric feelings of the adrenalin wear off, officers enter the shock or disruption phase. Second guessing, feelings of rage, anger, and guilt start turning officers' world upside-down. Roger Solomon interprets this rage and anger as feelings of vulnerability and lack of control. He cautions that officers may not get over this anger until they can accept the vulnerability and lack of control that lies underneath it.[70] To help officers get through the first night, Calibre Press advises officers to implement calming techniques, autogenic breathing; watch their beverage selection avoiding caffeine and alcohol; talk about the event to family or friends; stick with their normal routine; and above all, ignore the news media.

BOX 8.3   Perceptual Distortions Survey N=72

Percentage Who Answered in the Affirmative to These Various Distortions

88 DIMINISHED SOUNDS. You did not hear sounds at all, or the sounds had an unusual distant, muffled quality. (This applies to sounds you ordinarily would obviously hear, such as gunfire, shouting, nearby sirens, etc.)

82 TUNNEL VISION. Your vision became intensely focused on the perceived threat and you lost your peripheral vision.

78 AUTOMATIC PILOT. You responded automatically to the perceived threat, giving little or no conscious thought to your actions.

65 HEIGHTENED VISUAL CLARITY. You could see some details or actions with unusual clarity and detail.

63 SLOW-MOTION TIME. Events seemed to be taking place in slow motion and seemed to take longer to happen than they really did.

61 MEMORY LOSS FOR PARTS OF THE EVENT. After the event you came to realize that there were parts of it that you could not remember.

60 MEMORY LOSS FOR PARTS OF YOUR ACTIONS. After the event you came to realize that you could not remember some of your own actions.

50 DISSOCIATION. There were moments when you had a strange sense of detachment, as if the event were a dream, or like you were looking at yourself from the outside.

36 INTRUSIVE DISTRACTING THOUGHTS. You had some thoughts not directly relevant to the immediate tactical situation, such as thinking about loved ones, future plans, etc.

19 MEMORY DISTORTION. You saw, heard or experienced something during the event that you later found out had not happened.

17 INTENSIFIED SOUNDS. Some sounds seemed much louder than normal.

17 FAST-MOTION TIME. Events seemed to be happening much faster than normal.

11 TEMPORARY PARALYSIS. There was a brief time when you felt paralyzed.

Source: Alexis Artwohl and Loren W. Christensen, *Deadly Force Encounters: What Cops Need to Know to Mentally and Physically Prepare for and Survive a Gunfight* (Boulder, Colorado: Paladin Press, 1997) 49–50.

War Is Hell

This is the most painful and devastating stage for officers as life becomes almost unbearable. During this phase, officers will experience some, if not all, of the traumatic stress early warning signs discussed previously. Along with these symptoms, officers may feel sorrow for taking a human life, feel "fear and anxiety about the next time it happens," and "fear that they will be fired, criminally charged, or sued in civil court."[71] Some officers feel the **mark of Cain.** They sense they are marked for life as family members, neighbors and friends treat them differently, and their children are taunted at school about their parent—the killer.[72] Officers stuck in this phase will suffer stress-related illnesses, divorce, alcohol or drug abuse, and may turn to suicide to escape the pain.

Growing Wings

During this phase, officers are adjusting to what happened through coping strategies oftentimes involving a therapist. What they are actually doing is formulating a response to the question "How can I take what has happened to me and make it helpful to me?"[73]

This Ain't Heaven, But I Sure Feel Strong

In this stage, officers accept what happened and move on in life. Although the memories of the event will always be present, officers feel stronger for having lived through the experience. Calibre Press advises that they should accept and learn from one of three conclusions "I know I did what was right, I know I screwed up, or I know I did the best I could."[74]

Critical Incident Debriefing Teams (CISD)

The use of critical incident stress debriefing teams over the past ten years has had a compelling success rate[75] in alleviating the painful effects of the incident, in preventing the subsequent development of post-traumatic stress disorder, and in restoring the individual to the pre-incident level of functioning as quickly as possible.[76] CISD allows victims to verbalize their stress, thereby reframing the event before false interpretations become affixed in their minds. For the best chances of success, the critical incident debriefing should take place within 24 to 48 hours after the event.

The typical debriefing team consists of one mental health professional or a member of the clergy and of one to three peer support personnel. The team leader is required to hold an advanced degree in the mental health field and must work as a mental health provider in a professional setting. The debriefing is essentially a group counseling session, involving the primary victims, those directly traumatized, and co-workers who were involved in the traumatic event. Family and friends, to whom the event was communicated, are sometimes involved.[77] To help achieve openness, participants have the right to ask anyone with whom they are uncomfortable to leave.

POST-TRAUMATIC STRESS DISORDER

Admittedly, the "police culture" is suspicious of outsiders with a reluctance to admit that officers are affected by traumatizing events, and that they need help. The resulting suppression of emotions and avoidance of preventive strategies, such as psychological debriefings after a traumatic event, can set them up for a potentially serious condition called post-traumatic stress disorder (PTSD).[78]

Once thought of as only a combat-related syndrome, there is evidence today that **post-traumatic stress disorder (PTSD)** has the potential to arise out of virtually any life-threatening experience and is an accumulation of stressor experiences and exposure to certain events, such as the loss of personal property or physical injury.[79] It is considered "the most severe and incapacitating form of stress-related disorder, capable of ending [an officer's] functional life in a matter of moments."[80] According to Larry Blum, a police psychologist, what makes PTSD such an ominous threat to law enforcement is that two-thirds of officers suffer post-traumatic stress symptoms sometime in their career and one-third will have a profound reaction.[81] For a model of Post-Traumatic Stress, see Figure 8.5.

For most officers, acute stress reactions begin at the scene of a traumatic event or within 24 hours after the event. Yet, some officers will have little or no reaction to a traumatic scene. Instead, their delayed stress reaction tends to show up days, weeks, months, and in some extraordinary cases years after the event. Post-traumatic stress is confusing to the officer who can not pinpoint the exact incident that caused the reaction. Nonetheless, the reaction is as real and painful as if it occurred at the time of the crisis event.[82] Some of the common warning signs of PTSD are:

1. Flashbacks—intrusive memories of the trauma that may occur hourly, daily, and so forth. The officer may feel the same anxiety and discomfort that was present during the event. Sights, smells and sounds associated with the event can trigger the flashbacks.

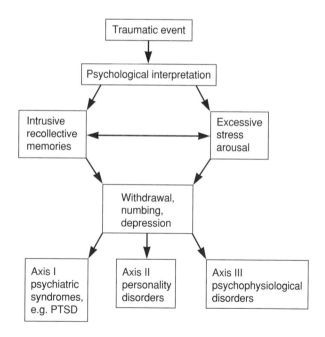

FIGURE 8.5 A Model of Post-Traumatic Stress

Source: Jeffery T. Mitchell and George S. Everly, *Critical Incident Stress Debriefing: (CISD) An Operations Manual for the Prevention of Traumatic Stress among Emergency Services and Disaster Workers* (Ellicot City: Chevron, 1993) 37.

2. Sleep problems—the most common warning sign. The officer may be haunted by traumatic images that replay the incident exactly as it happened in real life or as bizarre distortions in nightmares and daydreams. Physiological responses could include breaking out in a cold sweat even months after the incident, nausea, muscle tremors, or a startle response. When asked how many have dreamed about their bullets rolling out of the barrel onto the ground or the bullets striking the assailant with no apparent effect, over a third of the Street Survival® audience responded affirmatively.[83]

3. Anger, irritability, and difficulty controlling hostility—as a defensive reaction, anger is a secondary emotion closely tied to frustration and disappointment.

4. Concentration problems—delayed stress manifests itself in a deterioration of the thinking process. It involves mental confusion, a lowered attention span, difficulty making decisions, or performing problem-solving activities.

5. Distancing—one of the most common behavioral manifestations. The officer avoids contact with friends and family. He or she will not discuss anything with them.

6. Infidelity—cops suffering from trauma or cumulative stress often cheat on their spouses.

7. Avoidance of recreation and fun activities—frequently involves destructive behavior such as alcohol abuse or extreme decision making that is not in the person's best interest.

8. Exaggerated territoriality—will not share possessions.

9. Hitting spouses and citizens—occurs in the last stages.[84]

Early treatment of traumatic stress through Critical Incident Stress Debriefing Teams (CISD) or professional counseling is essential to stop the psychiatric manifestation of PTSD. Although CISD teams are helpful, they may not be adequate for some individuals since PTSD symptoms typically do not manifest themselves until much after the event.[85] For effective intervention, officers and spouses should become familiar with the early warning signs of a critical incident. If several of the early warning signs are evident in a fellow officer or a loved one, further evaluation and possible professional help are needed.

POLICE SUICIDES

During the last two decades (1970–1990), there has been a one and one half fold increase in police suicides.[86] Police officers are killing themselves at a rate 8.3 times greater than those who die at the hands of criminals.[87] Yet, at present, little is known about police suicide. The results from several studies vary considerably, depending on the demographics of the group studied.[88] What we do know is that the vast majority of police officers who commit suicide have a diagnosable mental disorder—most commonly, depression, alcohol, or drug abuse. For example, the New York City police survey of 18,000 officers listed depression, relationship losses, or conflicts as leading causes of suicide.[89] We also know that a critical incident may "trigger" a post traumatic stress disorder, but it is the exposure to long-term hassles that accounts for the impact a critical incident may have.[90]

In most cases the underlying problems that caused the suicide are, in fact, fully treatable. Police officers, like other citizens, do not kill themselves because they want to be dead. As described by a former New York officer, they are simply trying to escape unbearable pain:

> All I wanted to do was be a cop in my life, but I did not know it came with all these horrors and no training to back them up and nobody who cares about you.
>
> What was I doing there? I was giving Christie Masone mouth to mouth and he came up in my throat and I tasted his blood. And he stills lives with me today. And he will always live with me blood or no blood, but the taste of that blood was the most horrible thing that anyone could ever live with because no matter what you taste you will always taste that blood.
>
> They told me they were going to take care of me. They never once ever asked me: How do you feel? How are you? Is this too traumatic? Is this too emotional?... But I was too proud. How could I go to somebody and say, "Hey. I'm going to kill myself." What support would I get? Who would help me? They would tell me, "You're crazy. You're not a cop. You're crazy. You don't belong on the job."
>
> I know I can't be a cop again. I'm smarter. I know it. If I went out on an incident of a dead baby or something to recall the horror, I would go to the edge again.
>
> I went straight to hell and there was nobody there. I went straight to hell and I couldn't come back no more.[91]

For the above officer, the promise of an inspiring career ended in despair, isolation, and finally emotional pain so severe that suicide seemed the only viable relief. It is a story that is being repeated too often in law enforcement, as evidenced by the steady increase in police suicides. This trend is even more alarming given that police officers during the past three decades have undergone psychological testing and extensive background investigations to select recruits that are of sound character, with above average levels of emotional stability and intelligence.[92]

Nancy Davis, a psychologist who specializes in treating PTSD, gives several tips to officers who believe co-workers are contemplating suicide. First, use guilt—use whatever it takes to intervene. Constantly challenge the belief that the world will be better off without them. Second, tell the officers that their parents will never get over the suicide, nor will their children. Remind them that their suicide will increase the chances that their children will also kill themselves. Third, bring up the officer's spouse describing what the aftermath will be like for her or him. "Being blunt with people contemplating this act is much better than being soft."[93] Davis further advises officers to "never keep the suicidal thoughts or intentions of another officer to yourself.... Involve other officers to help you support [your co-worker]. Especially tell the people most involved with the officer."[94]

Davis gives additional advise to officers to help co-workers who have attempted suicide: First, ask if there is anything you can do to help them. Second, tell them you're sorry you didn't recognize their level of depression and that you want to be there for them when they're feeling bad in the future. Third, say you are glad the attempt was not successful. Be direct.... Do not ignore the incident, hoping the problem will go away."[95]

SUMMARY

The contextual analysis of stress presented in this chapter suggests that policing is an extremely stressful job. Its stress would be much more manageable if it merely took place on the streets, but the stress is ever greater because departments view occupational stress as an employee problem, not an organizational problem.[96] The stress of a police career also affects the officer's family. Spouses, as well as children, do not find it easy to have a police officer in the family.

Cumulative and critical incident stress are major problems for police officers and have contributed to high rates of alcoholism, divorce, various physical ailments, emotional problems, job "burnout," and suicide. Cumulative stress is almost totally preventable if officers take care of themselves, know the danger signs, and keep their work and home lives in a state of balance. Critical incident stress can lead to post-traumatic stress disorder, increasingly found in law enforcement, and can result in the total breakdown of a police officer. Severe reactions due to critical incident stress can be avoided through the use of CISD teams, mental health professionals, recognition of the early warning signs of traumatic stress by co-workers and family members, and a willingness to seek help. Psychological services or suicide prevention programs can only work if officers feel free to take advantage of them.

Although helping officers manage and cope with stress is important, it still has not cured the unhealthy workplace.[97] The fact is that police organizations must change if officers are to manage stress in more constructive ways. Richard Ayres, George Flanagan, and Marilyn Ayres recommend implementing six management strategies to achieve a healthy working environment:

1. examining the work place to identify internal stressors and develop plans needed for change
2. providing a clear direction to alleviate ambiguities, inconsistencies, and conflicts among peacekeeping, community service, and crime fighting roles of the line officer
3. encouraging upward communication
4. pushing autonomy by defusing the hierarchical structure of a paramilitary organization
5. ensuring fairness
6. caring about people[98]

KEY WORDS

after-burn	mark of Cain
critical incident	occupational stressors
Critical Incident Debriefing Teams (CISD)	post-traumatic stress disorder (PTSD)
cumulative stress	street-related stressors

DISCUSSION QUESTIONS

1. Why is police work stressful? Of the three main stressors, which one would be more difficult for you if you were a police officer?

2. Explain what is meant by cumulative stress. Why is it such a problem in policing?

3. Why are there often perceptual distortions during a crisis event?

4. What is post-traumatic stress disorder? What are some of its effects? Can it be cured?

5. Why are suicide rates so high in police work?

6. How would you handle a person about to commit suicide?

EXERCISE

Job Stress/Burnout Questionnaire

Police officers should take the following test to determine their stress levels. It probably would not be a bad test for college students either. Check any items that apply to you.

1. I am dissatisfied with my job.

2. I am pessimistic about my work.

3. My work affects my home life.

4. I cannot wait for my shift to end.

*5. I sometimes use alcohol or other drugs to forget work.

6. I often wish to change jobs.

7. I take a lot of sick days.

8. I feel I cannot talk to anyone about what my job is like.

9. I often feel like crying or breaking things.

10. I have less energy than I used to have.

11. My work absenteeism is up.

12. I feel under stress.

*13. It is rare for me to be completely relaxed.

14. I am gaining or losing weight.

15. My sex life has deteriorated.

*16. My job performance is deteriorating.

17. I think more and more about my job.

*18. I often feel depressed.

19. I am not sleeping well.

20. I do not feel like helping citizens anymore.

21. There is no one I can trust.

22. I am sometimes underaggressive or overaggressive.

23. I do not have many outside interests anymore.

*24. I sometimes feel I will explode.

25. I no longer take good care of myself.

26. No one understands me.

*27. I think of suicide.

*28. I often flash back to unpleasant things in the past.

*29. My family and peers are worried about me.

*30. I keep hoping for a major change in my life.

31. My spiritual life is not satisfying.

*32. I feel like I am on a treadmill and cannot get off.

*33. My life is becoming unmanageable.

*34. I feel very bad about several aspects of my job.

Scoring:

*Critical Items: Any one or more of these items indicates a problem requiring professional assessment.

If **0–3** noncritical items are checked, you may be handling stress well and may not be approaching burnout.

If **4–10** noncritical items are checked, you are moderately stressed and heading for burnout. You will probably need some help soon, if not immediately.

If **11–15** critical and noncritical items are checked, you are probably highly stressed and experiencing burnout. You need help now.

If **16** or more items are checked, your rate of stress and burnout is probably at a life-threatening level.

Source: Reprinted with permission from EAP Digest (Jan/Feb, 1990). Performance Resource Press, Troy, MI.

FURTHER READING

Anderson, Dennis, and Charles Remsberg. "Street Survival® '97: The Tactical Edge® Seminar; The Win® Seminar." Northbrook: Calibre Press, Mar. and May 1997.

Ayres, Richard M., George S. Flanagan, and Marilyn V. Ayres. *Preventing Law Enforcement Stress: The Organization's Role.* Washington DC: The National Sheriff's Association and Bureau of Justice Assistance, 1990.

Everly, George S., Jr. *A Clinical Guide to the Treatment of the Human Stress Response.* New York: Plenum, 1990.

Finn, Peter, and Julie Esselman Tomz. *Developing a Law Enforcement Stress Program for Officers and Their Families.* Washington DC: U.S. Department of Justice; Office of Justice Programs; National Institute of Justice, Dec. 1996.

Kurke, Martin K., and Ellen M. Scrivner, Eds. *Police Psychology Into the 21st Century.* Hillsdale: Erlbaum, 1995.

Mitchell, Jeff, and Grady Bray. *Emergency Services Stress: Guidelines for Preserving the Health and Careers of Emergency Services Personnel.* Englewood Cliffs: Prentice–Hall, 1990.

Mitchell, Jeffery T., and George S. Everly. *Critical Incident Stress Debriefing: (CISD) An Operations Manual for the Prevention of Traumatic Stress among Emergency Services and Disaster Workers.* Ellicott City: Chevron, 1993.

Remsberg, Charles, Thomas M. McTernan, and Ronald J. Adams. *Street Survival: Tactics for Armed Encounters.* Northbrook: Calibre, 1980.

Violanti, John M. Ed. *Police Suicide: Epidemic in Blue.* Springfield: Charles C. Thomas, 1996: 104.

ENDNOTES

1. L. B. Johnson, "Job Strain among Police Officers: Gender Comparisons," *Police Studies 14* (1991): 12–16.

2. T. Martelli, L. Waters, and J. Martelli, "The Police Stress Survey: Reliability and Relation to Job Satisfaction and Organizational Commitment," *Psychological Reports 64* (1989): 267–273; J. Violanti and F. Aron, "Sources of Police Stressors, Job Attitudes, and Psychological Distress," *Psychological Reports 72* (1993): 899–904; F. Graf, "The Relationship between Social Support and Occupational Stress among Police Officers," *Journal of Police Science and Administration 14* (1986): 178–186; and N. Norvell, D. Belles, and H. Hills, "Perceived Stress Levels and Physical Symptoms in Supervisory Law Enforcement Personnel," *Journal of Police Science and Administration 16* (1988): 75–79.

3. This is a common expression with police officers.

4. Jeff Mitchell and Grady Bray, *Emergency Services Stress: Guidelines for Preserving the Health and Careers of Emergency Services Personnel* (Englewood Cliffs: Prentice–Hall, 1990) 4.

5. Jeffery T. Mitchell and George S. Everly, *Critical Incident Stress Debriefing: (CISD) An Operations Manual for the Prevention of Traumatic Stress Among Emergency Services and Disaster Workers* (Ellicott City: Chevron, 1993) 29–32.

6. Jerome E. Storch and Robert Panzarella, "Police Stress: State–Trait Anxiety in Relation to Occupational and Personal Stressors," *Journal of Criminal Justice 24* (1996): 99. See also D. L. Conroy, and K. M. Hess, *Officers at Risk: How to Cope and Identify with Stress* (Placerville: Custom, 1966); and M. Reiser and S. P. Geiger, "Police Officer as Victim," *Professional Psychology: Research and Practice 15* (1984): 315–323.

7. David H. Bayley, *Police for the Future* (New York: Oxford, 1994) 71.

8. Storch and Panzarella, 99.

9. R. T. Sigler, C. N. Wilson, "Stress in the Work Place: Comparing Police Stress with Teacher Stress," *Journal of Police Science and Administration 16* (1988): 151–162; and R. T. Sigler, C. N. Wilson, and Z. Allen, "Police Stress and Teacher Stress at Work and at Home," *Journal of Criminal Justice 19* (1991): 361–370.

10. B. L. Patterson, "Job Experience and Perceived Job Stress among Police, Correctional, and Probation/Parole Officers," *Criminal Justice and Behavior 19* (1992): 260–285.

11. M. Pendleton, E. Stotland, P. Spiers, and E. Kirsh, "Stress and Strain among Police, Firefighters, and Government Workers: A Comparative Analysis," *Criminal Justice and Behavior 16* (1989): 196–210.

12. William J. Lewinski personal interview, May 1997.

13. John M. Violanti, "What Does High Stress Police Training Teach Recruits? An Analysis of Coping," *Journal of Criminal Justice 21* (1993): 415–416.

14. Storch and Panzarella, 99–107.

15. John M. Violanti and Fred Aron, "Police Stressors: Variations in Perception among Police Personnel," *Journal of Criminal Justice 23* (1995): 287.

16. Barry J. Evans, Greg J. Coman, and Robb O. Stanley, "The Police Personality: Type A Behavior and Trait Anxiety," *Journal of Criminal Justice 20* (1992): 439–440.

17. Evans, et al., 440.

18. John P. Crank, John D. Hewitt, Bob Regoli, and Robert G. Culbertson, "An Assessment of Work Stress among Police Executives," *Journal of Criminal Justice 21* (1993): 313.

19 Steven R. Standfest, "The Police Supervisor and Stress," *FBI Law Enforcement Bulletin* (May 1996).

20. Ellen Kirschman, *I Love a Cop: What Police Families Need to Know* (New York: Guilford, 1997) 17.

21. Quoted in Wayne Anderson, David Swenson, and Daniel Clay, *Stress Management for Law Enforcement Officers* (Englewood Cliffs: Prentice–Hall, 1995): 193.

22. C. D. Speilberger, L. Westberry, K. Grier, and G. Greenfield, *The Police Stress Survey: Sources of Stress in Law Enforcement* (Tampa: Human Relations Institute, 1981); and T. Martelli, et al., 267–273.

23. D. L. Carter, "Theoretical Dimensions in the Abuse of Authority by Police Officers," *Police Deviance,* 3rd ed., ed. T. L. Barker and D. L. Carter (Cincinnati: Anderson, 1994) 276–277.

24. John M. Violanti and Fred Aron, "Ranking Police Stressors," *Psychological Reports 75* (1994): 825.

25. Richard M. Gist and Vickie Harris Taylor, "Co-Workers and Their Families," *Concerns of Police Survivors, Inc.* (Washington DC, 1991) 1.

26. Personal Interview with Sharon A. J. Felton, President of Concerns of Police Survivors, Inc., reference COPS 1985 survey, Buffalo, New York (January 1997).

27. Constance Clark, *In the Line of Duty: The Service and Sacrifice of America's Finest* (Washington, DC: Potomac, The National Law Enforcement Officers Memorial Fund, 1989) 40.

28. Steve Herbert, *Policing Space: Territoriality and the Los Angeles Police Department* (Minneapolis: U of Minnesota P, 1997) 80.

29. APB Staff, "Above and Beyond the Call," *American Police Beat IV,* 4 (May 1997): 1, 27.

30. Ellen Kirschman, *I Love a Cop: What Police Families Need to Know* (New York: Guilford, 1997) 17.

31. "HBO under cover: Memphis P.D.," *HBO,* 7 July 1997.

32. Gist and Taylor, "Co-Workers and Their Families," 1.

33. Peter Finn and Julie Esselman Tomz, *Developing a Law Enforcement Stress Program for Officers and Their Families* (Washington DC: U.S. Department of Justice, Office of Justice Programs, National Institute of Justice, December 1996) 14–16.

34. Anthony J. Pinizzotto, Edward F. Davis, and Charles E. Miller, III *In the Line of Fire: Violence Against Law Enforcement, A Study of Felonious Assaults on Law Enforcement Officers* (Washington, DC: National Institute of Justice, 1997) 19.

35. Cited in *On the Front Lines: Police Stress and Family Well-Being* (Washington, DC: USGPO, 1991) 87.

36. William Westphall quoted during keynote speech at The Tenth Aslet International Training Seminar, Dallas, Texas (January, 1997).

37. Personal interview, 1997.

38. Martelli, et al., 267–273; Violanti and Aron, "Sources of Police Stress," 899–904; Graf, 176–186; and Novell, et al., 75–79.

39. Personal interview, Aug. 1997.

40. Kirschman, 52.

41. Kirschman, 64.

42. Richard M. Ayres, George S. Flanagan, and Marilyn V. Ayres, eds., *Preventing Law Enforcement Stress: The Organization's Role* (Washington DC: The National Sheriff's Association and Bureau of Justice Assistance, 1990) 11.

43. Kirschman, 54.

44. Lance W. Seberhagen, "Human Resource Management," *Police Psychology into the 21st Century,* Kurke and Scrivner eds. (Hillsdale: Erlbaum, 1995) 437.

45. Vivian B. Lord, "An Impact of Community Policing: Reported Stressors, Social Support, and Strain among Police Officers in a Changing Police Department," *Journal of Criminal Justice 24* (1996): 503–522.

46. Mitchell and Bray, 52.

47. Steve Albrecht, "The Police Officer's Companion: Pain and Grief," *The Informant* (official publication of the San Diego Police Officers Association) reprinted in Personal Resource Guide, "Street Survival® '97" (Northbrook: Calibre Press, 1997): 72.

48. Mitchell and Bray, 52.

49. Mitchell and Bray, 53.

50. Mitchell and Bray, 55.

51. Mitchell and Bray, 51–58.

52. Mitchell and Bray, 101–124.

53. Mitchell and Everly, 5–6.

54. Cited in Finn and Tomz, *Developing a Law Enforcement Stress Program for Officers and Their Families* (Washington DC: U.S. Department of Justice, Office of Justice Programs, National Institute of Justice, December 1996) 126.

55. Joseph Wambaugh, *The Onion Field* (New York: Delacorte, 1973).

56. Wambaugh, 159.

57. Wambaugh, 164–169.

58. Personal Resource Guide, "Street Survival® '97," 62.

59. Mitchell and Everly, 63; and Mitchell and Bray, 29.

60. Harvey Schlossberg, former police officer and police psychologist, in "Cops On The Edge," *A & E Home Video* (1995).

61. Lecture notes, "Street Survival® '97.

62. Nancy Bohl, "Professionally Administered Critical Incident Debriefing for Police Officers," Editors, *Police Psychology Into the 21st Century,* ed. Kurke and Scrivner (1995), 169.

63. Mitchell and Bray, 29.

64. William J. Lewinski, personal interview, 1995.

65. David Grossi, "Principles of Officer Survival," in *Total Survival* ed. Ed Nowicki (Powers Lake: Performance Dimensions, 1993) 185.

66. Charles Remsberg, Thomas M. McTernan and Ronald J. Adams, *Street Survival: Tactics for Armed Encounters* (Northbrook: Calibre Press, 1980): 283–290.

67. William A. Geller and Michael S. Scott *Deadly Force: What We Know, A Practitioner's Desk Reference on Police-Involved Shootings* (Washington DC: Police Executive Research Forum, 1992) 333.

68. George S. Everly, Jr., *A Clinical Guide to the Treatment of the Human Stress Response* (New York: Plenum, 1990) 32–34.

69. Lecture notes, "Street Survival® '97.

70. Roger Solomon, "Street Beat," *Law Enforcement Television Network (LETN)* (Dallas: Westcott, 1992).

71. Geller and Scott, 289–290.

72. Class notes from a lecture by Massad Ayoob, Officer Survival Course, Chapman Academy Springfield, Missouri (1982); Information also provided at the Calibre Press Inc. "Street Survivor ® '97 Seminar (1997).

73. Slide from "Street Survival® '97" (1997).

74. Personal Resource Guide, "Street Survival® '97," (1997) 78.

75. Mitchell and Everly, 127.

76. Seberhagen, 173.

77. Mitchell and Everly, 59–107.

78. Mitchell and Bray, 31.

79. George S. Everly, Jr., *A Clinical Guide to the Treatment of the Human Stress Response* (New York: Plenum, 1990) 321.

80. Mitchell and Everly, 126.

81. Geoff Boucher, "A Force of One: Welcome to the In-Your-Face World of Larry Blum, Cop Shrink. He Comes on Strong, But Ends up Earning the Trust of Officers in Pain," *Home Edition, Los Angeles Times,* Life style, 18 July 1994: 1.

82. Mitchell and Bray.

83. "Street Survival® '97: The Tactical Edge® Seminar; The Win® Seminar," (Calibre Press, Mar. and May 1997).

84. Mitchell and Bray, 44–49; Mitchell and Everly, 35–40; Nancy Davis cited in "Police Suicide, Part 1: What To Look For, How To Help," Street Survival *Newsline® 146* (Calibre Press, 3 March 1997).

85. Julie Klco, founder of My Officer Needs Assistance, personal interview, Aug. 1997.

86. John M. Violanti, *Police Suicide: Epidemic in Blue* (Springfield: Thomas, 1996) 13.

87. Violanti, *Police Suicide,* 24.

88. M. J. Davidson and A. Veno, "Stress and the Policeman," *Victorian Police Association Journal 49* (1984): 35–61.

89. Michael Blumenfield, "Psychiatry Today" *Gannett News Service,* 22 June 1995.

90. C. J. Lennings, "Suicide Ideation and Risk Factors in Police Officers and Justice Students," *Police Studies 18* (1995): 40.

91. "Cops On The Edge," *A & E Home Video* (Broadcast News Networks, and A & E Television Networks, 1995).

92. Elizabeth K. White and Audrey L. Honig, "Law Enforcement Families," *Police Psychology into the 21st Century,* eds., Kurke and Scrivner (1995): 201.

93. Nancy Davis as cited in "Police Suicide, Part 1: What To Look For, How To Help," Street Survival *Newsline® 146* (Calibre Press, 3 March 1997).

94. Davis, 2.

95. Davis, 3.

96. Joseph J. Hurrell Jr., "Police Work, Occupational Stress and Individual Coping," *Journal of Organizational Behavior 16* (1995): 27.

97. Ayres, Flanagan, and Ayres, 36.

98. Ayres, Flanagan, and Ayres, 25–26.

9

NATURE OF POLICE BRUTALITY
AND DEADLY FORCE

I am a cop. Have been for nine years. Have left pieces of my body strewn over much of the community where I work because I am aggressive in my adherence to my oath. Pins, plates, missing portions of bone and chronic pain are some of the rewards that I have received in addition to my paycheck. The realization that I could be next on the NLEOM [National Law Enforcement Officer's Memorial] wall is reinforced not just by having been there, what I see and hear or what I am told, but also by memories of my own life and death struggle with a suspect to maintain control of my own gun. With that in mind I do not take lightly the reasons for continuing to serve my brother and country in this way. Often I re-evaluate it and often I must consider the request of my family and spouse to walk away.

—Ken Stiver, Hayward, California Police Department,
quoted in Calibre Press Street Survival Newsline® No. 169.

This chapter addresses the issue of police abuse of force. In the words of Jack Enter, speaking to an audience of police officers, "You are policing probably the most violent society on the face of the earth. And this is one of the most complicated times in our history."[1] The opening to this chapter aptly expresses one officer's experiences with this violence. Police officers, particularly those of the inner cities, have to work in conditions that, according to George Kelling resemble the political dilemma faced by the soldiers who fought in Vietnam. Kelling claims "the terms war on crime' and 'war on drugs' encourage and even demand an all-out attack by police upon criminals"—no holding back, no quarter given. "But like American solders in Vietnam," Kelling adds, "the police are fighting an unwinnable war, assuming large social responsibilities that belong more to politicians than to policemen; and as in Vietnam, atrocities are being committed, on both sides."[2]

At the same time that the police are dealing with a violent society, there are scores of incidents in which strong evidence exists that excessive force was used by the police. The best known of these was the 1991 television broadcast of Rodney King's beating by officers of the Los Angeles Police Department (LAPD). In the 90 second tape, viewers were horrified by the sight of a group of Los Angeles police officers acting out their anger, fears, frustration, and prejudices on the body of an African American man who had led them on a high-speed chase.[3] Other disturbing instances of excessive force were the 1996 television broadcast of the beating of Mexican immigrants Alicia Soltero and Enrique Flores by sheriffs in Riverside, California; the live footage from a television helicopter of Kim Hong II who was shot 15 times by LAPD officers in 1996[4]; and the 1991 video tape recorded by a television news crew's cameras of half a dozen officers in Kansas City, Missouri beating a young African American male with night sticks and shocking him repeatedly with a stun gun.[5] Equally as shocking, if not more so, was the media coverage of the 1997 alleged police assault on a 33 year old Haitian immigrant, Abner Louima, at the New York Police Department's 70th precinct. Louima was sodomized with the handle of a toilet plunger causing internal injuries. The assault took place in a precinct bathroom out of view from the public and most officers in the precinct.[6]

Police abuse of citizens, whether complaints of intimidation, excessive force or police brutality, or deadly force, has been debated for years, but never more intensely than after the repeated showings of the Rodney King tape or the "trial" of Mark Fuhrman in the O. J. Simpson murder trial. The King beating, the Simi Valley acquittal of the four police officers, the subsequent riots, and the federal trial of those officers acquitted in the Simi Valley courtroom will make the issue of police brutality a major concern for years to come (see Box 9.1 on the Rodney King beating).[7]

EXCESSIVE FORCE DEFINED

No single, accepted definition of "excessive force" exists among police, researchers, and legal analysts."[8] Albert Reiss Jr.'s early definition judged force to be improper or unnecessary under the following conditions:

1. a police officer physically assaulted a citizen and then did not make an arrest
2. a citizen did not, by word or deed, resist an officer
3. an officer, even though resistance to the arrest took place, could have restrained the citizen in other ways
4. a large number of officers were present and could have assisted in subduing the citizen
5. the subject was handcuffed and made no attempt to flee or offer resistance
6. the citizen resisted arrest, but the use of force continued even after the citizen was subdued[9]

More recently, David Carter has defined police abuse of authority as "any action by a police officer without regard to motive, intent, or malice that tends to injure, insult, trespass on human dignity, manifest feelings of inferiority and/or violate an inherent legal right of a member of the police constituency."[10] According to Jerome H.

BOX 9.1   The Beating of Rodney King

It all started when George Holliday brought home a camcorder, a Sony CCD–F77 on Valentine Day, 1991. The 33 year old recently married former rugby player, general manager of a local office of Rescue Rooter, a national plumbing company, hadn't had time to load it until March 2, the day before one of his employees was scheduled to run in the Los Angeles marathon. After setting his alarm for 6 A.M. so as to arrive in time for the race, Holliday went to bed early and was awakened at 12:50 A.M. by a blast of siren noise and screeching rubber. The racket was coming from Foothill Boulevard, the main thoroughfare of a middle-class, ethnically mixed Los Angeles suburb with a population about 60 percent Latino, 10 percent black, and the rest Asian and white. When Holliday, who is white, pulled the window shade aside, he could scarcely believe what he saw. The powerful spotlight of a police helicopter was shining on a white Hyundai surrounded by a half-dozen police cars. His first thought was, "Hey, let's get the camera!"

The videotape Holliday shot showed a large black man down on hands, and knees, struggling on the ground, twice impaled with wires from an electronic TASER gun, rising and falling while being repeatedly beaten, blow after blow after blow—dozens of blows, fifty-six in all, about the head, neck, kidneys, ankles, legs and feet—by two police officers wielding their 2-foot black metal truncheons like baseball bats. Also visible was a third officer, who was stomping King, and about ten police officers watching the beating along with a number of Holliday's neighbors.

Actually, twenty-three LAPD officers responded to the scene (an interesting number in light of the later claims that the Department is severely understaffed to respond to emergencies). Four officers were directly involved in the use of force; two hovered overhead in the heli-

copter; ten were on the ground and witnessed some portion of the beating; seven others checked out the scene and left. Four uniformed officers from two other enforcement agencies— the Highway Patrol and the Los Angeles Unified School Districts—were also there.

Both Holiday and Paul King, Rodney's brother, tried to report the police abuse. Neither succeeded. When, on Monday morning, Paul King went to the Foothill station to report that his brother had been beaten, the officer at the front desk told him to wait. After waiting and growing impatient, Paul King returned to the desk. Finally, a sergeant came out of the back of the station and proceeded to give Paul King a bureaucratic hard time.... Paul King testified at the Christopher Commission that when he left Foothill station, "I knew I hadn't made a complaint."

...On Monday, March 4, he [Holliday] telephoned the Foothill station, intending to offer his videotape to the police. He told the desk officer that he had witnessed the beating of a motorist by LAPD officers and asked about the motorist's condition. The desk officer told him that "we [the LAPD] do not release information like that." He neither asked questions about what Holiday had seen nor recorded a personnel complaint form as a result of Holliday's call. The officer seemed so uninterested in Holliday's information that Holliday decided to try another tactic and called Channel 5 (KTLA) in Los Angeles. The station made arrangements with Holliday to bring the tape in, and it was broadcast Monday evening. CNN gave it national and international exposure, playing it repeatedly until it was seen everywhere in the world, from Tokyo to London to Zaire. The beating of Rodney King became the lead story for several days on the major networks as well, the most explicit and shocking news footage of police brutality ever to be seen on television.

Skolnick and James J. Fyfe, one impediment to the police controlling and understanding use of force "is that even the police and some of their most sophisticated critics frequently fail to distinguish between brutality and unnecessary force."[11]

Skolnick and Fyfe define brutality as a conscious and venal act committed by officers who take great pains to conceal their misconduct. It is usually directed against persons of marginal status and credibility.[12] In a later writing, Fyfe divided force into extralegal violence or police brutality, and unnecessary force. **Extralegal violence** is "the willful and wrongful use of force by officers who knowingly exceed the bounds of their office."[13] He contends that this form of violence rarely causes police–community friction because generally it takes place out of sight of spectators as brutal police officers take precautions to avoid detection.

In contrast, **unnecessary force** results from "ineptitude or carelessness, and occurs when well-meaning officers prove incapable of dealing with the situations they encounter without needless or too hasty resort to force"[14] This type of force is usually unplanned and in the open as officers find themselves caught up in evolving circumstances that have gotten out of control. It usually begins with police intervention in a minor incident that escalates because of police haste or failure to establish communication with the individuals involved.[15] The videotaped beating of the illegal emigrants in South El Monte by Riverside County sheriff's deputies falls into the category of unnecessary force. The officers in this incident became involved in a long and dangerous pursuit. Once stopped, the deputies pulled immigrants from their vehicle and struck an unresisting arrestee several times with a PR–24 police baton. This incident took place on a public highway during the daytime, in full view of passing motorist and news media helicopters circling over head. Helicopters make considerable noise. These officers were caught-up in the evolving circumstances of the event and adrenaline rush caused by the danger of the pursuit. Joseph Wambaugh, 14 year veteran of LAPD and author, writes "…that when police officers lose self-control after a long and dangerous pursuit, the ethnicity of their quarry matters not at all. And the Riverside County sheriff's deputies clearly lost control during the South El Monte incident."[16]

EXTENT OF THE USE OF FORCE

The use of **coercive force** by peace officers has always been accepted as an intricate part of the profession. According to Skolnick and Fyfe "Anybody who fails to understand the centrality of force to police work has no business in a police uniform."[17] There are still physical, emotional, legal, and financial risks for the officer who uses reasonable force. Justifiable use of force is often seen as illegitimate by some in the community causing distrust, strained police–community relations, riots, and future violence towards the police.[18]

Skolnick and Fyfe propose that police brutality has "diminished in the past fifty years, even in the past twenty years."[19] In view of the publicity given of recent cases of police brutality, this seems to be a questionable conclusion. Yet they support their position by saying, "We need to recall how much worse, how routine, police brutality used to be."[20] An examination of the brutal nature of policing in the nineteenth century, some of the court cases in the twentieth century that document the extensive use of the third degree during police proceedings, and the widespread brutality findings of the 1931 Wickersham Commission certainly support Skolnick and Fyfe's thesis that police brutality has gone down.[21]

A number of studies have examined the extensiveness of police use of coercive as well as excessive force. These studies have generally found that the use of coercive force by police is a rare event.[22] Data from research indicate that between 1 to 6 percent of arrests involve some type of coercive force.[23] Table 9.1, which contains the results of a national survey of complaints and sustained complaints of excessive force during 1991, reveals the small numbers of coercive force found among city police departments. Even the Christopher Commission, formed to investigate police brutality complaints in the Los Angeles Police Department, found that only 1 percent of arrests involve police use of force. Los Angeles's violent crime is twice the national average and second highest among the six largest cities.[24] This commission also discovered that of the 44 officers who had six or more complaints for **excessive force**—none were female officers.[25]

TABLE 9.1 **Reported Incidents of Police Use of Force per 1,000 Sworn Officers During 1991 in City Departments**

Type of force	Rate per 1,000 sworn officers
Handcuff/leg restraint	490.4
Bodily force (arm, foot, or leg)	272.2
Come-alongs	226.8
Unholstering weapon	129.9
Swarm	126.7
Twist locks/wrist locks	80.9
Firm grip	57.7
Chemical agents (Mace or Cap–Stun)	36.2
Batons	36.0
Flashlights	21.7
Dog attacks or bites	6.5
Electrical devices (TASER)	·5.4
Civilians shot at but not hit	3.0
Other impact devices	2.4
Neck restraints/unconsciousness-rendering holds	1.4
Vehicle rammings	1.0
Civilians shot and killed	0.9
Civilians shot and wounded but not killed	0.2

Source: Antony Pate and Lorie Fridell, as cited in Tom McEwen, *National Data Collection on Police Use of Force*. U.S. Department of Justice, Bureau of Justice Statistics, National Institute of Justice (Washington, DC: USGPO, Apr. 1996) 34.

Studies based on participant observation, focusing on "potentially violent" police–citizen contact, suggest that up to 10 percent of the encounters involve police use of force. These studies also indicate that police use of force occurs at least twice the rate suggested in police use of force reports, which they attribute in part to the undercounting bias in official reports. They still found that the average officer will only use coercive force one to three times a year.[26] It is when officers go beyond reasonable force in making an arrest that citizens become the victims of police, and the confidence in them plummets.[27]

Statistics on the prevalence of excessive force vary considerably. Elizabeth Benz Croft and B. A. Austin's 1987 study found that between 5 and 10 percent of use of force incidents resulted in complaints about excessive force. This would translate into rates of 50 to 100 complaints per thousand arrests. Other studies had a variety of results—some as high as one in three and others as low as 3 percent of suspects experienced excessive force.[28]

Tom McEwen's *National Data Collection on Police Use of Force* cited three recent studies to illustrate the variety of approaches to collecting data and to show the importance of definitions. The studies include Anthony Pate and Lorie Fridell's *Police Use of Force*, the Use of Force Report by the Virginia Association of Chiefs of Police (VACOP), and Joel Garner and John Buchanan's *Understanding the Use of Force by and Against the Police.* The Pate and Fridell study was a survey at the national level, gathering statistics for 1991 on use of force and citizen complaints. The VACOP survey encompassed 360 departments in Virginia in 1993 and 1994. The Garner and Buchanan study was based on survey information from officers and interviews, with a representative sample of 1,585 custody arrests in the Phoenix, Arizona Police Department during a two week period in June 1994.[29]

Pate and Fridell, whose objective was to obtain a national picture on the police use of force, evaluated 1,111 completed surveys from a representative sample of 1,697 agencies throughout the United States (see Table 9.2). The results of the study were statistically weighted based on the number of agencies in the population, type of agency, and population category. Pate and Fridell also asked respondents to provide the number of citizen complaints of excessive force, and the number of complaints sustained. For the purpose of their study, excessive force was defined as "police use of more force than is necessary in seizing or detaining an individual."[30] Rates of citizen complaints for responding city departments were 11.3 complaints per 100,000 population. Although males accounted for 48 percent of the population, they accounted for 73 percent of the complaints and 83 percent of the sustained complaints. This overrepresentation may be due in part to the male overrepresentation in crime statistics.[31]

The Virginia Association of Chiefs of Police sent survey forms to 360 departments. The response rate for the survey was low (16.1 percent and 23.1 percent respectively), undermining the anticipated representativeness of the findings. Another significant limitation of the study was the subjective definition of "police force." The underlying motivation that inspired the VACOP study was that "police across the country do an outstanding job of resolving literally millions of encounters without resorting to any force."[32] One representative stated, "I don't believe police use of force is a widespread problem, but until we get the data, we can't

TABLE 9.2 Complaints and Sustained Complaints of Excessive Force for City Police Departments During 1991

	Number	Percent	Number of responding agencies
General population	72,036,089		215
Male	12,910,899	48	
Female	14,125,190	52	
Complaints	3,053		215
Male	2,224	73	
Female	829	27	
Sustained complaints	480		73
Male	398	83	
Female	82	17	

Source: Antony Pate and Lorie Fridell, as cited in Tom McEwen, *National Data Collection on Police Use of Force*, NCJ–160113. U.S. Department of Justice, Bureau of Justice Statistics, National Institute of Justice (Washington, DC: USGPO, Apr. 1996) 35.

prove it."[33] Other participants supported this view.[34] Some of the results from the study are as follows:

- The responding agencies made a total of 1,101,877 arrests and used force in 1,697 arrests, or about 0.15 percent of the total. The survey from the previous year showed that 0.3 percent of arrests involved force.
- A total of 897 officers were assaulted during the year, 26 of whom were off duty at the time.
- The agencies received a total of 119 complaints from citizens about use of force, of which 99 complaints were determined to be unfounded and 20 were sustained. An additional 25 complaints were made from within the agencies, of which 19 complaints were determined to be unfounded and 6 were sustained.
- The median age of officers receiving complaints was 31 years, and the median length of experience was 7 years.[35]

In June 1994, the Phoenix Police Department, in conjunction with Rutgers University and Arizona State University, conducted a two week study on the role of force in arrest tactics, policy, and training. The goal of the study was to describe the amount of force used by police officers and the characteristics that precipitated that force. Although the study represents police use of force in only one department, it did provide insights that led to the eventual decision by the National Institute of Justice and the Bureau of Justice Statistics to replicate the study.[36] Garner and Buchanan examined both police and suspect use of force during 1,585 arrests to determine the frequency of specific officer and arrestee behaviors along five dimensions:

1. Voice—officer/suspect spoke in a conversational tone, articulated threats, issued commands, shouted, or curse.
2. Motion—mode of officer pursuit and suspect flight.

3. Restraints—mechanical devices used by police to control arrestee, for example, handcuffs, body cuffs, or hobble.
4. Weaponless tactics—officer/suspect grabbing, twisting, shoving, pushing, biting, punching, kicking, scratching, scuffling, wrestling, scuffling, and use of control holds or pressure points.
5. Weapons—suspect possession or officer/suspect threatened or actual use of martial arts or a baton, flashlight, blunt instrument, knife, chemical agent, canine, handgun, shotgun or rifle, or use of a motor vehicle as a weapon.[37]

The use of force in the Phoenix Police Department was found to be infrequent and typically at the lower end of the Control Continuum. Other key findings were:

• Police used some physical force in about one of every five arrests [22 percent]. Suspects used some physical force in about one in every six arrests.
• Phoenix police officers were required to restrain only felony or belligerent suspects. In 20 percent of all adult custody arrests studied, officers opted to use no restraints.
• When force was used by the police or suspects, it was typically at the low end of the severity scale.
• Weapons were used by the police in 2 percent of all arrests. The weapon most frequently used by the police was a flashlight (12 times in 1,585 arrests).
• Of 41 factors examined, only 9 consistently contributed to the prediction of police use of force.
• The single best predictor of police use of force was suspect use of force.
• Two-thirds of the variation in the amount of force used by police remain unexplained.[38]

Other consistent predictors included increased number of police; previous arrest for a violent offense; presence of bystanders; the suspect's use of force; gang involvement; alcohol impairment; and police knowledge of the suspect to be resistive or assaultive or to carry a weapon. The study also showed that more force was used when both the suspect and officer were male. (For the types of use of force, see Figure 9.1.)[39]

REASONABLE FORCE

A discussion of the Control Continuum, of the possible justifications of force, and of the relevant United States Supreme Court decisions constitute the most important concepts in the police use of reasonable force.

The Control Continuum

The **Control Continuum,** also known as the Force Continuum, generally has six levels of force: the officer's presence, verbal commands, low-level compliance,

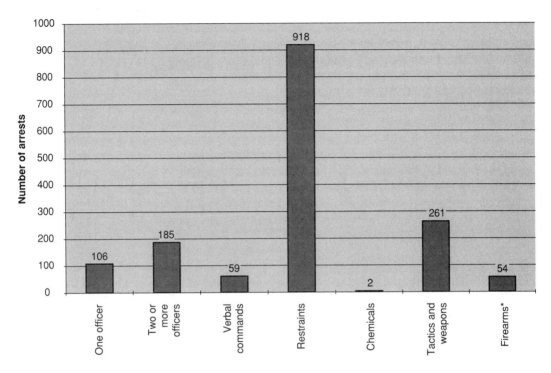

FIGURE 9.1   Measure of Continuum of Force Used by Police

*This category includes any use or threatened use of a firearm. During the 2-week period, one suspect discharged a firearm. During this same period, there is no indication that the police discharged a firearm.

Source: Joel Garner, John Buchanan, Tom Schade, and John Hepburn, "Understanding the Use of Force by and Against the Police," (National Institute of Justice: Research in Brief, Nov. 1996) 6.

intermediate-level compliance, impact weapon, and deadly force (see Figure 9.2). The underlying principle of the Control Continuum is that the officer's actions are always in response to the subject's actions. During a response, police officers must maintain the position of advantage, focusing on proper police action that is a balance of safety and efficiency. Safety is a primary concern for the officer and the person with whom the officer is dealing. This requires an officer to move at least one step higher on the Control Continuum than the resistance offered by the subject including calling for backup. For example, when the Illinois State Police tested the ASP tactical baton, they had 17 uses that amounted to just opening the expandable baton. The presentation of the baton was all that was needed to gain compliance.

Officers are always permitted to disengage from a confrontation, when that is possible, or to escalate the amount of coercive force that is needed to take proper

FIGURE 9.2 Control Continuum for Line Officers

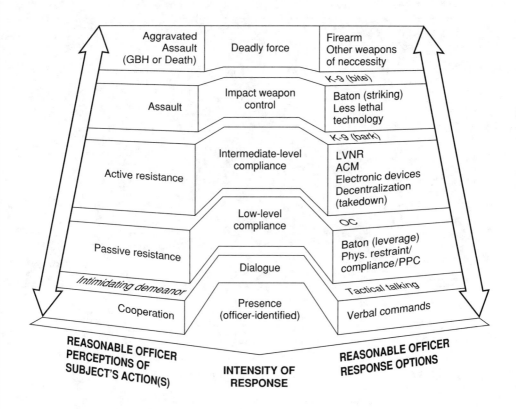

REASONABLE OFFICER PERCEPTIONS OF SUBJECT'S ACTION(S)	INTENSITY OF RESPONSE	REASONABLE OFFICER RESPONSE OPTIONS

GBH   Great Bodily Harm
ACM   Active Countermeasures
LVNR   Lateral Vascular Neck Restraint (Lindell system)
OC   Oleoresin Capsicum
PPC   Pressure Point Control

Your force decisions as a law enforcement officer are scrutinized from several perspectives. Some who assess your actions will be concerned whether they were **legal.** Others may focus on how much **medical** damage was done to the subject. Still others will evaluate what you did from a **tactical** standpoint: did you successfully stop the threat?

In selecting a **justifiable** level of force to control a subject, you must accommodate, at least to some extent, all of these perspectives.

There will never be a unanimous agreement on any ranking of force options. However, a

USE OF FORCE DILEMMA

(continued)

232

FIGURE 9.2 *Continued*

good Control Continuum does offer a guideline that will help you keep your use of force reasonable, and allow you to articulate a good explanation of it after the confrontation is over.

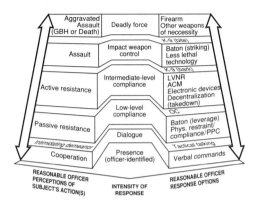

This Control Continuum, designed by Calibre Press for the Street Survival ® Seminar, is different from the models that have been standard in law enforcement for the past decade. It shows a relationship between a suspect's behavior and your appropriate response. It includes certain response options that are prevalent today and whose relative ranking in terms of force intensity is confusing to many officers. And it allows for adaptation, according to your training and experience, to your department's policies, and to new tools, techniques, and legal decisions that may develop in the future.

Understand that any Control Continuum is merely a **starting point** for discussing a very complex issue: the justification for the use of force. It represents an ideal, orderly world—not necessarily the real, chaotic, bizarre world on the street, where officer actions in the midst of violent turmoil often are judged long afterward in calm and distant settings.

Resistance and response are dynamic. The suspect's behavior and your use of force to control it may move up and/or down on the Continuum during any given encounter, as indicated by the two-way arrows. Moreover, this movement will not always be in an incremental step-by-step sequence. In selecting your use of force, you may need to skip one or more entire

steps on the Continuum, depending on how you "normally" read certain **key variables,** namely:

Threat Assessment Observations. What factors bear on your perception of dangerousness? Your evaluation should include the subject's:

- emotional state
- resistive tension
- early warning signs
- pre-attack postures
- access to weapon(s)
- apparent willingness to sustain injury.

Officer/Subject Factors. How do the strengths and weaknesses you bring to this encounter compare to the subject's strengths and weaknesses? Your evaluation should include your respective:

- age
- sex
- size
- strength
- skill level (training/experience)
- backup (yours/subject's).

Special Circumstances. What is unique about this confrontation, if anything, that requires a higher or lower level of response than would "normally" seem justified? Your evaluation may include:

- a sudden, unexpected assault
- your physical position
- your reasonable perception of danger
- subject's ability to escalate force rapidly
- your special knowledge about subject
- your/other officers' injuries or exhaustion
- timing, tools, tactics, training
- other factors necessitating unusual control measures, such as crime rate in the neighborhood, nature of the call, etc.

These important variables should always be reviewed and explained in your report and/or testimony, if pertinent, to document **in detail** that the level of force you used was nec-

(Continued)

FIGURE 9.2 *Continued*

essary and appropriate, considering all the circumstances. This Control Continuum should also be presented to Administration for inclusion in training and Departmental policies and procedures.

Appreciation is gratefully acknowledged to the following trainers and use of force ex-

perts: Bob Willis, Dave Grossi, Mildred O'Linn, Larry Hahn, Sam Faulkner, Joseph Scuro, Jr., Gary Klugiewicz, Ed Nowicki and Greg Connor. Their concepts about proper use of force stimulated and influenced Calibre Press' Control Continuum.

Source: From the *Street Survival® Seminar,* produced by Calibre Press Inc., Northbrook, IL.

police action. Proper action includes withdrawing from a dangerous situation until backup arrives. Gary T. Klugiewicz instructs officers to ask themselves before continuing or entering into a dangerous situation, "Am I winning?" or "Is this worth dying for?"[40] An officer rushing blindly into a hazardous situation only increases the danger to all involved. For example, an officer responding to an alarm at one of the local convenience stores rushes in the front door only to be confronted by an armed robber. The clerk, customers, the officer, and the robber are facing serious injury or death. In addition, other officers hearing the first officer's radio pleas for help will rush at high speeds to assist, endangering themselves and other motorists. The old school where a machismo attitude prevailed and disengagement symbolized cowardliness is no longer an acceptable standard.

Communication skills are integrated throughout the Continuum, being used before the force is applied to gain compliance; during the application of a technique to enhance the effectiveness by telling the subject what is expected; and after control is established to calm the arrestee and to conduct a initial medical assessment.[41] Finally, the ultimate justification of coercive force "is a perception based on the officer's training and experience and the facts of the situation."[42]

Bob Willis, primary presenter for Calibre Press, Inc. Street Survival Seminar®, makes understanding the Control Continuum easier for line officers by dividing it into three categories of people: First, "Yes People" are those who will comply without any physical contact by the officer. They are located below the low-level compliance on the Control Continuum. Two, "Maybe People" are located in the low-level compliance area. They are uncertain if they want to comply with the officer's legal order. A mild persuasion using physical contact, such as grabbing the person's arm, a wristlock, or pressure point application, is usually all that is needed. "Maybe people" will soon comply without offering any assaultive resistance. Finally, "No People" occupy the rest of the Continuum. They will not comply with the officer's lawful commands unless considerable coercive force is applied. Sometimes, this is as simple as decentralizing the subject to the ground for handcuffing. Other times, the officer is required to use force that can cause injury or death.

Justification of Force

Police officers are granted discretionary powers in enforcing the law and in the use of coercive force. As no two calls are exactly the same, no two use of force incidents are exactly the same. Each involves human interaction and the multiple variables that they represent. The decision to use coercive force is even more convoluted by the volatile, fast evolving, emotional environment in which the decisions are made. These variables are subject to many different interpretations, even among officers based on their training and experience. For example, the average 50 year old officer will be at a considerable disadvantage confronting a larger 20 year old male than would be a younger officer of equal or greater size than the subject. This older officer, consequently, would then be expected to escalate more quickly to a higher force option than the younger officer. Age, size, gender, skill level, and number of participants on both sides are taken into consideration in the officer's reasonable response.

The justification for police use of force revolves around the question "what would a reasonable officer have done in the same facts and circumstances." The "reasonable officer" standard implies training and experience not privy to the average citizen. The average person does not have a frame of reference of an officer trained to recognize danger signs. Officers operate, or at least they should, in a state of hypervigilance, sensing danger cues much faster than the average citizen.

An example of what appears to be reasonable force is officer John Wilbur's use of deadly force when his hand was closed in a suspect's rear door, and he was dragged on asphalt at 70 miles per hour, peeling skin and muscle from most of his lower body.[43] Wilbur later made a telling statement: "I believe I have every right to try to save my life as much as anyone else does. Because I'm a police officer, my life is not any less valuable than anyone else's."[44]

Unlike the average citizen, officers cannot act solely on intuition. They must be able to articulate the reasonable suspicion or probable cause that prompted their use of coercive force or it is unjustified. There are few absolutes as most use of force decisions fall within a gray area of variables. These decisions can be divided into misconduct by omission, involving too little force and resulting in needless injury or death of the victim; and misconduct by commission, involving unnecessary force or brutality and also resulting in injury or death of the victim (see Figure 9.3).

Again, the only difference between proper police action and misconduct is justification. A major component of justification is the officer's ability to articulate his

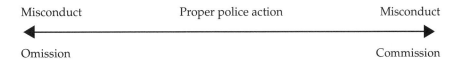

FIGURE 9.3   Proper Police Action Graph

Source: Gary T. Klugiewicz, *Active Countermeasures: Instructor Certification Training Manual* (Milwaukee: Active Counter Measures Instructional Systems, 1994) 78. © 1990 ACMI ®.

or her response to the subject's actions. Klugiewicz advises officers when writing their use of force reports:

> Your report is *your* account of what happened. Many people will read it. Be sure to indicate your "reasonable suspicion" and probable cause. Quote the subject directly if possible. Be chronological and show the "totality of the circumstances." List *all* factors that contributed to the incident. Detail the debriefing and care rendered to the subject after *control* is effected. State your perceptions at the time of the occurrence based on your training and experience."[45]

An officer's discretionary decisions concerning coercive force are guided by department policies and directives, state law and state case law, Federal statues, Appellate Court decisions, and the United States Supreme Court decisions. State law and agencies' policies and directives vary among states and departments. To illustrate, the cardiovascular neck restraint is accepted in some departments as a viable force option while others ban its use (see Table 9.3 for the variation between criminal act and proper police action).

SUPREME COURT DECISIONS CONCERNING EXCESSIVE FORCE

In 1989 the United States Supreme Court's landmark decision *Graham v. Conner* (1989) placed all excessive force claims under the analysis of the Fourth Amendment's "reasonableness" standard:

> Today we make explicit what was implicit in *Garner's* [*Tennessee v. Garner*, 471 U.S. 1 (1985)] analysis, and hold that *all* claims that law enforcement officers have used excessive force—deadly or not—in the course of an arrest, investigatory stop, or other "seizure" of a free citizen should be analyzed under the Fourth Amendment and its "reasonableness" standard.[46]

The Court also rejected the notion that all excessive force claims brought under Section 1983 are governed by a single generic standard. The courts must first "iden-

TABLE 9.3   Control Theory

Criminal act	Proper police action
Disorderly conduct	Dialog
Assault	Control techniques
Battery	Countermeasures
Aggravated battery	Impact weapon (baton)
Murder	Firearms

Source: Gary T. Klugiewicz, *Active Countermeasures Instructor Certification Training Manual* (Milwaukee: Active Countermeasures Instructional Systems, 1994) 77. © 1990 ACMI ®.

tify the specific constitutional right allegedly infringed by the challenged application of force," and second "judge the claim by reference to the specific constitutional standard which governs that right."[47] In essence, if an officer's actions are determined to fall within the constitutional standard of the Fourth Amendment, the appropriateness of the force used to affect the arrest must be assessed using the reasonableness standard. To determine if the force was reasonable "requires a careful balancing of 'the nature and quality of the intrusion on the individual's Fourth Amendment interests' against the countervailing governmental interests at stake."[48]

The Court recognized that "reasonableness under the Fourth Amendment is not capable of precise definition or mechanical application. [H]owever, its proper application requires careful attention to the facts and circumstances of each particular case." This includes "the severity of the crime at issue, whether the suspect poses an immediate threat to the safety of the officers or others, and whether he is actively resisting arrest or attempting to evade arrest by flight."[49] *Graham* added that what is most important is whether "the officers' actions are 'objectively reasonable' in light of the facts and circumstances confronting them, without regard to their underlying intent or motivation."[50] At the same time, the Court recognized the perils and complexities officers face in making crucial decisions, "The 'reasonableness' of a particular use of force must be judged from the perspective of a reasonable officer on the scene, rather than with the 20/20 vision of hindsight."[51]

In ***Sherrod v. Berry*** (1988) the court stated, "When a jury measures the objective reasonableness of an officer's actions, it must stand in his shoes and judge the reasonableness of his actions based upon the information he possessed and the judgment he exercised in responding to that situation."[52] Only the facts known to the officer before the use of force are relevant to assessing the objective reasonableness of the officer's actions. The discovery that a suspect was using an imitation gun after a police shooting is not admissible as evidence in the post hoc analysis of reasonableness of the officer's judgment. Simply, the jury would have more knowledge than the officer possessed at the time he or she had to make the crucial decision, although it could be argued that the officer should have known. The court continued:

> *It is not necessary that the danger which gave rise to the belief actually existed;* it is sufficient that the person resorting to self defense at the time involved reasonably believed in the existence of such a danger, and *such reasonable belief is sufficient even where it is mistaken. In forming such reasonable belief a person may act upon appearances.* In other words, it is sufficient that the danger was reasonably apparent."[53] (Court's emphasis)

The Court does not set a standard higher than "probable cause" for officers to apply coercive force. If an officer's actions were restricted to the "beyond a reasonable doubt" standard, officers would be shot, stabbed, or hit before they could act. This standard would be far too dangerous. The Court stated in Graham:

> The Fourth Amendment is not violated by an arrest based on probable cause, even though the wrong person is arrested, nor by the mistaken execution of a

valid search warrant on the wrong premises. With respect to a claim of excessive force, the same standard of reasonableness at the moment applies: "not every push or shove, even if it may later seem unnecessary in the peace of a judge's chambers violates the Fourth Amendment."

The calculus of reasonableness must embody allowance for the fact that police officers are often forced to make split-second judgments—in circumstances that are tense, uncertain, and rapidly evolving—about the amount of force that is necessary in a particular situation."[54]

EXCESSIVE FORCE

The police sometimes fall short of the reasonableness standard discussed above. Explanations for the inappropriate or excessive use of force include the inability to handle social protest and collective behavior, the police subculture and its support of different norms of behavior, and racist feelings on the part of the police.

Social Conflict and Excessive Force

The police have been continually called upon to control mass protest. This public order function of the police took place on a regular basis in the nineteenth century and became even more frequent in the early decades of the twentieth century. For example, in addition to the race riot in New York in 1900, there were race riots in Springfield, Ohio in 1904; Greensburg, Indiana in 1906; and Springfield, Illinois in 1908. The large riots in East St. Louis, Illinois in 1917 and Chicago in 1919 were also attributed to racial tensions. Then, there was the Detroit race riot of 1943, but in the 1960s, riots became a way of life for many cities, including Los Angeles, Cincinnati, Cleveland, Newark, and Detroit. Indeed, the United States Civil Disorder Commission found that there were 167 disorders of varying intensity during the first nine months of 1967. Thirty-nine cities were considered to have major outbreaks.[55]

The criticisms of the police handling of riots skyrocketed during the 1960s. In one of the violent encounters in Birmingham, Alabama, the nation was shocked to see police using dogs, firehouses, cattle prods, and nightsticks against civil rights marchers, many of whom were children. The nation sat glued to their television sets in the spring of 1965, watching a peaceful civil rights march, led by the Reverend Martin Luther King, Jr., being forcibly interrupted by state troopers and local police. In March of 1966, the National Advisory Commission on Civil Disorders wrote: "Negroes firmly believe that police brutality and harassment occurred repeatedly in Negro neighborhoods. This belief is unquestionably one of the major reasons for intense Negro resentment against the police."[56] In 1968, the Civil Disorder Commission singled out the police as the activating cause of the urban riots taking place across this nation: "Harlem, Watts, Newark, and Detroit, all the major outbursts of recent years," the report stated, "were precipitated by arrests of Negroes by white police for minor offenses."[57]

In the late 1960s, the police were confronted with political protest of the war in Vietnam. The most damaging to the credibility of the police were the events that took place during the Democratic National Convention, August 25–29, 1968. What occurred was a disorderly and violent confrontation between students who compared the Chicago police to the Soviet troops occupying Prague at the time, and the thin blue line who viewed themselves as attempting to maintain order in the midst of anarchy. Without question, the police were provoked. In addition to obscene epithets, all manner of objects, including rocks, sticks, and human feces were hurled at them. What outraged the public was how the police responded. Skolnick and Fyfe put it this way:

> Yet the police, like an urban army run wild, responded with vicious obscenities of their own, plus gas, mace, and club attacks directed partly at bands of provocateurs but also at innocent bystanders, peaceful demonstrators, and large numbers of residents who lived in the convention vicinity or were walking through the parks and streets. Because these persons had "broken no law, disobeyed no order, made no threat," the violence against them was all the more shocking. Reporters and photographers were singled out for assault, and their equipment was deliberately damaged....[58]

Daniel Walker's report of this riot, *Rights in Conflict,* concluded that the police response "was unrestrained and indiscriminate police violence, on many occasions, especially at night...in what can only be called a police riot."[59] In view of the fact that the convention was extensively covered by every form of media, journalists and television reporters offered to the American public a compelling and unassailable verification of this four day event.[60]

Nor did the police respond any better to the protests against the Vietnam war on college campuses, especially the 1968 riot at Columbia University, or to the antiwar protest in Los Angeles in 1967. The police, it was reported, ran wild. Other words used to describe police behavior were "indiscriminate," "capricious," and "arbitrary." Perhaps a partial explanation for the police's response can be attributed to strong personal feelings about the war. As Skolnick and Fyfe expressed it, "Each side felt itself to be morally and politically justified." The reason for this is that "the students believed they might be drafted to fight in an unwinnable and unjustifiably destructive war, while to cops who had brothers and cousins actually fighting in that war the student protests were considered unforgivable traitors who were offering aid and comfort to the enemy."[61]

Finally, the 1988 riot in Tompkins Square Park on the Lower East Side of New York City brought more brutality charges against the police. This time the recipients of police action were a bizarre alliance of homeless men and women who used it as an open-air toilet and sleeping quarters, punk rockers, neighborhood eccentrics, musicians, and poets. On August 6, at 1:00 A.M., the police were delegated to enforce a curfew on occupancy of city parks in Tompkins Square. However, sweeping the park did not prove to be an easy task for the assembled police officers, including a full column of mounted troopers. When someone threw a firecracker at the mounted column, the helmeted police officers began clearing the park and the street in front of it. The vicinity of the park soon resembled a war zone, and in the midst of mass confusion and disorder, the police were involved in senseless acts of brutality.[62]

It is no easy matter for the police to maintain order in the midst of the chaos or social protest. Both of the authors have been involved in riots, either on the streets or in institutional settings, and we know the rush of emotions, including fear and anger, at this time. The use of reasonable force during collective disorder demands the very best of policing in this nation. On too many occasions, this nation has experienced the very worst—police officers running wild and out of control, indiscriminately victimizing everyone in their path.

The Subculture of Violence

The "rotten apple" explanation of police deviancy is again challenged by the systemic nature of police brutality. Police use of excessive force typically takes place in departments in which a supportive subculture condones this behavior. It is this subculture that turns new members of the force into wrongdoers. It is also this subculture that encourages units to compete to be the baddest.[63]

One norm of the police subculture, according to William Ker Muir Jr., is that "The nastier one's reputation, the less nasty one has to be"[64]; that is, "the stronger one's reputation for being mean, tough, and aggressive, the less iron-handed one actually has to be."[65] This norm proposes that an officer has to manufacture a reputation of "badness" or being a "hardnose" on the streets. Such a reputation, so suggests this norm, will gain respect and actually be good survival insurance. Yet Ker Muir contends that "Police who rely on coercive force to make the world a less threatening place make it a more dangerous place for themselves and for other cops."[66]

A second norm is the demand for submissiveness from citizens. A citizen who complies with police authority is considered an ordinary citizen but one who does not is regarded as an outcast. The outcast citizen is labeled a "wiseguy" who must be dealt with in a firm and commanding way. Paul Chevigny found from his study that wiseguys would be typically arrested if they persisted in defying police authority. Too much persistence, Chevigny's respondents revealed, would result in a beating and then being charged with resisting arrest, in addition to the original charge.[67]

Police pursuits represent the cardinal sin of motorists fleeing from police custody.[68] Studies, which have examined this topic, have come to agreement on the following: (1) pursuits are highly dangerous; (2) pursuits need to be controlled; and (3) involvement in a pursuit results in the increase of adrenaline and excitement.[69] It is at the end of the pursuit that motorists may receive a good dosage of "street justice." Geoffrey P. Alpert and Roger Dunham's study of several agencies in the Miami area between 1985 and 1987 found that approximately 30 percent of injuries suffered by suspects took place after the vehicles were stopped and the suspects were being taken into custody.[70] In a more recent study, with data collected from the 1990s in departments in Mesa, Arizona, Miami, Florida, and Omaha, Nebraska, Geoffrey P. Alpert, Dennis Jay Kenney, and Roger Dunham found that "officers acknowledged that force was used in 53 percent of the pursuit-related apprehensions, supervisors reported that it was used in 47 percent of the apprehensions, and suspects said they were beaten 57 percent of the times that they were apprehended."[71]

The best known police pursuit took place on December 17, 1979, when Arthur McDuffie, an African American, was riding his motorcycle on the streets of Miami, Florida. According to police accounts, he gave the finger to a near-by police officer and accelerated the motorcycle. The police officer gave chase and was eventually joined by more than a dozen Miami patrol officers. When McDuffie stopped his motorcycle, at least six European American officers jumped McDuffie. It was not long before he lay motionless on the ground with his head split open. He died four days later as a result of these injuries.[72]

A less known but equally irrational incident took place in April 1988, when Lydia Ferraro, a 33 year old European American New Jersey mother of two, allegedly ran a red light in New York City. Her vehicle was pursued by police officers through East Harlem, at non-excessive speeds. During the pursuit, a NYPD sergeant fired at her moving vehicle. When a roadblock of police cars forced her to stop, a total of five police officers fired 13 shots into her automobile. The unarmed Ferraro was killed in this incident, which the Center for Law and Social Justice described as a "massacre."[73]

A third norm is that the two Americas receive different justices. One America is made up of good citizens who deserve respect, until they push it too far. But the other America is made up of the underclass. The police typically have little tolerance for any type of disrespect from members of this group. The horror stories that emerge too frequently from police interactions with minority groups simply have no place in a free and democratic society. One such story is that in 1987 an African American woman in Brooklyn was standing in front of her house. She paid little attention to a police car parked nearby, but by the time she realized that an African American officer in the car was ordering her inside her own house, it was too late. The enraged officer allegedly handcuffed the woman who was three months pregnant. As she attempted to resist, she was beaten, dragged on the ground, and placed in a chokehold. Her mother attempted to intervene, but she too was beaten and then handcuffed. When other family members tried to intervene, they too were beaten. In addition to the woman and her mother, a total of eight people in the woman's family were beaten.[74]

A fourth norm is that of secrecy. William Westley noted that the police "would apply no sanction against a colleague who took the more extreme view of the right to use violence and would openly support some milder form of illegal coercion."[75] Skolnick and Fyfe add that this code of secrecy "decrees that cops protect other cops, no matter what, and that cops of higher rank back up working street cops—no matter what."[76]

It appears that the chief's leadership in a department may have some influence over how much the subculture of violence is present. For example, Gerald Uelman's examination of the 50 police departments in Los Angeles County in the 1970s revealed that the best predictor of the rate at which officers killed citizens was not the level of violence they faced but the policies and personal philosophies of their chiefs.[77] Two of the best examples of chiefs' promoting a subculture of violence was the long reign of Daryl F. Gates as police chief of the Los Angeles Police Department and Frank Ruzzo who was both chief of police and mayor in Philadelphia.[78]

Racist Police and Brutality

During the 1950s and 1960s, police were used to enforce the Jim Crow laws and the policies of segregation. As the police were attempting to bring order out of the chaos of the time, including racial tensions, they were labeled as racists and bigots. The media transmitted police racism and brutality into our living rooms until our consciousness registered the horrors.

In the decade of the 1990s, we are again struggling to come to grips with our racial tendencies. At the same time that we are becoming aware of the gaping racial differences in our society, the police officer is being stereotyped as bigoted and prejudiced. Peace officers, like other members of American society, are shaped by the beliefs and norms of that society. It is not surprising, then, that racists and vicious criminals can be found wearing a badge. Although bigotry is not unique to law enforcement, a bigoted peace officer still defiles a sacred belief in human dignity. When a horrific or embarrassing incident about police misconduct is publicized, peace officers throughout the nation are embarrassed and angered by the hatred expressed in that encounter and by the understanding of society's propensity to generalize and stereotype.

In spite of a great deal of examination of the importance of race in affecting police discretion (see Chapter 3), there remains the question of what we do know. Hubert G. Locke concludes that the evidence appears to be indisputable that, in comparison with general population distributions, "persons of color are disproportionately represented among those subjected to police use of force, where the discharge of a firearm is involved. Beyond this finding," he adds, "there is little that researchers can assert empirically about the police use of appropriate and excessive force that is not in dispute."[79]

What we do not know is how much effect racism has on the police use of unnecessary force. Skolnick concludes, "We don't know how much racism is involved, but I believe that racist police are more likely to be brutal and brutal police are more likely to be racist."[80] In following Fyfe's definition of police brutality as willful, intentional violence, racism would provide the dehumanizing element needed to rationalize such abuse.

The fact still remains that racism does exist in the United States, that some police officers are racists, and that racism takes place in some police actions towards the public. Ira Harris, executive director of the National Organization of Black Law Enforcement Officers (NOBLE), makes a severe indictment when he comments:

> Police need more training in conflict resolution, all police supervisors, especially street supervisors, must be accountable, and misconduct must bear a tolerance level of zero. A climate has been created where white officers really aren't afraid of reprisals for their actions.[81]

USE OF DEADLY FORCE

The International Association of Chiefs of Police defines deadly force as "any use of force that is likely to cause death or serious bodily harm. Serious bodily harm may include: severe tissue damage, broken bones, major disfigurement, and permanent paralysis or impairment."[82]

Controversy always surrounds a shooting involving police. Possibly no other act sets into motion, and justifiably so, the scrutiny of the court, district attorney's office, internal agency investigation, civilian review, and the media. The split-second decision to use lethal force will be evaluated for months or even years to determine if the officer acted appropriately. The decision to convene a grand jury or pursue a criminal indictment rests with the district attorney or attorney general depending on the jurisdiction. The ultimate decision will be made by a jury in a criminal or civil proceeding.

The understanding of the police use of deadly force has changed rather dramatically over the past 15 years. First, many states have passed statutes modifying the common-law "fleeing felon" doctrine that has allowed police officers to use deadly force for the purpose of apprehending fleeing felons who would otherwise have escaped. Second, in *Tennessee v. Garner* (1985), the U.S. Supreme Court has ruled that shootings of any unarmed, nonviolent fleeing felon violates the Fourth Amendment of the Constitution. Third, nearly all major urban police departments have enacted administrative policies regarding deadly force that are more restrictive than state law. Fourth, the U.S. Supreme Court has made it less difficult for a citizen to file a lawsuit and collect civil damages as a result of a questionable shooting. Finally, a substantial body of research has examined many aspects of the deadly force question, including such concerns as the frequency of the use of firearms and whether that usage is increasing or declining.[83]

Over time, the fleeing felon doctrine has gradually become unacceptable as a standard for the police use of deadly force. By the early 1970s, six states and a number of police agencies developed a standard that allowed deadly force only in instances of violent felonies such as rape, robbery, and murder. In addition, two states and several more departments moved to a standard that authorized deadly force only necessary for a direct defense of life.[84]

On October 3, 1984, an incident took place that would change the deadly force standard for police. Two Memphis police officers answered a "prowler inside" call that night. At the scene, a woman pointed toward an adjacent house, saying that she had heard glass breaking. Upon going behind the house, one officer observed the suspect, Edward Garner, run across the backyard and stop at a fence. With the assistance of a flashlight, the officer observed that Garner was 17 or 18 years old, 5 feet 5 inches to 5 feet 7 inches tall, and unarmed. When Garner began to climb the fence, the officer shot him. Taken by ambulance to a hospital, Garner died on the operating table.[85] Following two sets of appeals, the U.S. Supreme Court eventually ruled in *Tennessee v. Garner* (1985) that police use of deadly force was inappropriate "unless it is necessary to prevent the escape and the officer has probable cause to believe that the suspect poses a significant threat of death or serious physical injury to the officer or others,"[86] and that the officer must have precluded other options for preventing escape including a warning that he or she is about to shoot, when feasible.[87]

Jeffrey L. Chudwin tells officers what not to do when making the critical lethal force decision. An officer must (1) never use deadly force against a misdemeanor offender; (2) never use deadly force based on mere suspicion; (3) never use deadly force based on mere words alone, no matter how antagonistic; and (4) never use deadly force against a non-violent, unarmed felony offender.[88]

The decision to use lethal force is not a simple one. An officer is typically reacting to the assailant's actions. Anytime during the process of a verbal warning (when that is feasible), placing a hand on the firearm, drawing that firearm, pointing it at the assailant, placing the finger on the trigger, and shooting, the subject could have stopped his or her life-threatening action. While taking these actions, the officer has to assess the subject's attack potential and his or her response considerations. The attack potential involves a three part formula of:

1. Intent (jeopardy)—Are the suspect's words or actions meant to place you in fear of serious injury or death? The threat has to be imminent.
2. Weapon (ability)—Does the object and its use have the ability to cause serious injury or death? This object includes not just a firearm or knife, but hands, feet, and teeth.
3. Delivery system (opportunity)—Is the means available to carry out the intent with the weapon? Is the belief reasonable?[89]

The officer's response considerations must include:

- Preclusion—Have I eliminated any other reasonable alternative?
- Target identification—Have I properly identified the target? Will the threat still be present if I shoot?
- Target isolation—If I miss, what will I hit?
- Parties at risk—Are third parties at risk?[90]
- Legality—Am I legally justified in shooting?
- Feasibility—Can I actually make the shot I need?[91]

The assailant only has to make one decision in this process—that is to shoot!

PREVENTING POLICE BRUTALITY AND UNNECESSARY USE OF DEADLY FORCE

A study conducted by several major chiefs and the FBI concerning the use of unauthorized force reached a consensus that there were six major reasons law enforcement officers use more force than is necessary:

1. Poor training in how to avoid confrontations or how to prevent confrontations from escalating.

2. Poor training in defensive tactics and having too few force options between words and firearms.
3. Personnel involved are psychologically unfit for duty—either when hired or because of drug or alcohol use.
4. Peer pressure involving a "them versus us" mentality.
5. Extreme cowardice compensated for by over-reacting and trying to prove themselves.
6. Racism, sexism, cultural ignorance, and a "holier than thou" attitude.[92]

A 1994 study sponsored by the National Institute of Justice (NIJ) interviewed 65 police psychologists, representing 50 of the largest department and serving populations exceeding 100,000, in order to learn more about the characteristics of officers who abuse force and police psychologists' recommendations. The study produced three key conclusions: (1) Reasons for excessive force are complex. Individual officer characteristics make up one element, but organizational practices are also implicated; (2) excessive force can be reduced by strengthening supervisory oversight and providing training that builds resistance to prevocational patrol situations; and (3) comprehensive prevention strategies are preferable to a crisis response for managing excessive force and are a better use of scarce resources.[93]

The Justice Department study produced five different profiles of officers with excessive force problems:

1. Officers with personality disorders such as lack of empathy for others, and antisocial, narcissistic, and abusive tendencies.
2. Officers with previous job-related use of force experiences, such as involvement in justifiable police shootings.
3. Officers who experienced early career stage problems having to do with their impressionability, impulsiveness, low tolerance for frustration, and general need for strong supervision. [Young and immature officers "frequently seen as "hotdogs," "badge happy," and "macho."]
4. Officers who have a dominant, heavy-handed patrol style that is particularly sensitive to challenge and provocation.
5. Officers who have personal problems such as separation, divorce, or perceived loss of status that cause extreme anxiety and destabilized job functioning.[94]

Department Monitoring

A majority of police departments use some form of monitoring.[95] In the National Institute of Justice study, police psychologists evaluated this method as of questionable value. By the time the warning is issued, the excessive force behavior may be well developed and entrenched, making it more difficult to change.[96] New York City created a computerized warning system ten months before the shocking assault on Haitian immigrant Abner Louima mentioned earlier. None of the four accused officers gave cause for suspicion. New York Police Commissioner Howard

Safir is now considering changes in psychological screening of new officers, but he comments, "I'm not sure any system could predict this kind of horrific act."[97]

Another police strategy, the marker behavioral method, represents a proactive stance getting supervisors to intervene before excessive force happens, instead of a reactive approach that creates institutional barriers to effective intervention. The most preferred method involves supervisors tracking "marker" behavior that signifies intervention is needed. The supervisor's trained observations, combined with the expertise of a psychologist, will determine appropriate interventions and what follow-up is needed. Some examples of behavioral markers include when "an officer acquires nicknames signifying forceful arrests, an officer's prisoners accumulate injuries, an officer's insubordinate behavior begins to increase, and squad concerns develop about an officer getting someone hurt."[98]

Partner Intervention

The "Rodney King" affect is present when a fellow officer witnesses an excessive force incident and does nothing. This effect is understandable (but not excusable) in terms of the police code that "you do not mess around with another person's bust." It is also understandable that officers from one department do not want to interfere with the arrest procedures of officers from another department. Yet, of all the sad days of law enforcement, it is the worst of all days when a group of officers watch but do not prevent an out of control officer or officers from brutalizing a citizen. It is such totally indefensible instances that have led some to label the police as racists and sadists.

Intervention by fellow officers appears to be one of the most effective means of controlling such forms of excessive force. Considering the frustrations and hostilities faced by line officers every day, it would be logical to assume that a breaking point will be reached at some point in the officer's career when he or she "loses it." When an agency has trained its officers in intervention techniques to prevent abuse, the following process are more likely to take place: (1) the stigma of not interfering with another officer's arrest disappears; (2) the angry officer realizes that he or she can turn the prisoner over to another officer for transport and booking without losing face; (3) the transporting officer accepts the request without question because he or she realizes the risks involved and the favor may be returned someday; and (4) it allows an officer to grab a partner who is out of control, pulling him or her away from a suspect before injury is sustained.[99]

Professional Training

Police officers receive a minimum amount of training for the physical skills that they are expected to have. Once they are appointed to the force, they get little ongoing training, if any, because departments are not provided with the personnel, the budgets, the equipment, and the logistical support needed to accomplish the task.[100] Fyfe advocates that the purpose of professional training is to prepare the individual officer to handle work-related problems better than a lay person. Brutal police officers do not pass this test. They are no better than a group of lay people, Fyfe claims, subduing an outnumbered individual with no regard for injury. He adds, "Police who handle tough situations brutally do so because of uncontrolled rage and/or because they are calculatedly oppressive.... Both hot tempers and proclivity toward violence are conditions that can be addressed in training."[101]

Two organizations have had a major impact on reducing police use of inappropriate force: Calibre Press, Inc. and The American Society of Law Enforcement Trainers (ASLET). Calibre Press is best known for its Street Survival® Seminar that started touring the United States in 1981. Initially, the seminar centered on officer survival training in response to the 1970s, the most deadly decade for police officers in United States history. By 1985 the curriculum changed to a more holistic approach, covering officers' legal, physical, and mental survival. A major portion of the seminar is spent on the justifiable use of force, including deadly force. Since its inception, over 200,000 officers have been trained by Street Survival®. The effects are far reaching, as police trainers, administrators, and police academy directors have attended the seminar. Recently, Calibre Press, Inc. introduced an e-mail service, Newsline, which sends out instructional material to over 18,000 subscribers in the United States and 12 foreign countries, with a readership estimated at between 50,000 and 60,000.[102]

The American Society of Law Enforcement Trainers was organized by trainers for the purpose of sharing valuable information. The organization brings together some of the best and most talented instructors in the world and provides a publication every two months covering training issues. An international seminar is held each year, combining lecture and hands-on instruction. The curriculum covers ten different tracks of instruction, ranging from legal and management issues to defensive tactics and hands-on training. Since its inception in 1987, the membership has grown to over 6,000 police trainers in the United States and 20 other countries.[103]

SUMMARY

Policing takes place in a context in which force is a dominant feature. As a reminder of this context of force, the police officer is armed with a gun, baton, and handcuffs and is granted the authority to detain and arrest, to search for and seize evidence, and to use deadly force. The police officer is expected to use reasonable force, but too frequently, especially in some departments across the nation, excessive force takes place during the process of policing society.

Little is truly known about the nature and extent of excessive force. What is known is that police officers work with the most hopeless and deprived members of society, as well as society's most violent members. How long can officers experience the hopelessness, the violence, and the utter futility of the population with whom they are working before they become numbed by the experience? How long can officers work in such a toxic environment before they too become contaminated? A quote from Nietzsche is most appropriate, "Whoever fights monsters should see to it that in the process he does not become a monster. For when you look long into an abyss, the abyss also looks into you."[104]

This context of the hopelessness, the violence, and the utter futility that some police officers face on a regular basis still does not exonerate excessive force or brutality toward citizens. The issue of excessive force is particularly troubling because it is directed too frequently toward minorities. Although the degree to which racism is involved in extralegal violence or unnecessary force is still under debate, there is little doubt that racism with some officers provides the dehumanizing vehicle to carry out heinous acts. According to Charles Vert Willie, "racial discrimination represents a failure in relationships between the minority and majority populations because one or both groups do not recognize that they are interdependent, that they need each other, and that the welfare of one depends on the other."[105]

One of the strongest influences to reduce the extent of police brutality is the increasing political power of minorities. Their political power has helped to elect politicians who understand that their tenure in office depends on the reduction of police brutality. Accordingly, they appoint police chiefs who, in turn, understand that their tenure in office depends on communicating to officers that brutality will not be tolerated. These chiefs are also expected to project a set of values more sensitive to inner city contexts.[106]

Without realizing it, officers who use excessive force endanger the lives of fellow officers. As in any use of force incident, there is at the very least resentment and often raw hostility felt by the person on whom force was used. The exception to this is the officer who has used reasonable force and who communicated with the individual after control was established. But unlike coercive force which suspects can understand, brutality is felt to be totally unjustifiable and unexplainable. This can only fuel the fires of hatred and cause future resistance, possibly injuring or killing an officer who was not involved in the original brutality. Officers need to stop brutal officers who are endangering their personal safety.

Perhaps Sergeant Larry Capps has captured what is needed to reduce police brutality in his "Peacemaker's Creed." The spirit he projects in this creed is much different than the mind-set of those police officers who employ excessive force:

> I am superior to no one
> I am subordinate to everyone
> I am not the master of all
> I am the servant to all
> I am not at the top of the hill
> I am at the bottom of the hill
> I am not above the law
> I am subject to the law
> I seek not personal comfort

> I seek comfort for society
> I stand with you—not against you
> I dispense compassion freely,
> exert force reluctantly,
> and cherish freedom
> I am the peacemaker; loved by
> many, feared by a few
> —and needed by all.[107]

> *The Peacemaker's Creed,* Sergeant Larry Capps.
> Reprinted with permission from *The Ethics Roll Call,* summer 1996,
> Center for Law Enforcement Ethics, Southwestern Law Enforcement Institute.

KEY WORDS

coercive force

Control Continuum

excessive force

extralegal violence

Graham v. Conner

Sherrod v. Berry

Tennessee v. Garner

unnecessary force

DISCUSSION QUESTIONS

1. Two officers are on patrol when they receive a dispatch of the description of two armed robbery suspects. One officer thinks he knows someone who fits the description and who has a history of robberies and purse snatchings. After receiving another communiqué that the suspect has returned to the area, the officers return to the crime scene. There, they spot a car with two males in it. One of them is this subject. When the suspects leave the parking lot, the officers attempt to stop their vehicle. Feeling this is a high-risk stop, both officers upholster their firearms and assume positions outside the police vehicle with their firearms pointed at the suspects. Following procedure, the suspects are ordered to raise their hands. They do not comply. The order is repeated three more times before the suspects comply. During this time, the passenger keeps looking at the driver. While the passenger officer covers his partner, the officer approaches the suspect's vehicle with his firearm raised. As he reaches the driver, the driver makes a quick movement with his hand into his coat. At that point the officer fires, killing him instantly. The suspect was unarmed. The trial court permits the introduction of evidence concerning the fact that the suspect was not armed. Is the court correct in permitting the unarmed evidence to be used? Was the officer correct in using deadly force?

2. You are a police officer. Officers in your department are known for their brutality. You have just witnessed an abusive incident. However, to report it to your supervisors would label you a troublemaker, resulting in a transfer and possibly the end of any chance for career advancement. What would you do?

3. What are the most important concepts in the police use of reasonable force? Explain each of them.

4. Discuss the norms in those departments that have a violence subculture.

5. Does collective protest represent a "no win" situation for the police? Is there any way to handle these situations in a reasonable way?

6. What can be done to prevent police brutality?

7. In your opinion, how much does racism contribute to police brutality?

FURTHER READING

Artwohl, Alexis and Loren W. Christensen. *Deadly Force Encounters: What Cops Need to Know to Mentally and Physically Prepare and Survive a Gunfight.* Boulder: Paladin, 1997.

Chevigny, Paul. *Edge of the Knife: Police Violence in the Americas.* New York: The New Press, 1995.

DeSantis, John. *The New Untouchables: How America Sanctions Police Violence.* Chicago: The Noble Press, 1994.

Geller, William A. and Michael S. Scott. *Deadly Force: What We Know, A Practitioner's Desk Reference on Police-Involved Shootings.* Washington, DC: Police Executive Research Forum, 1992.

Geller, William A. and Hans Toch. *And Justice for All: Understanding and Controlling Police Abuse of Force.* Washington, DC: Police Executive Research Forum, 1995.

Klugiewicz, Gary T. *Active Countermeasures Instructor Certification Training Manual.* Greenfield: Active Countermeasures Instructional Systems, 1994.

McEwen, Tom. *National Data Collection on Police Use of Force.* U.S. Department of Justice, National Institute of Justice, Office of Community Oriented Policing Services, Washington, DC: USGPO, 1996.

Moore, Mark H. and Darrel W. Stephens. *Beyond Command and Control: The Strategic Management of Police Departments.* Washington, DC: Police Executive Research Forum, 1991.

Ogletree, Charles J., Jr., Mary Prosser, Abbe Smith, and William Talley, Jr. *Beyond the Rodney King Story.* Boston: Northeastern UP, 1995.

Rothwax, Harold J. *Guilty: The Collapse of Criminal Justice.* New York: Random House, 1995.

Skolnick, Jerome H. and James J. Fyfe. *Above the Law.* New York: The Free Press, 1993.

Willie, Charles Vert. *A New Look at Black Families,* 4th ed. Dix Hills: General Hall, 1991.

ENDNOTES

1. Jack Enter, "Why You'll Never Want for Work," Street Survival® '97 *Newsline* (26 August 1997) 1.

2. Lance Morrow, "Rough Justice," *Time,* 1 April 1991: 16.

3. Jerome H. Skolnick and James J. Fyfe, *Above the Law: Police and the Excessive Use of Force* (New York: The Free Press, 1993) 3.

4. Carl Dix, "Police Violence: Rising Epidemic/Raising Resistance," *Black Scholar* 27 (1997): 59.

5. Victor E. Kappeler, Richard D. Sluder, and Geoffrey P. Alpert, *Forces of Deviance: Understanding the Dark Side of Policing* (Prospect Heights: Waveland, 1994) 146.

6. Jim Williams and Aaron Brown, "Justice Dept. Asked to Investigate NY Brutality," *ABC World News*, 16 Aug. 1997.

7. Skolnick and Fyfe, xvi.

8. Tom McEwen, *National Data Collection on Police Use of Force*, U. S. Department of Justice, National Institute of Justice, Office of Community Oriented Policing Service (Washington, DC: US-GPO, April 1996) 5.

9. Cited in Kenneth Adams, "Measuring the Prevalence of Police Abuse of Force," *And Justice for All: Understanding and Controlling Police Abuse of Force*, eds. William A. Geller and Hans Touch (Washington, DC: Police Executive Research Forum, 1995) 63.

10. D. L. Carter, "Theoretical Dimensions in the Abuse of Authority of Police Officers," *Police Deviance*, 2nd ed., eds. Thomas Barker and David Carter (Cincinnati: Anderson, 1991) 200.

11. Skolnick and Fyfe, 19.

12. Skolnick and Fyfe, 19.

13. James J. Fyfe, "Training to Reduce Police–Civilian Violence," *And Justice For All: Understanding and Controlling Police Abuse of Force*, eds. William A. Gellar and Hans Toch (Washington, DC: Police Executive Research Forum, 1995) 163.

14. Fyfe, 163.

15. Fyfe, 165.

16. Joseph Wambaugh, "But What Do Advocates Say About Mexican Police?" *Los Angeles Times*, Home Edition, 14 Apr. 1996.

17. Skolnick and Fyfe, 37.

18. William A. Geller and Hans Toch, *Police Violence* (New Haven: Yale UP, 1996) 293.

19. Skolnick and Fyfe, 18.

20. Skolnick and Fyfe, 18.

21. Judge Harold J. Rothwax described the third degree that resulted in the 1936 case called *Brown v. Mississippi* as "pervasive in the United States then, especially in the South." Brown was beaten by the sheriff using a metal-buckled leather strap to solicit a confession to a murder. See Harold J. Rothwax, *Guilty: The Collapse of Criminal Justice* (New York: Random House, 1995) 71–72.

22. McEwen; see also Robert E. Worden, "The 'Causes' of Police Brutality: Theory and Evidence on Police Use of Force," *And Justice For All*, ed. Geller and Toch; and Joel Garner, John Buchanan, Tom Schade, and John Hepburn, "Understanding the Use of Force By and Against the Police," National Institute of Justice: Research in Brief (Nov. 1996).

23. Adams, "Measuring the Prevalence of Police Abuse of Force," in *And Justice for All*, 70–71.

24. Adams, 205.

25. Quoted in Geller and Scott, *Deadly Force: What We Know, A Practitioner's Desk Reference on Police-Involved Shootings* (Washington, DC: Police Executive Research Forum, 1992) 178.

26. Adams, 70–71.

27. McEwen.

28. Adams, 72–73.

29. McEwen, 31–32.

30. McEwen, 33.

31. McEwen, 32–35.

32. McEwen, 37.

33. McEwen, 37.

34. McEwen, 36–38.

35. McEwen, 36–37.

36. McEwen, 62.

37. Garner, et al., 2.

38. Garner, et al., 1–2.

39. Garner, et al., 7–8.

40. Gary T. Klugiewicz, *Active Countermeasures Instructor Certification Training Manual* (Greenfield: Active Countermeasures Instructional Systems, 1995) 67.

41. Klugiewicz.

42. Klugiewicz, 6.

43. "Officer's Terror Ride," *Real-Life Street Survival*, videotape, Northbrook: Calibre Press Video, 1997.

44. John Wilbur, "Quote of the Week," *Caliber Press Street Survival Newsline 181* (June 27, 1997): 4.

45. J. G. Smith, "The Force Option Continuum" *Active Countermeasures Instructional Systems* (Greenfield: Active Counter Measures Instructional Systems, 1992).

46. *Graham v. Connor*, 490 US 386, 1989, 395.

47. *Graham v. Connor*, 387.

48. *Graham v. Connor*, 396.

49. *Graham v. Connor*, 396.

50. *Graham v. Connor*, 397.

51. *Graham v. Connor*, 396.

52. *Sherrod v. Berry*, 856 F.2d 802., 7th Cir. 1988, 804–805.

53. *Sherrod v. Berry*, 807.

54. *Graham v. Connor*, 396–397.

55. *Report of the National Advisory Commission on Civil Disorders* (New York: Bantam, 1968).

56. Report of the National Advisory Commission on Civil Disorders, 206.

57. Report of the National Advisory Commission on Civil Disorders, 206.

58. Skolnick and Fyfe, 81.

59. Daniel Walker, *Rights in Conflict: The Violent Confrontation of Demonstrators and Police in the Parks and Streets of Chicago During the Week of the Democratic National Convention of 1968*, a report to the National Commission on the Causes and Prevention of Violence (New York: Bantam, 1968) xv.

60. Skolnick and Fyfe.

61. Skolnick and Fyfe, 83.

62. John DeSantis, *The New Untouchables: How America Sanctions Police Violence* (Chicago: Noble, 1994) 85–90.

63. Skolnick and Fyfe, 181, 191.

64. William Ker Muir, Jr., "Power Attracts Violence," *Annuals of the American Academy of Political and Social Science* (Chicago: U of Chicago P, 1977): 101–126.

65. Ker Muir, 101–126.

66. Ker Muir, 101–126.

67. Paul Chevigny, *Police Power: Police Abuses in New York City* (New York: Vintage, 1969).

68. Skolnick and Fyfe, 111.

69. Geoffrey P. Alpert, Dennis Jay Kenney, and Roger Dunham, "Police Pursuits and the Use of Force: Recognizing and Managing 'The Plucker Factor'—A Research Note," *Justice Quarterly 14* (June 1997): 371.

70. G. Alpert and R. Dunham, *Police Pursuit Driving: Controlling Responses to Emergency Situations* (New York: Greenwood, 1990).

71. Alpert, et al., "Police Pursuits and the Use of Force," 381.

72. Kappeler, et al., 56.

73. DeSantis, 52–53.

74. DeSantis, 11.

75. William A. Westley, "Violence and the Police," *American Journal of Sociology 59* (1953): 37.

76. Skolnick and Fyfe, 7.

77. Gerald Uelman, "Varieties of Public Policy: A Study of Police Policy Regarding the Use of Deadly Force in Los Angeles County," *Loyola of Los Angeles Law Review 9* (1973): 1–65.

78. See Skolnick and Fyfe, 139–141, 169–170.

79. Hubert G. Locke, "The Color of Law and the Issue of Color: Race and the Abuse of Police Power," 139.

80. Skolnick quoted in Alex Prud'Homme, "Police Brutality! Four Los Angeles Officers Are Arrested For a Vicious Beating, and the Country Plunges Into a Debate On the Rise Of Complaints Against Cops," *Time*, 25 Mar. 1991, 16.

81. "Clinton Asked for Summit on Police Misconduct," *Oakland Post* (Stamford: Ethnic NewsWatch SoftLine Information, 4 December 96).

82. As cited in *Street Survival '95 Personal Resource Guide* (Calibre Press, 1995) 43.

83. Mark Blumberg, "Controlling Police Use of Deadly Force: Assessing Two Decades of Progress," *Critical Issues in Policing: Contemporary Readings* (Prospect Heights: Waveland, 1989): 442.

84. Jeffrey T. Walker, "Police and Correctional Use of Force: Legal and Policy Standards and Implications," *Crime & Delinquency 42* (Jan. 1996): 145.

85. Walker, 145–146.

86. *Tennessee v. Gardner*, 471 US 1, 1985.

87. *Street Survival '95 Personal Resource Guide* (1995) 48.

88. Jeffrey L. Chudwin lecture and handout given out at the 1994 American Association of Law Enforcement Trainers Association National Convention, Milwaukee, Wisconsin. Also see *Tennessee v. Garner*, 105 S. Ct. 1694, 1985.

89. *Street Survival '95 Personal Resource Guide*; and Gary T. Klugiewicz, *Active Countermeasures Instructor Certification Manual* (Greenfield: Active Countermeasures Instructional Systems, 1997).

90. Klugiewicz, *Active Countermeasures*.

91. *Street Survival '95 Personal Resource Guide*.

92. *Street Survival '95 Personal Resource Guide*, 281.

93. Ellen M. Scrivner, "The Role of Police Psychology in Controlling Excessive Force," *National Institute of Justice Research Report* (Apr. 1994): 1.

94. Scrivner, 8–13.

95. Kevin Johnson, "More Cities Watching Cops Closely," *USA Today*, 27 Aug. 1997.

96. Scrivner, 8–9.

97. Johnson.

98. Scrivner, 9.

99. From one of the author's personal experiences after having trained his department.

100. Mildred K. O'Linn, personal interview, Jan. 1995. Interview with a board member and legal advisor for American Society of Law Enforcement Trainers, and an attorney who has specialized in the representation of law enforcement personnel and agencies in civil and criminal litigation.

101. Fyfe, 163.

102. Personal interview, 1997.

103. Personal interview, 1997.

104. Nietzsche quoted in Gavin De Becker, *The Gift of Fear* (New York: Little, Brown and Company, 1997) 47.

105. Charles Vert Willie, *A New Look at Black Families,* 4th ed. (Dix Hills: General Hall, 1991) 32, 235.

106. Skolnick and Fyfe, 20.

107. Larry Capps, "The Peacemaker's Creed," *The Ethics Roll Call,* Summer 1996, Center for Law Enforcement Ethics, Southwestern Law Enforcement Institute.

10

POLICE CORRUPTION

When one cop takes a bribe, there is a blind rush to assume most cops are on the take and when one officer tramples the Constitutional rights of a suspect, it is immediately presumed that most cops are of a similar persuasion. We are quick to blame all of them for the misdeeds of a few, only seeing one shade of blue. Remarkably, while we hungrily embrace the suggestion that one rotten cop spoils the barrel, we reject such leaps of logic when it come to other professionals such as doctors, lawyers and judges....

The enforcement of the law is a highly individualized process guided not only by an officer's experience and intelligence, but by his compassion and, most importantly, his moral fiber.... And despite recent high profile attacks on them, the reality is that the overwhelming majority of law enforcement officers responsibly carry out and act in the public's best interest. However, we rarely hear about these officers. Bad cops make good news, good cops make no news.

—Paul Mones, "Where Have All the Good Cops Gone?" *American Police Beat III,* No. 9, (November 1996), p. 10.

The author of this quote is very right in his comment that bad cops always make the news and provide all the evidence necessary for generalizing and stereotyping. He is also correct that police officers are guided by their experience, intelligence, compassion, and most of all, by their moral fiber. He further makes a sound point that the vast majority of police officers "responsibly carry out and act in the public's best interest." But there is far more question about the "bad apple" theory of police corruption that appears to be implicit in his statement.[1]

According to the "bad apple" theory, bad officers are morally corrupt individuals, rotten on the inside and only out for themselves. This individual pathology theory blames police corruption on a few aberrant officers who act on their own in isolation from the social environment, without peer or organizational support.[2]

The 'bad apple" theory assures us that the majority of the officers (the remainder of the apple barrel), are morally upstanding and beyond excess or temptation. The rotten apples, of course, need removed so that the barrel's other apples will not be contaminated. What is concealed in this argument is that the barrel might itself be contaminated or even that it might be the source of the problem.[3]

Police corruption, like other forms of police deviancy, is structurally and organizationally induced.[4] Corruption is influenced by such external factors as the economic, social, and political structures of society and by such internal factors as the cultural history of the department, departmental policy, peer groups, and leadership style.[5] This structural account of police corruption is aptly described by Julian B. Roebuck and Thomas Barker:

> Police corruption is best understood not as the exclusive deviance of individual officers, but as group behavior guided by contradictory sets of norms linked to the organizations to which the erring individuals belong, i.e., organizational deviance.[6]

The pervasiveness of corruption is reflected in Lawrence W. Sherman's statement that every police department has probably witnessed some form of organized corruption or major scandal since the 1920's. According to Paul Chevigny, "most police corruption has been part of the larger pattern in the government as a whole, whether of election fraud or graft taken from vice rackets."[7]

Police corruption is also frequently linked with brutality. The sorry career of Michael Dowd in the New York Police Department aptly demonstrates the link that sometimes exists between corruption and excessive force. Early in his career, Dowd testified before the Mollen Commission that assaulting drug suspects in front of other officers became a test of these officers' tolerance for further acts of corruption.[8] "You kick some punk down the stairs in front of 10 cops and you have 10 friends," Dowd said. "Young officers…tested one another. How much bad could you be trusted to see, the old-timers wanted to know, before you ratted on another cop?"[9]

Herman Goldstein defines **police corruption** as "the misuse of authority by a police officer in a manner designed to provide personal gain for the officers or for others."[10] Even though police corruption is systemic, you still cannot factor out the individual equation. Just as socialization into the police culture is a process, there is also process for the individual to become corrupt. The process of corruption, as is aptly described by Del Fisher's "Nayes and Yeas" (see Box 10.1), ranges from political favoritism for personal gain, ignoring crime, and accepting gifts for favors, to outright theft and extortion (see Table 10.1).

Although corruption has been a problem of varying degree from the very beginning of policing in this nation, the widespread availability of drugs has increased the opportunity for wrongdoing. Officers assigned to drug enforcement units, of course, are constantly faced with wrongdoing. Patrol units also encounter large supplies of drugs and cash. The fact that they usually have less oversight than do specialized units provides both greater temptation and opportunity.[11]

BOX 10.1 "Nayes and Yeas"

General George Patton believed that a soldier's entire career amounted to a "three minute accumulation of nayes and yeas." In other words, a three minute recital of important yes–no questions encountered throughout a career and the answer to those questions determine how a soldier reaches any given point. From reputation to rank to survival, the answer to those "yea–nay" questions leaves a trail that can be traced, and at each possible fork in the trail, the "yea–nay" choice has a significant impact on the final outcome.

Could the same be true of a police officer's career? Do our answers to affirmative–negative questions lead us down a road to the final point, the end of our careers? If so, here's what a police officer's "accumulation of nayes and yeas might consist of:

"I want to be a police officer when I finish school, so should I do this illegal act I'm considering? Should I lie on my application with the PD? Should I cheat on the academy test? Will I call in sick when I'm not? Should I drop my non-police friends and activities? Do I write the off-duty officer a traffic ticket? Do I challenge inappropriate behavior among my peers? Do I ignore the officer abusing his prisoner? Do I respond with profanity when citizens use profanity? Should I turn in the money I found? Can I justify this search? Is police ethics more than an academy topic? Do I handle people differently based on their race or sex? Am I using racial slurs? Is my behavior sexual harassment? Do I badge my way out of this questionable situation? Do I drink too much and still drive? Will I take that half-price meal? Will I show my badge to get into a football game free? Will I put on my uniform and take my family to the restaurant so all of us can eat free? Do I "go the extra mile" to resolve a citizen's problem? Will I hand out business cards for my friend, the wrecker driver? Will I falsify a report to protect another officer? Will I commit perjury to get a criminal what he deserves? Do I listen to both sides of the story before acting? Do I believe in and practice the code of silence, the "brotherhood," "professional courtesy," and "us versus them?" Will I violate this person's rights? Will I refuse him an attorney? Do I ignore her request for medical assistance? Do I spray him with OC spray for "contempt of cop"? Do I use more force than needed to subdue him? Do I believe in "it's not what you did, its how you write the report?" Will I conceal things from my supervisor? Do I sleep on duty? Will I tolerate social drug usage among my non-police friends? Spend most of my time on-duty conducting personal business? Use my police position inappropriately? Abuse my office? Conduct more bar checks in topless bars than warranted? Risk lives in high speed pursuits for traffic violations? Do I care what citizens think of me or the Department? Will I make the correct, ethical choice in this situation?

General Patton went on to say that not only individual military careers, but history itself was shaped by the soldier's "yea–nay" accumulation of answers. Could the police professional be any less influential? Have we not already influenced society and history by the answers we have given and are given to the above question? Consider this impact the next time you find yourself in a conversation that begins with someone saying, "I don't know why we're talking about this ethics stuff…

Source: The Ethics Roll Call, Fall 1996, Center for Law Enforcement Ethics, Southwestern Law Enforcement Institute.

TABLE 10.1   Patterns of Police Corruption

Pattern	Acts	Organization
Corruption of authority	Free meals, liquor services discounts, rewards	No organization
Kickbacks	Money, goods, and services from those who service clients of the police (garages, bonds-man, towing companies, etc.)	Higher; collision
Opportunistic theft	Thefts from arrestees, victims, crime scenes, and unprotected property	None
Shakedowns	Money, goods, or other valuables from crim-inals or traffic offenders	None
Protection of illegal activities	Protection money from vice operators or companies operating illegally	High; often highly unorganized
The fixes	Quashing of prosecution proceedings or dis-posal of traffic tickets	Medium; fixers could be on the payroll
Direct criminal activities	Police officers engaged in such crimes as burglary, robbery, etc.	Low; small groups
Internal payoffs	Sale of work assignment, off-days evidence, and promotions	Low to high; depending on other forms of corruption present

Source: From Tom Baker, *Police Ethics: Crisis in Law Enforcement* (Springfield: Thomas, 1996) 38. Courtesy of Charles C. Thomas, Publisher, Ltd., Springfield, Illinois.

This chapter on corruption is one of the most important in this text because the damage done by police corruption has been devastating. As the current credibility crisis of the police vividly demonstrates, corruption has undermined the confidence of the public, reduced the respect for law, and harmed police morale.[12]

THE ENDURING NATURE OF POLICE CORRUPTION

Corruption, as suggested in Chapter 1, was found in American policing from the very beginning of colonial law enforcement. With the development of municipal policing in the nineteenth century, corruption increased in scope and magnitude. The fact that police departments become adjuncts to political machines led to widespread corruption and brutality and cost the police public respect and confidence. Their receptivity to graft made some police officers extremely wealthy as they were well paid for ignoring laws related to gambling, drinking, and prostitution.

An insight that can be gleaned from an examination of policing in the nineteenth century is that some police departments became cultural pockets of corruption. New York, Philadelphia, and Chicago were the most notorious centers of corruption. In response, reform-minded mayors brought police administrators in to clean up the department. In some cases, it appeared that these administrators were making progress, but all too soon, they would be gone and the corruption would return to being as extensive or even more so than before.

In the midst of the rise of professionalism during the early decades of this century, corruption received little attention but continued to be found in law enforcement, especially in urban departments. Then, the knowledge of the extensiveness of corruption exploded in New York City and became a department-wide scandal. Indeed, the Lexow Committee investigated corruption in 1894, followed by the Curran Committee in 1913, the Seabury Committee in 1932, and the Brooklyn Grand Jury in 1949.[13] In 1972, the **Knapp Commission**, or the Commission to Investigate Allegations of Police Corruption and the City's Anti-Corruption Procedures, was formed to investigate police corruption. The findings of this commission presented wide-spread corruption throughout the New York City Police Department, rejecting the "rotten apple" theory, and contending instead that the problem was systemic and that it involved all sectors of the department. Its report indicated that both uniformed and plain clothes officers were:

- keeping money and/or narcotics confiscated at the time of an arrest or a raid
- selling narcotics to addict-informants in exchange for stolen goods
- passing confiscated drugs to police informants for sale to addicts
- storing narcotics, needles, and other drug paraphernalia in police lockers
- accepting money or narcotics from suspected narcotics violators as payment for the disclosure of official information
- introducing potential customers to narcotics pushers
- revealing the identity of a government informant to narcotics criminals
- providing armed protection for narcotics dealers[14]

In finding that police corruption ranged from relatively harmless acts to illegal behavior, the Knapp Commission referred to the two basic types of corrupt officers as "**grass eaters**" and "**meat eaters.**" Grass eaters are officers who accept only those payoffs that police work would happen to bring their way. Meat eaters, on the other hand, are officers who aggressively misuse power for personal gain. The Knapp Commission, as well as other studies, found that the majority of corrupt police officers are grass eaters.[15]

Tom Baker, expanding on the Knapp Commission study, developed a continuum of officers in corrupt departments. In addition to grass eaters and meat eaters, Baker added "white knights," "straight shooters," and "rogues." **White knights,** positioned on the extreme left of the continuum, are honest and proclaim honesty almost to a fault. They often take an extreme position on ethics becoming rigid, judgmental, and vocal about ethics in a profession that requires discretionary decision making. **Straight shooters** are honest cops who remain silent, overlooking patterns of corruption and misconduct feeling that there is nothing they can do— they are uncomfortable turning in another officer. **Rogues** are on the far right of the continuum. They are an aberration even among meat eaters. The rogue often commits "highly visible shakedowns of citizens, felony fixes, and even direct criminal activities…. Actions on the part of both white knights and rogue officers have led to scandals." What usually takes place is that a white knight blows the whistle to the media or an external agency, or the outrageous behavior of a rogue officer is so far out that it cannot be covered up (see Table 10.2).[16]

The revelations of Detective Frank Serpico, depicted in the movie "Serpico," were another disclosure of police corruption in New York City in the 1970s. The drug corruption episodes of the Special Investigation Unit, dramatized in both the movie and book *The Prince of the City*, were a further portrait of this eroding problem. Detective Bob Leuci, who worked undercover for Knapp Commission prosecutors for 16 months, provided evidence on corrupt bondsmen, lawyers, and judges and explained to prosecutors how the robbing of drug dealers took place:

> The SIU detectives, having conceived an overpowering hatred for these people [South Americans], began to dispense their own justice. Sometimes they talked of killing one or another prisoner, though this had never been done to Leuci's knowledge. Instead, they simply began to rob them. They would take whatever money the dope dealer had, order him on to the next plane to South America, and applaud themselves for accomplishing what no court seemed able to accomplish, a heavy fine followed by instant deportation. The only trouble was, it was stealing. But since they were all doing it together, it didn't seem so bad.[17]

In the 1980s, a number of other American cities conducted investigations of police corruption. In Philadelphia, 31 police officers were convicted of police corruption in a federal investigation. In Miami, a ring of police officers were convicted of running a drug distribution enterprise. Indeed, by 1988, 77 Miami police officers had been fired, suspended, or accused of misconduct after they resigned.[18] In Boston, several officers were convicted of extorting payoffs from vice providers. Since 1989, 201 Washington, DC police officers have been arrested (some more than once) on charges ranging from drug dealing and shoplifting to rape and murder.[19] In San Francisco, suspecting widespread corruption led public officials to reexamine the controls maintained over the police force.[20]

In New York City, the ugly face of corruption became apparent again when a group of police officers, who worked in the 77th precinct from around 1980 to the latter part of 1986, became known as the "Buddy Boys." Thirty-eight officers even-

TABLE 10.2   Continuum of Officers in Corrupt Departments

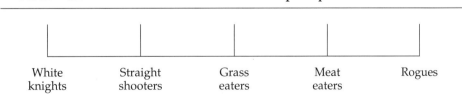

| White knights | Straight shooters | Grass eaters | Meat eaters | Rogues |

Source: From Tom Baker, *Police Ethics: Crisis in Law Enforcement* (Springfield: Thomas, 1996) 41. Courtesy of Charles C. Thomas, Publisher, Ltd., Springfield, Illinois.

tually were disciplined by the department. The Buddy Boys were involved in nearly every form of drug-related corruption—they extorted money from crack dealers, and they used drugs themselves on and off the job.[21] M. McAlary sketched a picture of officer drug use in the precinct:

> Certainly the 77th Precinct had a drug problem. Some officers smoked marijuana in their patrol cars on the late tour and snorted cocaine in the locker room lounge. Many more used drugs off duty, snorting cocaine with girlfriends they had met in the precinct while working. It was not at all unusual for a cop in the 77th Precinct to leave his wife and kids in the suburbs for a prostitute in the slum.[22]

In 1992, Detroit Police Chief William Hart was sentenced to federal prison for ten years for tax evasion and for embezzling $2.6 million from a secret police department fund. The 68 year old Hart had been police chief of Detroit since 1976. His was the most recent of a series of charges against Detroit police officers. In New Orleans, Louisiana, 50 police officers have also been arrested, indicted, or convicted on criminal charges ranging from murder to drug trafficking since 1993.[23] In 1993, the Mollen Commission, headed by former Judge Milton Mollen, held 11 days of hearings on police corruption in New York City. Officers spoke of dealing drugs, of confiscating drug funds, of stifling investigations, and of beating innocent people. There was also evidence presented at these hearings that high-ranking police officers attempted to hide embarrassing incidents in a "phantom file."

Sergeant Joseph Trimboli, a highly decorated member of the New York City Police Department, has been widely praised for his testimony before the Mollen Commission. In his testimony, he spoke about his six year effort to build a case against a group of rogue cops led by former officer Michael Dowd, and the frustrations and the lack of support he received from the agency in that effort.

In a speech Trimboli made at the Law Enforcement Ethics Center dinner, he tells about the first time he saw Dowd during 1986 at the precinct where he worked. Even that first impression of Dowd bothered Trimboli: "But for some reason, and you all know the feeling, the hair on the back of my head stands up and it's the feeling that I used to have working the streets when I looked at somebody and [knew he was a problem.]" But, Trimboli adds, "With the cases coming in on Mr. Dowd, I no longer believed that he was a cop. He was using a gun and a badge for his own purposes, and we had to catch him doing it."[24] He continues:

> In 1988 we learned of a ring of cops, led by Michael Dowd, who were transporting large quantities of cocaine in their own cars, who were sticking up drug locations and reselling the drugs back to the dealers, who were doing all kinds of things out there on the street. Unfortunately, this information was not well received in Internal Affairs.... Eventually, Internal Affairs called me down to their main offices and the first thing they did was accuse me of trafficking drugs from South America. I guess that was their way of attempting to demonstrate to me

that if I didn't stop doing what I was doing, they could make all kinds of accusations against me and probably make them stick.[25]

However, Trimboli courageously did not stop his investigation and suffered the consequences over the next few years. His car was broken into on a regular basis by key entry, as opposed to forced entry. Dowd and his cronies opened his mail, tapped his telephone, and followed him home from work. They did everything they could to intimidate Trimboli, but he stood tall and helped bring this rogue down. Dowd was eventually prosecuted and sentenced to prison.[26]

THE SOCIALIZATION PROCESS AND POLICE CORRUPTION

New officers generally do not quickly become corrupt. Typically unfamiliar with their precincts and the people in them, they are usually uncomfortable with doing any more than observe what takes place. Even if new officers have the opportunity to make extra money or engage in some form of corruption, their idealistic beliefs or fear of getting caught usually influences them to turn it down.

New officers have three options when confronted with corruption in the department. First, they can attempt to maintain the high ethical standard instructed in the academy and make an arrest. Second, they can inform a supervisor of the activity. Third, they can do nothing. What makes the decision more complicated is that the supervisor receiving the complaint may be the violator's best friend or involved in the corruption. Additionally, the senior officer, most likely the officer's field training officer, may be involved in the corruption or brutality and could start the termination process by a bad evaluation or by labeling the new officer as incompetent through the rumor mill. Even if the officer survives the probationary period, it may take years to live down this label.

For example, an officer who had just retired after 20 years of service confided to one of the authors that he witnessed colleagues stealing merchandise on his first burglary call, a common practice for that department. He was very angry when telling his story, "I'm retired now. I told them I would not participate nor would I report them. I stayed clean—I stayed clean!" A few months after his retirement, eight officers, half of the department, were arrested for theft. He never did receive a promotion, although he was one of the most gifted police trainers in the United States.[27]

Officers faced with this conflict between the ideal and the real may be tempted to undergo a shift in their standards. For those who succumb to this temptation, they must find a way to justify to themselves that what they are doing is not wrong but is necessary and, therefore, acceptable under the circumstances. Corruption, as with other forms of deviation, usually begins with a small step. This slight compromise in moral standards is usually normative within the department and can be more easily justified than corruption that has clearly crossed the line into criminal behavior.

Those who have grown up in neighborhoods similar to those they patrol may regard the transition from straight to corrupt as no more than a step back toward the only lifestyle they know. But for others, they need a cause to make corruption acceptable. Their step toward corruption may require the failure to be promoted, financial worries, the feeling that they have little or no recognition of achievements, the lack of management support, the desire to attain certain material possessions, or pressure from peers. New officers, regardless of what motivates their receptivity toward corruption, usually need to be led into corruption by fellow officers who are already corrupt before they are willing to step into corruption.

One of the many reasons that corruption is so problematic in law enforcement, as well as in corrections and the courts, is that it is almost always a one way street. That is, once an officer takes a small step toward corruption, he or she finds it nearly impossible, at least in that department, to return to the role of the "straight cop." Even if an officer could regain that sense of the intact moral self put aside by the corrupt act, fellow corrupt officers now have a "dirty" colleague and are reluctant to permit him or her to "go straight." A "dirty" colleague no longer has the right to judge other corrupt officers and, even more important, no longer presents the legal threat that a clean colleague does.

DEPARTMENTAL CORRUPTION

Most police corruption scandals in the 1970s and 1980s presented little evidence for the "rotten apple" theory. The "rotten structure" or "rotten to the barrel" argument seems to better explain most police corruption scandals, and it is the rotten structures or rotten barrel that make the problem of corruption appear unsolvable. Countless examples prove that corrupt officers can be weeded out of policing. Officers who have extorted money from defendants have been indicted or forced to resign. Those who have profited from scams have been convicted of income tax evasion. Those who have been caught in the sale of drugs have been indicted and even sent to prison. In other words, specific problems of corruption can be identified, isolated, and solved.[28]

The **rotten structures** of corruption mean that the tentacles of corruption extend throughout the department. Sometimes it goes to the top, other times it reaches the command staff, and it almost always encompasses the informal circle of power. In the 1970s the Knapp Commission found corruption spread throughout the New York City Police Department and that this systemic problem included all sectors of the department. In the 1990s the Mollen Commission's investigation of corruption found the persuasiveness of corruption in the NYPD. Indeed, it is significant that the Internal Affairs Unit, set up to weed out wrongdoing in a police agency, was not only aware of this corruption in the NYPD, but put great pressure on Sergeant Joseph Trimboli to look the other way and ignore what was taking place.

Another example of corruption extending to the top occurred in the Forth Worth, Texas police department when a tip came in that people were dumping construction debris, asphalt shingles, asbestos tiles, paint, solvent cans, antifreeze, oil jugs and used tires into a dump, all of which could contaminate ground water.

For refusing to look the other way because a local politician owned the dump, Deputy Marshal David Zimlich was suspended several times and demoted. It was then that the deputy marshal decided to file a lawsuit. This case had a positive outcome when a 1996 jury awarded this whistle-blowing deputy $2.1 million.[29]

Department-wide corruption is so difficult for the "clean officer" because he or she must deal with the top–down protection of illegal activities. In view of the fact that loyalty is highly valued in policing, the value-driven officer does not want to be accused of disloyalty. There is also the policy of suppression within the corrupt department; the costs of breaking the "code of silence" will, in one way or the other, probably mean walking away from a police career. It is certainly a career ending move to take legal action against the department. Even if an officer wins in court, the troublemaker's reputation follows whenever he or she applies for another law enforcement position.

STAGES AND TYPES OF POLICE CORRUPTION

Lawrence W. Sherman divided the process of becoming corrupt into five stages.[30] The first stage consists of accepting such "perks" as coffee, meals, drinks, cigarettes, or theater tickets. These offers may come as early as the first few days on the job. See Box 10.2 for an unusual twist on refusing perks.

There is considerable disagreement in the law enforcement community over whether the slippery slope of corruption begins with accepting a small gratuity, including the infamous free cup of coffee. Michael Feldberg, for example, claims that "small vices have small effects, and we need not begrudge police officers their free cup of coffee, half-priced meals, and the sense of welcome that they convey." He adds that "they are a relatively innocent transaction in a work universe in which the standard form of reciprocity…is extortionate rather than hospitable."[31]

In contrast, Tom Baker calls accepting gratuities a corruption of authority because citizens are expecting something in return. He contends that the acceptance of the gratuity creates the impression that the officer has been compromised as only law enforcement officers are selected for these perks.[32] Some restaurant owners offer police a free cup of coffee or half-priced meal as a gift of kindness, while others want at least the officers' presence in the restaurant.[33] This is especially true around bar closing time when the officers mere presence diverts trouble. Some restaurant owners have gone as far as offering free meals without realizing how much some officers can eat. After a few visits, the practice is usually stopped.

Perks may actually become more prevalent as officers are reintroduced into the neighborhoods through community policing. Community policing involves officers and chiefs attending neighborhood meetings and giving speeches at dinners. Is it wrong to accept a free cup of coffee, a soda, or a free meal at these gatherings, or would it be considered cold and unfriendly to refuse? There is little doubt that these respectable citizens want something in return. In the end, it is the community that decides the quality of law enforcement and conduct expected of its officers.

BOX 10.2   Food Fight

While out of town for training, several officers from the Columbus, Nebraska, Police Department visited a pizza restaurant for lunch. When the bill was presented, it had been reduced by half because, according to the waitress, "we always give police officers half price." The officers thanked her and pointed out "we can't take this; it's against our policy," but she insisted that she could not remove the discount.

The officers finally took the bill to the manager and explained their dilemma. After more discussion, the manager agreed to accept the full amount, adding, "but your sodas are free." The officers politely, firmly, and repeatedly declined the offer until the manager accepted full price for both the meal and the drinks.

Upon exiting the restaurant, one of the officers happened to look up at the marquee over the restaurant. There, for all the world to see, and everyone to enjoy, was the sign "FREE DRINK WITH MEAL PURCHASE!" Truly, these officers can be said to take their ethics seriously.

Source: Chief Bill Gumm of the Columbus, Nebraska, Police Department submitted this to the Law Enforcement Ethics Center, July 22, 1997.

Perhaps, then, accepting perks in one community may be wrong, but in another, acceptable and encouraged.

The second stage consists of taking free drinks or five or ten dollars to keep a bar open another hour after closing time. The third involves such behavior as taking five, ten, or $20 dollars handed over with a driver's license (an updating of Sherman's study today would probably say $50 or $100) when a citizen is stopped for speeding and accepting merchandise from drivers unloading trucks in no parking zones. The fourth stage includes the major step of beginning to accept payoffs from gamblers. In accepting such offers, officers solidly entrench themselves with other corrupt officers. Finally, in this demise of the moral career in which they slide from clean to corrupt, officers accept money obtained from the sale of narcotics. What makes this such a major step is the money from drug use is regarded as "dirty," since drug use involves harm to others.

With the rise of cocaine use and the "crack" epidemic in the mid-1980s, drug-related deviancy has become the most serious form of police corruption. The enticement of drug trafficking is so tempting because of the tremendous amount of illicit cash that fuels this market and the lucrative illegal drug trade. In Miami, for example, three 1985 drug raids on the Miami River demonstrated how serious this form of police misbehavior has become. In the first raid, police officers seized 850 pounds of cocaine hidden beneath the deck of a boat at the Tamiami Marine Boat Yard and arrested the smugglers. This largest seizure in the history of the Miami Police Department required an internal investigation because one of the smugglers maintained that over 1,000 pounds of cocaine were actually on the boat. A second incident took place at the Tamiami Marine Boat Yard, in which at least ten Miami police officers, some in uniform, boarded a boat that held 400 kilograms of cocaine. They threw the smugglers into the water and confiscated the drugs. In the third incident, eight Miami police officers, some in uniform, stormed the Mary C at the Jones Boat yard. The six smugglers unloaded 350 kilograms of cocaine and jumped in the water, where three of them drowned. Known as the "River Cops," 19 police officers were eventually convicted for their part in these incidents. Six received sentences of 30 or more years.[34] In 1996, Len E. Davis and eight other New Orleans officers were arrested and charged with protecting a warehouse filled with cocaine in exchange for $97,000 in bribes.[35]

David L. Carter, in examining 13 law enforcement agencies across the nation in terms of drug-corruption investigations, found that there were two distinct types of drug corruption:

- Type 1—characterized as a "Search for Illegitimate Goals," involved such activities as bribery, theft, and similar activities. This type was motivated by either a "user-driven cycle" or a "profit-driven cycle."
- Type 2—labeled "In Search of Legitimate Goals," pertained to corruption in the criminal justice process, in which officers perjured themselves, violated criminal procedures, and planted evidence as a means to facilitate drug-law enforcement.[36]

Robert M. Morgenthau, District Attorney of New York County, delivered a July 28, 1993 speech to a meeting of the Citizens Crime Commission that poignantly communicates the importance of reducing police corruption:

Let me begin by stating what should be obvious: Nothing is more essential to the health of our city—indeed to the very fabric of a democratic society—than the integrity of our police officers. If our citizens believe that the police are dishonest, they will be dishonest. If officers flout the law, respect for the law will be diminished, and the rule of law will be eroded. As the Knapp Commission observed, "for most people, the policeman is the law."[37]

In sum, corruption emerges from both the values and norms of the police culture and from the local community. It is a short step, especially in large, urban departments where corruption is widespread, for a young officer to justify a moral shift in their standards. But once minor forms of corruption become acceptable behavior, then more serious and illegal expressions of corruption become more acceptable.

THE DANGERS OF DECEPTION

There are many interesting debates in the criminal justice system. One of the repeated questions is: Can people who have done bad things change? As the basis of rehabilitative philosophy, there are countless examples where those who have had extensive histories of criminality turned themselves around and lived lawful and productive lives. Indeed, many of the gang prevention and control programs, as well as drug therapeutic communities, are staffed by individuals who, in their day, brought fear to law-abiding citizens. A further interesting question is: Can good people do bad things? The history of law enforcement documents a long list of well-known leaders of law and order who, at the same time, were ruthless agents of crime and disorder. Finally, there is another disturbing question: Can those who are good be around evil and not be contaminated by it? Or is it possible to stand tall against the power of evil?

This latter question is particularly relevant in law enforcement today. Police officers are faced with so much evil and total human degradation that they understandably want to get these "low-lifes" off the streets." It is not surprising that **"noble cause corruption"** is used as a means to justify whatever means are required. "Noble cause corruption" suggests that illegal actions that violate the rights of citizens are morally right or excusable if a higher or greater purpose is accomplished.[38] The ends, when they are noble (such as getting "low-lifes" off the streets), will then justify whatever means are necessary. It is this moral justification that encourages perjury on the stand, planting evidence, excessive force, and other forms of police deviancy.

This relationship between ends and means needs a little more consideration. According to Edwin J. Delattre, who has a national reputation for teaching ethics and moral philosophy to police officers, "a good end cannot justify a means in a context that makes it wrong and evil." But it still leaves the question "whether we should ever excuse the use of evil means because the end is undeniably good, lesser means are ineffective, and the motives of the agent are unquestionably noble."[39] Consider the hypothetical case that Delattre proposed:

> Suppose you have a perpetrator in custody who is known to have kidnapped a victim. The victim is known to be buried alive, and the perpetrator is known to have the information sufficient to rescue the victim.
>
> Time is short. The perpetrator will not divulge the information under ordinary legal interrogation, even though it is conducted very shrewdly. Is it morally right to exceed your authority and use physical coercion to get the information?[40]

Delattre warns that once we justify doing wrong for an honorable end, it may become easier the next time. As one of Delattre's colleagues observed: "When we violate a suspect's Constitutional rights, we deviate from fundamental principles. That can be the beginning of a substantial erosion. There's a fine line in these things, but once you step over it, you tend to justify subsequent acts by the former one."[41]

Richard Dunn, an inspector with the Illinois State Police, designed a creative court scenario to illustrate the relationship between deception and law enforcement. In a courtroom scene, he has a Special Agent being cross-examined by a defense attorney. The defense attorney wants to know if he always tells the truth. The Special Agent assures him that he always tells the truth. The attorney questions, "You don't always tell the truth, do you?" The special agent qualifies his answer,

"When I am under oath I always try to tell the truth." The defense attorney questions, "What I am asking you is whether you always tell the truth when you are about your business as a Special Agent." The Agent answers, "No, I do not always tell the truth when I go about my business as a police officer." He receives a short retort, "Let's not mince words, Special Agent. The truth is! Let me say that again, Special Agent. THE TRUTH IS THAT YOU LIE, ISN'T IT?" Restricted to the yes and no format of this type of cross-examination, the Agent has to answer, "When the circumstances call for it, yes." The defense counsel is able to get the court to strike "when the circumstances call for it" from his testimony. The State Attorney tries to come to the rescue: "You know what it means to testify under oath, don't you?" Even though the defense attorney objects, the court permits the Agent to answer:

> The best way I can answer is to compare testifying under oath to my work as a police officer. As a police officer I am sworn to uphold the law. It is my duty to investigate allegations of criminal activity. In doing so I must use all the resources available to me. Sometimes in investigating an alleged crime I find myself in situations where it would be very dangerous for me or for someone I am working with to tell the truth. For example, I'm not going to tell a drug dealer that I know the fellow standing next to him is really an undercover law enforcement officer. Sometimes I lie because I believe it is necessary to gain the trust and confidence of a suspect. I contrast those situations to my testimony here. Here I know of no exception to my obligation to tell the truth. I have sworn to tell the truth. I do my very best to tell the jury truthfully what happened.[42]

In this discourse, the Special Agent maintained that police deception is absolutely essential in police work. To do their jobs, police officers use tactics like undercover agents, "stings," and paid informants. In addition, the police sometimes help criminals obtain narcotics or plot the details of a burglary. They fabricate events, establish fake friendships, and make use of a wide range of deceptive ploys.[43]

Yet deception remains a very dangerous tactic. It clouds the truth, often confusing the facts and inviting undependable relationships for the user and the recipient. Deception can induce criminal behavior in innocent people and can overcome the good the police attempt to protect.[44] Perhaps there are situations where it is essential, but the deception of a state that enforces political means on its people is a problematic activity in a free and democratic society.

HOW MUCH IS POLICE CREDIBILITY WORTH?

In February 1995, a civil jury handed down an award that was the largest ever leveled against a police agency in the United States: $15.9 million in damages plus $2.3 million in attorney's fees and costs. Overshadowed by the O. J. Simpson trial, the case and award did not get much national coverage. The incident in question boiled down to the L. A. County Sheriff's Office response to a loud party call on February 11, 1989, at the middle-class residence of an American Samoan, Arthur Dole. Before the evening was over, dozens of officers had stormed the house, 35 people were under arrest, and several wedding shower party guests were hospitalized, some with allegedly permanent injuries.

A publication for attorneys, "The California Lawyer," interviewed jurors to see what they took into account in awarding such a decision. A female juror who worked in the accounting department of a law enforcement agency provided such insight to the journalists. In terms of the escalation of the confrontation, she said, "A lot of police have an attitude—you kowtow to them or they will get out of hand." She acknowledged that the Samoan family and friends were verbally abusive, but in the minds of the jurors, the officers went into a frenzy when faced with verbal resistance.

One of the Dole's neighbors videotaped some of the events of that night. When the tape was played during the trial, the video evidence called into question officers' decisions and their truthfulness. Ultimately, the case rested on the lack of credibility of the officers in light of this evidence and other discrepancies in their testimony. An alternate juror articulated how skeptical the jurors were of the officers' testimony:

> At the trial, it just really angered me that deputies could identify suspects from booking photos, people they never knew, and describe in detail what actions people did that night, people they hardly ever saw. And yet throughout the entire trial I don't think there was ever one deputy who was able to identify their fellow deputies or any of the actions that their fellow deputies did that night.[45]

What is highlighted by this case (now on appeal) is that policing appears to be in danger of squandering its long-standing image of integrity. Jurors may become increasingly reluctant to believe the testimony of officers. If this ever takes place, then the police will have completely lost the public trust.[46] Gary W. Sykes draws a challenging conclusion: "The antidote to the negative publicity generated in recent years, whatever its magnitude, is to avoid even the appearance of impropriety as part of our relationships with the public." He adds that "perception is reality and we clearly must be concerned about how people interpret what we do."[47]

THE COSTS OF POLICE CORRUPTION

Police corruption is costly both to the officer involved and to his or her family. Officers considering corruption must never forget the impact it could have on their lives. Corruption certainly robs an officer of the joy and fulfillment of a policing career because it makes the job a type of "rip-off." The perception of an officer toward the job is changed, and with this change of perception, the ideas and intentions bringing a person to policing are abandoned.

If officers' dishonesty is discovered, then they can be arrested, charged, tried, convicted, and sentenced for their illegal behaviors. The moment of truth, as well as embarrassment, comes when a fellow officer and perhaps a friend comes to the house to make the arrest. Placed in handcuffs, as an ordinary criminal, the officer is taken to the station to be booked. William Bratton, former police commissioner of the NYPD, was fond of personally arresting corrupt officers and taking their badges from them as they were placed in handcuffs.

The shame of being labeled a corrupt cop can be nearly overwhelming to an officer. It will likely cost the officer his or her job and a good bit of their self-respect. An officer shares his inner most thoughts after having been caught lying in a report and fired:

> I miss wearing my badge and my uniform the highly polished gear displayed with pride. That feeling of purpose, accomplishment and the prestige I felt deep down inside. The rush, the excitement, the tragedy and the pain. Each tour of duty was different—no two were ever the same. My neighbors and friends always waved in passing and often came to me for help. Now most turn away and ignore me, and that loss is sorely felt.
>
> The desire to return to the job occupies every moment of my day. It's a living hell, to hope for life to return to its former "Happier" way. I've never feared falling and always enjoyed the climb. I just can't seem to get off the ground this time. Seeing vacancies in other departments, I always got to apply. And regardless of my qualifications, I am rejected every time. I loved what I was and hate what I am. Because, if I can't be a cop—life isn't worth a damn![48]

Nor can an officer considering corruption forget the impact on his or her family when the misdeeds are discovered. These loved ones both wear the shield and suffer the consequences along with the dishonored officer. When Christopher Kerins, an undercover vice squad detective of the Trenton, New Jersey Police Department was visiting Cincinnati, Ohio for a law enforcement conference on combating drugs and gangs, he was arrested and charged with robbing a bank and then leading police on a six mile chase. After his arrest, Kerins admitted to the Ohio bank robbery as well as to four of the seven stickups the "camouflage bandit" had committed in the Trenton area since November 1995. Kerins, the married father of two teenage boys, likely failed to consider the effect on his family when he acted as he did. "His thirteen year old son, while being interviewed outside the family home on the night of his father's arrest, spoke with heartbreaking eloquence when he said, 'I won't believe it until he tells me he did it, and then I still won't believe it.'"[49]

Moreover, the costs of legal proceedings can more than take up the profits made through years of illegal activities within the department. There is the worry of what will happen from the court process. If officers are convicted, they will be terminated from the police departments and placed in the unfriendly arms of the criminal justice system. Imprisonment is another possible cost of corruption to the police officer. For the costs of imprisonment, see Box 10.3.

BOX 10.3   Prison Is No Place for an Ex-Cop

There are many problems with a police officer going to prison. Certainly, cops are not popular in prison. The media see to it that their identity is not protected, and so they are usually easily recognized. John Orr, a former investigator in southern California, in reflecting on his personal transition from "cop to con," comments: "Initially placed in isolation, I soon talked to the watch lieutenant, and we decided to let me try the general population."

The former police investigator was celled with a huge, heavily tattooed biker-type named Jimmy. As he made his bed, he felt Jimmy behind him. "I know who are you," he said quietly. He turned, expecting to use his "street" abilities to defend himself. "But it's cool with me man," he added. "I ain't got no beef with you and no problems roomin' with you, either." He held out his large hand and we shook.

The former cop was also fortunate that he was sentenced to a federal "joint," and federal prisons almost always have better facilities than most state correctional institutions. But he still had to do his time:

Let me assure you that prison is not a picnic, not this or any other institution. Violence is only a word or a glance away. The animals you are forced to live with make life here an on-the-edge-every-second experience. A view of the ocean from your dormitory or two man cell doesn't make doing time any easier. Our day rooms are seldom quiet.

The former cop in prison who chooses population [with other inmates rather than locked in isolation for twenty-four hours a day] will be forced to prove himself, perhaps over and over. If he is able to defend himself in these fights, and knives are more popular than fists with contemporary inmates, then the ex-cop has the further problem of not being observed by the keepers. Regardless of who initiated the contact, being observed by a guard would mean that "violent inmate" label would be added to his files. Parole boards are not terribly impressed by such labels and, even if a state no longer has parole boards, such forms of violence can result in losing "good time" and prolonging imprisonment.

In other words, prison is a hell of a place for a former cop to go. John Orr was serving a 30-year term for setting fires in retail stores. His fellow inmates at Terminal Island included at least five police officers.

Source: John L. Orr, "From Cop to Con: He's Living the Ultimate Nightmare: Going to Prison," Law Enforcement Ethics Center.

WHAT CAN BE DONE?

The means to reduce or eliminate corruption must take place on both the individual and the organizational levels. It is the organizational level that makes corruption seems so unsolvable.

Development of the Fourth Culture

The police officer is faced, particularly in corruption-ridden departments, with many impediments to doing what is right on the job. Integrity can come at a steep price when what is demanded is loyalty to the department and the chief, adherence to the conspiracies of silence, and obedience to the basic tenets of the informal code. When you love being a cop, it is extremely difficult to stomach the protection of illegal activities and the repression of those who stand up to what is wrong. This officer is especially vulnerable if he or she stands alone, against the collective forces of evil.

The development of the fourth culture has to do with the emergence of a culture based on values and ethics. In those departments in which integrity is receiving a major push, it is easier to become "one of the good guys" and support this culture. In corruption-ridden departments, it becomes mandatory to find kindred spirits who want to do what is right, who feel strongly that it is morally important for them to uphold their oaths, and who are aware that they must resist the evil surrounding them. These individuals, then, can develop a culture that stands apart from those developed by administrators, supervisors, and fellow officers.

The basic underpinning of this fourth culture is the loyalty to the ideas of public service as the primary source of moral order. This loyalty to public service translates into loyalty to the constitution and laws, to the mission of the agency, and to work productivity. It is aware that professionalism in policing means divorcing oneself from cult-like behaviors thriving on wrongdoing. It means refusing to go along with demonstrating loyalty to supervisors in order to make them look good, when they are actually involved in what is wrong. A former assistant chief of the New York City Police Department put it this way, "When an organization wants you to do right, it asks for your integrity; when it wants you to do wrong, it demands your loyalty."[50]

To put this in a more theoretical context, the three types of loyalties in the workplace are personal loyalty, institutional loyalty, and integrated loyalty. First, **personal loyalty** is mechanical in nature and constitutes the subordinate's unexamined obligation to accept, comply with, and support the desires and directions of a specifically identified superior. Personal loyalty would include the obligation of deputy sheriffs to be loyal to their sheriff. This form of loyalty is transient and seldom outlives the subordinate–superior relationship. Second, **institutional loyalty** is organizational in nature and is constituted by the obligation of all agency members, both subordinates and superiors, to accept, comply with, and support the department's mission and its goals. Institutional loyalty is expected to last for the officer's entire association with the department. Third, **integrated loyalty** is the highest and most virtuous level of loyalty in the workplace. Idealistic in nature, it constitutes genuine concern by each officer for the values and ideals of the profession. It honors accountability, rationality, fairness, and good will. An example would be the obligation to respect constitutional rights of all individuals and to protect the innocent against oppression. Integrated loyalty is transcendental and is expected to last throughout the officer's organizational life, regardless of the department where the work takes place.[51] It is what motivates an officer to do the right thing when nobody is around to know if he or she decides to do the wrong thing.

Organizational Level

There is no question that police corruption can only be minimized when the issue of integrity and its ethical implications are perceived as vital aspects of becoming a police officer. During academy training and throughout the officer's career, the values of the department need to be presented in such a way as to develop an *esprit de corps* where the values of the organization are paramount. Values should also be woven into all aspects of training, given in value statements during a swearing in ceremony, posted throughout the building, mentioned in disciplinary actions and commendations, articulated in evaluations, be a part of promotional examinations, be found in value statements carried by officers, and be illustrated by publicly praising those who demonstrate them.[52]

The chief police executive must also make it clear that corruption will not be tolerated. This is especially true for police executives hired as agents of change following a public scandal. Some of these executives have taken a stance against corruption that effected meaningful reform, at least throughout their administration. Former Baltimore Police Commissioner Don Pomerleau learned in 1972 of the existence of wrongdoing among some members of the department. He sought the assistance from the FBI and the U.S. Attorney's office in undertaking an extensive investigation. In January 1973, six active and two former police detectives, along with 18 civilians were indicted for violations of the Organized Crime Control Act of 1970. Five of these detectives were convicted in the next six months, and other command and patrol personnel were indicted.[53] Pomerleau said at the time:

> Corruption is corruption, and like a cancer, its malignancy spreads.... But one thing should be clear now. Baltimore is not permissive when it comes to paid winks at wrongdoing. The lowliest patrolman on the beat should feel at this stage that he can blow the whistle on payoffs, no matter who is involved, and that he will be backed up. His badge is just as big as anyone else's.... Members of the force...have been consistently reassured, as I reassure you, of my whole-hearted support of this most important endeavor—the ferreting out of those few among us who violate their public trust and solemn oath of office. It is our individual and collective, moral and legal obligation to do so.[54]

Patrick V. Murphy, who spearheaded efforts against corruption in the New York City Police Department, provides broad outlines for progressive police chiefs as he outlines five factors that contribute to police corruption. First, community standards very much affect whether and how much corruption exists. Murphy explains, "Where a community is generally corrupt, so are the police," and adds that "no police department can remain an island of integrity in a sea of corruption." Second, the attitudes of police chiefs can open the doors to corruption if they are reluctant to deal with it. This failure only encourages corruption's development and continuance. Third, the attitudes of the rank and file are one of the most important factors contributing to corruption. When police officers tolerate corruption from fellow officers and themselves engage in corruption that is accepted by the group, the entire organization can become corrupt. Fourth, the amount of discretion available to police officers makes opportunities for corruption more readily available. As Murphy notes, "unrestricted discretion at the hands of a corruptible police officer invites misconduct and abuse of power. Finally, prosecutors and court actions also affect the likelihood of corruption in police departments. When the actions of prosecutors and court decisions," Murphy concludes, "are not based on fact or case law but rather influences and corruption, it soon weakens the system and makes it ineffective."[55]

Some police departments are developing a code of ethics as a reminder of the importance of ethical behavior among its officers. In a code of ethics developed by the International Association of Chiefs of Police, these statements are found:

> I will keep my private life unsullied as an example to all; maintain courageous calm in the face of danger, scorn, ridicule, develop self-restraint; and be constantly mindful of the welfare of others. Honest in thought and deed in both my personal and official life, I will be exemplary in obeying the laws of the land and the regulations of my department. Whatever I see or hear of a confidential nature or that is confided to me in my official capacity will be kept ever secret unless revelation is necessary in the performance of my duty....
>
> I recognize the badge of my office as a symbol of public faith, and I accept it as a public trust to be held so long as I am true to the ethics of the police service. I will constantly strive to achieve these objectives and ideas, dedicating myself before God to my chosen profession...law enforcement.[56]

Lieutenant Jim Chaney of the Las Vegas Metro Police Department created for his Academy class "A short Course in Police Ethics" that can have personal impact for an officer wrestling with difficult decisions. The test proved to have such validity for the line officer that Calibre Press, Inc. introduced it in the Street Survival Seminar®. The test asks the following questions:

- Am I about to act out of anger, lust or greed?
- Are my actions constitutionally legal?
- If my family was standing beside me, would I still do this?
- How will this make me feel 20 years from now?
- Is this worth my job and my career?
- Would I still do this if I knew I was being videotaped?
- Would my loved ones be proud of or ashamed of me?

Other available means for the reduction of corruption are to make certain that all officers selected meet high recruitment standards, to implement a continuous in-service training program dealing with the issues of corruption and misconduct, and to increase the risks for the deviant officer. Possible ways to increase this risk are to develop an internal policing unit that seeks out corrupt officers and checks on conditions that tend to produce corruption; to identify potential problems, integrity breakdowns, and management weaknesses; to recruit officers known for their honesty and integrity to act as the "eyes and ears" of the internal policing unit; to encourage solicitation of anonymous complaints from officers and citizens;

to implement corruption patrols that would patrol and monitor possible corruption locations; to conduct random interviews with arrestees and officers who work in assignments conducive to corruption such as vice and narcotics; and to use **integrity tests**—a procedure that should be used judiciously and sparingly.[57] Examples of integrity tests are: planting money or other valuables in illegally parked or abandoned vehicles; posing as drunks to see if police officers or jail officials steal money; and turning over wallets containing money or other valuables to officers for safekeeping.[58]

SUMMARY

An examination of police corruption in the United States suggests that it is multidimensional and multifaceted in nature and structurally and organizationally induced. What this means is that the "bad apple" theory that blames police corruption on a few aberrant officers is far less adequate in explaining corruption than structural and departmental factors. The social, political, and economic forces of a society are structural factors that influence the extent of police corruption. The organizational context of police corruption includes the cultural history of the department, departmental policy, peer approval of deviant behavior, the existence of a subculture of deviance within the department, and the chief's leadership style.

Yet the individual context remains important in understanding police corruption. Tom Baker's statement on police corruption is a challenge for the officer to stand tall against corruption: "Police corruption exists only where it is tolerated by the police officers themselves. Only the police peer group can permit unethical behavior and only the police peer group can eliminate it." He then states, "Every law enforcement officer must recognize the hazards of corruption and be prepared to face it. Each law enforcement officer has the individual responsibility for maintaining the integrity of his/her agency." Baker adds, "A law enforcement officer should avoid all unethical acts because they are wrong, not because of any fear of departmental action or criminal prosecution."[59]

KEY WORDS

"grass eaters"	personal loyalty
institutional loyalty	police corruption
integrated loyalty	rogues
integrity tests	rotten structures
Knapp Commission	straight shooters
"meat eaters"	white knights
noble cause corruption	

DISCUSSION QUESTIONS

1. What would you do?

   You are on assignment on the drug squad and are in the process of serving a search warrant on a suspected drug dealer's house. The suspect is handcuffed, sitting on the bed in the back bedroom, where you find a suitcase with what appears to be a small amount of marijuana on top of several stacks of $20 bills that appear to be about $50,000. The suspect says, "That stuff was left here by a friend—forget the dope and I'll forget the money." No other detective is present or has seen the money. Your son, a leukemia victim, is in need of a bone marrow transplant that insurance will not cover.

   Would you:

   a. Arrest the suspect for possession of marijuana and bribery.
   b. Take the money and forget the marijuana, since its only marijuana and not cocaine or hard-core drugs.
   c. Take only that part of the money needed for the operation.
   d. Take part of the money and arrest the suspect anyway.
   e. Call your partner and ask his opinion.

2. A woman living alone called the police on several occasions because she believed someone was breaking into her home. The police came and investigated but could find nothing to account for the noises she reported. Finally, a police officer realized that the cause of the noise was a tree rubbing against the roof of the house. Grateful but embarrassed, she baked an elaborate cake and brought it to the police station. Should the police accept this gratuity or would it be better to rebuff this citizen?[60]

3. List several behaviors that police officers engage in today that would have been considered deviant 20 years ago? List several behaviors that were acceptable 20 years ago but would be regarded as deviant today. What social factors have contributed to the changes for both lists?

4. If a city's government is corrupt, does this mean that the local police department will be corrupt?

5. Why is there so much corruption in policing today? How do structural, cultural, and organizational factors contribute to widespread corruption? Do you believe there is more now than in the past?

6. Is it possible to "stay clean" in a corrupt department? How?

7. Can integrity be taught? Or do you either have it or you don't have it?

8. What are the costs of being charged and convicted of corruption?

EXERCISES

Are You An Honest Worker?

Many cities of the United States use different interpretations of right and wrong at work and in their personal lives. How about you? Answer the yes–no questions below, then follow the directions to add up your score.

1. Someone you work with asks you to cover while he or she takes a day off. Would you do it?

2. Do you think that exploring other job opportunities on company time is ethical?

3. Would you give your boss information you know to be false?

4. You're certain that going to bed with one of your colleagues will advance your career. Would you do it?

5. Do you think that telling minor lies on a resume is ethical?

6. You find out that a colleague is padding his or her expense account. Would you say anything?

7. Your boss gives you an order that involves you breaking the law. Would you obey the order?

8. Someone offers you a million dollars for your company's secrets. Would you accept the offer?

9. You find out your boss is cheating your company. Would you say anything?

10. Have you ever taken credit for someone else's work?

11. Would you lie to your boss to protect your job?

12. Would you ever conspire to get your boss's job?

13. You discover that your company is illegally dumping hazardous waste into the ocean. If you tell the authorities, you will risk the future of your company and all of its employees. Would you tell?

14. Have you ever taken home office supplies for your personal use?

15. Do you usually slack off a little when your boss isn't around?

16. Do you think making personal calls on your company's phone is ethical?

17. Have you ever lied to your boss about one of your fellow workers?

18. Someone you know is using drugs at work. Would you say anything?

19. Have you ever denigrated your boss to others?

20. You feel that your company is mistreating you. You know that you could sabotage its operations. Would you consider doing so to get even?

21. You learn that your best friend is stealing money from your company. Would you say anything?

22. Do you always give 100 percent on the job?

23. If you were the boss, would you hire someone like you?

Give yourself one point for any of the following questions marked

YES: 6, 9, 13, 18, 21, 22, 23

Give yourself one point for any of the following questions marked

NO: 1, 2, 3, 4, 5, 7, 8, 10, 11, 12, 14, 15, 16, 17, 19, 20

Add up your score: A score of 21–23 ranks in the top 5 percent; 20, the top 10 percent; 19, the top 20 percent; and 18, the top 30 percent. All of these are rated an ethical employee. These persons are probably unlikely to ever succumb to police corruption.

FURTHER READING

Baker, Tom. *Police Ethics: Crisis in Law Enforcement.* Springfield: Charles C. Thomas, 1996.

Cohen, Howard S. and Michael Feldberg. *Power and Restraint: The Moral Dimension of Police Work.* New York: Praeger, 1991.

Delattre, Edwin J. *Character and Cops: Ethics in Policing.* Washington, DC: American Enterprise Institute for Police Policy Research, 1989.

Kappeler, Victor E., Richard D. Sluder, and Geoffrey P. Alpert. *Forces of Deviance: Understanding the Dark Side of Policing.* Prospect Heights: Waveland, 1994.

McAlary, Mike. *Good Cop, Bad Cop: Detective Joe Trimboli's Heroic Pursuit of NYPD Officer Michael Dowd.* New York: Pocket Books, 1994.

Murphy, Patrick V. and Thomas Plate. *Commissioner: A View from the Top of American Law Enforcement.* New York: Simon & Schuster, 1977.

Sechrest, Dale and Pamela Burns. "Police Corruption: The Miami Case." *Criminal Justice and Behavior 19* (1992).

ENDNOTES

1. Lawrence W. Sherman, *Police Corruption: A Sociological Perspective* (Garden City: Doubleday, 1974).

2. Victor E. Kappeler, Richard D. Sluder, and Geoffrey P. Alpert, *Forces of Deviance: Understanding the Dark Side of Policing* (Prospect Heights: Waveland, 1994) 70.

3. Howard S. Cohen and Michael Feldberg, *Power and Restraint: The Moral Dimension of Police Work* (New York: Praeger, 1991) 10.

4. Kappeler, et al., 92.

5. Kappeler, et al., 57.

6. Julian B. Roebuck and Thomas Baker, "A Typology of Police Corruption," *Social Problems 21* (1974): 425.

7. Paul Chevigny, *Edge of the Knife: Police Violence in the Americas* (New York: The New Press, 1995) 120.

8. Sarah Glazer, "Police Corruption," *CQ Researcher 5* (24 Nov. 1995): 1,047.

9. Mike McAlary, *Good Cop, Bad Cop* (New York: Pocket, 1994) 25.

10. Herman Goldstein, *Policing a Free Society* (Cambridge: Ballinger, 1977) 93–94.

11. "Police Ethics: Building Integrity and Reducing Drug Corruption," *The Police Chief LVIII*(1) (Jan. 1991): 27.

12. Patrick V. Murphy, "Corruptive Influences," *Local Government Police Management,* ed. Bernard L. Garmire (Washington, DC: International Management Association, 1982) 53.

13. Kappeler, et al., 197.

14. *Knapp Commission Report on Police Corruption* (New York: Braziller, 1973) 1–34.

15. *Knapp Commission Report,* 1–34.

16. Tom Baker, *Police Ethics: Crisis in Law Enforcement* (Springfield: Thomas, 1996) 42.

17. Robert Daley, *Prince of the City* (Boston: Houghton Mifflin, 1978) 279.

18. Dale K. Sechrest and Pamela Burns, "Police Corruption: The Miami Case," *Criminal Justice and Behavior 19* (1992): 296.

19. Robert E. Moffit and Edwin Meese III, *Getting Backup: Twenty-One Steps Public Officials Can Take to Support Their Local Police* (Washington, DC: Heritage Foundation, 1997) 2.

20. For these accounts of police corruption, see John Dombrink, "The Untouchable: Vice and Police Corruption in the 1980s," *Law and Contemporary Problems* (Winter 1988): 202–232.

21. Kappeler, et al., 190.

22. M. McAlary, *Buddy Boys: When Good Cops Turn Bad* (New York: Putnam's, 1987) 106–107.

23. Bruce Alpert, "NYPD Deserves U.S. Rights Probe Lawmaker Says," *The Times Picayune,* New Orleans, 13 Sept. 1995, B8.

24. "Sergeant Joseph Trimboli Addresses Ethics Dinner," The Ethics Roll Call, Summer 1994,

Center for Law Enforcement Ethics, Southwestern Law Enforcement Institute.

25. "Seargent Joseph Trimboli."

26. "Seargent Joseph Trimboli."

27. Personal interview, Spring 1995.

28. Edwin J. Delattre, *Character and Cops: Ethics in Policing,* 2nd ed. (Washington, DC: AEI, 1994) 91.

29. "A Jury Does the Right Thing: Whistle-Blowing Deputy Gets 2.1 Million," *American Police Beat 4* (Apr. 1997): 4.

30. DeLattre, 80.

31. Baker, 26–29.

32. DeLattre, 80.

33. Lawrence W. Sherman, "Becoming Bent: Moral Careers on Corrupt Policemen," *Police Corruption: A Sociological Perspective,* ed. Lawrence W. Sherman (Garden City: Anchor, 1974) 191–208.

34. Sechrest and Burns, 295–296.

35. Jim Yardley, "New Orleans Police Corruption," *The Atlanta Journal of Constitution,* 15 Apr. 1996.

36. David L. Carter, "Drug-Related Corruption of Police Officers: A Contemporary Typology," *Journal of Criminal Justice 18* (1990): 85–98.

37. "Insuring the Honesty of Police Officers," *New York Law Journal,* 28 July, 1993, 2.

38. Delattre, 194.

39. Delattre, 194–195.

40. Delattre, 193.

41. Quoted in Delattre, 207.

42. Richard Dunn supplied this statement to the Law Enforcement Ethics Center, 1997.

43. Inspector Richard Dunn, "Would You Ever Lie?", Law Enforcement Ethics Center, July 1997.

44. Dunn, "Would You Ever Lie?"

45. Quoted in Gary W. Sykes, "How Much Is Our Credibility Worth?, Law Enforcement Ethics Center (July 1997): 1.

46. Sykes.

47. Sykes.

48. Anonymous. Internet: Law Enforcement chat-room, 1997.

49. "Heartbreak at Home," *The Ethics Roll Call,* Summer 1996, Center for Law Enforcement Ethics, Southwestern Law Enforcement Institute.

50. Quote and materials on loyalty are found in Sam Souryal and Brian W. McKay, "Personal Loyalty to Superiors in Public Service," *Criminal Justice Ethics 15*(2) (Summer/Fall 1996): 44–62.

51. Souryal and McKay.

52. G. Patrick Gallagher, "Value- and Integrity-Driven Police Organizations," paper presented to American Society of Law Enforcement Trainers, Annual Conference, Buffalo, 1997.

53. Delattre, 92.

54. Quoted in Delattre, 92.

55. Murphy, 60–65.

56. International Association of Chiefs of Police, Alexandria, Virginia.

57. Baker, 71–74.

58. Baker, 75–76.

59. Baker, 77–78.

60. Cited in Dorothy H. Bracey, "Police Corruption and Community Relations: Community Policing," *Criminal Justice: Contemporary Literature in Theory and Practice,* ed. Marilyn McShane and Frank P. Williams III (New York: Garland, 1997) 31.

11

WOMEN AND A CAREER
IN POLICING

I wasn't prepared. I, like a lot of kids growing up, had put cops up on a pedestal. Here are these people, and they are generally men, who you can go to to protect you, to keep you safe, to make sure you are OK. I was finding that these same people who I had once put upon a pedestal were not any better than the scum of the earth that I was arresting. In fact, on occasion I could bring myself to hate them more because of what they were doing to me psychologically. People on the street would come to accept me after I solved their case, after I arrested the guy that hurt them, after I got a confession out of the child abuser. Those people were thankful. They told me what a great job I was doing. They were giving me positive strokes. For officers I was working with, it really didn't matter how good I did the job, or how hard I busted my butt. I was still a female, I was still a threat to them because I was a female in a male's position. If I did score better than them on a promotional exam, there was the chance they weren't going to get the promotion or they weren't going to get the job they wanted. Their efforts to put me down really tore me up inside. I did not have, at that time, a support system at home. There weren't many people I could talk to. My faith in God carried me though. I have a very strong faith in God, and as long as I knew that what I was doing was the right thing, I could get past all the pain.

—name withheld, interviewed in 1997.

This female police officer describes with considerable pain how difficult policing has been for her. She, like so many other policewomen, was not welcomed into a traditionally white male occupation. Although she had put cops on a pedestal all her life, she found her treatment and abuse by fellow officers disillusioning. Indeed, she accuses the officers with whom she worked of not being any better than the scum of the earth she was arresting. She feels that she has experienced sexual harassment—rejected by her coworkers because she was female. She also suggests that sex-based discrimination presented itself when it came to promotions and job assignments.

Entry into policing has never been easy for a woman. Considering this difficulty, why do women want to join this traditionally all male club? The first and obvious answer is the freedom to have the same privileges, rights, and responsibilities that men have.[1] Pure economics is another reason. Departments in the 1960s and 1970s had a hard time filling vacancies with qualified male applicants due to the poor image of police, low salaries, and sometimes deplorable working conditions officers faced.[2] Women, on the other hand (even those with higher education than male applicants), were attracted to the higher salaries not offered in other traditionally female occupations.

Perhaps even more importantly, many women enter policing because they have a great deal of enthusiasm for and commitment to becoming a police officer. Many see policing as a career in which they can make a difference. Or they may anticipate that policing is an exciting job. Similar to men who enter policing, women want to put the uniform on and feel that adrenalin rush when the action goes down. Or they may be attempting to prove something—that they can do the job just as well as a man. As one former policewoman noted, "When you are in a car with a male police officer, you got to show that you are just as calm as he is, and you're breaking out in a cold sweat—and you can't show it."[3]

Regardless of their motivation, policewomen almost always have three general experiences during their careers. The first is the difficulty of acceptance in this predominantly male world. This difficulty of acceptance may start on their first day in the academy and not end until their retirement. It may include male officers calling in sick so they do not need to be a partner with a female officer; male officers refusing to provide backup for female officers; male officers excluding female officers from various aspects of police culture; and male officers continuing their resentment, skepticism, and hostility to female officers throughout their careers in policing.[4] This difficulty of acceptance extends also to citizens in the community. They may experience what one officer called "female fever," which "she diagnosed as a disorder brought on by seeing women in uniform and on patrol for the first time."[5]

A second experience involves the career adjustments women must face in order to make it in policing. Policewomen learn very quickly that they must prove themselves over and over. They must display and identify with a "masculine" role (competency, intelligence, and independence), but the catch-22 is that this may result in their being typecast as pushy, unfeminine, and aggressive.[6] Excluded from police culture, women must find ways to establish their own networks and support groups. Female police officers must decide whether they want to be respected as crime fighters and hang in there with the men or whether they want to become specialists in community policing, in juveniles, or in vice. Then, there is the matter of promotion, and if promotion to sergeant or higher is attained, the supervision over male and other female officers presents other obstacles and challenges.

A third experience concerns abuse and harassment. Each policewoman must decide how much is too much. Sexual harassment is a subject repeated so frequently in female officers' accounts of their careers that it merits extensive coverage in this chapter. Susan L. Webb constructed a comprehensive definition of sexual harassment including the following characteristics:

1. The behavior in question must be sexual in nature or sexually-based.
2. The behavior must be deliberate and repeated.
3. The behavior must not be welcomed, asked for, or returned.
4. The more severe the behavior, the fewer times it needs to be repeated before it can be reasonably defined as harassment, and the less responsibility the receiver has to speak up.
5. The less severe the behavior is, the more times it needs to be repeated, and the more responsibility the receiver has to speak up.[7]

Sexual harassment erupted as a politically charged issue in the 1990s. One of the reasons for this surge of concern was that the alliance of liberal politics and tolerant sexual attitudes existing since the 1960s began to weaken. Spokespersons for the women's movement also frequently made the case that the sexual revolution was too often an arena in which dramas of oppression against women, ranging from harassment to spouse abuse, were played out.[8]

Another influence was the number of notorious cases catapulting sexual harassment onto the front pages of popular news papers and magazines and onto television news programs. Sportswriter Lisa Olsen claimed she was sexually harassed by players for football's New England Patriots who displayed their body parts in close proximity to her face while she attempted to conduct interviews in the players' locker room.[9] Dr. Frances Conley, a well-known neurosurgeon, left her position at Stanford University because of "ongoing verbal and physical harassment by her fellow surgeons."[10] Three months later, the nation watched as Law Professor Anita Hill accused Supreme Court nominee Clarence Thomas of creating a hostile working environment "laden with inappropriate sexual overtones."[11] The alleged conduct occurred when they both worked for the Equal Employment Opportunity Commission in the 1980s.[12] Three weeks before the Thomas–Hill hearing, the military's biggest sex scandal unfolded involving aviators at the Navy's annual Tailhook Association Convention.[13] The convention generated nearly 150 complaints of harassment.[14] Finally, several accusations of harassment continue to cloud the presidency of Bill Clinton. Clearly, sexual harassment has become one of the most important employment issues of the nineties.[15]

A HISTORY OF WOMEN IN POLICING

The policewomen's movement can be traced to demands by benevolent groups outside of the criminal justice system for prison, jail, and police matrons. In the 1820s, volunteer Quaker women, joined by upper-middle-class women, were motivated to reform female inmates and blamed their poor living conditions on "neglect and sexual exploitation by male keepers." For example, "Rachel Welch, one of a small number of women in Auburn prison in New York, became pregnant while serving a punishment sentence in a solitary cell. As a result of a flogging by a male prison official, Welch died after childbirth."[16] The pressure for reform that followed this scandalous event resulted in Auburn creating the position of prison matron to oversee women's quarters in 1832, and influenced the passing of the 1828 law requiring the separation of males and females in county prisons. Following the Auburn example, New York City officials responding to pressure from the American Female Moral Reform Society hired six matrons for its two jails in 1845.[17]

During the post-Civil War period, women again became concerned over the welfare of female prisoners noting "overcrowding, harsh treatment, and sexual abuse by their male keepers."[18] The Women's Christian Temperance Union and the General Federation of Women's Clubs demanded an expanded role for women in the caring for women and children in police custody. They helped create and finance the position of police matron in the 1880s—women's first entry into police departments, albeit, as social workers.

New York became the first city to hire full-time police matrons in 1845.[19] This effort was not without opposition, as demonstrated in 1887 by the Men's Prison Association's objection to placing matrons back in each stationhouse in New York City after they had been determined to be unnecessary by city officials. At this time, the "city detained 14,000 women prisoners and received 42,000 female lodgers for overnight shelter." The association based its objection "on lack of space for a matron, on the violent state of the women, and on their fear of a matron's physical inability to handle the women."[20]

The appearance of female police officers outside correctional settings in the early twentieth centuries was triggered by a series of social forces in the late nineteenth and early twentieth centuries. The expansion of the frontier, industrialization, the development of the steam engine, the extension of political democracy, and the development of new economic institutions all sparked intellectual debate about traditional values and life-styles. This was also an era of religious revivalism, utopian experiments, and increased social consciousness. People joined together to sponsor the temperance movement, institute public education and establish humane management systems for the insane, deviant, and delinquent.[21]

The experience of the female abolitionists, as well as such social problems as widespread poverty, breakdown of the family, child labor, and increases in juvenile delinquency and female-related crime provided some of the catalyst for the appearance of a renewed, white, middle-class women's movement.[22] One of the primary goals of this movement was to eliminate some of the social ills besetting women and children. Entailed in this reformist zeal was the "child-saving movement" and the development of the juvenile court and its *parens patria* philosophy.[23] Women's entry into law enforcement in a social worker capacity during this era was "due to the reformist zeal of the period, an acceptance of a limited and special role for women in law enforcement, and the efforts of a few dedicated progressive reformers."[24]

Reformers began to push for the appointment of female professionals who had the skills to work in the streets with prostitutes, runaways, and delinquents.[25] Some women were appointed to these duties. In 1905, Lola Baldwin, secretary to the protective group the Travellers' Aid Society, was taken on as a "safety worker," as part of the Lewis and Clark Exposition in Portland, Oregon. Her appointment was the first documented account of a woman with police power. Her duties were to protect girls and women from harassment as well as to stop girls and women from pursuing men. After the exhibition closed, the city government retained Baldwin as director of the Department of Public Safety for the Protection of Young Girls and Women.[26]

> Neither she nor the police department wanted women to be called "police-women," because neither wished to associate women with the concept or job of policemen. The women, called "operatives" or "safety worker," considered themselves social service workers.[27]

In 1910, Alice Stebbins Wells was officially classified "policewoman" in Los Angeles California, and her contributions to women in police were significant. She was hired after she convinced the city that a sworn female police officer could be effective. She entered at the rank of detective. The publicity about her hiring caused other cities to hire women, and in 1915 she founded the International Association of Policewomen.

Alice Wells was pictured in newspapers as "a masculine individual, grasping a revolver, and dressed in unfeminine clothing."[28] However, policewomen of her era did not consider themselves as "female versions of policemen, a concept they derogatorily termed "little men,"[29] Instead, they perceived themselves to be superior to policemen in social class, education, and professionalism. They "embodied the concept of the policewoman-as-social worker...seeking to bring social services and order into the lives of women and children...." At the same time they avoided "the trappings of police, opposing uniforms for themselves and choosing not to carry firearms even if permitted to do so."[30] Despite this limited role, their acceptance was only marginal. The demands for policewomen were almost always imposed upon police executives from outside sources.[31]

Frances Heidensohn concluded from her examination of this period that a number of factors shaped the development of female policing in both the United States and Britain. First, this movement had a moral basis in that the entrance of women into policing was "vigorously promoted by groups formed for moral protection, and sometimes feminist causes who did so to attain social purity, rescue, and welfare goals."[32] Second, volunteers had an important role in the origins of female police officers. A group of women sought to be police officers and were willing to volunteer their services on patrol. Third, there was considerable proselytizing for females in policing. Supporters of this movement, as well as the pioneers themselves, pursued their cause with missionary zeal. Fourth, the strongest opposition to policewomen came from both rank-and-file and senior police officers. Fifth, this movement advocated specialist work. What it sought was the right of women to work with women and children. They typically desired proper police powers rather than general police duties. Finally, women sought gendered control, because they wanted to protect their own sex and did not seek a mandate to police men.[33]

Women's place in policing became more secure following the First World War. In 1922, there were 500 women officers; by 1932, there were more than 1,500, but then it leveled off partly due to the Depression. In 1950, there were 2,600 policewomen, and in 1960 that number increased to 5,617.[34] The numbers were nearly to double in the decade of the 1960s due in part to this period of social experimentation. Both the Civil Rights Movement and the Women's Movement helped to shape the spirit of the times, and it was the Women's Movement that fueled the demands of women to have equal opportunity and career advancement in police departments.[35]

The demands for expanded roles in policing for women were spurred after a 1961 lawsuit that allowed policewomen to compete in promotional examinations. The New York Police Department promoted its first female sergeant in 1964.[36] In 1968, Indianapolis officers Betty Blankenship and Elizabeth Coffal were the first in the nation to break through the traditional social worker role to put on a uniform, strap on a gun belt, and drive a marked police vehicle, answering police calls like their male counterparts.[37]

The 1964 Civil Rights Act and the 1972 Equal Employment Opportunity Commission (EEOC) expanded the rules of state and civil service bodies and made it illegal to discriminate in employment. The EEOC rules, which pressure police agencies to change hiring practices and show why a female or minority individual is not qualified to become a police officer, had a major impact on the presence of women on the police employment lists.

On September 20, 1974, while attempting to arrest a bank robber, 24 year old Gail Cobb became the first African American policewoman to die of gunshot wounds.[38] Currently, The National Law Enforcement Officers Memorial has 121 female officer's names engraved on the memorial wall.[39]

WOMEN ARE NOT WANTED: THIS IS A MAN'S JOB

Policing has been one of the most resistant occupations to the acceptance of women.[40] Susan E. Martin described the initial resistance as "strong, organized, and sometimes life threatening."[41] In Catherine Milton's 1972 study, she reported that policewomen were used almost exclusively in clerical functions or in work with juveniles, that they were required to have additional education than policemen, that they were regulated by hiring quotas, and that they were allowed to compete for promotions or openings only in the women's bureau.[42] Donna Schaper writes about her experience:

> For me, the myth that women are physically less able than men found a remarkable rebuff one day in San Francisco 20 years ago. The San Francisco police department was in the throes of a lawsuit that would allow women to

become police officers. I was taking a group of teenagers on a tour of the police department when the officer guiding us said that the real reason women couldn't be on the force was that they could never pass basic training, which required carrying a 100-pound bag of sand in a straight line for 100 feet. Then, an 18-year-old horsewoman in our group spotted the sand bag in the weight-training room, hoisted it on her shoulders and carried it for the rest of the tour.[43]

Women clearly have made some gains in policing, which Susan Martin claims are related in large part to the "development of a substantial body of law requiring nondiscrimination on the basis of sex in terms and conditions of employment."[44] As of June 30, 1993, local departments had an estimated 474,072 full-time employees, and women comprised 8.8 percent of all full-time officers (see Figure 11.1).[45] Larger police departments tend to hire more women than smaller departments. In departments serving populations of one million or more, 15 percent of the officers are women; in small towns with a population of 2,500 or less, only 2.5 percent of officers are women.[46] In 1996, 15 percent of all uniformed officers in the New York

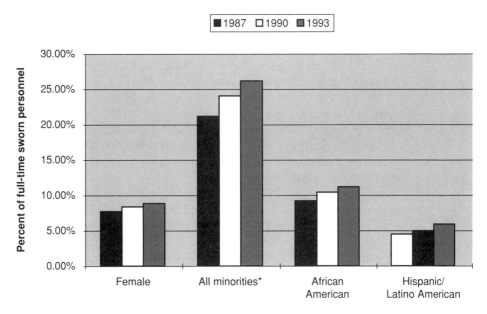

*Includes African Americans, Hispanic/Latino Americans, Asian Americans, Pacific Islanders, Native Americans, and Alaska Natives

FIGURE 11.1   Women and Minority Local Police Officers, 1987, 1990, and 1993

Source: Brian A. Reaves, "Local Police Departments, 1993," U.S. Department of Justice, Office of Justice Programs (Apr. 1996).

City Police Department were women.[47] The Madison, Wisconsin police department is an exception to this tendency as the total percentage of police women in this small university town's department is 25 percent, the highest percentage of any department in the nation.[48] But women nationally are still underrepresented among those who rise to a rank above entry level.[49] In 1996, only 9 percent of women in the NYPD were sergeants, 6 percent were lieutenants, 3 percent were captains, and 4 percent were above the rank of captain.[50]

The resistance toward women in policing must be ultimately viewed in terms of the patriarchal society. For the past three thousand years, Western society, as well as most other cultures, has been based on social, philosophical, and political systems in which men by force, direct pressure, or through tradition, ritual, custom, language, etiquette, education, and law determine what part women shall or shall not play. In this male-oriented, or patriarchal society, the female is everywhere subsumed under the male. In policing, women had the "audacity" to desire entrance to an all male occupation, one that male officers perceived to demand the traditionally masculine attributes of dominance, aggressiveness, superiority, and power.

In addition to the cultural barrier of the wider society, it is held that certain aspects of police work make it unsuitable for women. First, it is believed that women are unsuitable to police work because "they cannot cope with danger, do not command authority, and should not be exposed to degradation." Second, there is the fear that the introduction of women "will undermine male solidarity, threaten their security, and their self-image."[51] This could be regarded as the "porcelain policeman" argument; that is, male police officers "are so fragile and delicate that they will feel threatened and undermined, their solidarity shattered, and their loyalty over-stretched by the presence of women."[52] Third, women officers must cope with norms that create a disadvantage in interacting with male officers. Cursing, "raunchy" language, and sexual jokes, it is claimed, are an inevitable part of police culture and women should not have to deal with this "seamy" aspect of police culture. Finally, the argument for the exclusion of women is made that their lower status (in comparison with male officers) creates problems in arrest situations with both male and female citizens.[53]

Susan E. Martin's 1979 examination of women in policing found that women are considered only tokens for male police officers and that "they face performance pressure, isolation from co-workers, entrapment in stereotypic roles, and tests of loyalty." She concluded that the future is not bright: "It is likely that the dynamics of tokenism will continue to operate, leaving policewomen with a number of difficult choices in the face of the expectation that they think like men, work like dogs, and act like ladies."[54] In a 1997 article, Martin is a little more optimistic. She contends that "the status of women in policing today is uncertain....Nevertheless, as more women enter the occupation, move slowly into positions of authority, and serve as role models and sponsors for other women, there is reason for guarded optimism about the future of women in law enforcement, as well as a large number of questions waiting to be addressed."[55] In Box 11.1, Linda Cherry, past President of the International Association of Women Police, draws much more positive conclusions about the role of women in policing, especially in terms of the future.

COMPARISON OF MALE AND FEMALE OFFICERS' JOB PERFORMANCE

One of the criticisms of women who want to enter policing is that they lack the skills to perform well as police officers. In the 1970s, there was a flurry of research evaluating the performance of women police officers. These studies were conducted for Washington, DC; New York City; Denver, Colorado; Newton, Massachusetts; Philadelphia, Pennsylvania; the California State Highway Patrol; and St. Louis County, Missouri.[56] In these studies, as well as more recent ones, researchers have consistently demonstrated that women can handle the crime fighting, rescue, combat, peacekeeping, and social service aspects of police work as well as men, regardless of differences in biological constitution and socialization practices.[57] A number of other studies have found that women perform patrol in a similar and equally effective manner as men.[58] These studies also generally indicate that "men are in no more danger with women as partners than with men as partners."[59]

There were, of course, differences between male and female police officers in how they performed on the job. Policewomen were typically seen as exercising more restraint in using their firearms and in managing family disturbances; as being more sensitive to citizens' needs and using a style of policing more consistent with community oriented policing; as sustaining disciplinary action less frequently; and as using less sick time. Policemen generally had better shooting ability, superior strength and agility, and required less assistance in making arrests.[60] The findings from the second phase of evaluation at Philadelphia also reported that female officers were assaulted more often, had more vehicle collisions, and sustained more injuries.[61] Furthermore, some evidence exists that women have higher turnover rates than men in policing.[62]

SUCCESS IN A DIFFICULT CAREER PATH

Aware that they are at best accepted only at the fringe of the masculine culture of policing, women must decide upon how they plan to cope with their jobs. According to traditional gender stereotypes, women can decide to become either defeminized or deprofessionalized. **"Defeminized"** women become super-efficient and see themselves as good or better than their male colleagues. Their competence, then, serves to mask their femininity. **"Deprofessionalized"** women, in contrast to competing with male colleagues, accept subordinate status and concessions granted to them.[63]

Martin applied these extremes of adaptation to 28 female patrol officers in Washington, DC and described their adaptations as falling along a continuum consistent with Hochschild's typology. She renamed the two polar positions calling them "policeWOMEN" and "POLICEwomen." **POLICEwomen** focus on law enforcement rather than service. They show a high commitment to the job and even criticize fellow female officers. Similar to males' careers, they wish to do specialist work and be promoted. **PoliceWOMEN,** on the other hand, emphasize the feminine. In accepting

BOX 11.1   Interview with Linda Cherry

Question: Martin's *Breaking and Entering* was critical of police agencies because they made it difficult for women to break into the system. Do you think this has changed in the 1990s?

Cherry: I feel that great strides have been made with allowing men, women and minorities to break into the system. The age, the height and weight requirements, and specific physical agility tests have been modified through the court system, but the biggest difference over the years has been aggressive recruiting efforts early on in young people's lives when they are contemplating career choices.

I have observed a much broader picture being depicted in recruit advertising. This has included the positive use of women and minorities being displayed in all aspects of police work: patrol, detective, undercover, plainclothes, tactical units, supervision and chief. Today, there are more women and minorities in the profession for young people to look at as mentors, leaders and examples, as well as a better perception of minorities in police jobs on TV—"Cagney and Lacy" and "Hill Street Blues" compared to Angie Dickinson's "Police Women" and Don Johnson and company in "Miami Vice."

Question: Martin stated in a 1986 interview that "Once the women are hired there are still barriers to acceptance, including the assumption that they are not able to do the job." Is this statement true today?

Cherry: I don't agree that women police officers still have barriers to acceptance, including the assumption that they are not able to do the job. That stigmatism was indeed present in the 1970s when more and more women were making a career choice in the criminal justice field. Most departments hired one woman at a time on a case-by-case basis. But throughout all the scrutiny we endured, many of us have survived and have now become role models and examples which changed the macho preconceived notions that proceeded our entry into the profession.

Back in the 1960s and early 1970s, being big and strong and able to fight a whole block of bad guys by one's self were very important attributes for those chosen to be police officers. Fighting never has taken or required much educational knowledge, just the biggest and strongest will to survive. Today's officer does not fit that mold, and those officers who began their career during that era have had to make adjustments to keep up with their young counterparts. Today's society expects and demands officers of higher intelligence—college-educated, and able to negotiate situations into happy-endings without the use of force if at all possible. This demand by the public for a higher standard has assisted in police work evolving into a more respected profession in the 1990s.

A female joining today's law enforcement community can still expect to face many challenges. Times have changed, but there remain many in the criminal justice field who don't and won't accept women. Women are still being denied promotions and not being allowed to advance themselves through extra training. It is not as bad as it used to be, and pure dedication and determination will see one through. Others in society, the majority being women, also resent a female in a nontraditional role of authority. This will be the largest segment from which complaints against the female officer will arise.

Another challenge is that certain aspects of law enforcement may discourage women, particularly if they are married to someone in another field, divorced and/or have children. The job requires long hours, odd hours, shift work and working weekends and holidays. Unless one has a strong support system of family and friends who will be there and not expect the female to handle all of the domestic chores and responsibilities, it will be too difficult to survive the stress.

BOX 11.1 *continued*

Question: How would you change the entrance standards or the entrance testing to be more fair to women?

Cherry: I wouldn't change any of the entrance standards or testing. I believe that everyone should be able to attain the best scores based on the same tests and that exceptions shouldn't be allowed. My life may someday depend on another officer, and I want to know he or she completed the same agenda to get where we're at. I do not like and do not agree with the aspect of Affirmative Action that wants to push agencies to hire a certain percentage of females and/or minorities to make a quota. I do not care who you are, what sex you are, what race you are if you can't "cut the mustard" same as everyone else, then you shouldn't get the job. This job requires a special type of personality and makeup

to perform the duties and handle all of its demands, so hiring should ensure and guarantee that the "very best" are afforded the opportunity and are offered the job.

I never thought of or worried about having to arrest all the big bad guys. When I took the oath of office, received my badge, and graduated from the Academy, I felt confident and believed in myself. I was going to get the job done to the best of my ability and make the streets safer come hell or high water. When I hit the streets, I was never afraid or ashamed to ask for help in situations that required it. I never panicked or freaked. Many times after the situation was over, I'd get weak-kneed over the predicament and "what could have happened." It's always better to take cover, to call in reinforcements, and to go home each night than be a dead hero.

Source: Interviewed in the summer of 1995. Linda L. Cherry has been employed since 1990 as a Deputy United States Marshal, assigned to the Southern District of Iowa. She was previously a police officer with the Ankeny, Iowa Police Department for 14 years. Copyright © 1997 by Anderson Publishing Co./Cincinnati, OH. Reprinted with permission.

the male's invitation to function as a nominal equal, they actually function as an assistant or junior partner. They typically receive treatment and exemptions from work tasks that are inappropriate for a "lady."[64]

The women who survive in policing usually develop a thick skin. Male officers constantly pick on female officers, and if they discover their tender points, then they intensify their ribbing. One female officer, in acknowledging that those sensitive to abuse could not survive an eight hour shift, stated how she adapted: "I've got a skin like a table. Nothing bothers me. I just made up my mind that I had to take it and live with it and just move on from there and that's what I did. Truly, truly nothing bothers me jobwise."[65]

Another successful coping technique of female officers is to use the talents they have on the job. Many women use their verbal skills to deescalate confrontational or potentially violent situations. Jeanne McDowell put it this way, "cool, calm and communicative, they [women officers] help put a lid on violence before it erupts."[66] Another female officer expressed the importance of verbal skills a little differently:

So my theory is, you have to go in with your brain. I talk to people. And I talk to big guys and I talk to little guys and I talk to big women and I talk to little women. I talk to everybody. I think it comes in with this basic amount of respect for others as human beings. I don't take things personally. You can't. But see, a lot of people take things personally. As far as I'm concerned, the uniform walks into a situation all by itself. But it's not me.[67]

Women who are normally excluded from the culture of the police must establish their own supportive and nourishing networks if they intend to survive on the job. These networks may be organized in individual departments on a state level, or in national networks of associations of policewomen.[68]

Policewomen do appear to handle stress better than their male counterparts because of superior interpersonal relationship skills. According to a study by Patricia Lunneborg, 90 percent of the policewomen talked out their sources of stress, versus 45 percent of the policemen she surveyed.[69] Beermann et al. also found that the "double burden" of the unequal division of domestic duties, particularly for those with children, did not result in more severe psychosocial or subjective health impairments. This extra burden, in fact, may be a source of stress relief as policewomen are forced to change roles from cop to mom. This allows them to leave the job behind, avoiding the "live to work" mentality that traps male officers as they become couch potatoes (withdrawal and numbing of emotions) or associate with other officers after work. Accordingly, "being married and having children is a protective factor against completed suicide for women—but not for men."[70]

Female officers do experience the stressors of both low acceptance in the police agency and lack of access to the peer group support structures of male officers. The importance of access to this peer group support structure or police culture is that it helps to mitigate the strain of occupational stress by providing a forum within which individual officers can safely ventilate.[71] J. G. Wexler and V. Quinn's examination of the occupational stress experiences of female officers in a major metropolitan department in California found that women experienced a major stressor in attempting to demonstrate that they could be effective officers without compromising their femininity.[72]

Many women do report social and marriage problems caused by being a cop. They claim that some men are too intimidated to date or marry a female cop.[73] They appear to be intimidated by women who are assertive and self-confident, whose work is a driving force in their lives, who sometimes are tougher and stronger,[74] and who are authority figures that strap on a gun to protect society. An officer reflects on her dating experiences:

> If you're a single woman cop and you meet a guy, it's a three-month thing. That's it. Three months. At first, they love the fact that you're a cop. Then you notice a change. What's the matter? They're intimidated, they're disturbed that you're capable and intelligent.
>
> Well, try to understand. They work nine to five. They go home. You go out on midnights. You put on a gun so you can protect people. That's intimidating. They think they can handle it. But that's bullshit. They can't handle it. They're gone after three months.
>
> Now I don't tell people what I do.[75]

In addition, spouses are often troubled by the long hours of special assignments and the taxing hours of shift work that requires them to take over the responsibilities of housework, child care, and other tasks traditionally left to the wife. Husbands are well aware of the rumors of affairs with male officers and can become jealous of the close relationship between partners.[76] An Arizona State University study found the divorce rate of female officers to be twice that of the national average and three times that of male officers. In addition, female officers were almost twice as likely to be separated. Twenty-one percent felt that police work was definitely a factor in their divorce with another 20 percent undecided.[77]

Female officers also have fewer suicides than male officers. The fact that policing is dominated by white males is often given as a reason for the high numbers of suicides among the ranks of the police. The recorded suicide rate for white males in the general population is "1.9 times that for African American males, 3.9 times the rate for white females, and 9.0 times the rate for African American females." In their study of police suicides, Stack and Kelley determined that being white increased the odds of suicide 2.32 times and being male increased the odds of suicide 2.56 times.[78] Women are more likely than men to have stronger social supports and to be more willing to seek professional help which may contribute to them having a lower suicide completion rate than men. According to Susan Blumenthal, former head of the Suicide Research Unit at the National Institute of Mental Health, "being married and having children is a protective factor against completed suicide for women but not men.[79]

Policewomen are generally much less involved in deviant behavior than are policemen. For example, the Christopher Commission found that female officers handle suspects more successfully than men do as they are "less personally challenged by defiant suspects and feel less need to deal with immediate force or confrontational language."[80] Little evidence also exists that female officers are frequently involved in corruption. A widely quoted exception is Crystal Spivey, a NYPD police officer, who was videotaped accepted a $500 payoff to protect a drug dealer in the Buddy Boys corruption scandal of the mid-1980s. She justified her behavior by saying, "I'm a victim here...because of [officer] Henry Winter coercing me, over several months, to get involved in some kind of a dirty deal.... I began to feel afraid that being on his bad side would put me in a very life-threatening position."[81] More recently, in August of 1991, Arkansas undercover officer Ellen Randleman was convicted of possession and distribution of controlled substances.[82] On July 1, 1992, Washington, DC police officer Fonda Moore was indicted and charged with assisting a drug trafficking ring.[83]

HARASSMENT IN THE POLICE CULTURE

G. Patrick Gallagher defines employee harassment as "any explicit or implicit ridicule, mocking, derision, or belittling of any person or sexual harassment." This inappropriate attitude toward sworn and civilian personnel in an agency "in general will lead to and encourage sexual harassment, because both emanate from the same source—an absence of respect for the individual."[84] Gallagher concludes that "any form of harassment imposes tremendous liabilities on the organization." It does this by reducing productivity, mutual respect, departmental values, the philosophical bases for the agency's working relationship with the community, officers' safety, and the organizational climate.[85]

One of the most unbelievable accounts of sexual harassment is what Romona Arnold, the first female officer on the City of Seminole, Oklahoma Police Department, experienced. This case, decided on July 10, 1985, documented that in 1977 Arnold's problems began when she was transferred to the midnight shift under the supervision of Lieutenant Herdlitchka. He informed her that "he did not believe in women officers." He not only refused to speak with her and was hostile toward her, but "he told her that he would harass her until she quit or was fired."[86]

The sexual harassment became station-wide when "demeaning cartoons and pictures were posted for public view within the police station with the plaintiff's name written thereon." Her son was arrested and taken to jail in June 1979. Charges were eventually dropped "because it was determined that the arrest and detention of plaintiff's son were totally unjustified. Lt. Downing advised plaintiff that the arrest of plaintiff's son was pure harassment." Officers with less service and seniority were promoted over her. When new vehicles were obtained by the department, male officers got them. She was informed "that as a woman, she didn't know how to take care of it." The windows of her car were rolled down when it was raining so that her seats would become wet. Her name was removed from her mail shelf, and the shelf was eventually removed altogether. Her husband, "a fireman for the City of Seminole, was told that if his wife filed a discrimination complaint, both husband and plaintiff would be fired."[87]

On February 25, 1983, perhaps the most serious of all events in this sad account of police deviancy took place. Arnold received a call from Tommy Gaines, a known drug and alcohol addict, who wanted to see her. "He said it would only take five minutes and that it was urgent. When she arrived, Gaines told her that 'the County' had tapped his phone and was taping conversations." He also said that "in exchange for a reduced sentence," he "was to try to set plaintiff up in an illegal drug transaction." He assured her "that the Seminole Sheriff's office and the city police were involved."[88]

The court decision concluded that "the plaintiff suffers from sexual assault stress syndrome caused by the sexual harassment and discrimination detailed herein; in addition, she suffers from physiological problems induced by stress and anxiety." As a result, she "has been unable to return to work at the Seminole Police Department essentially since January 1, 1984, due to the deterioration of her physical and mental health as outlined above."[89]

Eighty plaintiffs have so far joined the growing class-action sexual harassment and discrimination lawsuit, *Tipton–Whittingham v. Los Angeles*.[90] According to the *Los Angeles Times*, many of the Los Angeles Police Department's female officers felt that the 1994 inquiry into sexual harassment at the West Los Angeles Division was a failure of department leadership because the department did not follow through on this inquiry's recommendations. The inquiry reported sexist and racist remarks, male police officers who failed to back up female officers needing help, and so deeply ingrained mistreatment that policewomen had come to accept it as a part of life. The true scope of the problem will never be known as many female officers were reluctant to complain for fear of retaliation. As expressed by officer May Elizabeth Hatter who has joined *Tipton–Whittingham,* "Management has thumbed its nose at this problem.... I had to prove myself every single day as a police officer. How can management just turn its back on me?"[91]

There are a number of other tragic examples of sexual harassment found in other parts of the nation. A two week academy cadet was victimized when a firearms instructor approached her from behind, reached around, and grabbed her left breast as she was practicing. In repulsing the advance, she made it very clear that it was unwelcome and offensive. As a result, she failed her marksmanship test. This same instructor refused to send the cadet's broken firearm in for repair claiming she could not shoot. He told the cadet the next day that she had "better learn to shoot," and called her "stupid" and "a dumb broad." Moreover, this same cadet was assaulted twice by a classmate who "pulled her against his body, and told her that he wanted to feel her body and that her body felt good."[92]

An African American policewoman was working in the traffic division when she returned to her desk to find seven of her case files ripped and soda poured into her typewriter. She was harassed on other occasions by her personal vehicle being vandalized, including tires slashed, windshield wipers removed, and paint scratched. Furthermore, there were pornographic pictures placed in her personal desk drawer and sexist terms addressed to her by her male coworkers. Another disturbing incident involved items of her clothing, located in the officer's locker, which had a lime substance placed on them that caused severe burns to the officer's back.[93]

An European American policewoman in the same division was harassed by sexually foul and lascivious language addressed at her. The males in the unit laughed at her when she found sexual devices and pornographic magazines in her desk drawer. Officers also removed files from her desk, coworkers refused to help her with work, and she received obscene phone calls to her unlisted home phone number. After complaining to her supervisor about a case file removed from her desk, he warned her, "You know, you're no spring chicken. You have to expect this working with the guys."[94] For another example of an European American policewoman's experience with sexual harassment, see Box 11.2.

R. Max Mendel and Elizabeth Shoenfelt's study even demonstrates bias in the appraisal process for new recruits. They surveyed a random sample of 226 police chiefs, serving populations over 80,000, to determine what administrative action they would use based on an actual arrest where a male training officer was shot and his female trainee–partner was fired for cowardice. Mendel and Shoenfelt found that for "precisely the same actions, police departments are significantly more likely to terminate female trainees than male trainees."[95] This predisposition toward biased judgments on policewomen's performances not only questions disciplinary actions against female officers, but contributes to why female officers are reluctant to report harassment.

BOX 11.2   My Experiences with Sexual Harassment

I was first exposed to sexual harassment after joining a department almost twenty-five years ago. I was shown the ropes by a sergeant whom I thought of as a grandfatherly type because of the differences between our ages. He was driving me around the town, showing me all the hot spots. For break, he said, "Let me walk you through a couple of these different buildings." We went up to the third floor of this abandoned building which had some old furniture around. The sergeant lays down on this davenport. At first I thought, "Ok, this guy must be a little bit tired." Then, he reached over and patted the davenport, indicating for me to lay down beside him. I looked at him and said, "I certainly hope you're just patting that to get the dust out of it." The war was on from that point on. After that, I got every kind of rotten duty he could think of.

I tested for a larger department two years later and was hired. I was told, out of kindness, by one of the officers that several officers had already told the captain that they were not going to ride with me. They paired me with an officer who would not allow me to drive. He made it very clear that I wouldn't be driving the car telling me that I was a female and he was a man, and he would drive the car for the entire night. That same night we were sent to a bar fight ending in an arrest after having to fight this guy tooth and nail. After the arrest, my partner handed me the keys to the car telling me I had earned my way. Although my contacts were knocked to the middle of my eyeballs making it very uncomfortable to drive,

I drove to the station not wanting to pass up my big chance.

That same officer, while I was still on my one-year probation, became very angry at a prisoner who had escaped from him. He began to kick the prisoner in the stomach. In spite of the fact that he was my senior officer, I was not going to let this happen. I stepped in front of it, and took two really good kicks to the gut from this officer. I was bruised the next day, all green, yellow, and blue. He called me and asked, "What are you going to say if we have to go to court on this? And they ask you about my striking him. What are you going to say?"

That incident, even more than the other one, set the tone for the rest of my career. I told that officer that I would always tell the truth. If asked under oath, it was my responsibility to tell the truth, and I would do so. Afterwards, I went into the bathroom and puked my guts out. This was my senior officer training me.... Toward the end of my probation, this same sergeant told me that I would not make it through my probation even if he had to lie about me to make sure that I would not make it. I also encountered a lot of open sexual comments from the other officers. One sergeant would whistle a particular tune every time he saw me. Then he would grab his crotch and make pelvic thrusts. He would make comments about getting a piece of me sometime. Most of the time, he thought I did not hear. I heard most of it. I heard him talking to the other guys about me....

Source: Interviewed in 1997.

Many of the same harassment problems endured by female officers in large departments are likewise experienced by policewomen in small town law enforcement, which make up 85 percent of municipal departments in the United States. A study on stressors and problems in small town police departments by Bartol, Bergen, Volckens, and Knoras reported that 53 percent of female officers had been sexually harassed, predominately by male supervisors, with two respondents reporting that they had been sexually assaulted by male supervisors. Eighty-three percent felt that male supervisors frequently communicated negative attitudes about women in policing. One female officer wrote, "The most stressful factor is the belief that the attitude of male supervisors toward female police officers is not likely to change anytime in the near future or during my career as a law enforcement officer."[96]

Connie Fletcher interviewed 106 female officers and observed an underlying theme that women in law enforcement consistently feel that the system fails to protect them against enemies or harassers within the organization, while they view most male officers as neutral or even encouraging to their women counterparts.[97] Although the interviews conducted were not a scientific random sampling of the population of female police officers but consisted rather of officers referred to her, Fletcher does provide insightful observations. She continues:

> I was surprised by the almost universal picture of police work that emerged from these very diverse sources: Policing is a club for men...; the club still operates in a culture of socializing and informal contacts impervious to legislation; people who are not wanted in the club may be harassed, ostracized, denied desired assignments, days off, shifts, or promotion; speaking or "grieving" (filing a grievance) about what happens within the club breaks the code and, thereafter, breaks the officer. This is a club where harassers can get away with virtually anything because no one, male or female, can afford the punishments that follow ratting on a fellow cop. And this is a club where you can get killed if people don't like you.[98]

The next section of this chapter examines legal protections, court decisions, and the costs of harassment to police agencies. It is clear that the issue of harassment and gender bias must be a primary concern for police officials if they are interested in overcoming the stereotype of the police officer as a nonprofessional. Supervisors who engage in sexual harassment reinforce the tendency in others to do the same, creating a culture in which sexual harassment is the norm. Police management must develop leadership styles that instill the principle of fairness and integrity and that uphold the belief in human dignity and value.[99]

LEGAL PROTECTIONS

There are four categories of law that cover sexual harassment in the work place: (1) the United States Civil Rights Acts of 1964 and 1991; (2) state statutes on fair employment practices; (3) common tort and criminal law; and (4) Statute 42 of United States Code Section 1983 (Civil Rights Act of 1871).

United States Civil Rights Act

The **Civil Rights Act of 1964** makes discrimination on the basis of race, color, religion, sex, or national origin illegal. Title VII of this Act "prohibits employers from, among other things, discriminating on the basis of sex with respect to compensation, terms, conditions, or privileges of employment."[100]

Congress established the Equal Employment Opportunity Commission (EEOC) as the enforcing agency, but restricted its oversight to employers with 15 or more employees and placed a back pay liability limitation of two years prior to the filing of charges.[101] In addition, Title VII did not apply to local governments, including police departments, until almost a decade later when Congress passed the Equal Opportunity Act of 1972.[102] Until then it was rare to see policewomen in a patrol function.[103]

By 1980, as a result of pressure from women's groups, the Equal Employment Opportunity Commission ruled that sexual harassment was a form of sex discrimination covered under Title VII issuing guidelines on discrimination because of gender.[104] These guidelines did not have the force of law, but were acknowledged by the United States Supreme Court in its first ruling on sexual harassment *Meritor Savings Bank, FSB v. Vinson, et al.* Sixteen years after the *Meritor* decision, Congress passed the **Civil Rights Act of 1991** to correct some inadequacies in the Civil Rights Act of 1964.

The new law made possible a jury trial if punitive damages are alleged. Punitive damages are available under Title VII providing the employer acted with reckless indifference or malice to federally protected rights. The limits on punitives ranged from $50,000 to $300,000 depending on the size of the workforce.[105] If an employee is successful, the Civil Rights Act provides redress of reinstatement and promotion, back pay and benefits, a limited amount of money damages, injunctive relief to prevent similar harassment from taking place in the future and a portion of or all of attorney's fees.

In 1998, the United States Supreme Count expanded the Civil Rights Act making "sex discrimination consisting of same-sex harassment actionable under Title VII."[106] The court held in *Oncale v. Sundowner Offshore Services, Inc., et al.* that Title VII prohibits discrimination "because of sex" in "terms" or "conditions" of employment protects men as well as women.[107] In assessing the severity of the harassment, the Court emphasized "common sense and an appropriate sensitivity" to the social contexts in which the behavior occurred "to distinguish between simple teasing or roughhousing among members of the same sex, and conduct which a reasonable person in the plaintiff's position would find severely hostile or abusive."[108] The Court used the example of a coach smacking a professional football player on the buttocks as he heads out to the field as not severely or pervasively abusive—"even if the same conduct would reasonably be experienced as abusive by the coach's secretary (male or female) back at the office."[109]

Fair Employment Practices (FEP)

Legal definitions of sexual harassment, as well as laws governing the enforcement of sexual harassment laws, vary from state to state. Although some states have no laws at all, most state **Fair Employment Practices (FEP) agencies** have similar powers to seek remedies as the EEOC. In addition, various states' FEP laws provide remedies for recovering substantial monetary damages for personal injuries without limitations, while other states have no remedy. Moreover, states vary widely as to the amount of compensation they allow for damages. Only about half of the states allow for punitive damages. Several states require an administrative claim to be filed with the enforcing agency before relief can be pursued under the FEP laws in court. Finally, counties and cities often have their own laws and administrative agencies prohibiting and punishing sexual harassment.[110] A complainant may find better relief filing with a state agency, but research and possibly legal advice is required to seek the best avenue for a remedy.

Tort Laws and Criminal Charges

A **tort** claim in state court may be the best solution for some victims; indeed, it may be the only remedy for victims who work for a small agency,[111] or whose governing entity's aggregate employment is less than 15 employees.[112] A tort is a "breach of duty, other than a breach of contract, for which the offender will be subject to legal responsibility"[113] Common law torts include assault, battery, intentional infliction of emotional distress, wrongful discharge, and defamation.[114]

Providing a wider range of remedies than those available under the Civil Rights Acts of 1964 and most states' FEP laws, torts include both compensatory damages for the emotional and physical distress suffered from workplace harassment and the possibility of large punitive damages aimed at punishing the wrongdoer.[115] Unlike the Civil Rights Acts that only pertain to the employer, common tort actions can penalize the predator with punitive damages. The following are two examples of common tort claims based on sexual harassment. A woman who quit her job because of sexual harassment was entitled to unemployment benefits even though she voluntarily resigned. The Court found that she had been subjected to severe sexual harassment and that any prudent person would have quit. She was awarded unemployment benefits and attorney fees. The court of Appeals in Atlanta ruled that a female who brought suit under Title VII against an employer for sexual harassment was properly permitted to bring state law tort claims. The woman was awarded under $3,000 in back wages under Title VII, and a jury awarded her $10,000 for common law battery and $25,000 in compensatory damages for invasion of privacy under state law.

In addition to tort claims, criminal charges can be filed against the perpetrator for such actions as assault, battery and sexual assault. As witnessed in the O. J. Simpson trials, filing criminal charges does not preclude taking civil action. In fact, the criminal action will often precede the civil for the purpose of solidifying a claim or as a fact finding measure.

Statute 42 United States Code Section 1983

Until the Civil Rights Act of 1991, there was more incentive to file under **United States Code Section 1983** to obtain punitive damages and a jury trial. Unlike the Civil Rights Act of 1991, Section 1983 provides the opportunity to file for punitive damages against the offending party establishing personal liability. Punitive damages allowed by Title VII are against the employer; Section 1983 can be against the predator.[116] Section 1983 states:

Every person who, under color of any statute, ordinance regulation, custom or usage, of any State…subjects, or causes to be subjected, any citizen of the United States…to the deprivation of any rights, privileges, or immunities secured by the constitution and laws, shall be liable to the party injured in an action at law."[117]

Mildrew K. O'Linn, an attorney who has specialized in the representation of law enforcement personnel and agencies in civil litigation, reminds law enforcement officers that "Statute 42 of the United States Code 1983 provides for civil remedies if an individual acting under color of law violates the civil rights of another individual." She adds that

if you are a peace officer, you are acting under color of law whenever you are on duty or off duty if there is a strong enough nexus or connection made between whatever your actions were and the fact that you are a police officer. Simply put, you are still acting under color of law if you are using the powers of your office. Under that statute, if you violate an individual's civil rights as a police officer in the form of sexual harassment, you can be sued under section 1983.[118]

In *Monell v. New York City Department of Social Services,* the Court concluded that "sexual harassment can violate the equal protection provisions of the 14th Amendment, thus creating a basis for an award of damages under Section 1983."[119] In addition, Section 1983 offers incentives for attorneys as employers can also be sued as persons[120] (deep pocket theory) and attorney's fees are recoverable pursuant to 42 U.S.C. § 1988.

THE COURTS AND FINDINGS OF SEXUAL HARASSMENT

Harassment violations were first considered by the court in 1972 in *Anderson v. Methodist Evangelical Hospital* requiring employers to maintain a work atmosphere free from racial and ethnic intimidation and insult.[121] Since that time, sexual harassment law has rapidly evolved as courts interpret federal, state, and local anti-discrimination statutes. According to Sarah E. Burns, the most important unresolved issues concern the amount and kind of proof required to establish certain elements of sexual harassment claims and the employer's liability for harassment by nonsupervisory personnel. Other important aspects concern the application of the law to the factual circumstances of a specific case, the evaluation of the parties' claims and proof, and the determination of proper damages.[122] Nonetheless, courts have shown their disdain for sexual harassment practices:

Sexual harassment which creates a hostile or offensive environment for members of one sex is every bit the arbitrary barrier to sexual equality at the work place that racial harassment is to racial equality. Surely, a requirement that a man or woman run a gauntlet of sexual abuse in return for the privilege of being allowed to work and make a living can be as demeaning and disconcerting as the harshest of racial epithets.[123]

Sexual harassment has been categorized in two forms: (1) **quid pro quo** (something for something) **harassment**—sexual favors as a condition for receiving a tangible benefit; and (2) **hostile work environment**—an offensive environment that unreasonably interferes with the employee's job performance. The first two sections of the Equal Employment Opportunity Commission's definition of sexual harassment pertain to quid pro quo harassment, the last refers to a hostile work environment.

Until the United States Supreme Court's ruling in *Meritor Savings Bank, FSB v. Vinson, et al.*, there was considerable debate in the lower Courts as to whether harassment fell under the legal definitions of sexual discrimination.[124] The Supreme Court concluded: "The EEOC Guidelines fully support the view that harassment leading to noneconomic [sic] injury can violate Title VII.... Since the Guidelines were issued, courts have uniformly held, and we agree, that a plaintiff may establish a violation of Title VII by proving that discrimination based on sex has created a hostile or abusive work environment."[125] In addition, the Supreme Court held that: "...The correct inquiry is whether respondent by her conduct indicated that the alleged sexual advances were unwelcome...."[126]

According to some critics, the **unwelcome standard** actually places the plaintiff on trial in a way similar to a rape victim. A plaintiff is "routinely required to explain why, if she was being subjected to sexual harassment, consistent with her claim of unwelcomeness, she failed to complain, remained politely silent, appeared flattered, joked, or even affirmatively participated in reciprocal slurs."[127] In essence, she becomes the accused having to defend her actions. The proof of unwelcomeness "is usually determined by the sufferer's testimony corroborated by evidence that either she behaved as if the conduct were 'unwelcome' to her or the conduct was the kind likely to be obviously unwelcome or both."[128] To prove or refute a claim of sexual harassment can be very difficult, a he said–she said paradox centering on who is the most creditable person.

The Reasonable Woman Standard

The 9th Circuit in *Ellison v. Brady* (1991) focused the severity and persuasiveness of sexual harassment on the perspective of the victim, applying the **"reasonable woman" standard**: "We hold that a female plaintiff states a prima facie case of hostile environment sexual harassment when she alleges conduct which a reasonable woman would consider sufficiently severe or pervasive to alter the conditions of employment and create an abusive working environment."[129]

The Circuit Court felt that the "reasonable man" or "reasonable person" did not take into account the concerns women share. "For example, because women are disproportionately victims of rape and sexual assault, women have a stronger incentive to be concerned with sexual behavior than men."[130]

The *Harris v. Forklift Systems, Inc.* decision of the Supreme Court two years later was its second decision on sexual harassment and took the middle ground to resolve a conflict among the circuit courts holding "that to be actionable under Title VII 'abusive work environment' harassment, the conduct need not seriously affect an employee's psychological well-being or lead to the employee suffering injury."[131] The Court did leave vague what standard the plaintiff needed to prevail on such a claim (reasonable woman, reasonable victim, or reasonable person standard).[132] In using the test of an objectively reasonable employee, the Court did provide guidance saying that the totality of the circumstances needs to be considered according to the five categories:

1. How often the conduct occurs.
2. How serious the conduct is.
3. Whether the behavior physically threatens the victim, or stops at offensive comments.
4. Whether the behavior unreasonably interferes with work performance.
5. Whether the victim perceives the environment to be abrasive.[133]

Anita Bernstein argues in a 1997 article in *Harvard Law Review* that sexual harassment can be better explained using the concept of respect. She defended the legal virtues of a legal rule that affirms respect, saying that these virtues

> include the resonance of respect as a value among ordinary people, the history of inclusion based on human dignity that informs respect, the orientation of respect around the conduct of an agent (rather the reaction of a complainant, the focus of current rules) and congruence with a tradition, found in many other areas of American law, of calling on citizens to render respect.[134]

This standard of respect is actually being used to guide behavior in many businesses. For example, 3M Corporation's "The Appropriateness Test" raises the following questions: "Would I be embarrassed to discuss my language and behavior at work with my family? Would a newspaper account of my language and behavior at work embarrass me or my family? Would I be embarrassed to discuss my language and behavior at work with my supervisors and members of management?"[135] Rosemarie Skaine provides more in-depth questions for men to ask themselves to aid in assessing their behaviors:

> Would I mind if someone treated my wife, partner, girlfriend, mother, sister, or daughter this way? Would I mind if this person told my wife, partner, girlfriend, mother, sister, or daughter about what I was saying or doing? Would I do this if my wife, partner, girlfriend, mother, sister, or daughter were present? Would I mind if a reporter wanted to write about what I was doing? If I ask someone for a date and the answer is "no," do I keep asking? If someone asks me to stop a particular behavior, do I get angry and do more of the same instead of apologizing and stopping? Do I tell jokes or make "funny" remarks involving women and/or sexuality?[136]

COSTS OF SEXUAL HARASSMENT

Sexual harassment in policing has both personal and departmental costs. The daily costs of sexual harassment for a police officer is overwhelming, but the tangible costs of sexual harassment to a department are also staggering.

Personal Costs

According to the American Psychological Association, sexual harassment can devastate psychological health, physical well-being and vocational development of the victim.[137] Reportedly, 90 percent of the victims of sexual harassment will suffer from a significant degree of emotional distress with approximately 12 percent seeking professional help.[138]

Adding to this trauma, a second victimization can occur due to retaliation from supervisors, coworkers, the predator, and from insensitivity or blame at home, a lengthy wait or negative result after filing a complaint.[139] This revictimization, representing a second injury, further reduces an individual's trust in other people and in society in general and may leave the victim with a sense of isolation and vulnerability in a world that may seem unjust and unpredictable.[140] Retaliation for filing a complaint was a common fear alleged by victims of sample court decisions in this chapter. According to the United States Merit Systems Protection Board study, 47 percent of victims who filed grievances or adverse action appeals reported that the action only made things worse, and filing a discrimination complaint was reported by 37 percent to make things worse (see Table 11.1).[141]

A sampling of cases that have gone through the courts reveals injuries resulting from a hostile work environment in police agencies. After complaining to an Equal Employment Opportunity Coordinator, a policewoman suffered more verbal harassment and ostracization from coworkers and supervisors causing her to resign.[142] A Philadelphia policewoman, after having experienced vandalism, obscene phone calls to her unlisted number, and being ostracized and harassed by coworkers and supervisors, was emotionally unable to work. Even though she was afraid to go out of her house, believing that someone was going to hurt her, she was terminated for failure to return to work.[143]

How a female officer will handle sexual harassment is as varied as the personalities involved and the severity of the offense. If an officer is isolated in a small agency, an adequate response may be difficult, particularly if the offending party is a supervisor. The pressure to belong to the group is great and so is the risk of being ostracized.

The responses can range from filing criminal charges, a lawsuit, filing an internal complaint or grievance, requesting an investigation by an outside agency, ignoring the behavior, asking the harasser to stop, avoiding the harasser, or responding with a vulgar comment, among others. The United States Merit Systems study of Federal employees found that most victims ignore the behavior, followed by asking the harasser to stop (see Table 11.2).

TABLE 11.1   MSPB 1994 Sexual Harassment Survey: Percentage of Victims Who Said That the Indicated Formal Action Made Things Better, Made Things Worse, or Made No Difference

Action	Made things better	Made things worse	Made no difference
Requesting an investigation by an outside organization	61	32	7
Requesting an investigation by employing organization	47	19	35
Filing a grievance or adverse action appeal	32	47	21
Filing a discrimination complaint or lawsuit	21	37	42
Other	61	24	16

Source: U.S. Merit Systems Protection Board, *Sexual Harassment in the Federal Workplace* (Washington, DC: USGPO, 1995) 73.

Departmental Costs

Administrators cannot ignore the tangible costs of sexual harassment to the department: First, there is considerable expense to an agency caused by voluntary turnover, the payment of sick leave to employees avoiding sexual harassment, and the cost of reduced productivity of harassed employees.[144] Second, there is the time lost by management involved in dealing with harassers and the problems of

TABLE 11.2   MSPB 1994 Sexual Harassment Survey: Percentages of Male and Female Respondents Who Said They Had Taken the Indicated Action in Response to Unwanted Sexual Attention

Response	Men	Women
Ignoring the behavior or doing nothing	44	45
Asking or telling the person(s) to stop	23	41
Avoiding the person(s)	20	33
Making a joke of the behavior	15	14
Reporting the behavior to a supervisor or other official	8	13
Threatening to tell or telling others	5	13
Going along with the behavior	7	6

Note: Respondents could choose more than one action.
Source: U.S. Merit Systems Protection Board, *Sexual Harassment in the Federal Workplace* (Washington DC: USGPO, 1995) 72.

the victims. Third, the expense of sexual harassment training for the workforce and management is another cost. Finally, there is the loss of good will in the community when the agency is adversely affected by the negative publicity of harassment charges.[145] The lack of community support can translate into loss of employment for the chief of police[146] or a police officer,[147] and possibly an election defeat for a county sheriff.[148]

The United States Merit Systems Protection Board estimated that sexual harassment cost the Federal Government $237 million in the year period preceding their 1994 study. This is a conservative estimate that did not include benefits paid to harassed workers, overtime for coworkers filling in due to absenteeism to avoid harassment, and the cost of dealing with informal complaints, processing formal ones, and handling litigation.[149] Litigation fees, if the case goes to trial, can be as high as $700,000.[150]

SUMMARY

The wider context of this chapter is the patriarchal society, which is made up of social, philosophical, and political systems in which women are subsumed under the male. But the more immediate context is the culture of the men's club of policing. This is a culture, according to male officers, that demands dominance, aggressiveness, superiority, and power. As part of this cultural barrier, it is held that the basic aspects of police work make it unsuitable for women. Thus, there are cultural and structural barriers to the gender integration of women in policing. In contrast to this misguided viewpoint, research has found that females may have somewhat different skills than male police officers, but that they are equally competent to their male counterparts.

This examination of sexual harassment reveals that the term itself is multidimensional and has expressed itself in various ways in law enforcement. There was the initial resistance to women entering the public sphere, and then the toxicity of sexual harassment expressed itself in the appraisal process of new recruits, in supervisory attitudes and treatment, in attitudes of male line police officers, and in promotional opportunities and career advancements. Yet research studies continue to mount that female police officers may have somewhat different skills than male police officers, but that they are equally as competent.

There is much that we do not know about sexual harassment in law enforcement. We do not know what the background of the offenders are. Is race and ethnicity a factor here? Are males from some groups more likely to harass females sexually than are males from other groups? Is education a factor? Are college educated male officers more or less likely to victimize female officers? Is satisfaction in police work a factor? What is the relationship between job satisfaction and sexual harassment? Is emotional maturity a factor? How well adjusted are those who sexually victimize others?

What we do know is that integrity, an on-going theme of this text, is vitally important in explaining sexual harassment in law enforcement. Although some police departments have made admirable progress in terms of eliminating sexual harassment, this progress ultimately depends upon individual male offenders and how they respond to their female counterparts. It depends on the integrity of administrators in establishing and enforcing policy against the violation of sexual harassment policies in their agencies. It depends on the integrity of male supervisors. Are they fair in their supervision of female officers? Do they give female officers support and encouragement? It depends on male officers on the street. Do they treat female officers as equals? Do they make sexual comments to female officers in which their wives or girlfriends would object?

Unquestionably, sexual harassment prevents police departments from attaining the professionalized and value-based vision found in this book. Sexual harassment is no longer acceptable with the courts, and it is increasingly under attack in both public and private workforces. The moral and financial costs are too great for this sad legacy of male dominance from the past to continue in present day police agencies.

KEY WORDS

Civil Rights Act of 1964
Civil Rights Act of 1991
"defeminized"
"deprofessionalized"
Fair Employment Practices (FEP) agencies
hostile work environment
POLICEwomen

PoliceWOMEN
quid pro quo harassment
"reasonable woman" standard
tort
United States Code Section 1983
unwelcome standard

DISCUSSION QUESTIONS

1. You're a sergeant. A female officer takes you into her confidence to talk to you about male officers making vulgar comments about women. One particular male officer keeps picking lint and taking pens from her shirt pocket. She tells you that she does not want to get anyone in trouble or to have the complaint followed up on. What should you do?

2. You're a sergeant. You meet with one of your officers to give an assignment. As you are talking to him, you notice a Playboy magazine lying on the front seat of the car. What would you do?

3. While attending a briefing, some officers start complaining about a female dispatcher. The Lieutenant responds, "That big titted bitch is not going to dispatch on my shift." As a patrol officer what would you do next?

4. A female officer joins the department. A group of male officers led by the shift sergeant refuses to back her up on calls. What would you do?

5. You're an officer on the Special Weapons and Tactical Team (SWAT) when a female officer joins the team. She is only allowed to participate in drug raids by driving the support vehicle. The team leader will not help her with her gear, and yells at her in front of the team for the smallest mistakes. After a particularly vicious encounter with the team leader, you notice her throwing-up behind the van, traumatized by her harsh treatment. What would you do?

6. As lieutenant, several female officers complain to you about three other female officers watching them in the locker room. They are very uncomfortable about this, and if you do not do something about it, they will start reporting for work late to avoid these officers. What would you recommend?

FURTHER READING

Fletcher, Connie. *Breaking and Entering: Women Cops Talk about Life in the Ultimate Men's Club.* New York: HarperCollins, 1995.

Heidensohn, Frances. *Women in Control? The Role of Women in Law Enforcement.* Oxford: Clarendon, 1992.

Lord, Leslie K. "Policewomen." In *The Encyclopedia of Police Science,* 2nd ed. Ed. William G. Bailey. New York: Garland, 1995, 627–636.

Martin, Susan E. *Breaking and Entering.* Berkeley: U of California P, 1980.

Petrocelli, William and Barbara Kate Repa. *Sexual Harassment on the Job,* 2nd edition. Berkeley: Nolo, 1994.

Schulz, Dorothy Moses. *From Social Worker to Crimefighter: Women in United States Municipal Policing.* Westport: Praeger, 1995.

Skaine, Rosemarie. *Power and Gender: Issues in Sexual Dominance and Harassment.* Jefferson: McFarland, 1996.

Webb, Susan L. *The Global Impact of Sexual Harassment.* New York: Master Media, 1994.

Webb, Susan L. *Sexual Harassment in the Workplace: What You Need to Know.* Master Media, 1991.

ENDNOTES

1. Donna Schaper, "More Women in Uniform Could Be a Force for Peace," *Newsday* (28 January 1997): 32.

2. Dorothy Moses Schulz, *From Social Worker to Crimefighter: Women in United States Municipal Policing* (Westport: Praeger, 1995) 135.

3. Frances Heidensohn, *Women in Control? The Role of Women in Law Enforcement* (New York: Oxford, 1992) 176.

4. See Heidensohn, 183–184; and Lesli Kay Lord, "Policewomen," *The Encyclopedia of Police Science,* 2nd ed., William G. Bailey (New York: Garland, 1995): 630.

5. Heidensohn, 166.

6. Lord, 631.

7. Susan L. Webb, "Step Forward: Sexual Harassment in the Workplace: What You Need to Know!" *MasterMedia* (1991): 26–29.

8. Lawrence Rifkind and Loretta Harper, "Conflict Management Strategies for the Equal Opportunity Difficult Person in the Sexually...," *Public Personnel Management 23,* (1 September 1994): 487.

9. Susan L. Webb, *Shockwaves: The Global Impact of Sexual Harassment* (New York: MasterMedia Limited, 1994) 4.

10. Webb, *Shockwaves,* 4.

11. Webb, *Shockwaves,* 4.

12. Webb, *Shockwaves.*

13. Rifkind and Harper.

14. William Petrocelli & Barbara Kate Repa, *Sexual Harassment on the Job,* 2nd ed. (Berkeley: Nolo, 1994).

15. Robert D. Lee, Jr. and Paul S. Greenlaw, "The Legal Evaluation of Sexual Harassment," *Public Administration Review 55,* 4 (July–Aug. 1995): 357.

16. Schulz, 10.

17. Schulz, 10–11.

18. Schulz, 11.

19. Bruce L. Berg and Kimberly J. Budnick. "Defeminization of Women in Law Enforcement: A New Twist in the Traditional Police Personality," *Journal of Police Science and Administration* (1986): 314.

20. Berg and Budnick, 15–16.

21. Lord, 627.

22. Lord, 16–17.

23. Anthony Platt, *The Child Savers* (Chicago: U of Chicago P, 1969) 76.

24. Lord, 628. See also Peter Horne, *Women in Law Enforcement* (Springfield: Thomas, 1980).

25. C. Feinman, *Women in the Criminal Justice System,* 2nd ed. (New York: Praeger, 1986) 81.

26. Heidensohn, *Women in Control?,* 43.

27. Feinman, 81–82.

28. Daniel J. Bell. "Policewomen: Myths and Reality," *Journal of Police Science and Administration* 10 (1982): 13.

29. Schulz, 4.

30. Schulz, 4.

31. Schulz, 2–5.

32. Heidensohn, 52.

33. Schulz, 52–54.

34. Schulz, 55.

35. Lord, 628.

36. Lord, 114.

37. Lord, 2–5.

38. Lord, 140.

39. "Law Enforcement Facts" *National Law Enforcement Officers Memorial Fund, Inc.* (Washington DC, 1998).

40. Joanne Belknap and Jill Kastens Shelley, "The New Lone Ranger: Policewomen on Patrol," *American Journal of Police 12,* 2 (1992): 47.

41. Susan E. Martin, " 'Outsider Within' " the Station House: The Impact of Race and Gender on Black Women Police," *Social Problems 41* (Aug. 1994): 389.

42. Catherine Milton, *Women in Policing* (Washington, DC: Police Foundation, 1972).

43. Schaper, 32.

44. Susan E. Martin, "Female Officers on the Move? A Status Report on Women in Policing," *Critical Issues in Policing: Contemporary Readings,* ed. R. Dunham and G. Alpert (Prospect Heights: Waveland, 1989): 315.

45. Brian A. Reaves, *Local Police Departments, 1993* (Washington, DC: Bureau of Justice Statistics, 1996) 1.

46. U.S. Dept. of Justice, 1996 survey published in *American Police Beat 3* (Oct. 1996): 24.

47. Barbara Raffel Price, "Female Police Officers in the United States" (Slovenia: College of Police and Security Studies, 1996) 1.

48. Jeanne McDowell, "Are Women Better Cops," *Time,* 17 Feb., 1992, 72.

49. Martin, "Female Officers on the Move?," 313.

50. Price, 1.

51. Heidensohn, 200.

52. Heidensohn, 216.

53. Martin, "Female Officers on the Move?," 321–322.

54. Susan E. Martin, "Policewomen and Police*women:* Occupational Role Dilemmas and Choices of Female Officers," *Journal of Police Science and Administration* 7 (1979): 314–323.

55. Susan E. Martin, "Women Officers on the Move: An Update on Women in Policing," in *Critical Issues in Policing: Contemporary Readings,* ed. Roger G. Dunham and Geoffrey P. Alpert (Prospect Heights: Waveland, 1997) 381.

56. Lord, 632.

57. Horne.

58. Horne, 314–323.

59. Feinman, 95.

60. Lord, 632.

61. Lord, 632.

62. William G. Doerner, "Officer Retention Patterns: An Affirmative Action Concern for Police Agencies," *American Journal of Police 14* (1995): 205.

63. A. P. Hochschild, "Making it: Marginality and Obstacles to Minority Consciousness," *Annuals of the New York Academy of Science 208* (1973): 79–82.

64. Susan E. Martin, *Breaking and Entering* (Berkeley: U of California P, 1980) 315.

65. Connie Fletcher, *Breaking and Entering: Women Cops Talk about Life in The Ultimate Men's Club* (New York: HarperCollins Publishers, 1995) 162.

66. McDowell, 70.

67. Fletcher, 24.

68. Heidensohn, 197.

69. Patricia W. Lunneborg, *Women Police Officers Current Career Profile* (Springfield: Thomas, 1989) 99.

70. Cited in Susan J. Blumenthal, "Suicide and Gender," *Lifesavers Newsletter* (New York: American Foundation for Suicide Prevention, Spring 1994): 3.

71. Lord, 631.

72. J. G. Wexler and V. Quinn, "Considerations on the Training and Development of Women Sergeants," *Journal of Police Science and Administration 13* (1985): 98–105.

73. Ellen Kirschman, *I Love a Cop: What Police Families Need to Know* (New York: Guilford, 1997) 203.

74. Kirschman, 203.

75. Fletcher, 187.

76. Wayne Anderson, David Swenson, and Daniel Clay, *Stress Management for Law Enforcement Officers* (Englewood Cliffs: Prentice Hall, 1995) 270.

77. House of Representatives, testimony of Leanor Boulin Johnson in a Hearing Before the Select Committee on Children, Youth, and Families (Washington, DC: USGPO, 20 May 91) 41–42.

78. Steven Stack and Thomas Kelley, "Police Suicide: An Analysis," *American Journal of Police XIII*, 4 (1994): 84.

79. Blumenthal.

80. P. Morrison, "Women Make Better Cops L.A. Probers Find," *Los Angeles Times,* 14 July 1991.

81. "60 Minutes," CBS News, transcript, 14 Feb. 1988: 4, 5.

82. *USA Today,* 16 Aug. 1991: 7A.

83. *USA Today,* 1 July 1992: 9A.

84. G. Patrick Gallagher, "When Will the Message About Harassment Be Acted Upon," *The Law Enforcement Trainer 11*, 5 (Nov. and Dec. 1996): 21.

85. Gallagher, "When Will the Message," 21.

86. *Arnold v. City of Seminole, OK*, 614 F.Supp. 853, D.C. Okl., 1985.

87. *Arnold v. City of Seminole.*

88. *Arnold v. City of Seminole.*

89. *Arnold v. City of Seminole.*

90. *Tipton–Whittingham v. Los Angeles.*

91. Jim Newton, "Harassment Complaints Continue to Dog LAPD; Police: Leadership has Not Heeded 1994 Inquiry, Many Women Say. Chief Says Managers Were Held Accountable," *Home LA Times, Home Edition,* 8 Dec. 1996.

92. James M. Daum and Cindy M. Johns, "Police Work From a Woman's Perspective." *The Police Chief* (Sept. 94): 49.

93. *Watts v. New York City Police Dept.,* 724 F.Supp 99, S.D.N.Y., 1989.

94. *Andrews v. City of Philadelphia,* 895 F.2d 1469, 3rd Cir., 1990.

95. R. Max Mendel and Elizabeth Shoenfelt, "Gender Bias in the Evaluation of Male and Female Police Officer Performance," paper presented at the Annual Convention of the Southeastern Psychological Association, New Orleans, 21 March 1991.

96. Curt R. Bartol, George T. Bergen, Julie Seager Volckens, and Kathleen M. Knoras, "Women in Small-Town Policing," *Criminal Justice & Behavior 19* (1 Sept. 1992): 240.

97. Fletcher, xi.

98. Fletcher, 151.

99. Stephen R. Covey, *The 7 Habits of Highly Effective People: Powerful Lessons in Personal Change* (New York: Simon & Schuster, 1989) 34.

100. Paula N. Rubin, "Civil Rights and Criminal Justice: Primer on Sexual Harassment," *National Institute of Justice: Research in Action* (October 1995): 1.

101. Mildred K. O'Linn, "Sexual Harassment," handout prepared for the American Society of Law Enforcement Trainers Convention, Anchorage, Jan. 1995: 2.

102. Berg and Budnick, 314; Schulz, 134.

103. Michael T. Charles, "Women in Policing: The Physical Aspect," *Journal of Police Science and Administration 10* (1982): 194.

104. Petrocelli and Repa, 1, 19.

105. Petrocelli and Repa, 1, 19.

106. *Oncale v. Sundowner Offshore Services, Inc., et al.,* Syllabus, 523 U.S., 1998, 1.

107. *Oncale v. Sundowner Offshore Services, Inc., et al.,* 7.

108. *Oncale v. Sundowner Offshore Services, Inc., et al.,* 6–7.

109. *Oncale v. Sundowner Offshore Services, Inc., et al.,* 6.

110. Petrocelli and Repa.

111. Petrocelli and Repa.

112. Mildred K. O'Linn, lecture for the American Society of Law Enforcement Trainers Convention, Anchorage, Jan. 1995.

113. *The New Lexicon Webster's Encyclopedic Dictionary of the English Language,* Deluxe Edition (Danbury: Lexicon, 1992) 1042.

114. O'Linn, "Sexual Harassment," handout: 5.

115. Petrocelli and Repa, 8, 2.

116. O'Linn, lecture.

117. *42 United States Code Section 1983.* In pertinent part as cited in *O'Neal v. DeKalb County,* 850 F.2d 653, 11th Cir., 1988.

118. Personal interview, 1997.

119. *Monell v. New York City Department of Social Services,* 436 US 658, 1978.

120. *Carrero v. New York City Housing Authority,* 890 F.2d. 569, 2nd Cir. 1989; and *Starrett v. Wadley,* 876 F.2d 808, 10th Cir. 1989 as cited in O'Linn, "Sexual Harassment," handout: 3.

121. Mildred K. O'Linn, "Sexual Harassment" in Ed Nowicki ed., *Supervisory Survival* (Powers Lake: Performance Dimensions, 1993) 181.

122. Sarah E. Burns, "Issues in Workplace Sexual Harassment Law and Related Social Science Research," *Author's Abstract, Journal of Social Issues 51,* 1 (1995): 193.

123. *Henson v. Dundee,* 682 F.2d 897, 1982, 902.

124. O'Linn, lecture.

125. *Meritor Savings Bank, FSB v. Vinson, et. al.,* 477 US 57, 1986: 66.

126. *Henson v. Dundee,* as cited in *Meritor Savings Bank, FSB v. Vinson, et. al.,* 67.

127. Burns, 194.

128. Burns, 195.

129. *Ellison v. Brady,* 924 F.2d 872, 9th Cir. 1991, 878–879.

130. *Ellison v. Brady,* 878–879.

131. O'Linn, "Sexual Harassment," handout, 18.

132. Burns, 193–196.

133. *Harris v. Forklift Systems, Inc.,* 114 S.Ct. 367, 1993.

134. Anita Bernstein, "Treating Sexual Harassment with Respect," *Harvard Law Review 111* (1997): 446.

135. O'Linn, "Sexual Harassment," 186.

136. Rosemarie Skaine, *Power and Gender: Issues in Sexual Dominance and Harassment* (Jefferson: McFarland, 1996) 401.

137. "Sexual Harassment: Myths and Realities," *American Psychological Association Office of Public Affairs,* Internet (17 Jan. 1997).

138. "Sexual Harassment: Myths and Realities."

139. Dara A. Charney and Ruth C. Russell, "An Overview of Sexual Harassment," *American Journal of Psychiatry 151,* 1 (Jan. 1994): 13–15.

140. Charney and Russell, 14.

141. Burns, 34.

142. *Watts v. New York City Police Dept.,* 724 F.Supp. 99, S.D.N.Y., 1989.

143. *Watts v. New York City Police Dept.*

144. Thacker and Gohmann, "Emotional and Psychological Consequences of Sexual Harassment: A Descriptive Study," 429–446; Burns, 23.

145. John Kohl and Paul Greenlaw, "The Who, How, What, and When of Sexual Harassment: Teaching Tips for Business Educators," *Journal of Education for Business 68* (1 July 93): 358.

146. Darryl Enriquez, "Oak Creek Fires Chief of On-duty Sex Scandal," *Milwaukee Journal Sentinel,* 4 Oct. 1996.

147. Olivia Winslow, "Firing of Cop in Harassment a First." *Newsday* 21 Aug. 1996: A08; Marie Rohde, "Fox Point Police Chief Seeks Officer's Removal," *Milwaukee Journal Sentinel,* 29 Oct. 1996.

148. Jeff Cole, "Deputy Claims Sex Harassment," *Milwaukee Journal Sentinel,* 14 Aug. 1996.

149. Burns, 23–24.

150. Webb, 42.

12

THE MINORITY POLICE OFFICER

As a young cop in New York City, Mike Singleterry (not his real name) got an early history in police racism. Singleterry was assigned to the Hasidic Jewish section of Crown Heights in Brooklyn. The white lieutenant in charge instructed his officers to issue traffic summonses to residents only if absolutely necessary. But when the officers were shifted to the neighboring black community, the order changed, "I want summonses," the lieutenant demanded....

From the beginning, he says, white cops tended to treat young black males more harshly than whites. Singleterry believes it's because they saw blacks as more threatening.

"Ten or 15 white boys getting in a phone booth is considered fun," he says. "Five or six blacks getting in a phone booth is considered vandalism. That was the attitude."

Singleterry remembers working a demonstration that had turned into a confrontation between white and black students. One of the white kids started verbally harassing a white cop. Singleterry watched the officer take it "for a good half-hour before he finally grabbed him and shoved him. But then three days later, I saw a black kid say something out of the way to him and instantly he was in handcuffs."...

Singleterry said he rarely saw the racial hostility escalate to brutality. But when it did, he says, it was usually white on black violence. Junior black cops did not report the incidents or protest to fellow officers, he says, because they often feared a beating or other harassment themselves. Supervisors generally condoned the behavior.

"In most cases, what's bad is that the supervisors basically agree with what the cops are doing," Singleterry says. If a cop brought a bleeding suspect into the precinct, Singleterry says, "normally the desk officer would say, 'It didn't happen as far as I'm concerned' and the suspect was considered resisting arrest."

—Quoted in Sarah Glazer, "Police Corruption,"
CQ Researcher 5 (November 1995) 1,050.

In this statement, an African American former police officer describes the racism he experienced when he was a police officer on the mean streets of New York City. At times it came from other officers on the streets. At times it took place in the station. But he quickly acknowledged that whatever discrimination he and other minority officers received from fellow officers was mild to what suspects, especially minority suspects, faced when they came in contact with the police.

This chapter attempts to glimpse into the world of the minority police officer and to examine what obstacles and challenges confront an African American or a Native American who enters policing. Unfortunately, the gaps in the literature do not permit the same type of analysis for Hispanic/Latino American and Asian American police officers. Another type of minority officer considered in this chapter is the officer whose sexual orientation separates him or her from other officers. Like any other minority officer, the gay police officer experiences discrimination and sometimes outright hostility from other officers.

This chapter finishes a series of four chapters depicting the dark side of policing. Chapter 9 focused on the use of force, and it revealed that much police deviancy is expressed in the excessive use of force, sometimes the unnecessary fatal use of force. Chapter 10 examined corruption, emphasizing the systemic nature of corruption and how it tarnishes the badge of police officers across the nation. Chapter 11 considered the female police officer. Beyond the difficulty she experiences and the means by which she copes with this rejection, particular attention was paid to the issue of sexual harassment. This chapter investigates the issue of racial and sexual discrimination and how this inappropriate police response affects the officers involved.

RACIAL MINORITIES IN POLICING

Discriminatory treatment of minorities in policing has encompassed appointments, entrance and promotion testing, assignments, evaluations, treatment by supervisors, and salaries. The race riots of the 1960s and the federal laws that followed placed pressure on local police agencies to hire more minority officers. The African American police officer has been better received into police culture than other minorities and women, but the struggle has not been easy. In 1993, the percentage of full-time sworn African American police officers was 11.3 percent (9.1 percent male and 2.2 percent female); the percentage of full-time sworn Hispanic/Latino American police officers was 6.2 percent (5.5 percent male and 0.7 percent female); and the percentage of full-time sworn Native American, Asian American, and other groups of minority police officers was 1.5 percent (1.4 percent male and 0.1 percent female). Table 12.1 (on pages 312–313) also reveals that police departments serving large populations have much greater minority representation than smaller departments.

African American Police Officers

African Americans have always been policed by a separate standard in this nation. Early on, policing was linked to this nation's reliance on slave labor; later, young African American males were defined as a dangerous class that needed to be targeted by the police; and more recently, it is African Americans' poverty induced involvement in drug trafficking that receives so much attention from the police. During the first three centuries of the presence of African Americans in North America, few African Americans had the opportunity to serve as police officers.[1] The history of African Americans in policing over the past century has continued to be one of discriminatory treatment by both white officers and the public. Even within their own communities African American's involvement in police work has been questioned. This involvement in policing is a classic example of role conflict. In 1969, Nicholas Alex's excellent study of African American police officers illustrates this dilemma:

> He is much more than a Negro to his ethnic group because he represents the guardian of white society, yet he is not quite a policeman to his working companions because he is stereotyped as a member of an "inferior" racial category. He may find it necessary to defense his serving as a police officer and to explain it largely on the basis of economic necessity—that this was one of the best paying jobs that was available to him. But often he feels that he is subject to criticism by his ethnic peers derived from premises inapplicable to his situation—that is, they may consider him a traitor to his race because his race does not benefit from the protection that he officers. Yet he may defend his race because he is a Negro and inextricably bound up in the current struggle for civil rights and the demands of Negroes for social and legal equality. It is difficult for him to play both roles....[2]

A Brief History of African Americans in Policing

The first African American police officers in this nation belonged to the New Orleans City guard. It was no accident that the first African American officers appeared in this city. People of African descent had played an important role in the history of New Orleans. Many African slaves had won their freedom and became **free men of color** because they served in the militia with the French and then Spanish rule in several wars against the English and Native Americans. Another aspect contributing to the uniqueness of New Orleans was the miscegenation and intermarriage that occurred there.[3]

Following the acquisition of New Orleans by the United States, the city government tried four police organizations—the Gendarmerie (1805–1806), the first city guard (1806–1806), the lamplighter–watchmen and the constables (1808–1809), and the second city guard (1809 and after). Free men of color served on all four police organizations, chiefly because there were never enough white men able to fulfill these police functions. One of the chief responsibilities of the first African American police officers was to serve as slave catchers and to control the behavior of slaves in New Orleans. In order to preserve their own precarious position in a society where skin color generally determined status and conditions of servitude, these early free men of color were forced to patrol, police, and suppress other people of color who were still slaves.[4]

Gradually, as policing became more important in New Orleans, men of color lost their positions on the city police force. African Americans did not regain the

TABLE 12.1   Race and Ethnicity of Full-Time Sworn Personnel in Local Police Departments by Size of Population Served, United States, 1993[a]

Percent of Full-Time Sworn Employees Who Are:

Population served	Total	European Americans			African Americans			Hispanic/Latino Americans			Other[b]		
		Total	Male	Female	Total	Male	Female	Total	Male	Female	Total	Male	Female
All sizes	100	80.9	75.2	5.7	11.3	9.1	2.2	6.2	5.5	0.7	1.5	1.4	0.1
1,000,000 or more	100	69.2	61.7	7.5	17.7	12.8	4.9	12.0	10.0	2.0	1.2	1.0	0.2
500,000 to 999,999	100	66.2	60.1	6.1	21.0	16.1	5.0	7.0	6.1	0.9	5.8	5.4	0.4
250,000 to 499,999	100	71.9	64.5	7.4	17.7	14.3	3.4	9.0	8.2	0.9	1.4	1.2	0.2
100,000 to 249,999	100	80.6	74.2	6.3	12.4	10.4	2.1	5.4	4.9	0.4	1.6	1.5	0.1
50,000 to 99,999	100	86.3	80.7	5.5	7.2	6.3	0.9	5.1	4.7	0.5	1.4	1.3	0.1
25,000 to 49,999	100	89.8	85.1	4.6	5.4	5.0	0.5	4.3	4.1	0.2	0.6	0.6	(c)
10,000 to 24,999	100	91.6	87.1	4.5	5.1	4.8	0.3	2.6	2.5	0.1	0.6	0.6	(c)
2,500 to 9,999	100	92.8	88.9	3.9	4.1	3.8	0.3	2.6	2.4	0.1	0.5	0.5	(c)
Less than 2,500	100	91.7	89.3	2.3	5.3	5.0	0.3	1.9	1.8	0.1	1.2	1.1	0.1

Note: (c) = less than 0.05%.
[a]Percents may not add to total because of rounding.
[b]Includes Asian Americans, Pacific Islanders, Native Americans, and Alaska Natives.

Source: U.S. Department of Justice, Bureau of Justice Statistics, *Local Police Departments, 1993,* (Washington DC: U.S. Department of Justice, 1996) 4, Table 6.

TABLE 12.1 *continued*

Race and Ethnicity of Full-Time Sworn Personnel in Sheriffs' Departments By Size of Population Served, United States, 1993[a]

		Percent of Full-Time Sworn Employees Who Are:										
		European Americans			*African Americans*			*Hispanic/Latino Amercians*			*Other[b]*		
Population served	Total	Total	Male	Female	Total	Male	Female	Total	Male	Female	Total	Male	Female
All sizes	100	83.1	72.1	11.0	10.0	7.4	2.7	5.8	5.0	0.8	1.1	1.0	0.1
1,000,000 or more	100	73.1	63.6	9.5	11.4	8.4	3.0	13.3	11.5	1.8	2.2	2.0	0.2
500,000 to 999,999	100	78.9	67.5	11.4	14.1	10.3	3.9	5.5	5.0	0.6	1.5	1.2	0.2
250,000 to 499,999	100	83.3	70.8	12.5	11.0	8.0	3.0	4.7	4.0	0.7	1.0	0.8	0.2
100,000 to 249,999	100	85.8	73.9	11.9	10.7	7.4	3.2	2.9	2.4	0.5	0.6	0.5	(c)
50,000 to 99,999	100	90.5	79.2	11.3	6.3	4.7	1.6	2.4	2.1	0.4	0.8	0.6	0.1
25,000 to 49,999	100	89.8	79.9	9.9	6.1	4.7	1.4	3.5	3.3	0.2	0.6	0.6	(c)
10,000 to 24,999	100	87.7	78.0	9.8	7.9	6.6	1.2	3.9	3.1	0.8	0.5	0.5	(c)
Less than 10,000	100	90.1	79.0	11.2	4.8	3.4	1.3	4.1	3.4	0.7	1.0	1.0	(c)

Note: (c) = less than 0.05%.
[a]Percents may not add to total because of rounding.
[b]Indudes Asian Americans, Pacific Islanders, Native Americans, and Alaska Natives.

Source: U.S. Department of Justice, Bureau of Justice Statistics, *Sheriffs' Departments, 1993* (Washington DC: U.S. Department of Justice, 1996) 4, Table 6.

right to become police officers, either in New Orleans or anywhere in the country, until following the Civil War. Then, African Americans became members of police forces throughout the South, serving in an extremely violent period in this nation's history. Most Reconstruction African American police officers performed the same duties as European American officers, and like European American officers, some were good and some were bad. In most southern cities, they had the right to arrest all citizens who broke the law.[5]

However, what W. Marvin Dulaney refers to as the **"first coming"** of African American police officers in the Reconstruction South was short-lived. He adds that **"Redemption"** ended African American political participation in the South and made law enforcement the exclusive preserve of white men.[6] Whites in some cities, such as Jacksonville, Florida and Charleston, South Carolina, used state intervention to eliminate men of color from their police forces.[7]

As African Americans lost their police jobs in the South, they were appointed to forces in the North. The political patronage system in the North is what played the critical role in this integration. African Americans' participation in northern political machines resulted in the appointment of a few African American men to police departments. Yet, just as in the South, the duties of African American police officers were limited. Racism remained the primary factor limiting the number of African American officers and ensuring that their status would remain little more than tokenism.[8]

On 5 August, 1881, Mayor King appointed the first four African Americans as policemen in Philadelphia. Charles K. Draper earned the distinction of being the first African American in a police uniform to patrol the streets of Philadelphia. As reported by the *Philadelphia Times,* a large crowd of African American spectators gathered at the 19th Police District and "by the time six o'clock struck headquarters the entire street was blocked. The crowd was inclined to laugh a great deal,... but there was no mistaking the fact that their heads were, figuratively speaking, bumping against the clouds, as they greeted their hero of the hour on his appearance on the steps of the station house." The article added, "with him moved the crowd, elbowing and pushing for a good look. Every window along the way was filled with faces to gaze and wonder."[9]

Around the turn of the twentieth century, large cities were responsible for hiring most African American officers, comprising about 2.7 percent of all "watchman, policemen, and firemen. However, the number of African American officers declined until in 1940 they only represented .9 percent of the total. This number steadily increased following World War II; nonetheless, unequal treatment of African American officers continued into the 1950s.[10]

This was nowhere more demonstrated than the common practice of not allowing African Americans to patrol white neighborhoods. The Southern Regional Council's 1959 survey of 130 cities and counties reported that 69 cities required African American officers to call for a European American officer when arresting European American suspects, and 107 cities restricted African American officers to patrolling African American neighborhoods.[11] Confining them to African American precincts or districts was not restricted just to Southern or border cities, but was an accepted practice in Northern cities as well.[12] The rationale behind segregated assignment practices was that African American officers knew their own people better, that they could command greater respect from them, and that they were stricter with African Americans than were white police officers.[13]

The 1967 President's Crime Commission noted that 18 of the 28 departments surveyed allowed African American officers to hold an European American felony suspect until an European American policeman arrived, unless there was none available. In 10 departments, they could only keep the suspect under surveillance until an European American officer arrived. When considering misdemeanor offenses, the arrest powers of African American officers were even more limited.[14]

Miami sadly illustrates this **"separate but equal doctrine"** and the resulting second class status of African American police officers. Indeed, in 1950, city officials built an African American police station with an African American judge and bailiff to administer a "black only" court. This "Negro police station and court," the only one of its kind in the South, established a legacy of inequality that affected the city's African American police officers long after 1963 when they were integrated into the regular police department.[15]

The ghetto riots of the sixties placed new emphasis on the hiring of African American officers to ease racial tensions and promote equal and fair treatment of minorities. In 1968, The National Advisory Commission on Civil Disorders (also known as the Kerner Commission) noted that, "Our Nation is moving towards two societies, one black, one white—separate and unequal...The abrasive relationship between the police and minority communities has been a major—and explosive—source of grievance, tension, and disorder. The blame must be shared by the total society."[16] Often the controlling factor on whether a disorder turned into a full scale collective violence was the degree to which police officials were able to effect control over their own officers. When control broke down "deep-seated racial prejudices surfaced and the desire to vent hostility and to reestablish dominance in the streets frequently became compelling motives for retaliation."[17] As the result of this study, the Kerner Commission recommended a review of police operations to eliminate abrasive practices and for departments to recruit African Americans and review promotion policies to insure fair promotions for African American officers.[18] In fairness to law enforcement, Kenneth J. Peak emphasizes that "at this point in time many departments were far ahead of other government agencies, private businesses, and educational institutions in employing and promoting minorities."[19]

The numbers of African Americans in policing have doubled since the early 1970s. The major factors spurring this increase have been the National Advisory Commission on Civil Disorders' 1966 report, the 1971 Supreme Court case *Griggs v. Duke Power Company* that banned the use of intelligence testing and other obstacles that were not job related, and the federal Equal Employment Opportunities Act of 1972.[20]

Growing Acceptance and Struggles Today
Nicholas Alex, who studied African American police officers in the New York Police Department, found that European American police officers were often accept-

ing of African American officers at the workplace but typically excluded African Americans in the social setting. He also found that African American officers faced the problems of not being accepted by his or her own race. Alex called this position one of "double marginality."[21] Paul Chevigny and D. Rafky also found this double marginality in the studies they conducted during this same time period.[22] But Valencia Campbell argues, based on her sample of 1,050 African American police officers, that double marginality is no longer an important aspect of African American officers' perceptions about either public involvement in policing or in the perception of police authority.[23]

Stephen Leinen, after intensive interviews with 46 African American New York City police officers, concluded that outright institutional discrimination has been all but eliminated in the department. African Americans are presently not only actively encouraged to join the department, but, once hired, are assigned to the same basic duties as European Americans, promoted through civil service without regard to race, often occupy command positions over European Americans, and have available avenues of grievance redress both within and outside the police organization. African Americans can also expect to be assigned to precincts on a more or less random basis.[24] Yet, Leinen adds, the African American officer may find that chances for upward mobility on the job are still restricted, especially in some units. Leinen found, consistent with Alex's earlier study, that African American officers typically do not fraternize with European American officers outside of work.[25]

African Americans have sought to protect their interests in policing by establishing police associations. The Texas Negro Peace Officers' Association (TNPOA), the first formal police association organized by African American officers in the United States, was organized by six African American officers on Houston's police force in 1935. In 1944, African American officers established the Miami Colored Police Benevolent Association (MCPBA) because the department would not accept them for membership in their Police Benevolent Association. In 1949, after a six year struggle, the Guardian Association became the representative government body for African Americans in the New York Police Department. In 1946, African American police officers in Cleveland established the Shield Club, and, like the Guardian Association in the NYPD, the Shield Club became active in community service.[26] Associations of African American officers were also formed at this time in Philadelphia (Guardians Civil League of Philadelphia), in San Francisco (Officers for Justice (OFJ) Peace Officers' Association), and in Los Angeles (Oscar Joel Bryant Association (OJB). In August 1972, the St. Louis Black Police Association hosted the "First National Conference of Black Policemen"—attended by officers from eight cities. The **National Black Police Association (NBPA)** emerged from the St. Louis conference and has held an annual conference every year since 1972. The National Organization of Black Law Enforcement Executives (NOBLE) was founded in 1976.[27]

In the 1960s, many African American police officers became radicalized and began to organize more aggressively to challenge the racist police of this nation's police departments. This new breed of police officer was more than willing to speak out against racism in policing and often adopted the methods, tactics, and strategies of the so-called "black militants" in the African American communities.[28] The Afro-

American Patrolmen's League of Chicago became the voice of this new radicalism in policing. Its organizational position powerfully identified its purpose:

> We are going to elevate the black policeman in the black community to the same image-status enjoyed by the white policeman in the white community; that is as a protector of citizenry and not as a brutal oppressor. We find it impossible to operate within the framework of existing police associations. For example, we disagree categorically with the position of the Fraternal Order of Police supporting "Stop and Frisk," and their position supporting the order to "shoot to kill" or maim looters during civil disorders. We will no longer permit ourselves to be relegated to the role of brutal pawns in a chess game affecting the communities we serve. We are husbands, fathers, brothers, neighbors, and members of the black community. Donning the blue uniform has not changed this. On the contrary, it has sharpened our perception of our responsibilities as black males in a society seemingly unresponsive to the needs of black people. We see our role as the role of a protector of this community and this is the role we intend to fulfill.[29]

African American Women in Policing

Some evidence exists that African American women entering policing have to face a much different reception than African American males. The combination of the effects of race and gender expose African American women to multiple disadvantages known as "double jeopardy."[30] According to some analysts, the African American's "unique social location at the interaction of different hierarchies has produced a distinct feminist consciousness different from that of white women." Susan B. Martin continues, "White women have ample contact with white men and the potential for increased power by association with one of them. But they have limited their influence by internalizing an image of helplessness and allowing themselves to be 'put on a pedestal.'" She concludes that "due to racism, black women have experienced far less protection and a far greater desire of fear based on white hostility, physical separation, and intimidation."[31]

Martin, in examining the interactive effects of race and gender in five large municipal police agencies, conducted in-depth interviews with 106 African American and European American officers and supervisors. One African American woman recounted:

> Males didn't want to work with females, and at times, I was the only female or black on the shift so I had to do a lot to prove myself. I was at the precinct 10 days before I knew I had a partner 'cause...[the men] called in sick and I was put in the station. The other white guys called the man who was assigned to work with me the 11th day and told him to call in sick...he came in anyway.[32]

Martin found that several African American women "observed differences in their treatment that reflect differences in the cultural images and employment experiences of black and white women."[33] European American women, especially those who were physically attractive or attached to influential European American men, were more likely than African American women to be protected from street patrol by being given station house duty. When European American women were assigned to the streets, they were more likely than African American women to receive protection from both European American and African American males.

This study also found that African American women's relationships to African American males were "strained by tensions and dilemmas associated with sexuality and competition for desirable assignments and promotions." Part of the explanation for these strained relationships was the competition "for position and promotions earmarked 'black' by affirmative action programs." Thus, within these five departments, African American women were, in a number of ways, the victims of "widespread racial stereotypes as well as outright racial harassment."[34] For an interview with an African American policewoman, see the interview with Sergeant Stephanie Bradley Peterson in Box 12.1.

Cumulative Stress and the African American Officer

Minority officers face stressors from their policing careers, "family and relatives, the minority community, other officers, and in some cases department administrations."[35] A male minority officer reflects on his career: "The biggest stress for me any more isn't a black thing, it's a blue thing. You're in a uniform, black, white, or whatever, and there's the public attitude of 'I don't care for you.' There's a hate there, an attitude…"[36] The stressors in the community can come from peers who accuse the African American officer of doing "whitey's work for him." At times, this can disturb relationships that have existed since childhood. Family members' reactions range from the dislike and distrust of the police reflected in the African American community to concern over the officer's safety. A policewoman comments on her family's reaction:

> My mother and father's negative reaction wasn't with the fact that a member of the black race was going to be a police officer; their feelings were more "my daughter is taking a dangerous job and I don't want her to get hurt…."[37]

In addition to family and community pressures, African American officers have to contend with distorted perceptions of their culture from fellow officers and departmental prejudice. The prejudice and hostilities faced by minorities breaking into a profession dominated by European American males has been well documented. But there is some evidence that racial antagonism and discrimination is decreasing in policing.[38] In a survey conducted by John M. Violanti and Fred Aron, using the 60 item Police Stress Survey developed by Spielberger, Westberry, Grier, and Greenfield, "racial conflicts" was ranked in last place behind "minor physical injuries as stressors for minority officers."[39] Receiving more support from:

- the climate of the organization where he or she works
- the degree of the organization's administrative and supervisorial support
- the degree of the organization's commitment to fairness to all employees

BOX 12.1   Interview of Sergeant Stephanie Bradley Peterson

Question: Is the history of African Americans in policing an important topic?

Peterson: I think you need to talk about blacks in policing from the early days. It does a disservice to black officers to just talk about blacks in policing from the 1970s on. It does not allow people to grasp the problems blacks have had with law enforcement unless they truly know the history.

I think that part of the race problem in America is that so much history is edited out. People question: What's the problem now? You have affirmative action. There are desegregation laws. But they don't realize that this has been an ongoing thing for a couple hundred years. It has just been in the last couple decades that things have significantly changed in some ways. And so without having the background and knowledge of history people don't always grasp that. I think one major difference between how black people and white people think is that when something happens to black persons, they view it as a continuation of past problems. Instead, whites will view it as an isolated incident.

Question: Is it more acceptable for an African male than female to be in policing?

Peterson: It is still more acceptable for a black male to be in policing than a black female. Black males have been in policing much longer. Just in the past twenty-five years have police departments actually recruited women and permitted them to carry guns and share the same capacity or similar capacity as a man. So I think, as a female, you end up fighting two different types of stereotypes: that it is a male profession and that you are a woman and doing a man's job. In our society, it is particularly tough for a black woman, because we are probably on the lowest social strata of society. As a black female, you not only get it from white males and white females, but you're likely to get it from black males, too. All men can be sexist and white women can be racist. So you may have to deal with both groups, and you may not fit into anybody's group. You are just different!

Question: How do you break through that?

Peterson: Well, it takes support. Lots of black women have gone into policing and have felt isolated because it is hard to get support. Even in my job I often feel isolated, because I don't feel I have a lot of friends in the department. True friends I should say. I have accepted the fact that, for the most part, I will be alone in law enforcement. I have gone to many conferences and workshops here in Wisconsin and nationally where either I am the only woman or the only black woman. I have just become accustomed to being alone. It has been a struggle, and it is a lonely experience.

Question: How much has affirmative action done for women in policing?

Peterson: There is a lot of white reaction to affirmative action now. They tend to view the pie as shrinking as opposed to just being divided up in a different way. If you think about how employment has taken place in this country, it was purposely developed for white males. And now you have women and people of color coming in and taking jobs that they should have been entitled to all along. Whites have become fearful. The fact is that policing is still controlled and dominated by white males. If there is a black police department anywhere in this country, it might be Washington, D.C.

Question: The Madison Police Department has the highest ratio of women of any department in the country. Has retention of women of color been a problem in this department?

(continued)

BOX 12.1   *Continued*

Peterson: When I came on the department in 1984, I was the fourth black female hired, but I have been only the third one to stay here for any amount of time. The first black female hired is still on the department. She has been here for over twenty years. Other black females have come and gone. So, retention has been a problem for black females. There have been a number of reasons why they have come and gone. A couple were fired in the academy. Another didn't make probation. Another didn't like law enforcement and went to probation and parole. I think it has been a combination of different things.

Question: What should we be doing differently in policing to help women of color feel more accepted?

Peterson: There should be an official mentoring program. If you already know someone in the department, mentoring goes on unofficially. But I would venture to say that black females probably receive the least amount of

mentoring. They might be fortunate enough to get a veteran officer to take them under their wing. We need to be told about how to really handle a call; how to really prepare yourself for promotion; how to get the necessary training that you need; and how the department really works.

Question: What are some of the major issues facing African Americans in law enforcement?

Peterson: Retention is one issue. Another is to have more people of color in positions of authority. A third issue is greater representation on important task forces, training positions, and areas of policy development. There are black chiefs, but these are still pretty much all male. I think there are only two black females in the country who head departments. One is in Atlanta, Georgia, and the other is also in the same county Atlanta is in. More people of color need to go beyond entry level officer positions to make decisions on how policing is done in a community.

Source: Interviewed in January 1998.

- community attitudes and politics
- prevailing norms in society at large
- the number of other minority officers working in the agency
- the officer's personality
- the officer's competence[40]

African American Police Administrators

"Winning access of police administrative positions," according to Dulaney, "proved to be an even more difficult task for African Americans than winning equal opportunity as law enforcement officers."[41] In 1937, Harvey Alston joined the Columbus, Ohio police department and in 1952 became the first African American outside of Chicago and New Orleans to attain the rank of police captain. He became the department's first African American inspector—second in command to the chief—but failed to be appointed chief of this major department. Several African American males in the 1950s and early 1960s were appointed chiefs in small departments. In 1958, Payton I. Flournoy became chief in Palmyra, New Jersey, a suburb of Philadelphia; in 1959, Baptist minister Robert Wesby was appointed chief in Aurora, Illinois; and in 1962, Theodore Wilburn became chief in Portsmouth, Ohio.[42]

Cleveland, Ohio became the first major city to hire an African American police administrator in 1970. In what proved to be his biggest political mistake, Carl Stokes, the city's controversial African American mayor, appointed Benjamin O. Davis, Sr. as public safety director. Davis was the United States Army's first African American four star general and a graduate of West Point. A liberal mayor and a conservative public safety director were a bad mix, as Davis opposed the mayor on issue after issue. He was replaced six months later, but the media and business establishment still blamed the Stokes administration "for allowing 'black militants' to end the tenure of one of the nation's leading military men as the top law enforcement officer in Cleveland."[43] Stokes' conflicts with Davis were one of the contributing factors that led to Stokes' own resignation from office.

Kenneth Gibson, the second African American big city mayor in Newark, New Jersey, appointed Lieutenant Edward Kerr as police director on December 10, 1972. The Newark City Council voted against his confirmation four times. Kerr served six months as "interim" police director before the council would confirm him. Kerr served only one year before Mayor Gibson replaced him with another African American, Lieutenant Hubert Williams, who was eminently qualified to become the new director. He had earned a law degree from Rutgers Law School and a master's in public administration from the City University of New York. He had also participated as a fellow at Harvard Law School's Center for Criminal Justice. The new director not only served longer (1974–1985) than any previous police director in Newark, but also introduced a number of innovations.[44] In two outside evaluations of his performance as police director, after eight and ten years of his leadership, both studies identified flexibility, innovation, and sound management in spite of personnel and funding reductions.[45]

In 1974, Maynard Jackson of Atlanta became the nation's third big city African American mayor. That same year he appointed A. Reginald Eaves as public safety commissioner. Jackson met considerable criticism for his appointment of this outsider and a person with no police experience (Eaves had served as Boston's penal commissioner). Eaves, the first African American to direct a police department in a major southern city, attracted considerable media attention, and he was more than up to his task. During his four year tenure as public safety commissioner, most of which was filled with political conflict, he took a tough stance on crime and reduced the number of major crimes in Atlanta, implemented the city's first team policing program, and began to change the composition of the police force to make it more representative of Atlanta's population.[46]

Eaves was forced to resign over a police cheating scandal, for which neither he nor the mayor had any knowledge, but his replacement was Lee P. Brown, who became Atlanta's second African American public safety commissioner. Brown began what turned out to be an extremely illustrious career in police administration, even superseding those of August Vollmer, O. W. Wilson, and Patrick V. Murphy. Brown had a Ph.D. in criminology from the University of California, Berkeley. He had held university positions at Portland State University and Howard University. He had been sheriff and director of public safety in Multnomah County (Portland) Oregon, and in 1978 was appointed director of the Law Enforcement Assistant

Administration (LEAA) with the Justice Department. Six months later he accepted the position as Atlanta's public safety commissioner.[47]

Brown continued the process of reforming and integrating the police force and became involved in coordinating the joint police–FBI investigation team concerning Atlanta's child murder cases. In 1982, Mayor Kathy Whitmire persuaded him to become police chief in Houston. This department had a national reputation for brutality against African Americans and Hispanic/Latino American citizens and was well known for a policy of shooting first and asking questions later. Furthermore, promotional opportunities for African American officers had been limited, and these officers remained assigned exclusively to African American communities. In Houston, Brown implemented a Director Area Responsibility Team (DART) patrol plan (a community policing strategy based on decentralized management and community involvement); increased the number of officers on the force and put more on the streets; saw violent crimes drop more than 10 percent during his first two years as chief; took a tough stand against the abuse of citizens; established new rules concerning the discharge of firearms; and implemented an affirmative action plan to hire and promote more minorities on the police force. In December 1989, Brown was appointed police commissioner in New York City. He had some early success in reducing the crime problem and was in the process of implementing community policing ideas when he abruptly resigned in 1992 citing his wife's illness as the reason.[48]

By the 1980s and 1990s, African American chiefs were no longer a novelty in cities in the United States. African Americans served as chiefs in 50 cities by 1982, and by the end of the 1980s, 130 African Americans were serving as police chief. Cities with police administrations headed by African Americans in the 1980s included Baltimore, Chicago, Detroit, Houston, New York, and Philadelphia.[49]

Hispanic/Latino American Police Officers

The label Hispanic/Latino American encompasses over 25 different cultural and ethnic groups from the Caribbean and Central and South America.[50] One of the important issues is the use of appropriate terminology for the different groups comprising Hispanic/Latino Americans:

> The term *Hispanic* means so many different things to so many different people. To the typical American, stereotypes of poverty, illegal aliens, laborers and uneducated come to mind. For those who are part of the "so-called Hispanic" group, there is really no agreement as to what we want to be called: Is it Latino, Hispanic or the people from the specific countries of origin like Mexican, Puerto Rican, Cuban, Salvadorean, Columbian, Dominican, Nicaraguan, Chilean, Argentinean, Brazilian, and other South and Central Americans?[51]

Hispanic/Latino Americans represent the fastest growing cultural group in this nation. For example, between the 1980 and 1990 censuses, the population dramatically increased by 53 percent, from 14.6 million in 1980 to 22.4 million in 1990.

Since this is a relatively young population with high birthrates, it can be anticipated that this skyrocketing increase of population will continue.[52]

At the same time that such population growth is taking place, there remains a significant underrepresentation of Hispanic/Latino Americans in federal, state, and local police positions. Not surprisingly, the small numbers of officers from these cultural backgrounds have hampered police departments in their attempt to serve Hispanic/Latino American communities. The reasons for such underrepresentation include:

- past history of law enforcement stereotypes and relationships with the Hispanic/Latino American communities
- interests of Hispanic/Latino Americans with respect to law enforcement careers
- image of law enforcement personnel in the Hispanic/Latino American communities
- lack of knowledge about the different careers and pathways in law enforcement
- concern with and fear of background checks and immigration status, physical requirements, and the application process
- ineffective and misdirected law enforcement recruitment and outreach efforts in the Hispanic/Latino American community
- lack of role models and advocates for law enforcement careers for Hispanic/Latino Americans[53]

The Amigos En Azul, the Austin, Texas, Hispanic Police Officers Association, focused on five key goals and objectives for its 1995 program. These goals and objectives reveal some of the main emphases nationally with Hispanic/Latino American police officers.

1. To enhance a proper image of law enforcement within the Hispanic community by participating in the mentor program at Mendez Jr. High and promoting the "Bowling for Badges" program.
2. To further broaden the lines of communication between the Hispanic community and law enforcement by participating in other Hispanic community organizations' programs and participating in established police community relations programs with the Hispanic community.
3. Develop formal lines of communication and camaraderie through planned social events by planning an annual picnic for the Hispanic police officers and their families, to emphasize family values, and by planning the annual police officers' Christmas dance.
4. Encourage recruitment of Hispanic youths into law enforcement careers and to provide a progressive image with which they can identify. Recruitment efforts include: Providing college scholarships to four youths from the community; conducting two annual fundraisers to expand the scholarship fund; conducting a minimum of two youth leadership seminars annually; and, conducting several police job fairs at local high schools.
5. Provide a definitive voice on issues facing Hispanics in law enforcement by advocating policies and programs that result in equitable representation and

treatment of Hispanics in the Austin Police Department; and, developing strategies and training programs that promote hiring, appointment and advancement of Hispanics in the Austin Police Department.[54]

Hispanic/Latino American and African American police officers are currently joining together to protest discrimination in police promotional practices. In 1994, 288 African American and Hispanic/Latino American Chicago police officers who applied for promotion to the position of sergeant filed a complaint in a civil action under Title VII of the Civil Rights Act of 1964. In a 1998 decision in the United States District Court, Judge John A. Nordberg ruled against the City of Chicago and awarded each plaintiff $10,000 as compensatory damages.[55] As evidence of this discrimination, the court cited the 1994 test for sergeant taken by 4,700 police officers, 57 percent of whom were European American and about 42 percent were African American and Hispanic/Latino American. Three of the first 114 promoted were African American and two were Hispanic/Latino American.[56]

At the same time that African American and Hispanic/Latino American police officers are joining together to protest discriminatory practices in policing, there appears to be increased tension among African American and Hispanic/Latino American populations in urban centers. Michael Fix, a senior research associate at the Urban Institute in Washington, DC, examines this issue: "The problems between blacks and Hispanics are not unlike the problems blacks have with whites. The difference is the amount of friction related to the daily commerce that takes place where people live." He adds that "Hispanics tend to move into areas that are predominantly black. And in a time of economic frustration, those frustrations get played out in the neighborhoods.... Congestion is the key. It is harder to accommodate change in a congested area."[57]

This sense of frustration between Hispanic/Latino Americans and African Americans is beginning to express itself through urban riots. According to Fix, "Miami and Washington D.C., are almost mirror images of one another. In Miami, the riot by blacks was sparked by a Hispanic police officer shooting a black. In D.C., the Hispanics rioted when a black police officer shot a Hispanic." He explained, "You also had opposite city leadership situations that added to the sense of frustration in those circumstances. D.C. is a black-run city and Miami is dominated politically by the Hispanics."[58]

Native American Police Officers*

Most of the hundreds of groups that occupied aboriginal North America enforced laws and customs through informal means. Some tribes, however, assigned law enforcement tasks to specific groups of men. Among some groups, notably the Pueblo Indians of the Southwest, the group that enforced the laws also played an

*Dr. Eric Henderson, an anthropologist and expert on North American Indians, contributed this section on the Native American Police Officer to this volume.

important role in religious ceremonies.[59] Yet, most of the tribes of the Plains and Prairies designated secular groups to function as police officers. For example, the Cheyenne tribe had six **"soldier societies"** who served as tribal police. These societies were under the authority of the council of tribal chiefs who each year designated one or more of the six societies to patrol the tribal camp, to maintain order at tribal ceremonies, and to enforce rules for hunting buffalo. The soldier societies also investigated cases of illegal activity and punished offenders.[60]

During the 19th century, Native American tribes lost most of their territory to the United States government, retaining only small tracts known as reservations. But under United States law, they also retained the authority to control the actions of their own members who lived within the reservation.

In the early part of the 19th century, some tribes began to make changes in their governments. The Cherokee of the southeastern United States developed a government with three branches—legislative, executive, and judicial, although the functions of each branch were not exactly like those in the contemporary United States. In 1808, the Cherokee National Council created a police force known as the **"Light-Horse."** Each Light-Horse company consisted of six men—one captain, one lieutenant, and four privates. Its original purpose was to suppress horse stealing and robbery of other property. In their early years, Light-Horse companies were authorized to investigate crimes, arrest suspects, try cases, determine the punishment for those convicted, and administer punishment.[61] Cherokee Light-Horse companies existed for a century even though the Cherokee Nation was displaced from the southeast and removed to "Indian Territory" (present-day eastern Oklahoma). The responsibilities of the Light-Horse changed during this time as the Cherokee courts took over the function of trying criminal cases. In the early 1900s, the United States government dissolved the Cherokee government and, thus ended the Light-Horse tradition.

In the late 19th century, many of the tribes that had recently been restricted to reservations were beset by problems of survival. On some reservations, corrupt federal officials diverted funds intended for food and clothing. Many of these officials attempted to suppress tribal religious practices and other elements of tribal culture. Tribal members, of course, resisted these actions. In the 1860s and 1870s, in order to deal with the rising disorder, several Federal administrators organized police forces and court systems for the reservations they supervised. They appointed tribal members as police officers and judges. Many of the police officers had been scouts for the United States Army, while judges were often tribal chiefs.[62] Initially, the police forces existed on only a few reservations, but by the late 1870s, Congress authorized the **Bureau of Indian Affairs (BIA)** to pay salaries to these officers and judges.[63]

The role of these Native American officers was often a difficult one. They were frequently resented by some members of their tribe because they worked for the United States government and enforced regulations that were unpopular. They were often denigrated by their employers because they were not "fully civilized." The most effective Native American police officers often acted as mediators between agents and the local population.[64]

In 1892, the BIA employed over 850 Native Americans as police officers. There were 58 agencies in the continental United States that employed such officers. Most were designated as "privates," but 57 officers held the rank of "captain." The number of officers varied greatly from reservation to reservation. The BIA police force at the small Hoopa Valley Agency in northern California consisted of two privates, while 67 officers patrolled the Pine Ridge Sioux (Lakota) Reservation in South Dakota. Captains and lieutenants received a monthly salary of $15. Sergeants and privates received $10 per month. In the 1930s, the United States government changed its policies regarding Native American affairs. The federal government encouraged tribes to take on more governmental responsibilities, but few tribes could fund their own police departments. This situation improved in 1968 when Congress established the Law Enforcement Assistance Administration (LEAA) to provide local governments with grants to improve criminal justice operations. Native American tribal governments were specifically designated as governments entitled to receive grants.[65]

Many tribes established **tribal police forces.** Since the 1980s, many tribes have gained significant revenues by operating casino gaming enterprises. Funds from tribally controlled gambling have often been used to enhance law enforcement operations. Thus, today, most tribes use their own police departments to maintain order within tribal territory, while a few others continue to rely on BIA police officers.[66] Tribes with smaller populations and large gaming enterprises often hire mostly non-Native Americans as officers. The police forces of larger tribes are composed mostly of Native American officers.

Both BIA and tribal officers participate in training sponsored by the FBI.[67] Most recently, tribal governments have received nearly $45 million in U.S. Department of Justice grants from the Community Oriented Policing Service.[68] Some of these monies have been used to fund 595 police officer positions.[69]

There are currently over 320 federally recognized Native American tribal governments in the continental United States. Each one of these tribes maintains a "government to government" relationship with the United States. Each tribe also has the legal authority to create its own police force to maintain order within its tribal territory. But most Native Americans no longer live within these territories. About three quarters of all Native Americans live away from reservations and over half live in metropolitan areas. Nevertheless, most (but by no means all) Native American law enforcement officers work on or near reservations.[70]

The **Sycuan Band** of Mission Indians of southern California provides an example of small tribal government that has funded a relatively large police department with gaming revenues.[71] The Sycuan Reservation is only one square mile and has less than 100 residents. Located near San Diego, the reservation casino averages more than 3,500 patrons per day. The tribal gaming center employs more than 650 people. The tribal police department was created in 1990 and by 1992 had 45 members, most with many years of prior experience in law enforcement. Only 5 of these officers were Native Americans.[72] The tribal police department combines the functions of a casino security staff and a local police department. By the early 1990s, the department had conducted over 1,300 background investigations of prospective casino employees, including such investigations for other tribes. The department also maintains close relations with other area law enforcement agencies.

The **Oneida Nation** of upstate New York is another tribe that has expanded its tribal police force, partially as a result of gaming revenues.[73] There are far more Oneida (over 8,000) in the United States than Sycuan, but in 1980 less than 900 Oneida lived in New York State.[74] The department has 40 sworn officers, averaging 18 years of law enforcement experience, primarily in police departments in other parts of New York. Apparently, most officers are non-Native Americans. The Oneida Nation officers are cross deputized as law enforcement officials in two counties near the reservation.

The Sycuan and Oneida tribal police forces are among the largest law enforcement agencies operated by Native American governments. They indicate an emerging trend in tribal law enforcement associated with the many non-Native Americans who are attracted to reservation casinos.

The Navajo

The largest tribal police force is that of the Navajo Nation. The Navajo territory, which spans parts of the states of Arizona, New Mexico, and Utah, is by far the largest reservation in the United States. It has about 17 million acres (about the same size as the state of West Virginia), and it also has the largest reservation population—more than 150,000 members. A nation of this size requires a large police force. But the Navajo voted not to allow casinos on to their reservation and, therefore, must support their government from other revenues such as oil and gas royalties, agriculture, lumber, and federal grants. There are less than 300 tribal police officers.[75] Unlike the Oneida and Sycuan, nearly all Navajo police officers are Native Americans, mostly members of the Navajo tribe.

Unlike their Pueblo neighbors and the more distant Plains tribes, aboriginal Navajo society did not include a group designated to fulfill police functions. The Navajo relied upon gossip, mediation by chiefs, and other forms of informal social control. The first Navajo police force was a temporary one, organized by the federal agent in charge of the Reservation in 1872 and disbanded the following year. A prominent chief, Manuelito, was appointed as head of this force.[76] The force not only retrieved stolen cattle, but apparently also "informally" executed about twenty individuals accused of "witchcraft" (but who were probably political opponents of Manuelito and a potential threat to the Indian agent's authority).[77] Ten years later a new police force was again organized by the BIA, which continued to fund all police operations until 1953.

At the turn of the century, Navajo police officers enforced BIA regulations, some of which were unpopular among tribal members—especially "recruiting" children for boarding schools. Despite enforcing some rules that undermined traditional Navajo culture, many of these officers eventually used their positions as law enforcement officers and their connections to the BIA agents to gain prestige within some sectors of Navajo society. John Daw (1870–1965) was one of the first tribal police officers. Daw reportedly had scouted for the U.S. Army prior to his assignment to the newly established Western Navajo Agency in 1905. Daw moved over 100 miles from his home community to take this position and brought some of his relatives to this area with him. He established kinship relations with several local families through marriage. At the time, Navajo men of high status often had more than one wife. Daw had six or seven wives by about 1915. His wages as a police officer allowed him to purchase sheep and horses, another source of status among the Navajo. He also established a large farm. By the 1920s, Daw derived high status from participation in both the European American and traditional Native American socioeconomic systems. His authority and his income as a police officer, his wealth as a livestock owner, large farm, numerous in-laws and knowledge of Navajo hunting ceremonies all contributed to his prestige. Many people relied upon his informal advice and sought his help in times of trouble.[78]

On the other hand, some of the wealthiest families in the region seemed to ignore his authority. Daw seems to have actively avoided confrontations that might have led to violence. Once, when a complaint was made against an individual associated with one of these families, this Indian agent sent non-Native American employees to effect an arrest. Thus, the first Navajo police officers (such as Daw) were not universally respected. Their authority seems to have rested on their ability to act in the way chiefs had formerly acted rather than on the possession of a badge and revolver.

During the 1950s, the Navajo Tribe took over the funding and control of most of the policing of the reservation.[79] By 1975, the reservation's police department budget was $3.5 million. There were about 200 uniformed officers, mostly tribal members. The tribe had established the Navajo Police Academy to provide a 13 week training course to male and female recruits. Officers also received advanced training from other institutions.[80] Officers most frequently took people into custody for misdemeanors, but this did not diminish the potential for the dangers inherent in police work. In 1972 tribal officers made nearly 8,000 arrests for disorderly conduct and an additional 1,500 for liquor violations. A few officers were killed in the line of duty during the decade.

Since the 1970s, the difficulties of Navajo police officers seem to have increased. The increase in the number of officers has not kept pace with the overall growth of the population they serve. Officers often work in, or are called to, remote locations—scores of miles from another officer who could provide back up. The Navajo population is more youthful than the society at large, and more than half of Navajo men between the ages of 18 and 35 experience problems with alcohol. In some of the small towns on the reservation, small gangs of youth have formed.[81] These gangs engage in acts of vandalism and occasional violence. Moreover, when John Daw was an officer, policing was among the better paying jobs available to Navajos. Today, there are many better paying employment opportunities for Navajos.

More than a century after the establishment of the first force of Navajo law enforcement officers, Navajo attitudes toward the Navajo police remain ambivalent. Many Navajo consider the force ineffective, noting slow response times. Navajo officers argue that with few officers, it is difficult to provide service to the sparsely populated areas of the vast reservation. The criminal punishments that Native American courts may impose are limited by federal law to no more than one year in jail and a $10,000 fine. According to Navajo officers, some younger Navajo men therefore feel there is little risk in challenging the authority of tribal officers. Navajo officers complain that assaults are treated too leniently by tribal judges given the limited penalties available.[82]

HOMOSEXUAL POLICE OFFICERS

Homosexual police officers are perceived to be the most marginalized of all police minority groups. This marginality is so extreme that in most police departments "coming out" would likely be a "kiss of death" to an officer's career in policing.

This issue of homosexuals in policing was brought to law enforcement attention on November 22, 1981 when Sergeant Charles Cochrane of the New York City Police Department testified before a city council committee in favor of a gay rights bill. When he announced that he was gay "and proud of it," the audience was stunned. This declaration later spawned the **Gay Officers Action League (GOAL)**, a movement for the acceptance of homosexuals in the New York City police and elsewhere. On June 9, 1992, this movement was awarded recognition when the New York City mayor attended a GOAL monthly meeting.[83]

Traditionally, the police community has strongly resisted hiring homosexuals. J. B. Swerling's study in 1978 found that 20 percent of the California police officers interviewed indicated their intention to quit the force if it started hiring overt homosexuals.[84] Arthur Niederhoffer and P. Jacobs' surveys also found that homosexuals were ranked by police among the most disliked categories of people on both the east and west coats of the United States.[85]

The International Association of Chiefs of Police (IACP) has stated, "every policeman should conduct his private life so that the public...regard(s) him as an example of stability, fidelity, and morality" and has interpreted this to mean that homosexuals are not ideal police candidates.[86] In response to the New York City Police Department embarking upon a program to hire homosexuals, Phil Caruso, head of the Patrolman's Benevolent Association, made this point even more strongly when he said that homosexuals "could not hold the dignity and image of a police officer."[87]

According to the sample of homosexual officers that Stephen Leinen interviewed, it is no easy matter to be both homosexual and a police officer. One explains:

> It's not a gay thing to be a cop. It's acceptable for a gay person to be an artist, a singer, instrumentalist. It's tolerated if you're a gay lawyer, banker, stockbroker. People in these professions aren't under the peer pressure as much as a cop. To be a cop is very hard. To be a homosexual and a cop, it's harder.[88]

Marc Burke's survey of currently serving and retired police officers in Great Britain found that being a "closet" homosexual puts considerable stress on a police officer. One officer reported that he lived in constant fear that he would be caught, so much so that he wouldn't let his sexual partners answer the phone while at his house, and they part company quickly if he is seen by a colleague.[89]

The movement to accept homosexuals, not surprisingly, has been very slow to gain ground in the police community. In 1992, only 10 departments in the United States had made any direct attempt to recruit homosexuals: Atlanta; Boston; Los Angeles; Madison, Wisconsin; Minneapolis; New York City; Philadelphia; Portland, Oregon; San Francisco; and Seattle. Many other cities refuse to hire homosexual cops; an example of the negative attitudes toward homosexual police officers is that in the 12,000-member Chicago police force, there were no publicly "out" homosexual cops.[90]

SUMMARY

Between 1980 and 1990, the United States population increased by 23 million. Of this increase, 40 percent (9.6 million) fell into the census' white/non-Hispanic category, with the remaining 60 percent comprised of those categorized by the census as Hispanic (6.4 million increase), African American (4.3 million increase), and Asian and other races (3.4 million increase). It is estimated by demographers that the birthrate for Hispanic/Latino Americans and Asian Americans will continue to outpace those of other racial and ethnic groups. Indeed, by the year 2020, a majority of children in California, Florida, Louisiana, New Mexico, New York, and Texas will be minorities—African Americans, Asian Americans, and Hispanic/Latino Americans. What all this means is that by 2010 "minorities" will become the "majority." This large scale population shift will have major impact on many institutions in society, including policing.[91]

As this chapter has documented, police departments across the nation have not treated minorities who wanted to become police officers well. For an example of how racism is still present in police departments, African American state troopers in an eastern state in 1993 alleged that fellow officers had distributed racist fliers, including cartoons of Ku Klux Klansmen tying a rope around the neck of an African American. The cartoons also depicted African American officers with watermelon faces.[92]

It took African American officers until the 1970s to gain any degree of equality with European American officers. Before that time, they faced discrimination in hiring, promotion, and job assignment. African American female officers, particularly, face double jeopardy, or the stigma of being both African American and female. As suggested in this chapter, they often have difficulty gaining acceptance and equality from either European American or African American officers.

Hispanic/Latino American officers have been nearly totally ignored in examinations of policing in the United States. Consequently, without the benefit of empirical studies, it is difficult to draw many conclusions about these officers as a separate group. There is a sense that these officers have profited from the hard-earned gains of African American officers and that they are increasingly used in the highly populated Hispanic/Latino American communities in the Southwest.

Native American officers, who predate other minority officers, have not had an easy time policing their own people on reservations. Native American officers, like African American officers, have faced the charge that they have aligned themselves with the enemy and have sold out their own people.

Homosexual police officers were also discussed in this chapter. The homosexual police officer has been traditionally viewed as a threat to the image of the police. In recent years, as more homosexuals have been coming out, the issue of sexual preferences is stirring debate and conflict within the policing profession. In the midst of this debate, a few departments, especially Minneapolis, New York, and San Francisco, have been actively recruiting homosexual police officers.

KEY WORDS

Bureau of Indian Affairs (BIA)	Oneida Nation
"first coming"	"Redemption"
free men of color	"separate but equal doctrine"
Gay Officers Action League (GOAL)	"soldier societies"
"Light-Horse"	Sycuan Band
National Black Police Association (NBPA)	tribal police forces

DISCUSSION QUESTIONS

1. How has the experience of the African male police officer been similar and dissimilar to the woman police officer?

2. What are some difficult obstacles for the African American woman police officer to overcome?

3. Why is history important to understand the experience of African Americans in policing?

4. What were some of the key moments in the history of African Americans in policing?

5. How has the experiences of the Native American police officer been different than the African American police officer?

6. Gays have not been well received in policing? Do they belong in policing?

FURTHER READING

Alex, Nicholas. *Black in Blue.* New York: Appleton–Century–Crofts, 1969.

Dulaney, W. Marvin. *Black Police in America.* Bloomington: Indiana UP, 1996.

Leinen, Stephen. *Black Police, White Society.* New York: New York UP, 1984.

Leinen, Stephen. *Gay Cops.* New Brunswick: Rutgers UP, 1993.

Llewellyn, Karl N. and E. Adamson Hoeber. *The Cheyenne Way: Conflict and Case Law in Primitive Jurisprudence*. Norman: U of Oklahoma P, 1941.

Shepardson, Mary. *Navajo Ways in Government: A Study in Political Process*. American Anthropological Association Memoir, 1963.

Shusta, Robert M., Deena R. Levine, Philip R. Harris, and Herbert Z. Wong. *Multicultural Law Enforcement: Strategies for Peacekeeping in a Diverse Society*. Englewood Cliffs: Prentice–Hall, 1995.

Strickland, Rennard. *Fire and the Spirits: Cherokee Law from Clan to Court*. Norman: U of Oklahoma P, 1975.

ENDNOTES

1. Kenneth J. Peak, "African Americans in Policing," in *Critical Issues in Policing: Contemporary Readings* (Prospect Heights: Waveland, 1997) 356.

2. Nicholas Alex, *Black in Blue: A Study of the Negro Policeman* (New York: Appleton–Century–Crofts, 1969) 13–14.

3. W. Marvin Dulaney, *Black Police in America* (Bloomington: Indiana UP, 1996) 8.

4. Dulaney, 9.

5. Dulaney, 13.

6. Dulaney, 8.

7. Dulaney, 19.

8. Peak, 356.

9. James N. Reaves, *Black Cops* (Philadelphia: Quantum Leap, 1991) 11–12.

10. Peak, 356–358.

11. E. Rudwick, "The Unequal Badge: Negro Policemen in the South, Report of the Southern Regional Council," in Peak, 358.

12. Stephen Leinen, *Black Police, White Society* (New York: New York UP, 1984) 13.

13. Leinen, *Black Police, White Society*, 13–14.

14. Leinen, *Black Police, White Society*, 14–15.

15. Dulaney, 56.

16. Steven G. Brandl and David E. Barlow, *Classics in Policing* (Cincinnati: Anderson, 1996) 37, 55.

17. Leinen, *Black Police, White Society*, 18.

18. Bandl and Barlow, *Classics in Policing*, 57–58.

19. Peak, 358.

20. Peak, 358.

21. Alex.

22. Paul Chevigny, *Police Power: Police Abuses in New York City* (New York: Random House, 1969); and D. Rafky, "Racial Discrimination in Urban Police Departments," *Crime and Delinquency* 21 (1975): 233–242.

23. Valencia Campbell, "Double Marginality of Black Policemen: A Reassessment," *Criminology* 17 (1980): 477–484.

24. Leinen, *Black Police, White Society*, 244.

25. Leinen, *Black Police, White Society*, 244.

26. See Chapter 6 in Dulaney for a history of these associations.

27. See Chapter 6 in Dulaney.

28. Dulaney, 73–74.

29. Position statement is in Renault A. Robinson, "Black People: A Positive Means of Social Change," in the Afro-American Patrolmen's League Papers at the Chicago Historical Society.

30. For the citations for these studies, see Susan E. Martin, "Outsider Within" the Station House: The Impact of Race and Gender on Black Women Police," *Social Problems* 41 (Aug. 1994): 383–384.

31. Martin, 384.

32. Martin, 390.

33. Martin.

34. Martin, 394.

35. Wayne Anderson, David Swenson, and Daniel Clay, *Stress Management for Law Enforcement Officers* (Englewood Cliffs: Prentice–Hall, 1995) 193.

36. Anderson, et al.

37. Anderson, et al.

38. Anderson, et al., 191–204.

39. John M. Violanti and Fred Aron, "Ranking Police Stressors," *Psychological Reports* 75 (1994): 824–826.

40. Ellen Kirschman, *I Love a Cop: What Police Families Need to Know* (New York: Guilford, 1997) 207.

41. Dulaney, 81.

42. Dulaney, 82–83.

43. Dulaney, 85.

44. Dulaney, 87.

45. *New York Times,* 8 Aug. 1974, and 15 Nov. 1974.

46. Dulaney, 89–90.

47. Dulaney, 92.

48. Dulaney, 95–96.

49. Dulaney, 102.

50. Robert M. Shusta, Deena R. Levine, Philip R. Harris, and Herbert Z. Wong, *Multicultural Law Enforcement: Strategies for Peacekeeping in a Diverse Society* (Englewood Cliffs: Prentice–Hall, 1995) 194.

51. A Hispanic/Latino American community organizer quoted in Shusta, et al.

52. Shusta, et al.

53. Shusta, et al., 210.

54. Web page of Amigos En Azul, City of Austin, Texas.

55. United States District Court for the Northern District of Illinois Eastern Division, No. 94 C 5727, 1998.

56. U.S. District Court for the Northern District of Illinois Eastern Division.

57. Quoted in Ernest Harris, "Coalition Impossible?," *Hispanic,* 28 Feb., 1995.

58. Harris.

59. Watson Smith and John M. Roberts, *Zuni Law: A Field of Values,* Papers of the Peabody Museum of American Archaeology and Ethnology 43 (1953) 38.

60. Karl N. Llewellyn and E. Adamson Hoeber, *The Cheyenne Way: Conflict and Case Law in Primitive Jurisprudence* (Norman: U of Oklahoma P, 1941).

61. Rennard Strickland, *Fire and the Spirits: Cherokee Law from Clan to Court* (Norman: U of Oklahoma P, 1975) 56–59, 169–174.

62. William T. Hagan, *Indian Police and Judges: Experiments in Acculturation and Control* (Lincoln: U of Nebraska P, 1966) 25.

63. These data are tabulated from the *Report of the Commissioner of Indian Affairs* House of Representatives (Washington, DC: USGPO; 52d Congress, 2d. Session, 30 June 1892). This report of the Secretary of the Interior was part of the Message and Documents communicated to the two Houses of Congress at the beginning of the second session of the Fifty-Second Congress (in five volumes) Volume II: 163.

64. *Report of the Commissioner of Indian Affairs,* 23.

65. Felix S. Cohen, in *Handbook of Federal Indian Law,* edited by Rennard Strickland (Charlottesville: Michie/Bobbs–Merrill, 1982) 737–738.

66. Cohen, 736.

67. 133 Congressional Record S6712, 19 May 1987. (Between 1982 and 1985, 2,463 tribal and BIA officers attended FBI training programs.)

68. Office of Community Oriented Policing Services (COPS), U.S. Department of Justice, Washington DC.

69. Federal Documents Clearing House, Congressional Testimony, 8 Apr. 1997.

70. The number of Native American law enforcement officers is difficult to estimate. The Bureau of Justice Statistics reported that in 1993 on the ethnicity of sworn officers in local police departments. American Indians were reported in the "other" category along with officers of Asian ancestry. Only 1.5 percent of all officers in local police departments, and 1.1 percent of officers in sheriff's departments were "other."

71. These data come from the Hearing Before the Select Committee on Indian Affairs, United States Senate, 102th Congress, Second Session Oversight Hearing on the Status of the Activities Undertaken to Implement the Gaming Regulatory Act (Washington, DC: USGPO, 5 Feb. 1992) 32–37.

72. Lee Romney, "It's a Great Deal for Tribal Police Graduate; Law Enforcement Sycuan Reservation Officer is First Native American Sent to Police Academy by a Tribal Force," *Los Angeles Times,* 25 Sept. 1992, San Diego County Edition, Metro; Part B; Page 1; Column 3.

73. Information from the Oneida Nation Website, internet.

74. C. Matthew Snipp, *American Indians: The First of This Land* (New York: Russell Sage, 1989) 327–343.

75. Federal Documents Clearing House, Congressional Testimony, 22 Feb. 1994 (Navajo Tribal Assistant AG states 232 commissioned officers and 28 criminal investigators; 139 Cong Rec S 16288, 16289; however, report 337 commissioned officers and 28 criminal investigators).

76. Mary Shepardson, *Navajo Ways in Government: A Study in Political Process,* American Anthropological Association Memoir (1963) 96.

77. Martha Blue, *The Witch Purge of 1878: Oral and Documentary History in the Early Navajo Reservation Years* (Tsaile: Navajo Community College Press, 1988).

78. For similar evidence of the prestige that was associated with turn of the century Navajo police officers, see Frank Mitchell, *Navajo Blemmingway Singer: The Autobiography of Frank Mitchell 1881–1967*, Charlotte J. Frisbie and David P. Mc-Alester, eds. (Tuscon: U of Arizona P, 1978).

79. Shepardson, *Navajo Ways in Government* 83; and Peter Iverson, *The Navajo Nation* (Albuquerque: U of New Mexico P, 1981) 76. Under federal law, federal law enforcement agencies have the duty to investigate and prosecute "major crimes."

80. Iverson, *The Navajo Nation,* 137–138.

81. For an examination of Native American gangs, see Barbara Mendenhall, "Formative Influences on Youth Gang Membership and Activities Among the Navajo: The Role of Key Socializing Factors—Families, Schools and Friends." Paper presented at the Annual Meeting of the Academy of Criminal Justice Sciences, March 10–14, 1998; and Troy Armstrong, "Law Enforcement, Drugs and Increased Gang Activity in the Navajo Nation: The Problem and the Law Enforcement Response." Paper presented at the Annual Meeting of the Academy of Criminal Justice Sciences, March 10–14, 1998.

82. Comment of Karl Atcitty, 17 year veteran of Navajo police in Bill Donovan, "Police Fear for Safety: Attacks on Officers Seldom Punished," *Arizona Republic,* Valley and State section, 17 Feb. 1997: B1.

83. Stephen Leinen, *Gay Cops* (New Brunswick: Rutgers UP, 1993) 244.

84. J. B. Swerling, "A Study of Police Officers' Values and Their Attitudes Toward Homosexual Officers," diss., California School of Professional Psychology, Los Angeles.

85. Arthur Niederhoffer, *Behind the Shield* (New York: Doubleday, 1967); and P. Jacobs, *Prelude to Riot* (New York: Vintage, 1966).

86. Cited in Leinen, *Gay Cops,* 8.

87. Cited in Leinen, *Gay Cops,* 32.

88. Cited in Leinen, *Gay Cops.*

89. Marc Burke, "Homosexuality as Deviance: The Case of the Gay Police Officer," *British Journal of Criminology* 34 (Spring 1994): 6.

90. Leinen, *Gay Cops.*

91. Shusta, et al., 9.

92. Shusta, et al., 23–24.

13

POLICE AND THE FUTURE

Our police are precious to us and we need policemen [women] whom we can trust and respect, who will act in ways giving us confidence in the…democracy of our community.

William W. Westley, *Violence and the Police: A Sociological Study of Law, Custom and Morality* (Cambridge: MIT Press, 1970) 192–193.

Experts writing on policing, as well as on the courts and corrections institutions, are painfully aware that predictions for the future are too often no more accurate than calling heads or tails when a coin is flipped. Optimists, pessimists, and statisticians have wrongly predicted the future of the police. In this chapter, we will try to be realists. The past thrusts its way into the future, but unknowable forces and events can be expected to drive the course of policing in the United States—for better or for worse—from the familiar channels of the present.

In the preceding chapters, we have narrated the history, structure, and functions of police agencies. We have described the difficulties of reaching the objectives that society has expected of these agencies. As we watch the last years of the twentieth century and look ahead at the twenty-first, the difficulties remaining to be surmounted look even more formidable. If the policy makers of the future are more imaginative than their predecessors, they may find that their problems offer opportunities for economy and constructive innovation. Those who prod on with the policies of the past will drag policing through endless crises.

Our task in this final chapter is to answer three questions: What is the context of the present and how does that affect policing in this society? What progressive changes in policing are taking place at the present? What are other changes that are needed to make a paradigm shift for policing in the future?

CRIMINOGENIC CONTEXT OF THE PRESENT

The new wave of toughness, the unsolvable nature of crime, and the toxicity of policing are consequences of this nation's crime problem.

The New Wave of Toughness

These are times when toughness on crime is an essential element of any politician's campaign plan. Criminal justice practitioners, criminologists, and informed observers differ on how severe the crime problem is in the United States. Perhaps it has been exaggerated by the media, or perhaps it is even worse than stated. However, there is general agreement that no matter how severe it is, it is a different problem both in its scope and in its nature than it was earlier in the history of the United States. There were plenty of thugs in the old days, but they were not armed with Uzis and AK–47's. The illicit sale of narcotics is nothing new, but distribution was never before so efficiently organized, and never before so lucrative. Under these circumstances, the hard line is a natural response. There is plenty to worry about, and the worse of it is that a hopeful solution is not in plain sight.

The Unsolvable Nature of Crime

The United States has a long history of seeking easy cures to the crime problem, but society has found no simple solutions to this perplexing problem. War has been repeatedly declared on one form of crime or another with less than resounding success. In fact, one of the most vexing characteristics of crime is its ability to survive all the policy attacks against it.

One of the reasons for the high rates of crime in the United States is that crime performs valued functions. It has become a means of making money, regulating business, furnishing economic options for the poor, and providing the psychological satisfaction of beating the "system." Al Capone noted that the American system gives everyone a great opportunity "if we only seize it with both hands and make the most of it."[1]

There are reasons why crime will, in the next decade or two, pose as great, if not greater problems than crime has in the past. First, juvenile homicides appeared to peak in 1994 or 1995, but juvenile murder rates have still skyrocketed since the late 1980s. What is disconcerting is that children of the underclass will experience a major growth cycle in the next few years, and this is likely to increase juvenile violence in the United States. Howard N. Snyder and Melissa Sickmund, two highly respected federal researchers, predict, "If trends continue as they have over the past ten years, juvenile arrests for violent crimes will double by the year 2010.[2]

Second, in the 1990s, using Uzis, AK–47s, AR–15s, and other semiautomatic weapons, street gangs across the nation have evolved into small criminal empires fighting for control of thriving narcotics, auto theft, prostitution, gun-running, and extortion operations. Drugs, particularly crack, or rock cocaine, are at the center of gang criminal operation. The crack trade, more than anything else, has transformed these street gangs into ghetto-based drug trafficking organizations. These gangs usually use juveniles in exploitative ways, but are led and controlled by adults. Estimates are that 75 to 100 gangs are involved in cocaine distribution nationally, and some gangs have sales totaling up to $1 million a week.[3] The most powerful gangs are the Bloods and Crips in Los Angeles; the Gangster Disciples, Vice Lords, and Latin Kings in Chicago; the 34th Street Players and Untouchables in Miami, and several Jamaican gangs.

There is reason to believe that in the future street gangs will expand in numbers and become more violent. The fact of the matter is that the majority of those attracted to street gangs feel that they have little or no alternatives to gang participation. In the 1980s and 1990s, law enforcement officers, especially federal agents, have had increasing success arresting the leaders of the major gangs, but other "gang-bangers" have quickly assumed leadership positions. The end result has frequently been greater intragang conflict and more violence and destruction to urban communities.

Third, domestic terrorism is becoming a major problem in this nation. The popularity of the militia movement has contributed to an anti-government form of terrorism. The 1984 and 1985 spree of terrorism by the Silent Brotherhood (the Order), the 1989 shooting at the Weaver cabin in Idaho, the 1993 Waco disaster involving the Branch Davidians led by David Koresh, and the 1995 bombing of the Alfred P. Murrah Federal Building in Oklahoma City are examples of the destructive possibilities of the militia movement in this nation. In addition, there seems to be a recent outbreak in various forms of hate crimes. This violent refusal of hate criminals to accept those who are different from themselves has led to an increasing number of attacks against people because of their race, religion, sexual orientation, or ethnic origin.[4]

Fourth, some forecasters predict that crime will become more sophisticated in the future. For example, Georgette Bennett predicts that "traditional criminals—young, male, poor, uneducated—will increasingly be displaced by older, more upscale offenders." She adds that "the street crimes that scare us will decrease in relation to more impersonal, far-reaching white-collar crimes. Computers, cashless money, technological secrets will become the new booty…and we will find new ways of cheating old institutions."[5]

It is no doubt true that crime will become more sophisticated in the future, but the changing nature of street violence will probably be much more disturbing to the public and its policymakers than the emerging forms of white-collar crime. During a 1997 speech to the International Association of Chiefs of Police, Jack Enter stated, "The nature of violence is changing. Now it's young, random and mentally disturbed…. In some urban centers, children are suffering from post-traumatic stress because of the amount of violence they live with."[6] Enter adds that it is estimated that "16 percent of young people in the United States are mentally disturbed and need psychiatric intervention. The most prescribed drug in this nation is antidepressants." Indeed, he concludes that "we are a country who breeds people who do not handle life well."[7]

Finally, the elderly represent the fastest growing and the wealthiest segment of the population. As the population ages in the next couple decades, this will probably change the face of crime and probably even more the role of law enforcement in protecting this group. By 2010, one in every four citizens of this nation will be 55 or older.[8] An older population may well become more vulnerable to personal victimization. It is also likely that the vulnerability of this group will make it more dependent on law enforcement services. At the same time, the United States will have an older police force.

Toxicity of Working with Criminals

One day, one of the authors asked his 12 year old daughter, Kristin, "What do you want to do when you grow up?" She answered, "I have no idea." The father responded, "Why don't you become a criminologist, like me?" Kristin, who has always had a way with words, quickly retorted, "It is too toxic."

Kristin was absolutely right. This text has put more emphasis than most on the **toxicity** that crime creates in this society. Victims of crime experience this toxicity when their houses are robbed, when they are personally attacked or even murdered, perhaps by intoxicated or addicted offenders. Victims further experience toxicity on becoming aware that the justice system cannot be trusted to take their needs seriously and to value them as persons of worth.

Neither are police officers strangers to toxicity. They experience it every time they receive verbal and physical abuse from citizens. It takes place when they are passed over for promotion because of gender or race. It becomes a way of perceiving those offenders who seem to have little going for them. It also occurs when officers are treated without respect by supervisors who communicate that what they have to say and how they feel is not important. The feelings of toxicity increase even more when their work alienates them from spouses, when their children are ridiculed because their parents are police officers, or when their spouses or children live in constant fear concerning whether they will survive another shift.

The toxicity is further exposed when the police commit deviant acts. These acts include various forms of corruption, use of excessive force, inappropriate use of deadly force, denying suspects their constitutional rights, lying on the stand and planting evidence, sexual harassment of female officers, discrimination toward minorities within the department and in the community, and the sexual victimization of women in the community. Police have enormous political power in the United States and when they violate this power in these dark sides of policing, they create a real sense of disorder in this nation. Without order, we cannot have justice, freedom, or democracy.

CONTEXTUAL ANALYSIS OF POLICING IN THE UNITED STATES

A major theme of this book is that policing occurs in, and is shaped by five contexts: the historical, the legal, the political, the sociocultural, and the economic. These five contexts do not exist in and of themselves; they are interrelated. A contextual analysis, then, is multidimensional and avoids the tendency to become entrapped in one context and to subordinate all the others to that particular frame of reference.

Historical Context

An understanding of history reveals several important insights that are pivotal to understanding policing today. First, modern policing is a product of the complexity and impersonality of industrial society and is shaped by the political, social, and economic trends of time and place. Second, the influence of social class has guided the role and function of the police. Third, a review of the past clearly reveals that police systems are a reflection of the social, moral, and economic makeup of a community. Fourth, political control has trapped police departments in the United States in a morally ambivalent posture that has reduced their effectiveness. Fifth, police abuse of power in the past is a reminder that the issue of controlling the controllers is always one of great importance in a free and democratic society. Sixth, although professionalism has made major improvements in the nature and function of police operations, history also reveals that professionalism has contributed to the widening conflict between administrators and line officers. Seventh, community policing has made a number of mistakes in the past, including a lack of planning, mission ambiguity in terms of uncertainty of who to serve and how to serve them, lack of efficiency, and potential for corruption. Finally, the presence of women and minorities in policing was nearly nonexistent until late in the twentieth century.

Legal Context

The legal context guides everything that a police officer does and also contains a number of important insights. First, one of the central issues of the criminal justice system is to maintain a balance between the rights of the individual and society. The Founding Fathers faced this balancing problem in framing the United States Constitution and the Bill of Rights, which treat individual rights and freedoms. Second, the very integrity of police agencies depends on upholding constitutional guidelines in enforcing the law. Yet the police are still mandated to enforce the law against sometimes very sophisticated criminals. Third, there is a feeling among police officers that the rules concerning search and seizure favor the criminal and encourage the police to lie and cheat in order to win. Fourth, the interpretation of criminal law sometimes changes from one court to another; for example, the Warren and the Rehnquist Courts have interpreted the rights of criminal suspects quite differently. Fifth, the ambiguity in criminal law does permit the police to interpret the legal mandates according to the demands of a particular context. Sixth, organizational and personal objectives sometimes encourage officers to commit "noble perjury," make "chump" arrests, and "stack" or "jack-up" charges against citizens. Seventh, a serious form of police deviancy is when police officers fabricate or plant evidence, perjure themselves while giving court testimony, or commit excessive force against a criminal suspect. Eighth, the legal context is involved in terms of case law for reasonable force, sexual harassment, discrimination, and officers' constitutional rights. Finally, it is in the criminal and civil courts that police officers are tried for various forms of police deviancy.

Political Context

The political context provides several insights for understanding policing in this society. First, political power is at the very core of the police's role in this society. This political power enables the officer to detain and arrest, to search for and seize evidence, and to use deadly force. All of these are involved in taking a person's freedom and perhaps, even his or her life. Second, the public policy of a "get tough" attitude on crime strategy puts pressure on police agencies to solve crime and, at the same time, provides some encouragement to dish out more street and vigilante justice against offenders. Third, the politicization of crime over the past 20 years is seen in the declarations of war on crime and drugs. Fourth, part of the reason why the war on crime and the battle over drugs is unwinnable is because politicians do not wish to pay the costs of winning these wars (i.e. neglecting the social causes of crime, keeping drugs out of the country, and enforcing the law against the big drug dealers and those who launder money who are often part of the social elite). Finally, the political context pervades everything that takes place in a police department. It includes the appointment or termination of the chief, the election of the sheriff, politicians' supervision over the decisions that police make in a local community, and the departmental decisions concerning promotions and suspensions.

Sociocultural Context

Emphasis on the sociocultural context assumes that knowledge of a particular social structure and the social processes within and through which that structure operates are important in understanding policing. This context has considerable effect on the daily lives of police officers. First, this context influences the values and norms that police officers bring to the job. The dark sides of policing so much of the time simply reflect the communities from which officers come. Second, the culture of a particular police department affects the socialization of officers, the development of an informal code, and the solidarity of officers with each other. Third, the culture of a department also determines to what degree women and minorities are accepted and whether or not they will receive harassment and discrimination. Fourth, the importance of the cultural context is also seen in the fact that so much police deviancy is systemic. Finally, the organizational variable, or the department itself, contributes much to the frustration, stress, and burnout levels in policing.

Economic Context

The economic context pertains to such factors as socioeconomic class, unemployment, and poverty. There is danger in either overemphasizing or underemphasizing the role of economics in understanding crime. Although growing up poor or being unemployed may increase one's likelihood of becoming a criminal, economics is only one of the contexts that affects individuals on a daily basis.

The economic context leads to the following insights about policing in this nation. First, individuals who live in disorganized and impoverished neighborhoods have greater exposure than middle-class citizens to drug use and trafficking, firearms, prostitution, and gambling rackets. Second, most repeat offenders come from lower-class and urban areas. Third, police enforce the law and treat people differently in the two Americas. The second America, made up of minorities and the poor, receives the blunt of street and vigilante justice. Fourth, the public's attitudes toward the police are more positive in the first America than in the second America. Finally, the poor are more likely to defile authority, and to assault or shoot police officers.

Interrelationships among the Contexts

It is in the interrelationships among the various contexts that social reality emerges on societal, organizational, and personal levels. In every period since the colonies were founded, political and economic forces have combined with sociocultural and legal forces to shape society's methods of policing society. The wave of optimism that swept through the United States during the Progressive Era influenced the development of police professionalism. Constitutional rights for criminal defendants emerged from the interrelationships among the sociocultural, economic, and political contexts. For example, the sweeping constitutional changes made while Earl Warren was Chief Justice of the United States Supreme Court can be understood by considering the complex social, political, and economic contexts of that time. Beginning in the 1970s, the conjunction of the social and political contexts led to the passage of new laws facilitating the widespread hiring and promotions of women and minority police officers.

PROGRESSIVE CHANGES IN LAW ENFORCEMENT

Unquestionably, policing in the United States is under extensive criticism today. Its credibility is under major attack and nearly every month another incident involving excessive force or corruption receives national coverage. The excessive force incidents have been particularly damaging to the image and reputation of law enforcement in this free and democratic society. However, there is also no question that policing in this nation has come a long way in the past century and even in the past decade or two. The progressive changes that have taken place in law enforcement include those dealing with structure and function, those having to do with technological advances, and those involved with the recent emphasis on integrity and ethics.

There are a number of structural and functional changes that have taken place in law enforcement departments across the nation. Some of these innovations are found only in progressive departments, while others have been implemented in the majority of police agencies. First, police departments are generally now made up of better educated officers than in the past. Some question exists as to how satisfied college educated officers are with their law enforcement careers, but a balanced treatment suggests that the more serious problems still surfacing among law enforcement personnel are generally found among those whose education ended with high school.

Second, police departments are increasingly involved in the process of accreditation. In 1995, 368 law enforcement agencies had received accreditation and hundreds more were in the process of being considered for accreditation. The most positive aspect of accreditation is that it encourages more police departments to attain a minimum level of performance, a level that only a few departments across the nation attained until recent years.

Third, the autocratic police chief is largely a relic of the past. Most chiefs of police today use some form of participatory management, in which middle managers and supervisors are brought into the decision-making process. In some police agencies, line officers are also involved in decision making concerning operations, procedures, or policies.

Fourth, in the midst of rising rates of police suicides, the fact is that most departments are today handling the stressors of police work more effectively than in the past. There is greater commitment to identifying and helping those with cumulative stress and post-traumatic stress disorder (PTSD). For example, the Critical Incident Stress Debriefing (CISD) team is widely considered and utilized as one of the most important mechanisms to reduce post-traumatic stress disorder.

Fifth, police departments across the nation are increasingly placing an emphasis on community policing, specifically employing community-oriented policing (COP) and problem-oriented policing (POP) strategies. Indeed, a 1992 survey of the 25 largest departments in the nation revealed that 78 percent practiced community policing, 13 percent intended to in the near future, and only 9 percent reported having no community policing program.[9] More recently, over 300 police departments claim to have adopted what Alpert and Moore call a "new paradigm of policing."[10] Jihong Zhao, Quint C. Thurman, and Nicholas P. Lovrich, in examining a 1993 national survey of police chiefs conducted by the Division of Governmental Studies and Services (DGSS) at Washington State University, reported that the majority of police departments in the United States had implemented some type of COP program. For example, education of the public (98.1 percent) block watch programs (97.7 percent), special tasks units (91.6 percent), and foot patrol (88.4 percent) are the most commonly adopted COP programs.[11]

Yet there is some question about how effectively community policing programs have been implemented. S. Sadd and R. Grinc's examination of police agencies in eight cities identified certain barriers to implementation. These include (1) confusion among line officers concerning what community policing means; (2) inadequate support from middle management; and (3) lack of support of citizens in the community.[12] Michael J. Palmiotto and Michael E. Donahue add that community policing currently lacks valid and reliable evaluation and, as a result, it is difficult to draw any firm conclusions about its effectiveness.[13]

Sixth, although there is still rejection, abuse, and sometimes sexual harassment against women and discrimination against minority police officers, police departments are now generally more diverse employing more women, African Americans and Hispanic/Latino Americans than in the past. When there is discrimination and biased treatment toward women and minority officers, the victimizers are also more likely now to receive recriminations, especially in civil suits.

Seventh, police organizations are now more likely to be integrative organizations than they were in the past. Formerly, too much of the time police agencies were segmentalist organizations, in which individual officers were not trusted, authority failed to flow to the bottom, problems were not shared, and natural bureaucratic resistance prevailed. In contrast, integrative organizations support the involvement and participation of all levels, reward change over tradition, collaboration over isolated specialists, and enhanced roles for both middle managers and line officers. The fact that officers are trusted and valued in integrative departments encourages positive attitudes, courage, and enthusiasm.[14]

Technological Advances

Some of the most impressive changes in law enforcement have been in communication and information management. The facsimile machine (fax) and video telephones now permit police departments to transmit information instantly. For example, what this means is that a police agency detaining a suspect in one jurisdiction can transmit fingerprints, pictures, and warrants to another agency, perhaps across the nation, in a matter of seconds.

The video telephone promises to make the job of the police officer even easier in the future. This works by one part of the screen allowing transmission of the image of the person to whom you are talking, while the other part of the screen can be used to transmit photographs of suspects, sketches, or official documents needed during an investigation.[15]

Computers are increasingly being used by law enforcement agencies. Some innovative departments make laptop or notebook and on-board computers available to officers so that they can make accurate reports at a crime scene, have direct access to state computers to run vehicle registration and wanted person checks, and to the large data bank of National Crime Information Center (NCIC) for stolen items and wanted or missing persons. Further, criminal investigators are using the current developments in artificial intelligence to track and profile serial criminals. The National Center for Analysis of Violent Crime (NCAVC) presently uses advanced computer systems to investigate unsolved violent crimes.[16]

Some large police departments are presently integrating technologies into total information systems. The Detroit Police Department uses a system called the Detroit Emergency Response System (DETERS) which integrates the 911 emergency calling, computer-aided dispatching, mobile data terminals, automated vehicle locators, and graphic workstations into a single system. The capability of this integrated system allows the department to pinpoint each police vehicle, calculating its time of arrival to a location. This system also enables a dispatcher to zoom in on a map of an emergency and to determine more efficiently which vehicles to send to a call.[17]

Video cameras, a mixed blessing in the minds of some police executives, have been increasingly used in law enforcement. The VCR camera can be mounted on the inside of the police patrol car on the dash and is activated when the officer turns on emergency equipment or by a convenient power switch. It records everything that is taking place in front of the patrol car, or the camera can be swiveled to record a prisoner's actions in the back seat. Officers can be further supplied with wireless microphones that create an audio record of any conversations between the officer and stopped motorists, or combatants of a domestic abuse incident when the residence is within the effective range.

Another innovation in criminal investigation has been the use of DNA (deoxyribonucleic acid) fingerprinting by the police. Proponents claim that the use of DNA permits the police and prosecution to identify a person based on the scientific examination of semen, blood, or even a single cell of tissue. It is clearly most helpful when the police already have a suspect and are attempting to establish that he or she was at the scene of a crime. However, as the O. J. Simpson case vividly illustrates, juries may still decide to discount or minimize the presentation and weight of the DNA evidence.[18]

There is considerable research being done in creating new technology for the future in law enforcement. The police may be able to use a computer-driven system to track bullets in flight from their source. This device consists of a sensor that identifies a speeding bullet from its signals and aided by a computer converts the signals into an image on a display screen.[19] There is also experimentation taking place with brain wave analysis to determine whether a suspect is lying. Electrodes are attached to a subject's head in order to measure the brain's electrophysiological reactions to specific stimuli such as words, phrases, or pictures.[20]

The future may also hold such technological wonders as private vehicles having a factory-installed kill switch that a nearby patrol can activate by depressing a button, thus preventing high-speed pursuits. Police officers may be spared from going to court by transmitting their testimony through a home computer and video system. Laser radar guns may be used for tracking speeders, for sighting devices on police weapons, and for fingerprinting discovery techniques.[21]

Integrity as a Mission for the Police

A major theme of this text is that police executives are becoming increasingly attracted to **integrity** as a basic mission of their agencies. The apparent erosion of integrity in policing has caused a legitimacy crisis for both the political leadership of this nation as well as law enforcement itself. It is the lack of integrity and ethics that have contributed to excessive force, corruption, sexual harassment of fellow officers, and the misuse of constitutional protections guaranteed by the Constitution and upheld by the courts.

An example of this interest in integrity among law enforcement executives was the 1996 National Symposium on Police Integrity that took place in Washington, DC. Its 200 participants included police chiefs, sheriffs, police officers, police researchers, community leaders, and members of other federal agencies. The international interest in the issue of police integrity was evidenced by the attendance at the symposium of representatives from the United Kingdom, Belarus, the Netherlands, Sweden, El Salvador, Haiti, and Honduras.

The foreword of this report concludes on a very hopeful note:

> ...we are confident that the National Symposium on Police Integrity represents a profound new beginning toward a renewal of respect for the police and a new drive by law enforcement personnel to protect the personal dignity of both victims and offenders and the public trust of citizens. We encourage all members of the law enforcement community to continue their commitment to work on this critical issue at all levels of our profession and to consistently demonstrate a willingness to act decisively whenever necessary to enhance the level of integrity in our democracy.[22]

Integrity has been traditionally defined by police leaders as the absence of negative traits and actions, such as excessive force, corruption, selfishness, racism, sexism, and disloyalty. Traditionally, this has meant that integrity is maintained by disciplining wrongdoings by police personnel.[23] This is a negative morale-reducing approach toward department personnel that offers very little support or praise for ethical officers—only the fear of punishment.

In contrast, Stephen R. Covey's *Principle Centered Leadership* defines integrity as: "honest matching of words and feelings with thoughts and actions with no desire other than for the good of others, without malice or desire to deceive, take advantage, manipulate, or control..."[24] As it applies to police services, this broader understanding means that integrity is a series of beliefs and practices that combined "provide structure to an agency's operation and officers' professional and personal ethics. These concepts and beliefs include, but are not limited to honesty, honor, morality, allegiance, principled behavior, and dedication to mission."[25]

There are many unanswered questions that will determine whether and how much integrity will provide a renewal of police agencies and will help regain respect for these agencies. Can leaders supporting integrity overcome a police culture that supports "a code of silence" or a "blue flu?" Can it overcome the belief that it is impossible to win the war on crime without bending rules and regulations? How aggressive can police chiefs be in weeding out corruption and instilling and maintaining integrity? Is it possible to speak about integrity in departments that have long histories and cultures of corruption and wrongdoing? Do the ends ever justify the means: that is, does a difference exist between wrongdoing and doing wrong for a noble cause? How would an incorporation of integrity into its beliefs and practices actually affect the police's performance of its basic role of crime control? Perhaps the most telling question is: Is it possible to create a culture in which there is genuine trust in present day law enforcement agencies?[26]

POSSIBILITIES OF A PARADIGM SHIFT IN THE FUTURE

Geoffrey P. Alpert and Mark H. Moore's article, "Measuring Police Performance in the New Paradigm of Policing" argues that traditional models of police performance (such as crime rates, clearance rates, overall arrests, and response time) are outmoded. They go on to say that although these aspects of police accountability should continue to be regarded as critical aspects of the total system, "police performance measures should focus on a new model of policing that emphasizes their charge to do justice, promote secure communities, restore crime victims, and promote non-criminal options—the elements of an emerging paradigm of criminal justice."[27]

Alpert and Moore are contending that policing in the United States must go beyond the vision of professionalism because this vision is no longer effective in reducing crime or the public's fear of crime. It actually distances the police from those who meet their services the most. The heart of their proposed paradigm is that police "engage in community-based processes related to the production and maintenance of local human and social capital."[28]

This new paradigm has at least three approaches. One approach involves making the police more cooperative with the public and stresses the importance of police attentiveness to minor crimes and disorders.[29] Another approach is "community building"—focusing on crime prevention, victim assistance, and building greater rapport with racial minorities.[30] A third approach is "problem-oriented policing," which encourages the police to let the community define the problems that will receive police attention. Rather than wedded to any particular strategy, this approach urges the police to address the underlying causes of problems.[31]

There are those who urge that a necessary paradigm shift for the twentieth century is for law enforcement's paramilitary hierarchy, with its rigid controls and strict chains of command, to give way to a structure that emphasizes network-type communication and flexibility. It is suggested that police supervisors in the future will be required to spend less time commanding and controlling and more time helping officers identify and find solutions to community problems. Line officers, at the same time, will have greater opportunities to give honest feedback without fear of reprisal and to be more deeply involved in the decision-making process. In organizations in which job enhancement, enrichment, and training are perceived as tools of success, more attention will be given to help employees grow, to reward good work, and to develop creative ways to deal with employee burnout.[32]

A third possibility of a paradigm shift is to combine these two models, which emphasize an expanded version of community policing and a radical change in the organizational structure of police agencies, with the emerging emphasis on integrity. A widespread incorporation of integrity depends on its acceptance by line officers to the point that they are willing to buy into a fourth culture of policing. This fourth culture, as described in Chapter 10 on corruption, has a much different set of norms than those typical of most police subcultures. It is not a culture based upon opposition to administrators, supervisors, or the public. Instead, it is a culture committed to doing what is right. Integrity, as suggested in the final section of this chapter, will be viewed as having positive attributes and as expressing these attributes on the job. At the same time, those committed to integrity will refuse to accept those attitudes and actions deviating from this value-driven understanding of police work.

MEANINGFUL CAREERS IN LAW ENFORCEMENT

We believe that a career in law enforcement offers significant challenges and opportunities to influence the lives of others in a positive way. Nevertheless, we are the first to acknowledge that this career is not for the faint of heart. Police work is challenging, frustrating, boring, and dangerous. Such problems as stress, employee "burnout," and lack of appreciation from the public are detracting. We want to conclude this book with a few comments one must consider in finding employment in law enforcement agencies.

Becoming Committed to the Goal of Making a Difference

How does one make a difference? It ultimately means becoming a person of integrity. A former professor once told one of the authors that integrity means to be clean as a hound's tooth. This internationally known scholar went on to define that being clean as a hound's tooth meant to do what is right, to avoid compromising one's principles, and to stand tall even when others are bending this way and that way.

Persons of integrity typically possess a number of personal attributes. They treat others with **fairness.** They avoid bias and discrimination based on class, gender, or race. Integrity also requires **honesty.** You can count on these persons to carry out what they promised and to keep their word. They make a point to avoid deviancy in any form. Persons of integrity are **moral.** They have moral principles and keep them. They are not ones who cheat on their spouses or find ways to belittle others. Persons of integrity are **responsible.** It is important to them to do a good job because competence on the job is a top priority. They have developed realistic goals and objectives. They will do right by you. Persons of integrity are **caring, concerned,** and **genuine.** They place an emphasis on the positive experiences of others, communicating that others have the capacity to change. They tend to have the right words to communicate support when others have failed.

Persons of integrity have learned how to **manage stress.** Law enforcement is extremely stressful, and the most stressful jobs are in policing high-crime areas. An East St. Louis police officer resigned from the force and became a full-time college student. He justified his move by saying, "It was too dangerous out there. I've been shot at ten times the past two years, and I wanted to get out while I was still alive."[33] A Washington, DC police officer commented on the enormous stress he experienced every day for 20 years, "When you deal with as much as we did every-day, it is no wonder that we smoked and drank too much. When you deal with all this pressure, you've got to find some way to let it off or it's going to blow."[34]

Furthermore, persons of integrity have well-developed **critical thinking skills** that enable them to make accurate decisions quickly, to organize their time wisely and to work effectively under pressure. Police officers make important political de-cisions concerning peoples' lives—decisions that can deprive them of their liberty, of their material possessions, of their reputations, and even of their lives. Some-times involving life and death matters, these decisions must often be made on the spur of the moment, without the luxury of taking the evening or weekend to think it over. For example,

- The decision made by a police officer at a disturbance call may mean the dif-ference between life and death for a battered spouse.
- The decision made by a police officer and social worker on a child abuse inves-tigation may have life-long consequences for a child.
- The decision made by a police officer when an opportunity for illegal but prof-itable behavior flashes before him or her may provide the start of a career of corruption.

This whole matter of making a difference is very hard to measure as we walk down the road of life. We are at times cognizant of our small successes and, occa-sionally, we are privileged to witness a big success. We say then, "Wow, I really made a difference." But, for the most part, we simply do not know the impact we are having on others. We also do not know how this impact is effecting their short-term and long-term behaviors.

Joining with Others Who Are Trying to Make a Difference

The fact is that our trying to make a difference may not be enough. The grim reality of policing is one that includes "crack" houses, child molestation, domestic abuse, rape, and murder. The history of policing is filled with those who tried to make a difference but were poorly treated by the agencies in which they were involved. They were sometimes fired. They were often ignored. They may have experienced complete burnout. They frequently received harassment. And they may have left their jobs broken.

We need to be proud of the fact that they made the difference they did in the midst of overwhelming odds. But, at the same time that we admire what they achieved, we need to be aware that their contributions were frequently limited be-cause they had to stand alone. They lacked encouragement and support from peers who believed in similar ideas and followed similar goals. They were unable to participate in an environment in which their contributions could be joined by others to make positive changes in their departments.

The lesson to be learned is that those who want to effect more humane, just, and effective police agencies must establish networks with others. As these individuals develop their networks in and outside the department, they will eventually form a **critical mass.** What is crucial here is the understanding that once a certain number of supporters are attained (the critical mass) a movement suddenly dramatically increases its power and persuasiveness.

SUMMARY

History is filled with those who perceived human transformation well before their time. They were aware that the way we treat others makes a difference, both to them and to ourselves. They realized the importance of human dignity and the possibilities of human development. Generally feeling alone, these individuals who attempted to make a difference were often misunderstood and were viewed as unrealistic dreamers.

In preparing to enter the twenty-first century, we have learned that humans can progress only by uniting and converging with others. The more we unite with others, the more our creative differences can bring significant structural changes to toxic systems, including police agencies. "This engagement of energies with others," as Pierre Teilhard de Chardin once put it, "does not reduce our individuality. Rather, it enhances the creative consciousness and the discrete development of each person to full capacity."[35]

KEY WORDS

caring	honesty
concerned	integrity
critical mass	manage stress
critical thinking skills	moral
fairness	responsible
genuine	toxicity

DISCUSSION QUESTIONS

1. Evaluate the changes that are taking place in law enforcement today. How much will they help to regain respect for policing in the United States?

2. What attributes are involved in becoming a person of integrity?

3. Is it possible to bring meaningful change in law enforcement?

ENDNOTES

1. Quoted in Ysabel Rennie, *The Search for Criminal Man: A Conceptual History of the Dangerous Offender* (Lexington: D.C. Heath, 1978) xiii.

2. Howard N. Snyder and Melissa Sickmund, *Juvenile Offenders and Victims: A Focus on Violence* (Pittsburgh: National Center for Juvenile Justice, 1995) 7.

3. "The Drug Gangs," *Newsweek,* 28 March 1988: 27.

4. Jack Levin and Jack McDevitt, *Hate Crimes: The Rising Tide of Bigotry and Bloodshed* (New York: The Free Press, 1993) vii.

5. Georgette Bennett, *Crime Warps: The Future of Crime in America* (Garden City: Anchor Books/Anchor Press, 1987) xii-xiv.

6. Quote contained in *Street Survival Newsline,* No. 197 (Calibre Press).

7. *Street Survival Newsline.*

8. Anita Manning and David Proctor, "Senior Bloom: The Future's New Wrinkle," *USA Today,* 31 January 1989: 1D.

9. Cited in Eli B. Silverman, "Community Policing: The Implementation Gap," *Issues in Community Policing,* eds. Peter C. Kratcoski and Duane Dukes (Cincinnati: Anderson, 1994) 36.

10. G. P. Alpert and M. H. Moore, "Measuring Police Performance in the New Paradigm of Policing," *Performance Measures for the Criminal Justice System: Discussion Papers from the BJS–Princeton Project* (Washington, DC: U.S. Department of Justice, 1993).

11. Jihong Zhao, Quint C. Thurman, and Nicholas P. Lovrich, "Community-Oriented Policing Across the U.S.: Facilitators and Impediments to Implementation," *American Journal of Police 14* (1995): 16.

12. S. Sadd and R. Grinc, "Innovative Neighborhood Oriented Policing: An Evaluation of Community Policing Programs in Eight Cities," *The Challenge of Community Policing,* ed. D. Rosenbaum (Thousand Oaks: Sage, 1994).

13. Michael J. Palmiotto and Michael E. Donahue, "Evaluating Community Policing: Problems and Prospects," *Police Studies 18* (1995): 50.

14. Silverman.

15. Larry K. Gaines, Victor E. Kappeler, and Joseph B. Vaughn, *Policing in America,* 2nd ed. (Cincinnati: Anderson, 1997) 414.

16. Gaines, et al., 415.

17. W. Hart, "DETERS: Integrating Today's Technologies in Tomorrow's Emergency Response System," *Police Chief* (Mar. 1990): 26–33.

18. Gaines, et al., 421.

19. Kenneth J. Peak, *Policing in America,* 2nd ed. (Upper Saddle River: Prentice–Hall, 1977) 394.

20. Gordon Witkin, "The Hunt for a Better Lie Detector," *U.S. News and World Report,* 14 June 1993.

21. Peak, 395.

22. Stephen J. Gaffigan and Phyllis P. McDonald, *Police Integrity: Public Service with Honor* (Washington, DC: U.S. Department of Justice, 1997).

23. Gaffigan and McDonald, 86.

24. Stephen R. Covey, *Principle-Centered Leadership* (New York: Simon & Schuster, 1990) 108.

25. Gaffigan and McDonald, 86.

26. Gaffigan and McDonald, 86–89.

27. Geoffrey P. Alpert and Mark H. Moore, "Measuring Police Performance in the New Paradigm of Policing," *Performance Measures for the Criminal Justice System 109* (Discussion Papers from the Bureau of Justice Statistics: Princeton University Study Group on Criminal Justice, 1993): 111.

28. Alpert and Moore, 113.

29. James Q. Wilson and George L. Kelling, "Broken Windows: The Police and Neighborhood Safety," *Atlanta Monthly,* Mar. 1982: 29–38.

30. John P. Crank, "State Theory Myths of Policing & Responses to Crime," *Law and Society Review 28* (1994): 325–351.

31. Stephen D. Mastrofshi, Robert E. Worden, and Jeffrey B. Snipes, "Law Enforcement in a Time of Community Policing," *Criminology 33* (Nov. 1995): 541.

32. Andrew J. Harvey, "Guiding an Organization Foundation for the Future," unpublished, 1966, and Michael L. Birzes, "Police Supervision in the 21st Century," unpublished, 1966.

33. Personal interview, July 1985.

34. Personal interview, Feb. 1987.

35. Quoted in Blanche Gallagher, *Meditations with Teilhard de Chardin* (Santa Fe: Bear, 1988) 80.

GLOSSARY

18 USC Sec. 241   Federal Civil Rights Act—criminal conspiracy statute.

18 USC Sec. 242   Federal Civil Rights Act—criminal statute.

42 United States Code Section 1983   Under color of law depriving a person of constitutionally protected rights.

42 United States Code Section 1985(3)   Outlawing a conspiracy to deprive a person of constitutionally protected rights.

Administration   The process whereby individuals are organized and directed toward the achievement of group objectives.

Autocratic management   A management style where the Chief is clearly "the boss," and that uses negative and punitive means in an attempt to control the entire organization.

Brewer v. Williams (1977)   A Supreme Court case in which it was ruled that once a suspect requests an attorney, the police cannot use subterfuge or trickery to elicit incriminating information from him or her.

Brutality, police   A conscious and venal act committed by officers who take great pains to conceal their misconduct, usually directed against persons of marginal status and credibility.

Call boxes   First communication system whereby officers could be called to the station house.

Caring   One of the characteristics possessed by persons of integrity.

Carroll Doctrine (1925)   A doctrine that allows a vehicle search when there is probable cause to believe that contraband is being transported.

Chief of Police   The top administrative figure of a law enforcement agency.

Chimel v. California (1969)   A Supreme Court case in which it was ruled that a search in a home incident to a lawful arrest must be limited to the area into which an arrestee might reach in order to grab a weapon or other evidentiary items.

Civil Rights Act of 1964   A law passed by Congress that makes discrimination on the basis of race, color, religion, sex, or national origin illegal.

Civil Rights Act of 1991   Civil rights law that corrected some inadequacies in the Civil Rights Act of 1964.

Code of silence   Known as the "blue curtain," it serves to protect those who become involved in corruption or use of unnecessary force providing a firm barrier against administrative knowledge. It is particularly formidable when enforced by management or the inner circle of power.

Coerced statements   Officers are denied constitutional protection against self incrimination when they are ordered to either cooperate with the Internal Affairs Unit or face disciplinary action.

Coercive force   Justifiable use of force that is an intricate and unavoidable part of law enforcement.

Community policing   A hope for the future. A policing practice in the United States that is committed to building strong relationships with institutions and individuals in the community. Forms of community policing include strategic policing, problem-oriented policing, and neighborhood-oriented policing.

Community services   Community services units have been developed within police departments to gain local support. The main emphasis of these units is to break down the barrier of prejudice and hostility between the police and the public and to assist the members of the public in fighting crime in their own neighborhoods.

Compensatory damages   Damages that are awarded to make the injured party whole.

Conceptualization   The ability to see the whole and to rise above organizational parts.

Concerned   One of the characteristics possessed by persons of integrity.

Concerns of Police Survivors (COPS)   National networking organization for surviving families of police officers.

Consent   When a person voluntarily allows the police to conduct a search.

Contingency management   Management theory based on the notion that organizations will vary the structures they use depending on the decisions that must be made.

Control Continuum   A list of coercive force options in response to a subject's actions.

COPS   Office of Community Oriented Policing Services established by the Justice Department to promote community policing and add 100,000 community policing officers as authorized by The Violent Crime Control and Law Enforcement Act of 1994.

Corruption   The misuse of authority for personal gain.

County sheriff   An elected official of the county who usually provides criminal law enforcement and maintains a short term correctional facility known as the county jail.

Critical incident   Any event that has a stressful impact sufficient enough to overwhelm coping skills.

Critical incident stress   The stress reaction from a critical incident that can lead to a condition known as post-traumatic stress disorder if left untreated.

Critical mass   The number of supporters required to suddenly and dramatically increase a movement's power and persuasiveness.

Critical thinking skills   The ability to perform thoughtful analysis of a problem.

Cumulative stress   Stress that occurs over a long period of time (i.e. an officer is exposed to occupational, traumatic, and nonwork-related stressors over a long period of time).

Dangerous poor   Unemployed immigrants of different cultural, ethnic, and religious backgrounds thought of as suspicious, dangerous, and responsible for the crime wave of the early 1900s.

Discretion   An inescapable element of police work referring to the unwritten rule that police officers have the right to be selective in how they do their jobs as long as they stay within widely prescribed departmental guidelines.

Distress   The negative, painful aspects of stress.

Drug Enforcement Administration (DEA)   Agency under the Department of Justice responsible for the development of the overall federal drug enforcement strategy.

Excessive force   Force that is unreasonable under *Graham v. Conner* (1988).

Exclusionary Rule   A rule that excludes any illegally seized evidence from use in a criminal trial.

Extralegal violence   Also known as police brutality. The willful and wrongful use of force committed by officers who take great pains to commit their act outside of public view.

Fair Employment Practices (FEP) agencies   State FEP agencies have similar powers to seek remedies for sexual harassment and discriminatory employment practices as the EEOC. In addition, various states' FEP laws provide remedies for receiving substantial monetary damages for personal injuries without limitations, while other states have no remedy.

Fairness   An important attribute to law enforcement professionals, it is the ability and inclination to treat everyone equally.

Federal Bureau of Investigation (FBI)   The agency whose duties include those of performing federal criminal investigations, and so forth.

Federal police   Agencies evolved for the purpose of investigating and enforcing federal laws.

Field training   On the job training—an evaluation program for probationary officers.

Garrity v. State of New Jersey (1967)   A United States Supreme Court case that prohibited coerced statements resulting from an internal affairs investigation from being used in criminal proceedings.

Genuine   One of the characteristics possessed by persons of integrity.

Good faith exception   Examines an overview of the actions of the police to determine whether they have acted within the scope of the Constitution, and, if not, allows evidence to be admitted at trial if the police at least acted in good faith.

Graham v. Conner (1989)   A United States Supreme Court case that placed excessive force claims under the analysis of the Fourth Amendment's reasonableness standard.

Grass eaters   Officers who accept only those payoffs that police work would happen to bring their way.

Hate crimes   Legally prohibited acts motivated by a victim's race, ethnicity, gender, sexual orientation, or religion.

Homelessness   Individuals and families caught in the dilemma of not being able to provide for their daily needs.

Honesty   An important attribute for law enforcement professionals, the capacity and inclination to be forthright with offenders and the public.

Hoover, J. Edgar   FBI Director from 1924 to 1972, instrumental in developing the FBI into the most modern federal law enforcement agency in the world.

Hostile work environment   An offensive environment resulting from sexual or gender harassment that unreasonably interferes with an employee's job performance.

Incident to arrest   Police are permitted to search a person or the surrounding area at the time of or immediately after an arrest.

Independent source exception   Evidence initially discovered by the police during an illegal entry may still be admissible if discovered from an independent source.

Inevitable discovery exception   The Supreme Court ruled that evidence found without a warrant is admissible if the evidence would have inevitably been found.

Informal code   The values of the police culture that vary between departments and are unwritten procedures not covered in the formal system.

Integrated loyalty   The highest and most virtuous level of loyalty in the workplace that constitutes genuine concern by each worker for the values and ideas of the profession and honors the ideas of accountability, rationality, fairness, and good will.

Integrity   A major goal of police executives traditionally defined as the absence of negative traits and actions such as incidents of excessive force, corruption, selfishness, racism, and disloyalty.

Integrity test   A test whereby a department tests the honesty of its officers by such methods as leaving money in an abandoned vehicle or in a wallet turned into an officer or stings to see if an officer will take a bribe.

Internal affairs division   A division within a police agency that investigates citizen complaints and officer misconduct.

Inventory search   A search and inventory of the contents of an impounded vehicle.

Justice of the Peace   An office created by Edward II to assist the mutual pledge system that soon took over the role of magistrate in asserting control over the sheriff and constables.

Knapp Commission   The most famous of the commissions formed to investigate police corruption in New York City, that found that more than half of the city's police department had been involved in some form of corruption.

Law Enforcement Assistance Administration (LEAA)   Title I of the Omnibus Crime Control and Safe Streets Act of 1968 creating state planning agencies, block grants, and supplying money for the training of criminal justice personnel, and so forth.

Line functions   The primary law enforcement tasks in the community, including patrol, investigations, and traffic control.

Manage stress   Police officers of integrity have learned how to manage stress.

Management   The day to day operations of a police agency.

Management by Objectives (MBO)   A participatory management style concerned with general organizational planning de-emphasizing the role of specific personnel in the planning process based on the principle that the best way to ensure success is through planning.

Management culture   The culture of those persons, usually progressive thinkers, that make up the upper management of a police agency and demand higher levels of professionalism from street officers.

Mapp v. Ohio (1961)   A case that extended the exclusionary rule to state trials.

Massachusetts v. Sheppard (1984)   A case that established an expansion of the good faith exception to the exclusionary rule by upholding the admission of evidence obtained by a search warrant that was technically defective.

Meat eaters   Officers who aggressively misuse power for personal gain.

Mechanistic scientific model   A worldview that everything is a machine and can be understood as a machine leaving no room for anything other than mechanical functioning.

Metropolitan Police Act (1889)   An act set up to establish regulations for the hiring, training, and supervision of police officers.

Militia   An army composed of ordinary citizens.

Militia of Montana (MOM)   The foremost organized militia group in the United States.

Miranda v. Arizona (1966)   A famous case in which the Supreme Court ruled that suspects taken into police custody must, before any questioning can take place, be informed that they have the right to remain silent, that anything they say may be used against them, and that they have the right to counsel.

Misconduct litigation   An entire body of very complex law covering a spectrum of applicable law ranging from municipal codes to the constitution involving issues where criminal and civil liability overlap.

Moral   One of the characteristics possessed by persons of integrity.

Moral chameleon   A person who is anxious to accommodate and please others to the point of quickly abandoning or modifying previously avowed principles.

Moral hypocrite   A person who pretends to live by certain standards while he or she actually lives by a different code.

Moral opportunist   A person who places primary value on his or her own short-term self interest.

Moral self-deceivers   Persons who perceive themselves as acting on a set of core principles while in fact they do not.

Morally weak-willed   A person who has a set of core values in place but usually lacks the courage to act on them.

Mutual Pledge   Birth of modern policing tracing back to Alfred the Great. Designed to provide a defense against an impending Danish invasion, it organized England from the smallest levels to the counties to make certain all members obeyed the law.

National Crime Information Center (NCIC)   A major computer network managed by the FBI, linking police agencies across the country. Information available through this computer network includes wanted persons, missing persons, and stolen property.

National Law Enforcement Memorial   A monument, located on the grounds of the United States capital building, dedicated to the surviving husbands, wives, mothers, children, sisters, brothers, and co-workers of fallen officers. Over 14,000 randomly inscribed names are on the Memorial's "Pathway of Remembrance."

New York v. Belton (1981)   Allows that a police officer may search the passenger compartment of an automobile when the officer has made lawful custodial arrest.

New York v. Quarles (1984)   A case significant because it established a public safety exception to the *Miranda* ruling.

Noble cause corruption   Justification for deception, perjury, or lying to obtain a conviction.

Occupational stressors   The most significant occupational stressors are those acting on an officer's value system demanding respect, fairness, honesty, and integrity.

O'Meara, Stephen James   Police Commissioner of Boston in 1906. His administration was regarded as one of the most successful community police forces in United States history using the beat system and officers from the local community to lessen the militaristic image of the force.

Parker, William H.   A man who played a key role in transforming the Los Angeles Police Department from a scandal-ridden department to an organization noted for being free of corruption.

Participatory management   A management style based on developing a team approach and on sharing the decision-making responsibilities throughout the organization.

Peel, Sir Robert   England's Home Secretary, who helped develop and organize a police system copied in many ways by American police.

Pendleton Act of 1883   A reform bill that established and set rules for a civil service commission to govern entrance examinations, promotions, and settle grievances within a police organization.

Plain touch exception   Evidence seized through a pat-down search that reveals an identifiable object through clothing.

Plain View Doctrine   Allows a search of items in plain view.

Poisonous fruit doctrine   Any evidence found or secured from an illegal search cannot be used because it is like poisonous fruit from a poisonous tree.

Police brutality   Extralegal violence.

Police integrity   A yardstick of trust, competence, professionalism, and confidence of a police officer and his or her agency.

Police spirit   The police spirit, exemplifies honor, courage, fairness, a commitment to risk one's life to save another, and to "stand tall" against corruption, brutality, and distress.

Posse Comitatus   Latin for "the power of the country." In United States history, it was used by the sheriff to place persons under his or her leadership and control for peacekeeping or other law enforcement duties.

Post-traumatic stress disorder (PTSD)   The most severe and incapacitating reaction to a traumatic event that a person can experience; it can lead to personality changes, to physical illness and even to suicide.

Private police   People hired by the private sector to perform policing functions with the exception of making arrests not committed in their presence.

Problem-oriented policing   A policing philosophy that encourages the police to let the community define the problems receiving their attention. The problem-oriented approach urges the police to address the underlying causes of problems.

Public safety exception   The exception noted by the Supreme Court holding that the "overwhelming" need for the safety of the public in some situations allows the police to act on probable cause without first obtaining a search warrant.

Punitive damages   Intended to punish egregious acts.

Quid Pro Quo harassment   Something for something harassment—for example, sexual favors used as a condition for receiving a tangible benefit.

Quota   A predetermined number of traffic citations or arrests by a police officer on a daily, weekly, monthly, quarterly, or yearly basis.

Reasonable woman standard   A standard for judging cases of sexual harassment set by the Circuit Court which felt that the "Reasonable Man" or "Reasonable Person" standards did not take into account the concerns of women.

Rogues   Rogue cops fall on the far right of the corruption continuum. An aberration even among meat eaters, they commit highly visible crimes.

Rotten structures   Counter argument to the rotten apple theory asking if the barrel is rotting the apples. This means that the tentacles of corruption extend throughout the command staff of a department and sometimes to the top, but almost always encompass the informal circle of power.

Search warrant   A document issued by a judicial officer that gives police officers the legal means to conduct a search.

Sheriff   In British history, the sheriff is the chief law enforcement officer appointed by the King to maintain order in the shires formed as part of the system of mutual pledge.

Sherrod v. Berry   A Supreme Court case that restricted the assessment of the objective reasonableness of an officer's actions to the facts known to the officer before the use of force.

Skinheads   One of the most violent contemporary supremacist groups in the United States.

Slave patrol   A distinctive and egregious form of American law enforcement created in the antebellum South to guard against slave revolts and to capture runaway slaves.

Socialization   The process of being introduced to and taught the ways of a particular culture.

Stop and frisk   A pat-down of a subject's clothing for weapon detection.

Straight shooters   Honest cops who remain silent while overlooking patterns of corruption and misconduct, feeling either helpless to do anything or uncomfortable turning in another officer.

Street culture   The lesson learned by a police officer from the informal code that fills in the void that the formal system does not cover.

Stressor   Anything in the environment that can cause or set the stage for a stress response.

Supervision   The direction of the organizational participants in their day-to-day activities.

Support functions   Those personnel in a police agency that provide assistance to the line function, including such areas as records, training, crime prevention, and internal affairs.

Tactical teams   A special team of officers that are well-organized, trained to work as a unit, and equipped with high-powered assault weapons to handle high-risk incidents such as armed barricaded suspects and hostage negotiations. Sometimes called SWAT (special weapons and tactics teams).

Terry v. Ohio (1968)   A case in which the Supreme Court ruled that when a police officer believes that a crime is about to be committed, he or she may search a suspect's outer clothing for dangerous weapons.

Thief taker   A private detective system in which individuals collected a fee or public reward for apprehending criminals.

Tort   Monetary award and injunctive or declaratory relief for a private injury.

Totality of the circumstances test   Used to determine whether or not probable cause exists for the issuance of a search warrant.

Traumatic stress   Also known as critical incident stress. The stress response to a traumatic event.

Turner Diaries, The   The two books most revered in the militia movement.

Under color of law   The actions taken by a peace officer when acting in his or her official capacity.

Uniform Crime Reports   A national compilation of crime statistics based on information provided to the FBI by local and state police agencies.

United States v. Leon (1984)   A case that established the good faith exception to the exclusionary rule.

United States v. Ross (1982)   A case that established that the scope of a warrantless search authorized by the automobile exception is no broader and no narrower than one that a magistrate could legitimately authorize by warrant.

Unnecessary force   Force that is unplanned and usually in the open resulting from a situation that has gotten out of control because of ineptitude or carelessness as officers hastily resort to force.

Unwelcome standard   The reasonable person standard adopting the perspective of the claimant taking into consideration the totality of the circumstances.

Use of force   A term used to describe a police officer's actions ranging from mere presence to deadly force.

Vigilantism   When people take the law into their own hands because the official agencies are considered too weak or simply do not exist.

Vollmer, August   Reform-mined police administrator who fostered police professionalism as town marshal and police chief in Berkeley, California, in the early 1900s.

War on crime   A "get-tough" response to crime declared by President Johnson.

Watch   Unpaid watchmen charged with patrolling a city guarding against fires, crime, and disorder. The watch eventually evolved into a paid profession.

Weeks v. United States (1914)   A case that established the exclusionary rule for federal trial (later overturned by *Mapp v. Ohio*).

White knights   Honest cops who blow the whistle to the media or an external agency.

Wilson, O. W.   One of the most noted police leaders who developed a progressive management philosophy while working as a patrol officer.

Wingspan search   A search of an area reachable by the suspect immediately after an arrest.

Working personality   The personality an officer assumes while on duty formed by elements danger, authority, and efficiency.

Zero-based budgeting   A new method of making budgetary decisions whereby internal managers strive for a common agreement on goals, developing coordination among related services thereby permitting consideration of alternatives that ordinarily would be considered too extreme.

NAME INDEX

Webb, Susan L., 281, 303n
Webb, Vincent J., 30, 31n
Webster, John A., 114
Weeg, Joseph P., 155n
Weinreb, Lloyd L., 152n
Weistheit, Ralph, 47n
Wells, Alice Stebbins, 283
Wells, L. Edward, 45n, 47n
Westberry, L., 197n
Westfall, E. A. "Penny," 140n
Westley, William A., 241
Westley, William W., 335
Westphall, William, 54n, 202n
Wexler, J. G., 290
Whaley, James D., 152n

Whitaker, Gordon P., 112, 113n, 114
White, Elizabeth K., 215n
Wice, Paul B., 46n
Wilbur, John, 235n
Wild, Jonathan, 4
Wildhorn, Sorrel, 49n
Williams, Hubert, 321
Williams, Jim, 224n
Willie, Charles Vert, 248
Willis, Bob, 234
Wilson, C. N., 195n
Wilson, Carlene, 115n
Wilson, James Q., 32, 33n, 65n, 113, 117, 346n
Wilson, O. W., 11, 12, 231

Winger, Keith H., 25–26
Winslow, Olivia, 303n
Wintersmith, Robert F., 7–8n
Witham, D. C., 88n
Witkin, Gordon, 344n
Wong, Herbert Z., 176n, 322n, 323n
Wooden, Wayne S., 177n
Worden, Robert E., 75n, 227n, 346n

Yentes, Nancy A., 55n

Zhao, Jihong, 102n, 110n, 129n, 342

SUBJECT INDEX